Popular Front Paris
and the Poetics of Culture

Popular Front Paris
and the Poetics of Culture

Dudley Andrew and Steven Ungar

THE BELKNAP PRESS OF

HARVARD UNIVERSITY PRESS

Cambridge, Massachusetts

London, England

2005

Pages 437–438 constitute an extension of the copyright page.

Library of Congress Cataloging-in-Publication Data

Andrew, Dudley, 1945–
Popular front Paris and the poetics of culture / Dudley Andrew and Steven Ungar.
p. cm.
Includes bibliographical references and index.
ISBN 0-674-01703-X (alk. paper)
1. Paris (France)—History—20th century.
2. Paris (France)—Intellectual life—20th century.
3. Paris (France)—Social life and customs—20th century.
4. France—History—1914–1940.   5. Motion pictures—France—History.
I. Ungar, Steven, 1945–   II. Title.
DC715.A48 2005
944′.3610815—dc22   2004060585

To Stevie and to Robin

Acknowledgments

This project took far longer than either of us imagined when we conceived it in 1985, and longer than the National Endowment for the Humanities wagered when they awarded us a three-year interpretive grant that greatly enlarged our ambitions. But today we are glad for the delays brought on by family events, by other books we wrote, by new scholarly paradigms we needed to digest, and even by an unthinkable loss of research material. For over the years our collaboration deepened and our enthusiasm spilled out onto a greater number of graduate students. Several of those students gathered research for us both in the United States and in Paris. With careers of their own now well underway, we meet them today as colleagues and share a camaraderie enriched by the spirit of the Popular Front.

This project began and concluded in the classroom. In 1984 we experimented by team-teaching an undergraduate course on interwar France—a course whose success led to three NEH summer seminars for college teachers. All thirty-six participants broadened our view of France in the 1930s, for they each researched a historical or cultural aspect about which they already knew a great deal and in which they sometimes could be counted experts. In the congenial but questioning arena of those seminars, our approach gradually became clear. Since then, both of us have taught more specialized seminars. At Yale, Andrew's course "The Archive of the Popular Front" involved three successive groups of gifted graduate students whose research and questions were indispensable in the latter stages of the book's composition. At Iowa, even as we conclude this project Ungar is leading twenty students on their own discovery-walk through the period, where they continue to point out new features of an inexhaustible terrain.

We pestered a number of obliging American and French colleagues with requests for information and advice. Their encouragement and friendship remain even more precious than their enlightening responses. Of all who helped, Sally Shafto and Nataša Ďurovičová contributed in such crucial ways over so many years that the book would have been much different—and much less—without them. The warmth of our gratitude to each of the following belies the alphabetical impersonality we are reduced to: Great thanks, then, to Anne Alfke, Sylvie Blum-Reid, Dana Benelli, Didier Bertrand, Anke Birkenmaier, Jonathan Buchsbaum, Francesco Casetti, Roger Chartier, Natalie Zemon Davis, Tom Doherty, Elizabeth Ezra, Christopher Faulkner, Debbie Glassman, Jen Hofer, Nathan Hoks, Denis Hollier, Sarah Kennel, Anne Kern, Ruedi Kuenzli, Michèle Lagny, Jim Lastra, Herman Lebovics, Mary Litch, Dennis Nastav, Panivong Norindr, Charles O'Brien, Roger Odin, Linda Orr, Alastair Phillips, Michael Raine, Keith Reader, Pierre-Edmond Robert, Geneviève Sellier, David Slavin, Pierre Sorlin, Pierre Verdaguer, Marc Vernet, Ginette Vincendeau, Shoggy Waryn, Jennifer Wild, Prakash Younger.

Our book was nourished under the wings of several benevolent institutions. In addition to our gratitude for the full support of the National Endowment for the Humanities, Steve Ungar thanks Danielle Haase-Dubosc, Mihaela Bacou, and Maneesha Lal for the welcome he received during a semester's stay at the Columbia University Institute for Scholars, Reid Hall, in Paris; while Dudley Andrew salutes Michael Pretina, director of the Camargo Foundation in Cassis, France, where he spent a wonderful term. A great deal of our research was conducted at the university libraries in Iowa City and New Haven; for the rest, we depended on the Special Collections of the UCLA library in Los Angeles, and the Bibliothèque de l'Arsenal, Bibliothèque Nationale, and Bibliothèque du Film in Paris. We thank the expert staffs of each of these institutions. We also thank Sandrine Bosser and Michèle Lefrançois of the Musée des Années 30, Boulogne-Billancourt, and Christophe Mauberret of the Association Française pour la Diffusion du Patrimoine Photographique. At Harvard University Press we were fortunate to have attracted the interest of Lindsay Waters, editor extraordinaire. He and Tom Wheatland kept the book on track and, once they were involved, on schedule. We also had editorial assistance from Maria Ascher, whose competence and care emanated from her enthusiasm for our topic. She made the always difficult final stages of editing and checking the manuscript a task we somehow enjoyed.

Our home institutions helped to ease the work and expense of producing this heavily illustrated book, through a generous award from the Hilles Publication Fund at Yale and through the offices of the Dean of Liberal Arts and the Vice-President for Research at Iowa. Both universities have been exceptional places to work and to incubate an interdisciplinary project. Andrew salutes his colleagues in Film Studies and in Comparative Literature at Yale, as well as a benevolent administration and wonderfully competent and cheerful office staff.

Having each spent thirty years at the University of Iowa, we are glad for this opportunity to praise so extraordinarily personal a public institution. We are particularly indebted to Jay Semel and his assistant Lorna Olson of the Obermann Center for Advanced Studies, where the first chapters of this book and its design were fashioned. Our project thrived under deans Gerhard Loewenberg, Judith Aikin, Linda Maxson, and Leslie Sims; we applaud the elevation of David Skorton, formerly Vice-President for Research, to current President of the University. They actively looked for ways to assist us in providing time, graduate assistants, and subsidies. Most important of all has been Iowa's intangible aura, an atmosphere fostering both the intensity and the sociability of scholarship. And so to our many, many friends in the Department of Cinema and Comparative Literature, and indeed throughout the humanities, we say: we are proud and happy to have been among you.

Contents

What are time's folds made of? . . . Time bends so that its holes coincide. . . . The holes that prophets make to peer into the future are the same as the ones through which historians gaze at the stuff of the past.

—John Berger and Alain Tanner,
Jonah Who Will Be 25 in the Year 2000

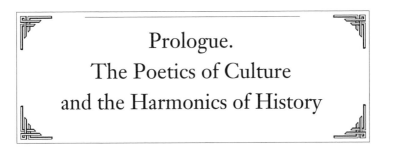

Prologue.
The Poetics of Culture
and the Harmonics of History

The term "Popular Front" (Front Populaire) designates more than a dramatic period during the final years of the Third Republic. It connotes social solidarity and the possibility of the democratic attainment of humane values. Yet this unified front came together only after street violence and heated rhetorical battles at meetings and rallies during 1934 had unsettled French society. The Popular Front then marched to electoral victory in May 1936, but reached its Gettysburg in the summer of that year. Weakened by labor strikes from within its own ranks, it retreated before debilitating onslaughts of economic and international pressure, relinquishing governmental authority in June 1937 and capitulating all along the line thereafter. Despite its shortcomings, the Popular Front remains a precedent for subsequent movements of solidarity and political change. Its legacy includes not only its grassroots electoral success plus the reforms enacted in its brief moment of power (the forty-hour work week and paid vacations), but also a vision of an authentic culture "of and for the people" that retains a strong affective charge of nostalgia even seventy years later.

The Popular Front is remembered fondly for the passion of its expressions, the fervor of its hopes, and the human scale of its social ambitions. But divisiveness and a certain martial impulse that are evident in its birth and baptism may have been necessary to its putative inclusiveness. And so we begin by questioning the metaphor of the "front," since it represents the social and political situation as a wide battlefield against right-wing extremists where a line is clearly drawn between opposing viewpoints, classes, and institutions. Like scouts, we need to pass through or circle around this line so as to explore the more general conditions (and perhaps the spirit) of the period. But to do so, we must learn to cross back and forth between scholarly approaches that have long been divided into disciplines guarded by departments.

When in the late 1960s both of us began teaching the literature and cinema of 1930s France, the issues seemed clearer than they do now. On one side—in our departments of literature and film—a list of novelists and cinéastes stood out prominently, a mass of canonical works surrounded by a coral reef of secondary material: philological, biographical, historical, and interpretive writings, as well as lesser literature and poorer films. On the other side—in the History Department, across the hall from French and Comp Lit—a relatively straight story accounted for France in the 1930s, telling of the rise and fall of the Popular Front before the debacle of the Nazi takeover in June 1940. The myriad monographs and articles on the period differed in approach and focus, but all built on this story.

The convenience of the canon and that of the skeletal story serve the disciplines of criticism and history respectively, and each field has often inspired the other. Still, their tasks, objects, and approaches have been separate and largely predefined. This, at least, is how it seemed a generation ago to two young professors of literature who designed courses that featured readings in history. By way of background, in order to allow powerful films, novels, and essays to stand out even more vividly, here is what we made sure our students knew.

The Straight Story

Even when sketched in a single paragraph, the story of the Popular Front is hardly straight. Though it may be linear, its line turns out to be an arc—or a rainbow, to those looking through the lens of nostalgia. The decade opened to a cacophony of cocky opinions blaring from manifestos by the Surrealists and other radical groups within the political and artistic arenas. After the Paris demonstrations of February 6, 1934, escalated into riots by protofascist gangs, these groups formed emergency coalitions and jockeyed for power on a dramatic and hugely consequential political stage. The momentum of the Popular Front movement in 1935, and its electoral victory the following spring under the Socialist Léon Blum, marked the apex of that drama and of a utopian moment in the late Third Republic. The fall of this government after scarcely a year in office produced an enervating disenchantment among those who had worked together in contagious fervor. This entropic course wound down with the dissolution of the Front following nationwide labor strikes in

November 1938. Ten months later, France declared war against Germany.

Now let us begin to widen this linear account. The Popular Front was a left-wing coalition of Radicals, Socialists, and Communists whose May 1936 parliamentary majority included a sizable Communist representation—72 out of 596 seats in the Chamber of Deputies. This majority had existed as early as 1932, but it was not until July 1935 that these groups agreed to set aside partisan differences in order to support one another. Julian Jackson has shown that the Communist gains came close to matching the decline in seats among the more conservative Radicals (from 157 seats in 1932 to 106 in 1936). Taken alongside the gains of the Socialists (from 131 seats in 1932 to 147 in 1936), the shift away from the Radicals was clear. Among all parties in the Chamber, this shift came at the expense of 38 seats lost between 1932 and 1936 by parties and independents on the political right, with losses of 44 seats incurred by the center left.[1]

In January 1936, the alliance had published the program that was negotiated more than six months after the interested parties had finally agreed to a strategy that would unify their constituencies in order to advance as many deputies as possible into power. That July 27, 1935, agreement had come less from backroom political maneuvering than from the surge of Popular Front energy on the streets during the Bastille Day demonstration two weeks before. Unforgettably, columns of Socialists and Communists linked arms on their way to the Père Lachaise cemetery in front of the Mur des Fédérés, symbol of the 1871 insurrection and Paris Commune. A genuine grassroots movement took shape that day. This glorious baptism followed the frantic mobilization of political parties and nonaligned groups on the political left in the wake of the February 1934 riots that augured a possible right-wing takeover and that left fifteen dead and nearly fifteen hundred wounded. Inklings of a united left can be found even earlier in the decade in isolated efforts by individuals and groups to combat the spread of fascism in Europe. But only when armed fascists and their sympathizers appeared on the streets of Paris did those on the left who had urged vigilance in the name of the French Republic scramble to organize a grassroots coalition that laid the groundwork of the Popular Front's electoral victory two years later.

The mixed record of the Blum government resulted from political and economic instability that preceded and outlasted it. Even before the administration was in place, labor unions went on strike to push leaders beyond their announced program of reforms. Those strikes were resolved in the June 1936

Matignon Accords, which established collective contracts, salary increases averaging 12 percent, a forty-hour work week, and annual paid vacations. Yet these concessions weakened domestic industry by prompting large companies to send capital out of the country. The outbreak of the Spanish Civil War on July 18, 1936, heightened pressure on Blum from political sectors reluctant to see France involve itself in a conflict likely to jeopardize the domestic economic recovery. By February 1937, Blum's call for a momentary pause in economic and social reforms in order to stabilize the nation heightened resistance among disaffected Communists and Radicals in the Chamber of Deputies. Four months later, after being in power for only 380 days, the Blum government unraveled.

Further disintegration of the economic and political situation led, in March 1938, to a second government under Blum that lasted less than a month. A general strike in November of the same year marked the formal end of the Popular Front movement. This final demise went virtually unnoticed, coming as it did two months after the Munich agreements that were intended as a response to the military expansion of Nazi Germany. Joining Neville Chamberlain in endorsing those agreements was Léon Blum's successor, the pragmatic Edouard Daladier. By the time Hitler's armies invaded Poland in September 1939, the Popular Front's ideal of solidarity across parties and classes had evaporated in a collective anxiety that colored what the French called the phony war *(drôle de guerre)* preceding the June 1940 fall of France. Thus, a mere four years separates the parliamentary vote supporting the Popular Front government and the vote relinquishing the French Republic to German occupying forces in a compromise that established the Etat Français under Philippe Pétain.

Popular fronts outside France emerged between the wars in Germany, Chile, and especially Spain in the name of antifascism, supported by the ambitions of the Comintern (Communist International) to overthrow bourgeois domination around the world.[2] The specific configuration of these coalitions varied from country to country, eroding the pretense of universal reach attached to a term like "Popular Front." Even within the national context, equating the French words *front* and *coalition* was debated, since the former, which was in vogue with the French Communist Party, was countered by the Radicals' preference for the word *rassemblement* ("gathering"). We, too, suspect that the term "Popular Front" designates something altogether too "frontal" to characterize or even suggest the less coordinated activities in the background that we deem significant. Our aim is to look into and around what stands front-and-center, in order to thicken the political dimension by bringing out its cultural depth.

From Narrative History to a Poetics of the Past

Stavisky . . . , a 1974 art film set in the 1930s, stamped our notion and our approach to the Popular Front. Exercising a radical form of historiography, its *auteurs*, the cinéaste Alain Resnais and the novelist Jorge Semprun, did far more than "bring the era to life" through filmed biography. In effect, they restaged a founding episode of the period by putting in play innumerable distinct aspects around even more distinct points of view. Suddenly, elements that had been anchored to their assigned roles within the overall narrative began to shimmer as their relations oscillated from one scene to the next. All at once, possibilities and strictures surrounding various individuals and classes could be felt. The simultaneous yet diverse perspectives of those people— agents and victims, we might designate them—opened up a genuinely multi-dimensional history, operating at various speeds or, to use the Heideggerian term, temporalities. A *ciné-poème* rather than a narrative, *Stavisky . . .* offers more than just another representation of a familiar past, even one adding something unfamiliar to what we know. It exchanges historical knowledge for historical *expérience*, using this term with its French connotation of "experiment."

We saw this film shortly before we met at the University of Iowa and discovered our shared enthusiasms. We understood it to be the apex of the *mode rétro*, that stylish return of fiction and film to the Vichy and prewar periods (often represented in comforting autumnal hues) that compensated for the widespread disillusionment after the failures of May 1968. Doubtless our fascination with the Popular Front had begun in that tumultuous year, which affected everyone in our generation. As students of twentieth-century French literature, philosophy, and cinema, both of us were primed to inquire into the precedents which grounded the solidarity among students and workers expressed so dramatically in Paris that spring.

And so we responded to *Stavisky . . .* in the register of elegy, and we discussed it in relation to another keynote film of the mid-1970s, Alain Tanner's *Jonas qui aura 25 ans en l'an 2000* (Jonah Who Will Be 25 in the Year 2000), which in turn deliberately peered through the lens of May '68 to recover Jean Renoir's social aesthetic of the 1930s. When several of those Renoir masterpieces were re-released to partake in the 1981 ascendancy of France's second Socialist government, we were ready to rethink the decade of the 1930s through them. Thus began our collaboration and the germ of this book. Eager to revivify the heritage taken up by François Mitterrand—especially in contrast to that of Margaret Thatcher and Ronald Reagan—we returned to the poignant novels, plays, films, paintings, and essays that had inspired us as students in large part because they were associated with a period of political optimism. The films of Resnais, Tanner, and Renoir had brought those politics and that era into our present.

And we returned to the Popular Front era with a new dispensation, for, as *Stavisky . . .* exemplified, historiography in the meantime had opened itself to the possibilities of fiction. Our conversations took on the terms of the Nouvelle Histoire, whose proponents were wresting authority from a tradition of writing history that gave priority to politics. In an academic ambience that Stephen Bann has aptly described as thick with historical-mindedness, we no longer wanted simply to read novels and films against a historical background, or to mobilize artworks to illuminate signal moments of history.[3] We joined colleagues in literary studies who were redirecting their skills in close reading and interpretation to venture headlong into topics previously reserved for professional historians. And we kept our eyes on those historians who were ready to discuss imaginative texts or to treat history as a field where the literary mode was an essential part of the historical endeavor rather than an accoutrement.[4] The effects of the Nouvelle Histoire were being registered in the United States as the New Cultural History, many of whose proponents (Lynn Hunt, Robert Darnton, Natalie Zemon Davis) worked on France. The titles of books such as *The Family Romance of the French Revolution, The Great Cat Massacre,* and *The Return of Martin Guerre* made one think of novels, or at least of the rapport between fascinating anecdote or episode and broader historical concerns.[5] Accordingly, a period's *mentalité*—its range of categories covering perception, concepts, expression, and actions—could be deduced from exemplary cases such as those of the sixteenth-century peasant Arnaud du Tilh in *The Return of Martin Guerre,* or a fifteenth-century Italian apostate in Carlo Ginzburg's *The Cheese and the Worms.* It could also be deduced from catalogues of items available in or valuable to a specific period, such as the inventory of devotional books in the so-called Bibliothèque Bleue, widely disseminated in eighteenth-century France, and putatively one index to a *mentalité populaire.*[6] The upsurge in the history of *mentalités* built on earlier Annales work, such as that of Lucien Febvre on the carnival and Philippe

Ariès on attitudes toward death. As a whole, this school sought to account for emotions and beliefs that standard histories of political, social, and religious institutions often elided.

Catalogues and anecdotes had also been instrumental to Michel Foucault's Faustian project to overturn the disciplines of philosophy, history, and literature. His notion of episteme—congruent with but more influential than *mentalité*—was famously introduced in reference to incommensurable catalogues and inventories each pertinent to a specific period. As for the anecdotes on which Foucault built his archeological analyses, a shocking example was that which he published under the title *Moi, Pierre Rivière, ayant égorgé ma mère, ma soeur et mon frère....* Foucault used this horrific family murder case to expose repressed aspects of the social system of nineteenth-century Europe. In 1976, René Allio made a feature film of Foucault's "historical" text.[7]

As a theorist of discourse and its uneven formations in history, Foucault emphasized the concept of *pouvoir/savoir* ("power/knowledge") over both reason and historical record. This concept doubtless encouraged the New Historicism, which swept into the United States at the outset of the 1980s. Literary scholars of the English Renaissance turned anew to social history by reexamining canonical texts (even Shakespeare) in conjunction with the mundane writings and sociocultural issues of the period. They unearthed diaries, logs, and tracts as materials for scrutiny. Using literary analysis, they meant to rethink how culture was represented as a noisy, cutthroat arena where words—including the sublime words of poets and playwrights—entered fully into struggles for economic and social domination. This New Historicism soon spread to the study of the nineteenth century and other periods of literature in English.

Working with French materials and methods, we did not explore possible parallels offered by the New Historicism, landing on the notion of "poetics of culture" to characterize our approach before learning about Stephen Greenblatt's coining of the phrase. We planned to introduce such a poetics to a period that is both beloved (because it incubated so many remarkable works) and significant (because those works and the figures who produced them precipitated out of an exemplary political moment). "Poetics" is an enticing term because it recognizes the dialectic between creativity and rules in artistic expression. A "poetics of culture" lodges those rules and regularities less in aesthetic universals than in the rapport between artist and contemporaneous social institutions and practices.

Greenblatt's supremely influential notion dates from his 1980 book *Re-*

naissance Self-Fashioning, which negotiates the relations of social structures to the presumed autonomy of literature, in the context of Renaissance Europe. The congruence of our project with Greenblatt's was evident when we encountered his 1987 essay expressly defining the phrase "poetics of culture."[8] For we, too, insist on the social relations that shape even the most fanciful products of the imagination and the most politically disengaged of artists. Much like Greenblatt, we accord a tethered freedom to artists, enough to allow their products some agency to speak back to, and even to alter, the structures they are inevitably caught up in. Less a theory than a series of methods and an attitude, the New Historicism introduced a dialectics of literary interpretation and historical research that would disclose the breadth of interchange between texts and social behaviors, institutions, and situations.

We follow this dialectical impulse when tracking major works that appeared within the social field of Popular Front Paris—principally the novels of Louis-Ferdinand Céline and André Malraux, and certain films of Jean Renoir. But passing well beyond masterpieces of the imagination, and doubtless beyond anything Greenblatt would countenance, we take culture itself as an indefinite text with its own patterns and rules, potentially codified through a greatly extended poetics—one related to reading the newspaper.

To regard the decade through the metaphor of the daily paper is to rummage in the culture of the French capital as in an archive. Since the 1970s, monographs, anthologies, and picture books have furnished a plethora of new statistics, writings, and visual documents to complement the chronicles of the mainly political drama of Paris in the 1930s.[9] But how should this burgeoning archive be mobilized for understanding? The project we undertake in this book, by no means an encyclopedia or a collection of anecdotes, looks for patterns across this enormously enlarged field of inquiry, as if it were an expansive discontinuous text. Hence the term "poetics," which promises to supplement the more common "politics of culture." If the latter aims to define the roles that popular practices and institutions have played in the conduct of public life as well as the role played by politics in education, entertainment, and other facets of everyday life, our poetics characterizes something of the specific qualities and tones felt by Parisians as they lived through and in the 1930s. Whereas the politics of culture produces chronologies and cause/effect sequences that depend on hierarchies of power, a poetics of culture ushers in a hermeneutics that must be as evocative as the active reading of poetry, where major and minor elements interact in dynamic though generally irregular syncopation.

And so we mean to read the city and its activities evocatively as if reading a poem, taking our cue from what we discover, while being aware that the text and its potential for meaning are limitless. At *our* limit, we experience something like the cultural sublime, where the vastness of the field and the minute intricacy of any of its sections make it utterly impossible to parse. Culture lifts itself from text into atmosphere, one might say, and then requires the investigator to use more than semiotics and hermeneutics in order to approach any of its significant moments or products.

From the Dailies to the Decade

Paris conveniently extrudes its culture as text in the ubiquitous newspapers of the period, both in the *quotidien* or "daily press" and in the abundant weeklies, political as well as sensational. A newspaper can shift the weight of history from continuous story to parallel attractions; it requires a peculiar kind of reading, a scansion of sorts. Resnais' *Stavisky . . .* points the way, for it is not merely a film full of newspapers, but one that emulates the form of a paper in its layout.

We have written this book to test our belief that the metaphor of the "front" has occluded other aspects and potential accounts of the period that are crucial to a historical understanding of the final years of the Third Republic. The political drama readily tracked in the headlines of the papers has kept off the page, and off the stage, aspects essential to the character and tone of the period. These neglected aspects often go under the name "culture." They emerge in the synchronic dimension of the topical, and they supplement the diachrony of political history. This pluridimensional sense of the times can be felt in *The Times*—that is, in the newspapers that serve as the constant metaphor for the cultural archive, since they record so many facets of public life.

Newspapers have always been of prime value to historians. They are peerless chronometers of change, monitoring and registering the day-to-day fortunes of a beleaguered nation or the parallel vicissitudes of some particular institution or individual. We, on the contrary, mobilize the newspaper in a quite different manner, using it less for its serial account or investigation of some topic than for the diversity of topics it exhibits in each issue. The 1930s constitute a golden age of illustrated newspapers and of the specialized magazines they spawned. Such publications were ubiquitous and inescapable; hundreds competed for high circulation. As Renoir pictures them in his 1936 film *Le Crime de Monsieur Lange*, newsboys pedaled through the capital to drop off bundles of papers and magazines at kiosks; thousands and thousands of readers went straight to the columns or sections that they followed by habit. Most must have scanned the headlines to keep up with the "news." But many went directly to the sports results, the theater schedules, or the *méteo* (weather reports), where daily changes were marked by reassuring continuity—repetition with variations. Day after day the newspaper conveyed familiarity and "oldness" to readers of the "news."

We mean to treat Paris in the 1930s as the newspapers of the time treated it. International and state politics were certain to be found on the front page, but one's eyes were invited to flit across parallel columns reporting on a great range of topics. Then, as now, the layout of the paper on any given day might feature columns with titles that we could readily adapt for our chapters: "Education," "Leisure," "Business," "International News," "Books," "Opinion," "The Arts," "Fashion," and "Sports." Thus, the daily newspaper opens up the decade for today's historians; it circulated through all strata of society and kept track of innumerable activities harboring the slightest public interest.

Of course many dailies, especially those backed by political parties, professed a slant (or *parti pris*), but their take on political events in France and the world seldom spilled over into their other, more mundane columns. Even *L'Humanité*, the organ of the French Communist Party, carried a daily sports page, as well as weekly features directed toward women. Newspapers were meant to be enticing. And so illustrations and photographs systematically break up the streams of words flowing down the columns. Captured by these pictures and by the sensual lure they tender in the midst of the reportage, we have tied our chapters to the images as well as to the texts of history. Overall, then, the ubiquity of the newspaper leads us to construct the equivalent of a historical layout (*la mise-en-page de l'histoire*) that emphasizes simultaneity and coincidence over hierarchy and scripted drama. Spread out on a table, the news of the decade is multiple; tellingly, it moves at different rates of change. Some columns jolt the reader with the shock of scandal or of sudden political decisions and turnabouts. Others scarcely develop over months or years. We hunt for patterns of change in the areas of theater, cinema, and music hall, in architecture, city planning, and transportation, as well as in the role of the media (radio, phonography, publishing). We mean to register the effects of disparate activities and institutions on one another and to model the multi-temporality of lives enmeshed in a tangled web where nationalism and modernity increasingly confound efforts to stabilize social and personal identity.

Circling behind the Front

Did the political drama really appear straightforward even to those in picket lines, voting lines, or lines marching down boulevards in demonstrations? It cannot, in any case, seem straightforward to us, who are circling around it through successive loops of re-vision from disparate vantage points: this moment of writing in 2004, as we prepare our study; or that of the fiftieth anniversary of the Popular Front, celebrated by Mitterrand's government in 1986; or that of 1974, when Resnais' *Stavisky . . .* premièred; or that of 1968, another generation's version of people's politics. Each time, a different impulse occasions a return to the 1930s; each time, a different set of concerns filters access to that past. Each time, a different set of images, accounts, statistics, and points of view present themselves in layered fashion.

The Popular Front may be prosaic (that is, represented through the logic of prose), but the era requires a more complex expression, a poetic or cinematographic form in which, as in *Stavisky . . .* , a jumble of elements and perspectives shape themselves into what Resnais termed the "harmonics of history." This analogy to a musical score, being time-based, seems superior to the metaphor of a painting and even to that of history as fresco. The analogy of a score also reminds us of the variety of registers and instruments that must be accounted for, many toning simultaneously, whereas historians often listen only to the violins or perhaps the horns. What about the background? What about the work of the timpanist, the bassoonist? And what about the peculiar effect produced by the interplay of, say, bassoon and timpani? Every historical period may be defined by its recognizable melodic line. But the period comes to life most vibrantly when we attend to the complexity of the full orchestra as well as to the weave of its myriad micro-musical events. After all, it is the orchestra that produces the melody, not the reverse.

How can one represent the simultaneity of sound that arises from so many different registers? Treating culture as a score, like reading it as a newspaper, challenges the linear layout of our own format, the monograph. And so we must struggle against convention to amplify certain of the harmonic effects produced by the interaction of cultural registers. To elicit something of the tone of the period, we must retard the momentum, if not the argument, implied by the serial order of chapters, most of which analyze a distinct cultural register (or sonic layer). Splitting the book into two parts halts the forward motion of the chapters, and initiates a recursive movement whereby topics in later chapters can be folded back onto those that arise earlier. For the two parts follow opposite trajectories, with the first descending from elite individuals and groups to street life, and the second rising from the sounds and images on those streets. Specifically, Part I observes the spectacle of impatient intellectuals mobilizing the expanded publics reached by the cinema and the illustrated press. To the hundreds of thousands of Parisians who paraded through their city on certain occasions in the years 1934–1936, one must add the millions more who followed these events at home through the newspapers. Mass media proffered the vain hope of rational mass movement.

Yet on most other days, Parisians were, as always, concerned first about the ordinary business of their lives. In Part II, we turn away from the cutting edge of the front to sample the atmosphere that people breathed across the city at large. We temper the dramatic history of discrete events (riots, elections, film premières, literary prizes) with accounts of habits and proclivities that pertain to the more banal realm of daily life whose aspects evolve more slowly over the decades. Nineteenth-century Parisians—indeed, pre-Revolutionary Parisians a century earlier—set up homes and shops, baked and bought bread, drank coffee or wine in neighborhood establishments in ways not so different from those of the 1930s. Still, even daily life is mutable in its trends and emphases, producing distinct tones, each characteristic of its era.

In sum, our focus shifts from forms of political engagement in Part I to daily life in Part II, from a concern with *populist politics* to simply *the popular*, from Jean Renoir's commissioned *film à thèse*, *La Marseillaise*, to René Clair's aptly titled entertainment *Sous les toits de Paris* (Under the Roofs of Paris).

The Circulation of Culture

The term "culture" has appeared so often in book titles over the past twenty years that it has become a default for identifying what the disciplines of the humanities have difficulty tying down. Nevertheless, we find ourselves picking up this term, in conjunction with "politics" and "poetics," precisely because it makes no methodological demands, merely pointing to a site of values yet to be identified. Whether one takes that site to be material (concrete institutions and practices) or intangible (the *mentalité* of a time, place, and people), "culture," as contrasted with politics, exhibits itself in countless ways and seldom announces its development or progress. This accounts for the series of metaphors we deploy to encircle it: culture as newspaper, as musical score, and now as atmosphere.

All three metaphors counter the military image of a Popular Front sweeping through Paris and across France, bringing political change; this offers too convenient a way to map people, forces, and events. If one follows the fluctuations of fronts and gauges the flows and pressure of ideas and images that surge behind them, the limits of this term become apparent. For fronts are hardly ready-made; they result from movement and friction that may ultimately organize people and nations into a comprehensible array exhibiting direction and purpose. Think of the chaos of molecular movement behind the formation of dramatic lines on a weather map. The fronts are the main features displayed (usually with colored lines and arrows). Behind them, we are told, turbulent air masses fluctuate and conflict, while these in turn result from temperature shifts, pressure gradients, constricting isobars, and other variables impossible to track. No wonder chaos theory immediately latched onto weather as its preferred example. Normal science could not calculate the innumerable causes and consequences of such complex systems.

Chastened by the limits of linear analysis and fascinated less by fronts themselves than by their formation, we have come to another meteorological metaphor—*circulation*—which de-dramatizes the period by urging us to look and listen for incessant rather than directed movements. Weather systems produce general climatic conditions, but they themselves often contain warm and cold fronts. We emphasize the term "contain" in order to subordinate the "fronts" of politics to the "circulation" of the cultural atmosphere. Slower-moving patterns suggest molecular rather than dynamic movement. Part II of our book attends to the modulation of culture, in contrast to the deliberate (even scheduled) street work of Part I.

The term "circulation" conveys not just the air that passes above and through Paris, but the essence of urban life in an era when it was lived more in the streets than it is today. On specific occasions—such as February 6, 1934, July 14, 1935, and May through July, 1936—masses of people representing a variety of groups converged on the Place de la Concorde, the Place de la Bastille, the Place de la Nation. Congestion, blockages, and even blockades resulted. But on more ordinary days, street movement circulated without such unified purpose or dramatic pressure. Individuals exchanged greetings, goods, and money; they performed or demanded services, took in entertainment of many sorts, and spent long hours in conversation and debate, often at buzzing cafés and restaurants. This activity was hardly scripted; it certainly formed no front. Rather, it exuded a tone that cultural historians of late have sought to articulate via histories of sounds, smells, anxieties—

qualities without distinct chronology. Our chapters in Part II measure the atmospheric pressure of the day, to keep up with the current of what's current: history from below, floating upward, perhaps to affect the ideas or the rhetoric of those who mean to direct it.

Much of the ambience of an era remains invisible and imaginary. Beneath, outside, or beyond the thoroughfares of public life, in a zone where fantasy and fear govern social inclination, lie *frontiers*—like that of colonial Africa. In the French fascination with Africa and what it represents, national identity falters and then strives to regain its footing. The 1931 Colonial Exposition in Paris signals the impossibility of understanding collective identity in conjunction with nation and republic, apart from the identity of Greater France *(la plus grande France)*. Yet this identity must, by definition, be vaster and deeper than the thin political line conjured up by the term "Popular Front." The colonies presented France with obvious and pressing political options. But their importance to the identity of France as republic and nation transcended the political process and the political imagination. Films, novels, paintings, and ethnographic studies all make plain that the colonies represented something beyond the limit of what fronts and borders stand for—something, in fact, that is powerful because indeterminate and imaginary. Our exploration of Parisian culture ends with the fantasies that form its underside.

How can we hope to address such an amorphous and inclusive conception of culture? What model allows the whole to resonate while elements in different layers play at their own tempo? This question surely stood before Resnais and Semprun as they undertook their collaboration on *Stavisky* . . . . The historical composition they arrived at may serve as an inventory of the elements that our book means to put into play. More important, it serves as a model that displays the simultaneity of the politics and poetics of culture at the inception of the Popular Front.

Introduction.
A Page in History:
Resnais' *Stavisky* . . . and the 1930s

To keep up with the Stavisky scandal—i.e., the French government—anyone would have to read the newspapers three hours a day, which is what everybody does. It is curious to be living in a land where the government is busy not governing, but sucking pencils over the scenario of a superproduction, thirty-million-dollar gangster film on which it will not get a penny back—if it can help it.

—Janet Flanner, *Paris Was Yesterday*

Cinema as History

What kind of access to the past can a feature film provide? What kind of historical understanding does it afford in an age in which authority is challenged everywhere, especially in the academy? For the past—whether we think of it through memory or through history—is necessarily an effect, hence a relative quantity and open to revision. Indeed, the fact that we recognize such different entryways to the past as private memory and public history demonstrates the existence of multiple perspectives that ultimately produce rival versions. Why not enter the past through whatever version seems most compelling and insightful? Particularly when that past appears to be inscrutable and contested, as is the case with which we begin: the case that goes by the name "The Stavisky Affair."

The tumultuous political events that rocked France January–February 1934 have been narrated in so many ways—from investigative reporting to tabloid exposés, political cartoons, and detective novels—that it is easy to confuse fact with fiction. From the start, divergent accounts surrounded the life and death of Alexandre ("Sacha") Stavisky—alias Serge Alexandre—who was discovered shot and near death on January 8, 1934, inside a chalet near the Alpine resort town of Chamonix. Stavisky's death at three o'clock the next morning ended a nationwide search by the Sûreté Générale, France's near-equivalent of the American FBI. At the time of his death, Stavisky was a key figure wanted for questioning in connection with a fraud involving the municipal loan office of Bayonne, a city on the Atlantic coast in southwestern France. The loan office was the tip of a pyramid scheme in which insurance companies bought millions of francs' worth of false bonds on the advice of politicians and government officials who, as it turned out, had been advised by Alexandre and his cohorts.[1]

No one will ever know for certain whether Stavisky was a suicide or a murder victim. Janet Flanner (writing under the pen name Genêt) stated in her "Letter from Paris" column for the *New Yorker* that fourteen of twenty-two French newspapers covering the story described Stavisky's death as a suicide.[2] The police, she continued, were going to have a hard time burying the corpse because many people believed the police had shot Stavisky to prevent him from revealing activities that might prove compromising to government officials, including the police themselves. A criminal lawyer reviewing the case later rejected the hypotheses of suicide and outright execution in favor of what he termed "suicide by persuasion."[3] Uncertainty surrounding the death fueled a scandal that within less than a month toppled an entire cabinet of ministers under Camille Chautemps. In addition, controversy over Stavisky's links with the Chautemps administration revealed the internal hostilities within France that would resurface to plague the Popular Front government under Léon Blum and the 1940–1944 Etat Français under Philippe Pétain.

We take Alain Resnais' *Stavisky . . .* as our point of departure first of all because it collects and interrelates a remarkable variety of elements from the period, laying them out in patterns linked to its mysterious title character, who arguably triggered the events that brought the Popular Front into being. More important, *Stavisky . . .* models a historiographic method we are intent on deploying, one that represents multiple perspectives and temporalities coexisting within a determinate period.

Rather than analyze the film, we follow it as an enticing representation of (and from) the past, and we do so at its own speed. Swept along in the wake of the film's visual and narrative movement, we submit, temporarily at least, to its vision and fate. Historians used to consider such simulated experience as an entertaining and refreshing supplement, a diversion or game for those with a taste for "art" and "literature." One could always return to the facts of the case after trying on the feel of a movie, a novel, or a biography. Today, however, few should be confident in those famous "facts of the case." Our vision of the past, whatever we take the *past itself* to be, is inevitably inflected— and even constituted—by every version that purports to show what happened, subjected to a hermeneutics either of suspicion or, in the attitude we adopt here, of critical acceptance.

So let us accept—critically—the vision of the 1930s in *Stavisky . . .* , while acknowledging the largely unforeseen consequences it may have for our sense of the events the film portrays and the era it marks. From the outset, Resnais tempts us visually to follow him. As the movie begins, a gently curving country road stretches far before us; then a single automobile—of 1930s vintage— speeds past, as though asking us to follow even if, as in the recurring nightmare later recounted by Stavisky's wife, Arlette, that car were inevitably to plunge over a cliff. We do, in fact, arrive at a cliff. And through the binoculars of a minor character, we close in on an amazing historical tableau of "grand"—that is, mythic—history in the making: Leon Trotsky, in an unmarked motorboat, entering France at the tiny harbor of Cassis, on the Mediterranean coast not far from Marseilles. At first glance, this would seem to be a film of grand characters and grand events, one seen, as here, at a distance from highly determined and therefore limited perspectives.

Resnais could count on a huge public of spectators to follow him to this past, because the release of *Stavisky . . .* in 1974 coincided with a resurgence of a nostalgic *mode rétro* relishing the cultures and artifacts of the 1930s and 1940s. *Stavisky . . .* also secreted the musky aroma of other notable *rétro* films of the time, such as Bernardo Bertolucci's *Il Conformista* (The Conformist), Vittorio De Sica's *Il Giardino dei Finzi-Contini* (The Garden of the Finzi Continis), and Jack Clayton's *The Great Gatsby*. James Monaco is precise on this point: "As an historical film set in the thirties, *Stavisky . . .* was perfectly set up to take advantage of the art-deco nostalgia which was cresting at just that time, especially since it starred [Jean-Paul] Belmondo, who had foreshadowed the fad for thirties clothes and lifestyles with *Borsalino* (1970), a film named after a hat!"[4]

Should we hesitate to take in the past through such films, to be "taken in" by the sheerly sensual lure of the colors, architecture, and music of those times? Not in every case, for films are texts before they are spectacles. And

1. A witness to history.

2. Trotsky arrives secretly in the French port of Cassis (July 24, 1933).

3. The pyramid in the Parc Monceau: symbol of unfathomable mystery.

like all texts, they often promote critical understanding and even self-critique. *Il Conformista*, for example, scarcely claims to account for Italian fascism. Instead, it explicitly questions its own staging of the past, in what amounts to a self-critique. At its center, unforgettably, Marcello (played by Jean-Louis Trintignant) and the exiled Professor Quadri rehearse Plato's allegory of the cave, complete with shadows thrown on the wall. In this dark psychoanalytic film, Bertolucci willingly leaves the truth of history inaccessible, instead projecting shadows—like those that play dimly around the threatening shell of Rome's Colosseum in the final sequence, when a hysterical Marcello repudiates his personal and political past to the outcasts huddled around makeshift fires.

Similarly, the last lines spoken in Resnais' film declare that Stavisky heralded the end of an era. In fact, that era would end in 1939 with a similar line and a similar scene when, in Jean Renoir's *La Règle du jeu* (The Rules of the Game), two aristocrats lament the passing of a way of life. Two months later, Hitler invaded Poland and the French government banned Renoir's film. The fatalistic lines on which *Stavisky* . . . concludes are spoken in voice-over by the anachronistic Baron Raoul (Charles Boyer), while the camera approaches an unidentified monument: the pyramid in the Parc Monceau. Even more than Bertolucci's Colosseum, this apparently ancient and anonymous monolith provides an ambiguous conclusion that suggests the troubling issues which continue to surround the historical events portrayed.

It is to maintain the essential ambiguity of Stavisky and of the constellation of major political events his name evokes that Resnais switches among very different perspectives, avoiding what most historical accounts represent in straight linear order. Resnais even takes the most ignorant of his characters seriously when he allows Baron Raoul to summarize Stavisky's death in the lines that conclude the film: "I realized it too late, but Stavisky was announcing death to us. . . . Not only his own, not only those of this past February, but the death of an era, of a whole period of history."[5] The Baron's peripheral status gives an ironic twist to his testimony as survivor. Even before the death of his friend Sacha, Baron Raoul was already a vestige of the recent past to which Stavisky, emblematic of new money, was drawn. The Baron's squandering of a vast fortune in casinos and risky investments foreshadows Stavisky's financial failures. In a sense, Raoul is a kind of false uncle who embodies the decadent French nobility to which, at least in part, Stavisky aspired. The ruin of aristocratic—that is, "family"—money associated with class and privilege prepares the ruin of devalued money of foreign origins associated with fraudulent schemes and corrupt officials. In the end, both fortunes are lost; neither ("good") French money nor ("bad") foreign money retains its value. The Baron's gloomy summary becomes a prophecy for the decline of the Third Republic: the Blum regime, the interval following the 1938 Munich agreement, and finally the "phony war" preceding the fall of France to the Germans.

The ambiguity and self-consciousness that pervade Resnais' rewriting of history are already evident in the three dots of the ellipsis contained in his film's title. How many figures does Stavisky (embodied in the figure of Jean-Paul Belmondo) represent in life and then in death? Monaco provides one answer to the question, in the form of a litany:

Serge Stavisky, the petty confidence trickster who seduces a woman to steal her jewels. Serge Alexandre, the suave image of the scandal newspapers and color magazines, and an international financier whose network of professional friends and lackeys extends throughout the fabric of French society in the thirties. Sacha, for whom living well is the best revenge. Stavisky, the Russian Jew who persists perversely in calling attention to himself in xenophobic, antisemitic France in the early thirties. Alexandre the theoretician of advanced decadent capitalism who explains that "the only way to attract money is to show it" and who understands probably better than most less successful businessmen of the time that style and image are at least as valuable as cold, hard cash and that cash is fictional in nature: credit is all.[6]

Sounding very much like a prototype of Charles Foster Kane in Orson Welles's *Citizen Kane*, Resnais' Serge Alexandre screams out, "No one knows who I am! None of you knows what I am capable of!" And like the reporter Thompson, the "historian" who leads us through Welles's film, an associate of Serge Alexandre concedes that all he can supply is "a single piece of a jigsaw puzzle." Because he skips about in time and from one perspective to another, Resnais has often been described as a maker of jigsaw puzzles. He has encouraged this view. Interviewed about *Stavisky . . .* , he said, "What I am striving for in a film is to try to construct a kind of compact object in which all the pieces or elements interrelate but . . . in isolation seem irrational."[7]

Like artists in the high modernist tradition such as Ford Maddox Ford, James Joyce, and the Cubist painters, and like filmmakers such as Federico Fellini, Resnais decomposes his subject so that he can reconstitute it through artistic intelligence. He chooses his point of departure in a series of events whose significance in a real past increases with gaps and resistances that are never overcome. The conventional questions raised by historical inquiry—what happened and what is the significance of what happened?—are sharpened by the lure of a detective story. To put it another way, the historical inquiry is supplemented by the desire to set individual facts and data concerning "what happened" into an integral whole, so that the historian's inquiry into a real past converges with the novelist's worry over emplotment. And so *Stavisky . . .* is a film very much in tension between its scenes and its structure, between fragments and spectacle.

Resnais thwarts our expectation of a faithful rendering of a real past by chopping up chronology from the very start and by setting the fairy-tale figure of Stavisky alongside the serious historical one of Trotsky (whose name is also a pseudonym). Up close, each scene, each figure stands out with hard edges: clear, autonomous, even beautiful, but unpredictable in the larger scheme. When seen from a distance through the structuring organization of the whole, these pieces meld into a totality that signifies eloquently just this complexity of history. To quote Resnais again: "What I'm trying to create are

4. Malraux and Trotsky: momentous meeting on August 15, 1933.

different kinds of harmonics, which, taken together, will make an emotional impact."[8]

Resnais' harmonics of historiography involve the intertwining of determinate facts (such as the various investigative dossiers) with fiction bordering on dream and fantasy. Midway through the film, Stavisky's physician, Dr. Mézy (Michel Lonsdale), declares: "In order to understand Alex, you sometimes have to forget the files. You have to dream about him, try and imagine what his dreams are." Accompanying this speech is a sequence of shots of Paris from the early part of the century, concluding with a shot of the pyramid in the Parc Monceau. The pyramid shot punctuates Mézy's account of Sacha's initiation into a life of pleasure. It objectifies a primal scene mixing pleasure and death. The pyramid itself serves as a metaphor for the secret and the unexplained, a mausoleum of unconscious drives and unfathomable personal truths. *Stavisky* . . . generously supplies us with material for inconclusive but evocative dreams. After Trotsky's clandestine arrival in Cassis, we peer into his everyday life, first through gates in Saint-Palais sur Mer and later over a stone fence in Barbizon. In one scene we glimpse him in extreme long shot, seated under an umbrella reading with his wife. In another a young man tells of a late-night meeting with Malraux—"Now there's one conversation I'd love to have overheard"—as we see headlights isolating Trotsky in the distance and a dark-haired man in a cape bounding from the car to embrace him. This scene, etched by Malraux himself in his memoirs, comes straight out of real history. A recent biography of Malraux virtually replicates Resnais:

> To keep Trotsky from being lynched by communist dockworkers, the French authorities had him and his wife secretly removed and taken by tugboat to the little port of Cassis before their liner docked at Marseilles. Just where Trotsky was hiding was a closely guarded secret. But thanks both to André Chamson . . . and to one of André Gide's Trotskyist friends, Malraux was able to obtain an appointment with the illustrious revolutionary. In Paris he was picked up by a stranger who only identified himself after they had driven well beyond the city's southern suburbs as Trotsky's son. . . . It took them a full day to cover the 500 kilometers and it was long after sunset when they finally drew up in front of a seaside villa situated in the village of Saint-Palais, near Royan. . . . Brilliantly illuminated by the two headlight beams, Trotsky came out to greet the visitor, dressed in light summer attire of white shoes and trousers. . . . Without wasting a moment, Trotsky led Malraux into his study. On the desk a revolver was placed like a weight on a sheaf of papers.[9]

Romantic pictures like this give the impression that history is under control, that it exists "out there" in time and space, so that we could capture it if we were only privileged enough to glimpse or to "overhear" it. The appearance of well-being that images beget is embodied in the film by no one more strongly than by Baron Raoul. In one tell-tale scene, he spies through his binoculars on Arlette and Montalvo (the Spanish aristocrat who desperately courts her) and asks, "What are they saying? She looks absolutely entranced."[10] The Baron is certain that Montalvo is seducing Arlette; but Montalvo is, in fact, mixing seduction with politics, as we learn when Resnais replays the same scene close up from another angle, allowing us to hear the words the Baron can only guess at. The two perspectives are not a stylistic quirk or a minor flourish. They remind us that although the Baron repeatedly volunteers accounts of the past, his attempt to interpret what happened is limited by the partiality of his position and personality. At the start, the Baron recounts Arlette's triumph modeling a fancy car at Biarritz to an avid Sacha,

5. Anny Duperey as Stavisky's glamorous wife: triumph at Biarritz.

6. Photo portrait of Stavisky's wife, Arlette, as model (1934).

7. Serge Alexandre (Jean-Paul Belmondo) descends into the lobby of the Claridge Hotel.

who savors every detail. At the end, he describes the aftermath of the scandal in his testimony at a government investigation into Stavisky's death. But how much does he really know? Resnais' reprise in close-up does more than revise and correct the Baron's view of Arlette and Montalvo; it insists that the past be built as a composite.

While *Stavisky* . . . purports to tell a story involving major historical characters, the film is replete with more ordinary figures like the Baron—a host of witnesses, snoops, and sycophants of various stripes who live off the events of the personages around them. Nor is any character, large or small, easy to read. This is a corrupt world full of gossip, blackmail, and seductive public spectacles. Arlette's role as a model allows her to control her emotions and to remain ever the center of attention. Such mastery of visual space is even more dramatically true of Serge Alexandre, whom we first see descending godlike in a glass elevator at the Claridge Hotel, with a red carnation in the lapel of his impeccable suit. In a later scene, he declares that the wealthy should show off their money, and he does so in various fashionable outfits. Yet Stavisky's "alias" signifies throughout the film that a complex being inhabits the body underneath those clothes. When the clothes are removed during a physical examination, the man regresses from Serge to Sacha by donning a false mous-

8. "Alexandre's Empire" theater, featuring the operetta *Katinka* in 1933.

tache and a cheap overcoat. Ironically, the very deceptiveness of this disguise reveals the authentic identity of Sacha Stavisky within the larger-than-life figure of Serge Alexandre.[11]

Resnais' Alexandre treats life as spectacle. Throwing elaborate banquets and filling hotel rooms with baskets of flowers, he asserts control over every mise-en-scène that involves him. His lifelong fascination with the theater has prepared him for this. The style of *Stavisky . . .* appropriately settles into several moments of genuine theatrical repose, removed from the flux of ordinary life. A theater called the Empire—known as a "temple du spectacle"—serves as a headquarters from which Alexandre oversees the production of operettas that are advertised in posters and on marquees.[12] Two extended scenes from plays of the period are rehearsed onstage, the first from Sacha Guitry's *Je t'aime* (I Love You; 1920) and the second from Jean Giraudoux's *Intermezzo* (1933).

The very mention of Guitry's name adds to the luster of Resnais' film. For Guitry shared with Stavisky a forename and Russian birth.[13] He shared, as well, an obsession with high life, theatricality, and disguise. Moreover, Resnais singled out Guitry as someone who pioneered the very sort of historical fiction that *Stavisky . . .* aimed to be: "He always made the spectator aware that it was he—Sacha Guitry—playing the king, whether Louis XIV, XV, or whomever."[14] Belmondo adopted this attitude as actor, while Semprun and Resnais endowed the character of Alexandre/Stavisky with something like Guitry's charm, as well as with the bravura of one whose smile challenged the world to unmask him. At this point, Resnais' cinematic adaptation mixes fact and fiction. Reporting on the events of July 24, 1933, the day the action of *Stavisky . . .* opens, the Paris entertainment daily *Comoedia* mentioned neither Stavisky nor Serge Alexandre. It did, however, mention Sacha Guitry, whose popularity was at a peak: four of his plays were being advertised on kiosks as currently running in Paris. When Stavisky went into hiding five months later, *Comoedia* was silent about him, even though he was the owner of a major playhouse. In what today reads like a displacement from one Sacha to another, the entertainment daily continued to monitor Guitry and *his* whereabouts: "Sacha Guitry has just changed hotels, moving to the Elysées-Palais." Then, trying to regain the affection of his new fiancée, the actress Jacqueline Delubac, Guitry fixed up a fantastic room at the Elysées-Reclus, complete with Louis XVI woodwork and designs by Fragonard and Watteau. News of Guitry lightened the pages of *Comoedia* during the February 1934 riots. He was touring Switzerland at the time, brushing off worries about the events: "It's only the government," he allegedly said in a phone conversation.[15] The question here is less one of a causal link between the lives of Guitry and Stavisky than of a stunning parallel that Resnais allowed to color the harmonics of his history.

This attempt to establish a different kind of harmonics between historical past and cinematic account resonates more complexly still when one notes a picture featured in the July 25, 1933, issue of *Comoedia*. Staring at us as "La Figure du Jour" ("The Figure of the Day") is "a figure formerly seen on the terraces in Montparnasse: no less a personage than Mr. Bronstein, . . . who became Trotsky. Exiled at present from Russia, he shows up as a solid middle-class citizen [*en bon bourgeois*] to rest and relax in France. What an ironic destiny!" Conjoined here are three Russian émigrés all facing the world *en bon bourgeois*, a phenomenon utterly fascinating to the French. Their names and their pictures crop up in publications of all sorts: entertainment journals like *Comoedia*, gossip sheets, serious literary magazines, and newspapers. Resnais focuses on Stavisky, but through this mysterious charlatan he also lets us glimpse the figures of Guitry and Trotsky, who bear some family resemblance to him.

With Giraudoux, contrast rather than resemblance creates the kind of

9. Trotsky *à la une* (on page 1) of the entertainment daily *Comoedia* (July 25, 1933).

"emotional effect" Resnais claims to be after. Perhaps less subtle here than with Guitry, Resnais uses Giraudoux to help tie up his text. In the film's concluding speech, it is by allusion to *Intermezzo* ("He was a herald of death . . .") that the Baron characterizes Alexandre's enigmatic existence. Like the Baron, all of us are drawn to the elegance of art as a means of restoring our peace of mind. All of us cling to set pieces and stagings in an effort to comprehend the incoherencies of history. Resnais plays on this need and tendency when he shows how the crumbling of Alexandre's empire coincided with a performance of Shakespeare's *Coriolanus* at the Comédie Française. Though in fact Corneille's *Horace* was at the Comédie Française that night, Resnais and Semprun had every reason to alter the playbill. For *Coriolanus* had been so prominent in the company's repertoire all month that it had caused a stir. Never in recent memory had the conservative Comédie Française taken aim at politics through its program the way it was now doing through Shakespeare. The very first review it received, on December 9, began: "Go see *Coriolanus*. You'd swear the play was written by a veteran of the Great War who has become disheartened by the baseness to which the victors and their virtue have fallen."[16] Two weeks later, on December 23, the day after Stavisky's empire began to unravel, actors and artists broke into the Commis-

10. Shakespeare's *Coriolanus* stokes debate over the Stavisky Affair.

sion of Finance at the Chamber of Deputies to protest the reduction in government funding for the Comédie Française. When one commissioner was asked if the budgetary slash was due in any way to the production of *Coriolanus*, he fumed that words unwarranted by the English original had been deliberately added to the French translation—words designed to bring the play's subject to bear on French politics. He pointed out that the translator was not French at all but Swiss, and a member of a fascist organization who obviously had it in for the current coalition of Radicals and other centrists.

Even without providing these details, Resnais surely expects us to nod knowingly at the tendentious reference to *Coriolanus*, whose plot turns on political duplicity and high-handed patrician behavior that inflicts great suffering on the citizens of Rome. Resnais includes on the soundtrack the boisterous reaction of the theater audience, which cheers and jeers the characters as if they were agents of the noisy politics of their own times. Theatrical representation, inflated here by the combined prestige of Shakespeare and the Comédie Française, promises to clarify all those micro-events of daily life that otherwise disperse themselves chaotically and confusingly on the streets.

Outside the theater, on those very streets, the organizing function of representation persists in the discourse of architecture and public gardens. Certain sequences of *Stavisky . . .* are composed of nothing more than a string of prominent French sites touched by—or "containing"—the drama the film recounts. Resnais often opens a sequence by tilting down from a tightly constructed long shot of the façade of some imposing building: the Claridge in Paris, the town hall in Cassis, or the Palais in Biarritz. These façades announce a mise-en-scène of public history in which Serge Alexandre seems most effective.

Resnais' film is party to this posing, setting itself on display much as does Stavisky's elegant wife, Arlette, happy to be photographed in such a settled, premeditated manner. The highly polished production, backed by Stephen Sondheim's sophisticated salon music, follows the practice of standard historical films—a genre that has always sought to blend public history, which we take pleasure in seeing on the screen, with the characters' private lives, which we dare to imagine. From *Madame Du Barry* and *Queen Christina* to *Reds*, cinema has catered to our historical yen by offering pleasing pictures, intriguing gossip, and narrative closure. In the early 1970s, this genre enjoyed such a vogue that the term *mode rétro* identified not just the pre-1945 setting of a number of prominent French films (*Lacombe Lucien*, *Il Conformista*, and so on) but an attractively cool style, which *Stavisky . . .* exemplifies to perfection.

But even as the genre renews itself through the public's desire for spectacle, *Stavisky . . .* frustrates this desire by trailing off into ellipsis. As the film concludes, the image of the mysterious pyramid returns, the prospect of a mysterious key that—like "Rosebud" in *Citizen Kane*—might unlock the protagonist's life if we knew how to use it. Resnais here takes his cue from the inconclusive judgment of historians and writers who have failed to unravel the full complexities of the case. The following remark by Joseph Kessel recalls Baron Raoul's apology for his harmonious but partial view of the situation: "If the bizarre inquiry conducted into Alexandre's mysterious activities—an inquiry full of holes, intentional gaps, hesitations, contradictions, and missing documents—nevertheless someday fills in the complete picture, I will surely be able to identify the factual source for the impression of resurrection that Alexandre used to convey. For the present, I remain in the realm of conjecture."[17] Kessel, we might note, was of Russian Jewish parentage and—like Stavisky—was caught up in the world of journalism and theater that Stavisky hoped in some measure to control. His 1928 novel *La Nuit des princes* (Night

11. An incongruous rehearsal: Stavisky and Erna read Giraudoux's *Intermezzo* on the set of *Katinka*.

of the Princes) celebrated the life of the Russian émigré community in Paris and probably brought him to Stavisky's attention. Living in the same milieu as Stavisky, Kessel should have been able to see through to the true story.

Perspectivism also shatters the gilded mirror of intelligibility held out by the various theatrical stagings we have cited. Each reference—to Shakespeare, to Guitry, to Giraudoux—is enmeshed in circumstances that further fragment and confuse the "affair" they were called upon to clarify. Resnais reiterates this point when Erna Wolfgang forthrightly introduces herself at the audition as a Jewish actress—"I'm Jewish; I've just arrived from Berlin"— whose latest role has been in Bertolt Brecht's didactic political allegory *Die Massnahme* (The Measures Taken). When the police closed the production, she adds, harsh politics sent her (as well as Brecht) into exile. Stavisky then volunteers to read a scene from Giraudoux's *Intermezzo* with Wolfgang. By contrast, he is anything but forthright, using the theater to mask his Jewishness while multiplying the roles he plays as Serge Alexandre.

Stavisky's passion for theater was symptomatic. After gaining control of the Empire in early 1933, he personally decided to produce *Katinka* (by Rudolf Friml and Otto Hauerbach) in the hope that the success of a Viennese-style operetta based on a Russian folktale would raise the level of entertainment at his theater. Soon, the official theatrical bulletins of the day recognized the Empire's upgraded status, elevating it from *music-hall* (this is the term used in French) to the more prestigious *théâtre comique et dramatique* ("comic and dramatic theater"). An echo of this subtle by-play of artistic distinction can be heard when Alexandre objects to a proposal for a new offering at the Empire, *Deux sous de fleurs* (Tuppence Worth of Flowers). He is concerned by the prospect that this low-grade entertainment might jeopardize the Empire's newfound prestige, as though his theater might be demoted even below *music-hall* to the catch-all category of *théâtre divers*. It is presumably for *Deux sous de fleurs* that the audition sequence in *Stavisky . . .* is held. Hence the resonant irony when Giraudoux's sweet dialogue is intoned against the backdrop of the sets for *Katinka*, which have yet to be struck. Giraudoux's angelic characters—so Christian and so conventionally French in a high "literary" text—come to life in the personae of two Jewish émigrés, Erna Wolfgang and Stavisky, reading their lines in front of a traditional snow-covered Russian building.

The audition scene stages a nightmare of the French right, in which foreign Jews wrest control of French literary culture. The actors in this scene, both immigrants, feed a growing xenophobia and anti-Semitism. Unlike Stavisky, Wolfgang seems to understand the symbolic threat she embodies when she invites Baron Raoul, a pure-blooded aristocrat, to read with her: "If it doesn't strike you as too insulting to the genius and spirit of France, I would like to do a scene from Giraudoux's *Intermezzo*. But for that I need a ghost." The Baron seems willing; but before he can answer, Stavisky interrupts from a balcony loge, offering his own services while he quips that the role of a ghost may be tailor-made for him. Stavisky and Wolfgang play their audition roles at a geographic crossroads of elite and popular cultures. A decade before Alexandre bought the Empire, Maurice Chevalier had made it one of the major music halls in Paris. The day after Stavisky's death, *Comoedia*'s front page lamented the fate of the Empire in terms better suited to the royalist daily *L'Action Française*: "It is unbelievable that we are invaded by so many foreign speculators from god knows where, who are determined to inundate Paris with foreign plays, foreign actors . . . and all with French money."[18]

While Guitry's *Je t'aime* was associated with light nostalgic drama, Giraudoux's *Intermezzo* was written with an entirely different sort of theater in mind—namely, Louis Jouvet's extraordinary Comédie des Champs-

12. Resnais insists on a genuine document of the period, *La Petite Illustration*.

Elysées. Jouvet's production of *Intermezzo* premièred on March 1, 1933, a few days after *Katinka* opened at the Empire. It ran for 116 performances, until June 8—exactly a week before *Katinka* closed. Pierre Renoir (Jean's brother) played the ghost—the role that Stavisky reads in the film—with Valentine Tessier (frequent companion of the publisher Gaston Gallimard) as the fragile Isabelle, alongside the well-established stars Jouvet, Robert le Vigan, and Odette Joyeux. The fairy-tale sets for *Intermezzo* have been described as creating a serene atmosphere that Francis Poulenc's score quietly extended.[19] The production contrasted starkly with the Empire's cruder rendering of traditional Russia in *Katinka* and the dubious status projected onto its owners by remarks such as those in the January 1934 pages of *Comoedia*, alluding to "foreign speculators."

Resnais amplifies the contrast between theater and real-life dramas by having Alexandre jump onstage from a loge to take on the ethereal role of the ghost just after we've witnessed a more personal drama in his office involving Borelli and the blackmailer sent by Inspector Bonny. The contrast makes Giraudoux's script resonate so strangely that Stavisky cannot help noticing it himself. The screenplay by Semprun reads as follows: "'All the dead are extraordinarily clever.' Alexandre stops in mid-speech, probably shocked by the words he has just read. 'All the dead are extraordinarily clever. They never stumble against the void. They never get caught on shadows. They never trip on nothingness. . . . And nothing ever illuminates their faces'"[20]

The audition episode's juxtaposition of Guitry and Giraudoux provides a compelling dramatic sequence. In line with Resnais' desire to create a complex harmonics, the scene also uses theatrical citations to evoke the complexity of Stavisky's character and its various personae. Far from a simple diversion or an extraneous curiosity, the episode allows Resnais to contrive a plausible interplay between avant-garde and music-hall theater, between French spiritualism and international black market, between ostentatious entrepreneurs and the "nothing" that "(n)ever illuminates their faces." More than just the evocation of interpenetrating levels in 1930s culture, this eerie sequence renders history as an unreachable past lorded over by the ghost of nothingness that Giraudoux introduces.

Brief though it may be, Resnais' inclusion of Shakespeare's *Coriolanus* is complex and ironic in the network of references it exposes. Like *Intermezzo*, *Coriolanus* was indeed on the boards in Paris during Stavisky's final year—but, in contrast, the production was openly entangled in the political strife coalescing around Stavisky. Even before the public knew the details of the bond scandal at Bayonne that forced Stavisky into hiding at Christmas of 1933, the Comédie Française production of *Coriolanus* was deemed a calculated affront to the Radical government. Once Stavisky's death had been reported and an apparent cover-up put into effect in January, the relevance of the play's theme became explicit. On February 4, 1934, the government summarily replaced the head of the Comédie Française—Emile Fabré—with a man named Thomé. Expressions of outrage were immediate and crossed ideological lines. As *Comoedia* commented in its February 4 issue, it was clear to all that "an innocent was paying for the sins of the guilty" and that Thomé had been given the job as consolation for having to leave his post as director of the Sûreté Nationale, after being deeply implicated in the scandal. Fabré was not only innocent; he was a widely loved and admired figure, and was at the height of his career. The highly charged atmosphere blurred conventional distinctions between life in the streets and life in the theater, to the point where otherwise mundane events suddenly took on symbolic overtones. This is just what happened with the February 4 première of Raymond Bernard's film *Les Misérables* at the Marignan Theater. *Les Misérables* was France's most ambitious—and most expensive—sound film to date. Bernard hoped and expected that it would open to a public appreciative of Victor Hugo's "timeless" ideas and his own careful rendering of the novel. But it opened instead to a volatile throng ready to use the energy of the occasion to mount a forceful response to the expanded politics of the moment. At the Marignan Theater, Emile Fabré made a spectacular entrance that momentarily stole attention from the film. Cheers broke out during the screening whenever the dialogue veered toward political or social issues. A line referring to the "sickness of the Republic" almost brought the house down. The spectators, said one reporter, had to contemplate the possibility of barricades in their own lives as they witnessed the heroism of the students of 1832.

If Fabré's entrance could attract such attention at a movie première, one can imagine the atmosphere at the performances of *Coriolanus* that continued to pack the Comédie Française. *Comoedia* reported that the February 3 performance was interrupted twice while the audience cheered Fabré (who was treated as the play's hero, according to one account) and shouted down the government officials in attendance.[21] Pressed on many sides, the government reversed itself: on February 6 Fabré was reinstated as head of the Comédie Française and Thomé found himself packing for Stockholm, in the vague position of France's "plenipotentiary." The story hardly ends here—the theater world had only a few hours to savor a rare victory of justice. At 6:30 that evening, crowds erupted in demonstrations that would result in some fifteen deaths and three hundred hospitalizations. The street violence in no way diminished the unusual rapport between staged representation and contemporary political life. Reviewers of *Les Misérables*, for example, could not resist commenting on the film's political overtones, even if it was unlikely that Bernard had intended any. The February 12 issue of *L'Illustration*, a weekly news and feature magazine with one of the largest circulations in Europe, ran seven pages of graphic pictures of carnage in the streets, followed by four full pages devoted to *Les Misérables*. The description of the riots was written by the same journalist who reviewed the Bernard film, Robert de Beauplan. Stage and screen converged with the spectacle on the street, all sites of Popular Front expression in the making.

Writing History: Fragment, Reportage, and Narrative

Stavisky . . . looks back on the events leading up to the February 1934 riots from a point beyond and above them. The last third of the film unrolls in a series of flashbacks provoked by the French government's April 1934 inquest into the affair. From this Olympian judicial height, the duplicities, jealousies, and whims of powerful characters are rumored to result in street riots in Paris and in the annihilation of peasants in Spain, but the bloody riots are never shown. Resnais' period piece remains as cool as Stephen Sondheim's score and as dapper as his hero's stylish clothes. The camera keeps its distance, whether on the cliffs above Cassis or in the glass elevator descending in the Claridge.

Yet this perspective affords no synoptic overview. On the contrary, each shot, no matter how crystalline, stands as merely one intricately cut fragment in a bewildering and complex ensemble. On the surface, these fragments continually satisfy our taste for beautiful spectacles. But like the Parc Monceau pyramid, their autonomy also evokes mystery. What lies beneath or behind perfectly composed images of perfectly composed characters, wearing their finest? We are tempted to pursue the film's vague references to politics, psychology, finance, and popular culture. Shattering the surface of the past to pursue its submerged connections is precisely the work of history.

Resnais brings to bear a full panoply of historiographic tools in *Stavisky . . .*, particularly in its final sections. Scenes showing interrogations by deputies and shots of secret dossiers exemplify history as official inquest. Borelli's trip to Bayonne to dig through ledgers portrays history as sleuthing fed by document and gossip. Inquiry of this kind barely differs from the French *écho* (news item) invoked by the would-be blackmailer who tries to plant a rumor of excessive gambling at Biarritz in hopes of discrediting Stavisky/Alexandre's financial schemes. Each sequence asserts the ties between event and text, especially when the latter is taken as its own kind of event. Throughout the film, history exists in word and image when we see newspapers clipped or documents burned. To be sure, history is also a product of personal testimony staged as though spoken and direct ("live"). Most troubling, history is apparently both unpredictable (who knows what the future will bring to Trotsky?) and inscribed in signs that the film's retrospective narration shows as predetermining its outcome (the vivid symbolism of the color red, or the discussions of suicide—especially that of Stavisky's father), culminating in Stavisky's bloody demise at the snowy resort of Chamonix.

The film's concluding flashbacks display the past in moving tableaux, while voices comment on them like the captions that accompany paintings. The effect is lustrous and eloquent in detail, but its significance remains unclear, so that the conclusion neither stages nor implies closure. Like Stavisky at the party in the Russian nightclub, each flashback seems to exclaim: "No one knows who I am or what I'm capable of!" In this sense, the film's *mode rétro* details go well beyond simple style or mood. For the crackling varnish that protects Resnais' stylish images also exposes them as sheer surface. As with the opening sequence of the automobile moving toward the cliffs overlooking Cassis, a visual lure invites us to be carried along. We try to follow the pattern of the crackled surface at the film's conclusion or merely slip through to some deeper understanding. But access to the fuller meaning that seemingly holds any sequence of images together remains closed and deferred.

This deferral persists and takes on increased significance, until it asserts—ironically, and as though by default—a system of meaning and nonclosure bordering on the pathological. Dr. Mézy describes Stavisky as emotionally paralyzed, paranoid, and in need of rest. His secret network of financial dealers and protectors is nervous, stretched too thin to bear the weight of still greater deals in the making. One of these deals spreads out beyond France as an international monetary plan he claims may save Europe from falling deeper into depression. Stavisky can be seen as a prophet of today's transnational finance. In a sense, Resnais' film shows the extent to which Stavisky's grandiose operations are his way of responding to—and defusing—the anti-Semitism and xenophobia beneath the cosmopolitan pretensions of his French accomplices. While Baron Raoul despairs of understanding the disturbances that ruffle the surface, Trotsky's young disciple thinks himself capable of following all the threads of these various systems and their interconnection. History, to him, is the dynamic reaction to one surface event—Stavisky's fall—visible on surfaces distant from it: the expulsion of Trotsky from France and the eventual failure of the leftist coalition. *Stavisky . . .* tempts us to pluck the chords that constitute this network and to listen for harmonic interplay.

Even more than the inconsistencies of history, the film shows the extent to which Stavisky relishes the ironies and variations that an obsession with the past produces. At his most complex and compelling, Resnais embeds in his scenes the seeds that gave rise to them. Surely the best example of this involves the deepest flashback of the film. Two pairs of men (government investigators on the one hand and Stavisky's associates on the other) are shown through parallel montage to be examining separate copies of the same July 26, 1926, issue of *Le Petit Journal Illustré*, whose garish cover depicts the ar-

13. Resnais discloses the genuine 1926 source of his tabloid style.

rest of Stavisky during a sumptuous dinner party. While one pair discusses this event in voice-over, we are shown an equally dramatic film sequence of the dinner party arrest rendered in a style keyed by that of the 1926 tabloid. In this case, Resnais' 1974 film stages two related dialogues set in late 1933 between men who discuss—at cross purposes—a 1926 magazine cover. But there is no reason to suppose that this mimesis is grounded in the event just as it occurred. Imitation in this instance is based on a previous representation, so that a spectator of *Stavisky . . .* would need to reckon the effect of at least two mediations through which a version of the original occurrence is transmitted.

In scenes like the 1926 arrest, Resnais exploits his dual role as filmmaker and historiographer. Unquestionably he provides an exciting account of events in a real past that continue to elicit wonder and gossip in France even today. At the same time, he constructs this version with a self-consciousness that indicates his doubt that any representation can actually grasp the past. Again and again, Resnais incorporates fragments of conflicting versions— fragments that break up the continuity of his visual and verbal account with archival documents such as newspaper headlines, clippings, and other press materials. These documents lend a certain authenticity to the film account, conveying a rhetorical force similar to that which Roland Barthes attributes to photographs: the power to state, "This has been" ("Cela a été").[22]

All of this is not to say that Resnais' version is equivalent to contemporary accounts of the period. For one thing, many of those accounts were invariably tendentious, using the figure of Stavisky to press a political point. "News" stories about Stavisky in 1934 were often accompanied by caricatures, or else by crude photographs whose point could not be missed. In contrast, Resnais' account is polyvalent in form and suitably complex in attitude, accumulating a multitude of indexes of the period as well as an array of views provided by narrators and witnesses, ranging from Baron Raoul and Arlette to Dr. Mézy and Inspector Bonny. The result is a composite portrait whose complexity represents the conditions out of which any social view—and all historical knowledge—arises. The protean Stavisky, whose unfinished name gives the movie its title, becomes for Resnais a marvelous magnet attracting disparate fragments from various archives. For example, in the back pages of the July 26, 1933, issue of *Comoedia*, which featured Trotsky on its front page, Resnais would have found a featurette on new styles in women's apparel for elegant beach resorts (Biarritz).

Because Resnais wanted to evoke the diverse details that coexisted within what might otherwise be seen as a more unified and monolithic "Stavisky Affair," his film gives the impression that he steeped himself in the public remains of French politics and everyday life from March 1933 to April 1934. At the same time, Resnais reveals the interpretive bias at work in his restaging of the past when he intercuts shots of Trotsky's retreat at Saint-Palais with others of Arlette modeling on the seashore at Biarritz. Proximity here is geographic, temporal, and symbolic. It serves as a measure of the various ways Resnais constructs his film around the "different harmonics" that constitute the rewriting of the past in *Stavisky*. . . . Geography and temporality or—more simply—space and time: Trotsky's second retreat lay very close to Bayonne, the city at the center of Stavisky's financial deals. It was also near Biarritz, where Stavisky and Arlette lived their ostentatious life of gambling and fashion. The real Stavisky may never have encountered his fellow Russian in person, but he might have run across ordinary individuals—like Erna Wolfgang—who had. Geographic, temporal, symbolic: Resnais constructs his portrait of the past in large part by creating the kinds of daily events and places in a fictional space-time that might have brought Stavisky and Trotsky to rub elbows.

In a sense, Resnais had little to invent. He ventured headlong into accounts of a period he had lived as an eleven-year old, recalling at one point that he had seen Stavisky's wax effigy at the Musée Grévin. Forty years later, this childhood memory makes it that much easier to imagine the adult filmmaker reproducing—in tones of brown and yellow—various images conjured up by newspaper articles, photographs, surviving architecture, and eyewitness accounts. In this sense, Resnais' version can be set alongside those by various witnesses who lived during that period. In *Stavisky: L'Homme que j'ai connu*, Kessel describes in detail the glass-walled elevator at the Claridge that Resnais used to stage a first view of the glamorous Serge Alexandre descending from on high. Kessel also portrays the Russian nightclub where Arlette was serenaded. On their own, these passages may seem mere curiosities. Yet such details give substance to Kessel's personal account of Alexandre, which was so different from those circulating in the media.

Kessel writes early on that he wants to use his personal acquaintance with the man to set the record straight: "I knew Stavisky. I sat at his table. We were on familiar terms."[23] The assurance born of direct contact is soon undercut by growing doubts. After losing contact with Stavisky in 1933, Kessel sees him only occasionally at the Claridge, when he goes to visit Colette. (Stavisky and Colette both had apartments at the Claridge.) When reports of the scandal begin to break, Kessel is stunned by their inconsistencies: one daily paper says that a warrant has been issued for "Alexandre, known as Stavisky," while another gives the name as "Stavisky, known as Alexandre." Kessel comments that headlines in the morning, noon, and evening editions of major dailies enlarged Stavisky's name at the top of the front page *(à la une)*: "With each passing hour, I saw Alexandre enveloped by a disturbing legend, taking on—through the distorting interplay of popular imagination, the crowds of rabid reporters, and the fear and hatred of the political parties—a kind of exaggerated, absurd, and trumped-up grandeur, just like the entire conclusion of his life."[24]

The excessive media coverage Kessel describes was fueled by politics. Yet the events surrounding the municipal loan office at Bayonne also tapped into a more dubious hunger for scandal that went well beyond politics and ideology toward an atmosphere of collective madness in which conjecture promoted the most unlikely rumors and falsehoods. Janet Flanner noted at the time that the entire country seemed to be taking notes while the French government worked out the scenario of a lavishly produced gangster film. Among those taking notes was Georges Simenon, whose imagination was fired by the case. At the time of Stavisky's death, Simenon had already written more than a hundred potboilers under some seventeen pseudonyms. In 1932, he had worked with Jean Renoir to adapt his detective novel *La Nuit du carrefour* (Night of the Crossroads) as a full-length film, with Pierre Renoir in the lead role of Inspector Maigret. Alongside his novels, Simenon wrote accounts of his personal travels—he preferred sailboats and ocean liners—for mass-circulation newspapers. A third set of writings straddled fiction and the daily press in the form of articles and interviews in magazines and tabloids such as *Voilà, Police, Détective, Reportage,* and *Témoignages de notre temps.* (A strange coincidence is Simenon's two-part interview "Chez Trotsky," conducted in Istanbul and published in the June 16–17, 1933, issues of *Paris-Soir,* about a month before Trotsky's arrival at Cassis.)

Simenon contrived to interview himself in the January 24, 1934, issue of Gallimard's illustrated weekly *Marianne.* In the opening paragraph, a fictitious reporter catches up with him coming out of a theater on a Saturday night (a theater in the entertainment district of boulevard nightlife, more akin to Alexandre's Empire than to the Comédie Française). What, the interviewer asks, is Inspector Maigret's opinion concerning Stavisky's death and the inquiries into it? Simenon starts by communicating Maigret's joy at the troubles of the Sûreté Générale, whom he describes as adversaries ("les gens d'en face") of Maigret's Police Judiciaire and thus as rivals he is always glad to see in a fix ("dans la mélasse"). Simenon/Maigret is especially delighted because the investigation into Stavisky's "suicide"—the term is always set within quotation marks—has embarrassed his rivals. As he puts it quite graphically, the Sûreté has "taken it on the chin" ("vient d'en prendre un bon coup"). But when the reporter asks Simenon whether he agrees with Maigret, Simenon replies that, on the contrary, the Sûreté has never before been so cunning and skillful—has never managed to block all leads and overturn all facts so that no one will ever know what happened. While everyone thinks that Stavisky's murder was staged to look like a suicide ("Stavisky a été suicidé"), the police have guaranteed that no one will ever prove it: "Nothing has been proven. Nothing ever will be. And in fifty years, in a century, I am certain that people will still talk about this historical enigma. Appearing clumsy is sometimes the shrewdest move of all. Especially when you appear to be messing things up out of stupidity, only to destroy what is causing you trouble. The peasants call this 'playing dumb to get what you want' ('faire la bête pour avoir du foin')."

The interview in which Simenon speaks for Maigret appeared a little more than two weeks after Stavisky's death and roughly two weeks before the February 6 riots. Its interest derives first of all from the opinions it expresses. Yet it also derives from the format of the political weekly that set those opinions at a point of convergence between the high literary culture of the Gallimard publishing house and the interconnecting worlds (milieux) of entertainment, politics, and crime that the inquiry into Stavisky's death had disclosed.

The French term *milieu* is especially suitable here, for its reference to the underworld of organized crime includes the gray zone of police informers and others who tried to work both sides of the law. The milieu surrounding Stavisky portrayed in the *Marianne* interview superimposes the world of criminals, police, and politicians evoked in Simenon's fiction onto a nonfictional present. It is as though real life had suddenly turned into a detective novel. Simenon later sustained this blurring of real life and fiction when he claimed to have located the stolen jewels that Arlette Stavisky had pawned to help her husband escape from France. Elsewhere he recounted having almost convinced one of Stavisky's cohorts, Georges Hainaut (known as "Jo-la-Terreur"), to sell him a checkbook with stubs recording payments to all those in the police and the government whose services and goodwill Stavisky had bought.[25] In his memoirs, Simenon tells the following anecdote: "One evening, as I was leaving the offices of *Paris-Soir* on the rue Royale, I was confronted by a longtime friend, a police inspector in charge of a large department. He pushed something hard against my stomach and said to me, 'Now, George, you're going to promise me that my name will no longer be on your list of suspects.' I drew my own gun and said to him, 'I'll print your name as long as you're under suspicion. I never said you were guilty.'"[26]

Like the editorial cartoons in publications and pamphlets all along the political spectrum, the *Marianne* interview with Simenon expressed a popular skepticism that went well beyond party and ideology. It tapped into an antiliberal strain whose origins in the late nineteenth century produced a native French fascism that, in Zeev Sternhell's expression, was "neither right nor left."[27] By the 1930s, mistrust of liberal republican ideals found a new public among the urban shopkeepers and semi-skilled laborers resentful of government policies that promoted an influx of foreigners who threatened France's economy. Crisis was often linked to a government widely viewed as corrupt and inept—nothing less than a threat to the nation. Maurice Pujo expressed the opinions of many on the right when he wrote in the January 7, 1934, issue of *L'Action Française* that no law and no justice existed "in a country where magistrates and the police are the accomplices of criminals. The honest people of France who want to protect their own interests, and who are concerned about the moral quality of public life, are forced to take the law into their own hands."[28] Hostility toward parliamentary rule grew to a point where calls for national revolution were coming not only from the left but also from center and right-wing groups wanting "to return France to the French."[29] This mistrust was doubled by a free-form resentment directed toward amorphous groups such as foreigners, "Bolsheviks," and Jews.

The Stavisky Affair undeniably involved shady aspects of French society in what it implied concerning the overlapping *milieux* of politics, crime, and entertainment. The first two months of 1934 predicted a "black year": Stavisky's death was followed by the casualties at the February 6 demonstrations led by army veterans and others calling for the dissolution of the Daladier government. Two weeks later, the mutilated body of Albert Prince was found near Dijon on the tracks of the main Paris-Dijon railroad line. Prince had headed the financial section of the Parquet (public prosecutor's office) and had been accused of failing to forward the dossiers on Stavisky's early swindles after investigators became suspicious of dealings at Bayonne in the fall of 1933. The prosecutor's office had been building a case against Stavisky since 1930, but the dossier had been "misplaced." Some skeptics surmised that it was "found" only when it could do real damage to the enemies of the government. Did Prince withhold the dossier on his own, or had he been ordered to do so by someone else? As with Stavisky, the death was officially listed as a suicide despite the fact that the body was discovered with one hand tied to the tracks and an autopsy showed that Prince had been drugged shortly before he died. Was it an accident or was Prince "suicided" *(suicidé)* because, like Stavisky, he knew too much? While *L'Action Française* called Prince's death "a Masonic and police crime," only the left-wing press considered the possibility that it might not have been a murder. Jean Prouvost, who had hired Simenon to write the series of articles on Stavisky's death for *Paris-Soir,* reportedly complained that he needed Prince's death to be a murder because a suicide meant the loss of two hundred thousand readers![30]

14. An illustrated weekly displays the wax effigy of Stavisky at the Musée Grévin (spring 1934).

When Resnais casts Stavisky as a "clever ghost" in the popular imagination, he picks up the sensationalist coverage of the time. Three months after Stavisky's death, his wax effigy entered the Musée Grévin, where it was soon the third most popular display, following Jesus and Napoleon.[31] Another haunting occurred some years later at the 1941 Palais Berlitz exhibit titled "The Jew and France," a major propaganda effort by the Institut d'Etudes des Questions Juives, under the Vichy regime. It drew more than 200,000 spectators—over 100,000 in its first three days in Paris—before traveling to Rouen and Bordeaux. Stavisky's picture appeared in a display devoted to scandals, below a heading that read: "Dans tous les grands scandales, on retrouve des Juifs" ("In all major scandals, Jews can be found").[32]

Stavisky's death led to numerous theories, ranging from the crude to the outrageous. Some beg to be taken seriously; others seem fanciful. One in particular is richly inventive. It concerned a December 24, 1933, train crash in the fog that killed two hundred people at Lagny, on the Paris-Nancy line. According to one commentator, Stavisky learned of the crash almost

15. Trotsky *à la une* again: a minor character scans the back page of *Le Matin* (April 17, 1934).

immediately. Looking for a convenient way to slip out of Paris undetected, he decided instead to disappear and ordered a police inspector on his payroll to go to the accident scene, find a body disfigured beyond recognition, and substitute his identity papers for those of the dead passenger. Arlette, purportedly aware of the plan, told her children and their governess that Stavisky was on the 7 P.M. train for Nancy leaving from the Gare de l'Est. Had Stavisky not inadvertently run into the governess later that night at the Claridge, this exchange of identities might well have succeeded.[33]

The account is probably fabricated. (Thévenin dismisses it and attributes it to Xavier Vallat's memoir, *Le Nez de Cléopâtre*.) Even so, it resurfaces in Jacques Prévert and Jean Renoir's 1936 film *Le Crime de Monsieur Lange*, when the head of a print shop in financial straits skips town in order to elude his creditors. The man—named Batala, and played to sleazy perfection by Jules Berry—is smoking in the company of a priest on a train seconds before a radio voice-over announcing a major train crash ends with the words: "On cherche un ecclésiastique disparu" ("A missing priest is still being sought"). Months later, Batala returns to Paris dressed in a priest's robes. While there is no hard evidence that Renoir had this incident in mind when he shot his film, he certainly played to audiences prepared to imagine financial scandals, disguised officials, and engineered public disasters.

To have lived in France in the 1930s was to have been surrounded by this material and these points of view. What we call French culture at the end of the Third Republic is a euphemism for myriad interested subgroups competing to identify what mattered. Taken individually, the hateful caricatures of Stavisky in the weekly *Gringoire*, the staged interview in *Marianne*, and even the presumably objective news reports in *Comoedia* are all monovalent. Yet because the significance of each view depends so thoroughly on the existence of opposing views, and because every fragment of the moment implies a context it can readily vivify, the social situation must always be taken as multiple and polyvalent. Resnais' *Stavisky . . .* demonstrates this early on when the Baron, after quoting a passage from a piece by Kessel in the right-wing Parisian daily *Le Matin*, acknowledges that he never reads the left-wing press. Serge Alexandre, pulling out other dailies, forces him to listen to a few choice phrases from "the other camp." The gesture is minimal, but one sees in its banality exactly the kind of detail—"tip of the pyramid"—through which the movie shapes a range of actions, images, and events into a significant entity, one that is clearly narrative and putatively historical. Toward the end of the film, Resnais repeats this effect by displaying the front page of a newspaper (once again, *Le Matin*) with a headline—"Trotsky ne doit pas être renvoyé en Corse" ("Trotsky should not be sent back to Corsica")—which is legible to us but which the character, reading the back pages, does not see. What is he reading that *we* do not see?

Resnais mimics the material workings of history by combining a plethora of coexisting elements with discrepant accounts that are only partly coordinated. One example: Trotsky leaves Cassis at the very moment that Stavisky descends into the lobby of the Claridge. A second example: Montalvo's schemes to provide armaments for Franco depend on Stavisky's money dealings, just as do Trotsky's unspecified plans for international revolution. In both cases, viewers must determine how the elements presented as spatially and temporally proximate are coordinated—whether causally or, to use Resnais' term, as a harmonics of history.

Three poses from the film raise the question of cinematic historiography by illustrating the conundrum Jean-Louis Comolli has dubbed "a body too much."[34] The first pose faces us directly on the page of *Le Matin*, where

16. Belmondo pasted onto *Le Matin*'s front page.

17. The actual image of *Le Matin* with caricature of "the handsome Alexandre" (January 4, 1934).

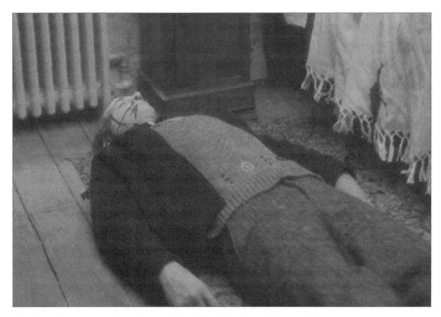

18. Resnais restages the photo of Stavisky dead (see Figure 19).

Resnais has substituted the face of Jean-Paul Belmondo for that of Stavisky. The second pose shows Belmondo's *body* in the precise position of Stavisky's *corpse* as seen in newspapers of the day. Resnais took the trouble to shoot on site at Chamonix, in an effort to restage "what really happened," though without harming his actor. The third pose, more complex still, presents itself first in a flashback narrated by the Baron. Anny Duperey, in the role of Arlette, stands beside a Hispano-Suiza while photographers register her elegance. Later, moments before his death, Belmondo (Stavisky) is seen cutting out newspaper photos of his wife. Two glamorous portraits of Duperey are set beside a third showing a woman next to a Hispano-Suiza. Is this Annie Duperey as Arlette, or is it the genuine newspaper photo of the real Arlette published in *Marianne* in January 1934? In this way *Stavisky* . . . juggles images drawn from three ontological states: the historical re-creation, the simulated newspaper, and the archival document. Far from being a collage designed to jar the viewer (the way Picasso or Juan Gris glued newspaper fragments over painted forms), *Stavisky* . . . uses Sondheim's score to blend elements of material history (monuments, buildings, and newspapers as existing samples of the fading era) into his narrative tableau of the period. The

19. The layout of a life in *Marianne* (January 31, 1934): a visual archive for *Stavisky . . .*

20. Pieces of a puzzle: a montage of genuine and doctored newspaper fragments.

"real" is already stylized, hence partial and tendentious. *Stavisky* . . . is a representation in *mode rétro*, but to the second degree. While the first degree holds up a comforting mirror image, the second degree—when another mirror is held to the first—engenders the instability of multiple perspectives and the vertigo of views that diminish toward a vanishing point in the past.

Resnais is fascinated by the pathology for coherence exhibited by everyone who announces a view, but even more fascinated by the inevitable disintegration of each provisional coherence. Belmondo's character is the most concentrated site of this pathology. Literally a specimen for the doctors who worry about how far he can stretch himself, he hopes to fabricate a personality that eliminates rough spots in his past, his existence as "Stavisky" first and foremost. He hopes to accomplish this by projecting a future in which he can lead an international cartel toward a fiscal plan that will save Europe. Here Serge Alexandre surely exhibits advanced paranoia. Yet doesn't his passion for totality (the fantasy of the international cartel) govern the film as well? Doesn't it govern the historical impulse itself?

In the chapters that follow, we too provide a view—or series of views—of France in the 1930s, adding another layer to a suite of perspectives, ours

coming thirty years after Resnais' film and seventy after the events themselves. By following Resnais, we may appear to project an interpretation that
aspires to the clarity of spectacle and the smoothness of music in the *mode
rétro*. Yet the movie also frustrates every totalizing impulse, be it Stavisky's,
Trotsky's, or ours. The historical dissonance of *Stavisky* . . . sets the complexity of the past into play, alongside our own complexity in trying to make
sense of it.

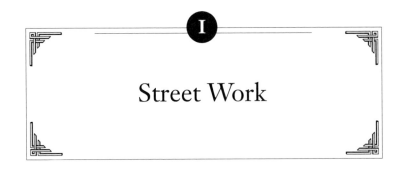

I

Street Work

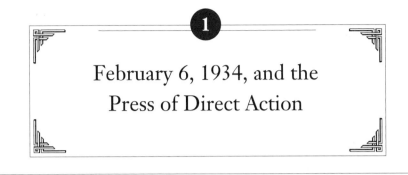

1

February 6, 1934, and the Press of Direct Action

Perspectives on Violence: Three Models of Presenting History

Our analysis of *Stavisky . . .* has emphasized questions of historiographic method that Alain Resnais, alongside Jorge Semprun, Sacha Vierney, and others involved with the production, contended with forty years after the fact in their evocation of France of 1933–1934. Working on artifacts of the same period, the anthropologist Marc Augé has written that one task of the historian who wants to understand a specific period is precisely "to imagine it in its present, to inventory its range of possibilities."[1]

Let us begin to imagine our period by zeroing in on what we take to be its most consequential drama. Looking back from 1997, Charles Rearick described the scene:

On the night of February 6, 1934, the nation's political fear and dark hatred joined in street battle in the heart of the capital. Right-wing veterans and leagues, outraged over the government's handling of a financial scandal, gathered in the Place de la Concorde late in the day with the intent of protesting and marching on the Chamber of Deputies. The scandal involved swindler Serge Stavisky, who represented all that the Right imagined and hated as the "other": he was foreign-born and Jewish. The leagues' offensives were more than a protest against Stavisky but less than a coordinated fascist conspiracy; they were aimed at changing the government whose high officials seemed to have protected the crook. Partisans of the Left—veterans associated with the Communists—came out for counteraction, and violent clashes ensued in the night. When the murky battle around the Place de la Concorde ended, fifteen people were dead and 1,435 had been wounded.[2]

Rearick paints this vivid fresco in such a way as to highlight the groups, people, and events that most affected the populace of Paris. But does he (in Augé's words) imagine this moment "in its present" and "inventory its range of possibilities"? Or does he fall into the illusion of retrospection? His clear prose, in any case, buffers the texts of the period he calls up in evidence. As opposed to standard histories like Rearick's, journalism of the period relays a vibrant immediacy.

It was to evoke the past as indeterminate rather than complete—in conditional mood rather than preterit tense—that we hitchhiked on Alain Resnais' film, which exemplifies an alternative historiographic model. In *Stavisky . . .* we find ourselves at the outset of the Popular Front in much the same position as the anonymous young man in the film's first scene, when he peers through binoculars from a cliff-side as a small boat carrying Trotsky motors into the harbor of Cassis. We, too, want to isolate events we are sure must matter; we, too, relish history in the making (as he says, "A page in history has turned"). Yet the young man's physical distance from "grand historical figures" and the slight temporal deflection that allows him to observe the present as history are greatly magnified in our case, since we write seventy years after the event and are looking across not a bay but an ocean.

This young man is the first of many witness-participants whose historical perspectives Resnais samples. Some characters think to bask in the luxury of hindsight (the film presents flashbacks from the inquest held three months after Stavisky's death), though their testimony is contradicted; others need to make decisions on the spot. Across this mosaic of memory—accessed through different subjects of history—Resnais wafts a single mysterious and unsettling aroma. Seen from his own point in time (thirty years prior to our own, forty after the death of his title character), both history and its various "presents" exist in simultaneity. Some characters (Stavisky and his gang) scheme to circumvent the law at the same time that others act out roles in a play *(Coriolanus)* about lawlessness. Resnais cuts from one to the next, as these and all characters living in proximity in December 1933 breathe the same atmosphere. He makes sure to place major figures of the day (Trotsky, Malraux) alongside minor players whom he brings center-stage (Stavisky above all),

21. Open revolt—from the left or right?—on the Place de la Concorde (February 6, 1934).

and also alongside ordinary citizens who lived in this epoch as witnesses and potential agents. All of these took up space in France, and all of them were jostled by the only partly predictable motion of history.

Resnais' modernist historiography inspires us to look to Paris as the site of the interplay among a spectrum of agents, institutions, and events, only intermittently coordinated as they bounce off one another to varying effect. Ultimately the sepia tone of cinematographer Sacha Vierny's images and the urbane coffeehouse tone of Stephen Sondheim's score filter Resnais' retrospection to provide precisely the *mode rétro* that became a negotiable, consumable style in the 1970s. Within the attractive package of the film are material remnants of the past—theater programs, magazines, newspapers, the pyramid at the Parc Monceau—that go undigested in the body of the film and that evoke uneasy feelings, reducing one's distance from a past which can seem again unresolved.

Marc Augé further implements Resnais' historiographic model when he describes the power of certain photographs to act like shards that tear the smooth fabric of the past, allowing the historian to feel the open potential of key moments. Our own sense of the incalculable import of February 6, 1934, may well come from one such arresting photograph that Augé collected in a 500-page compendium, *Paris Années 30*, whose images all come from the archives of the Roger-Viollet photographic agency. Jutting out from the hundreds of pictures in this book, one of the most reproduced images of the era thrusts individual agency before us with an affective force that is at once violent, exhilarating, and unpredictable. The image shows a man poised to throw a paving stone at police retreating on horseback. Whereas written accounts of the period (such as Rearick's) generally focus on recognizable agents like Stavisky, prefect of police Jean Chiappe, veterans-association leader François de La Rocque, and statesman Edouard Daladier, the photographed figure of the stone-thrower pitted against the mounted and retreating police is faceless. The significance of the image builds on a posture of opposition. Seventy years after the fact, the figure is a lone agent whose stance is an index of the street violence that in the following decade will draw others to take actions and risks only dimly understood in 1934.

Lampposts and columns visible in the background divide the visual frame of the photograph of the Place de la Concorde along a horizontal axis. A man dressed in overcoat and hat stands to the right of center, in a street or paved passageway. He is poised to throw something (a paving stone? a rock?) at a group of police retreating on horseback toward the left. The vertical lines of the lampposts and columns in the background are enhanced by another lamppost whose position to the left of center and closer to the foreground marks a divide between the stone-thrower and the mounted police. The visual field of the image is framed by onlookers in front of and behind the thrower. Those at the rear stand immobile; others closer to the front seem to be dispersing. Only one figure—at the center of the frame, just to the right of the lamppost in the foreground—has adopted a posture similar to that of the stone-thrower, whose extended left arm prolongs the horizontal line of the curb behind him. The triangle formed by the thrower's outspread arms and legs suggests willful action amid the dispersion surrounding him. The styles of clothing and shape of the lampposts mark the moment by evoking the early twentieth century. The fuzziness of the image sets the heat of the central action within a cooler overtone that conveys an earlier phase of technology.

Whereas still photography freezes a past moment, news photos such as the one in question are more like single frames of a film pulled out of se-

quence. The stone-thrower might qualify as the equivalent of a movie-set extra *(figurant)* in a scene packed with spontaneity and immediacy: history in
the making. Indeed Augé, commenting on this image and pictures like it,
reaches for a film metaphor when he writes: "During riots, strikes, and demonstrations, the actors—and to a lesser extent the extras (during the most intense clashes, there are always some onlookers waiting to be told to keep
moving)—constitute the whole spectacle. In a sense, they rebuild the set."[3]
Anonymous and faceless agents dramatize history by carrying us beyond conventional images and recognizable faces into untold stories of expectation, violence, and pain. Hence, the photograph of the stone-thrower on the Place
de la Concorde derives its force from the visibility of direct action in the
street.

We are all familiar with the fetishistic attraction of photographic details
attached to someone whose subsequent fate the viewer knows. This accounts
for the intimacy manufactured when recognizable objects are brought into
contact with famous individuals: Picasso and his cap, Kees van Dongen and
his beard, Tsuguharu Foujita and his eyeglasses. But voyeurism functions
more forcefully when the subject is unknown or anonymous, as in the image
of the stone-thrower. The photograph immobilizes and thereby sanctifies
this pure "gesture of expectation, hope, love, or boredom by an anonymous silhouette, on the threshold of a possible novel—a story that will never
be told."[4]

On the threshold of the possible, indeed. Such immediacy and indeterminacy
bring photography to the forefront of the media in the interwar period.
Whether or not action photos were illustrating newspapers, they exerted a
moral influence over the press. Journalists surely wanted their articles to
reach a wide readership. Whereas the literary enterprise continued to promote reflection, thoughtfulness, and good taste, photographs—often reproduced alongside articles—could bring the instantaneous into focus. Journalism, deriving from the journal (diary) or daybook, found itself emulating not
the diary entry penned in the calm of the evening after the day's events, but
the photograph snapped on the spot. To render speed and decisiveness, reflection had to succumb to instinct in what we term the "press of direct
action."

While such reportage constituted only a fraction of everything published,
that fraction billed itself as the cutting edge of the entire publishing industry,

an edge that influenced the form and content of editorials, reviews, essays, and original literary compositions. Formerly a spin-off of *maisons d'édition* (publishing houses), daily and weekly papers of the 1930s, many of which had circulations well above 100,000, influenced the way writers at all levels conducted themselves. Even the most refined authors could not help becoming involved in the cultural dimension of their publishing houses. In February 1934 many looked out on the streets, weighing their words as if hefting rocks in their hands. What was to be done?

Out of the Hands of Government: Riots and Coalitions

Less a failed coup d'état than a demonstration turned riot, the events of February 6, 1934, effectively jump-started leftist coalitions fearing a national revolution initiated by another set of loosely linked groups on the militant right. This emergent political culture incubated in the streets and other public spaces of Paris. The Stavisky Affair was neither a sufficient nor a necessary cause of the February 6 demonstrations. Yet it so forcefully conjoined economics, politics, and criminality that it has long symbolized the spirit of crisis associated with the decade. This conjuncture was palpable in press coverage of the demonstrations and in responses by writers in literary and political journals over the following months. Indeed, publishing served as perhaps the most central and most contested of public spaces at a moment when debates surrounding politics and culture were taking on extreme urgency. The participants on and near the Place de la Concorde that February 6 represented an array of groups, each of which went beyond any particular party doctrine or consistent ideology.[5] Rearick's preferred term—"street battle"—is a genteel way of describing a transition from demonstration to riot and from demonstrators to mob. Similarly, he characterizes the leftist responses of February 9 and 12 as only partly coordinated. That week Socialists and Communists marched with labor unionists, veterans, and others carrying no formal or implied affiliations.

Throughout January 1934, the right-wing press had hammered at what it termed the threat to the French nation posed by a corrupt and decadent government. In the January 7 issue of *L'Action Française*, Maurice Pujo urged the people of Paris "to come together in large numbers before the Chamber of Deputies, to cry 'Down with the thieves!'"[6] Two days later, one of the daily's most prestigious and virulent contributors, Léon Daudet, decried "this regime of thieves, pimps, murdering policemen called Republic, or Democ-

22. Antifascist march to the Place de la Nation (February 12, 1934).

racy," while another writer encouraged readers to stand "in large numbers before the Chamber and demand the end of . . . this dishonored regime."[7] Such calls coincided with demonstrations abetted by Jean Chiappe, the Parisian prefect of police who reputedly condoned violence on the part of his agents toward left-wing demonstrators. Between January 9 and February 4, more than a dozen demonstrations were staged in Paris by Action Française

23. "Tomorrow, General Strike!" (February 11, 1934).

and assorted right-wing groups, leagues, and associations. By early February, the Chautemps government had fallen and Chiappe had been fired.

The February 6 demonstrations involved some 5,000 to 6,000 militants, belonging to four distinct groups. These included right-wing leagues and associations, World War I veterans on the left and right, members of the French Communist Party (Parti Communiste Français, or PCF), and a small group of conservative municipal councilmen. Among the first group, the Association des Croix-de-Feu et Briscards (better known as the Croix-de-Feu, or "Cross of Fire") were geared up for action. Founded in 1927 by Maurice d'Hartoy, the Croix-de-Feu was initially an association of war veterans whose 1934 membership of 35,000 included 18,000 in greater Paris. By the middle of the decade, related groups accounted for as many as 100,000 additional supporters, membership being open to war veterans whose acts of courage under fire had been officially cited. In a shrewd move to recruit a disaffected minority, the Croix-de-Feu extended membership to those whose unacknowledged acts of courage were ratified as honorable by an extraordinary general assembly of association regulars.

The Croix-de-Feu sought, in its own words, to bring together the highest *(les plus belles)* national energies for the good of France and French patriotism, by defending the prestige of French military decorations, respecting treaties that were the fruit of sacrifices, and promoting the moral and material enhancement of France.[8] What set the Croix-de-Feu apart from other veterans' associations was the paramilitary reorganization of the group instituted in 1930 by its second president, Count François de La Rocque de Sévérac. The new Croix-de-Feu under de La Rocque included nearly 1,500 *dispos* (*disponibles*, or "available individuals") on call to defend the interests of the association throughout Paris and the provinces. Recruitment initiatives filtered into youth movements such as the *regroupement national* (national alliance) and *volontaires nationaux* (national volunteers), called on to swell the participation in rallies and demonstrations. In October 1933, the Croix-de-Feu's publication, *Le Flambeau* (The Torch), ran a six-point program of direct action to defend the nation's economy, workers, and family property against foreign interests as well as against excessive government control in areas of activity they believed ought to remain private.

De La Rocque, by most accounts less a man of ideas than of passion and charisma, was often compared with Benito Mussolini. Asked during a government inquiry into the February 6 events whether he considered his activities political, he asserted his right to defend the ambitions the Croix-de-Feu was struggling patriotically to attain. When his questioner, the Deputy Pétrus Faure, pushed him further, de La Rocque replied, "Nous nous occupons de la chose publique" ("We deal with public matters," or literally "with the public thing"), words that expressed his disrespect for the proceedings and for the Socialist-Communist affiliations of the man questioning him.[9] His response also expressed an impetus toward direct action: groups such as the Croix-de-Feu believed that the streets of Paris were the site for resolving matters of public concern—de La Rocque's "chose publique"—which governmental institutions had shown themselves increasingly inept at managing.

De La Rocque was most certainly in the streets of Paris leading the Croix-de-Feu on February 6. But where were the public intellectuals—the writers, artists, and other professionals who militated, wrote, and spoke out on civic matters? Among the generation born in the 1870s and associated with France's leading literary monthly, the *Nouvelle Revue Française* (or *NRF*), André Gide was in Sicily and Roger Martin du Gard on the Riviera. After February 6, they and their peers sought to be as visible in person and in print as their equivalents at *L'Action Française*. They wrote articles in newspapers and journals, signed petitions, made speeches. They did their best to establish links with a younger generation and to overcome barriers that several leftist groups, the PCF in particular, had set up so as to distinguish their ideology and political mission from those of other groups. The barriers finally fell on July 27, 1934, when the Communist and Socialist parties signed a pact of united action. Between February and July, leftist intellectuals militated and organized—but most of all they wrote, producing a stream of articles, tracts, and manifestos.

On February 11, the Socialist daily *Le Populaire* published a tract entitled "Appel à la lutte" (Call to Struggle). Progressing from incantation to incitation, it advocates concerted action by workers to block fascism ("barrer la route au fascisme"):[10]

CALL TO STRUGGLE
With unheard-of violence and speed, the events of recent days place us brutally before an immediate fascist danger.

YESTERDAY:
Fascist riots.
Defection of the government of the Republic.
Explicit claims on the part of *all* elements on the right to constitute an antidemocratic and prefascist government.

TODAY:
Government of holy union.
Bloody repression of workers' demonstrations.

TOMORROW:
Reappointment of the *coup d'état* prefect.
Dissolution of the Chambers.

THERE IS NOT A MOMENT TO LOSE!
The working class has yet to act in a unified way.
It must do so *immediately*.
We appeal to all workers, whether organized or undecided: block the road to fascism!

UNITED ACTION
It is necessary, urgent, and indispensable that the united action desired by the workers and required by the political parties arise through the *very spirit of conciliation* called for by the gravity of the situation.

This is why we address an urgent appeal to all workers' organizations: that they immediately constitute the necessary organizational structure, the only one capable of making united action a reality and a weapon.

Remember the terrible experience of our comrades in Germany. Let it serve as a lesson.

LONG LIVE THE GENERAL STRIKE!

February 10, 1934[11]

Rumor had it that André Breton, leader of the Surrealists, was a key instigator of the tract, whose ninety signatories included Alain, Paul Eluard, Jean Guéhenno, André Malraux, Henri Poulaille, and Jacques Prévert. (The name of the anarchist filmmaker Jean Vigo stands out as well.) Jean-François Sirinelli notes the documentary value of the tract as a measure of the shock wave caused by the February 6 demonstrations among intellectuals and political progressives.[12] Only in retrospect have commentators amplified the tract's importance into an expression of productive unity. In fact, its call to mobilize workers against fascism did nothing more than imagine and anticipate such unity. A full year would elapse before the unprecedented 1935 Bastille Day demonstrations and ceremonies marked the true onset of the Popular Front as a political movement.

"Appel à la lutte" cast its call to action alongside the efforts of two groups, the Association des Ecrivains et Artistes Révolutionnaires (Association of Revolutionary Writers and Artists, known as the AEAR) and the Amsterdam-Pleyel movement, both of which emerged within the milieu of international Communism. The AEAR took shape in 1932 under the leadership of Paul Vaillant-Couturier, editor of the French Communist Party daily, *L'Humanité*, and a founder in 1921 of the journal *Clarté*. Following his participation in the 1930 Kharkov conference, Soviet officials had delegated him to found a French section of the International Union of Revolutionary Writers. In July 1933, the AEAR began publishing a monthly journal called *Commune*, expecting to recruit PCF support from pacifists and antifascists, and from prominent members of the middle class such as Gide and Henri Barbusse, both of whom were now Communist sympathizers, or "fellow travelers." (Gide permitted his name to appear in *Commune*, but never became a formal member of the AEAR.) All these efforts to fashion a broad front of revolutionary intellectuals culminated in the June 1935 International Congress for the Defense of Culture. From this plateau, the Popular Front movement gained momentum into 1936 (an election year), with *Commune* broadcasting the PCF's program "in defense of culture." Until it shut down in 1939, the AEAR's monthly kept to the high road of leftist policies by endorsing the Popular Front's initiatives in regional Maisons de la Culture, backing Republican Spain, and denouncing the 1938 Munich agreements.

The Amsterdam-Pleyel movement likewise began with efforts on the part of Soviet Russia to mobilize progressive intellectuals throughout Western Europe. While the movement's charter emphasized united action beyond partisan allegiance, Communist Party influence was constant and obvious. Named for meetings held in the Dutch port of Amsterdam in 1932 and in Paris' Pleyel concert hall in 1933, the movement professed commitments to pacifism ("the struggle against imperialist war") and antifascism. Barbusse, once again a key figure, used his prestige to help recruit literary figures like Gide, Eugène Dabit, and Jean-Richard Bloch. By 1936, its leaders claimed a membership of some 250,000 among pacifists, syndicalists, and other antifascists.[13]

Drawing on the structure and momentum of these two Communist-directed organizations, but taking no orders from above, was a third initiative that spontaneously took shape in the immediate aftermath of February 6. The Comité de Vigilance des Intellectuels Antifascistes (Vigilance Committee of Antifascist Intellectuals, or CVIA) came up with a tri-partisan provisional leadership: the Socialist Paul Rivet, the Communist Paul Langevin, and the philosopher Alain, representing the Radical Party. Signaling solidarity, all three names appear at the bottom of the manifesto titled "Aux Travailleurs" (To the Workers), dated March 4, 1934:

TO THE WORKERS

United beyond all factions before the spectacle of the fascist riots of Paris and the popular resistance that alone confronted them, we declare to all workers, our comrades, our resolve to fight by their side in order to rescue the French people's hard-won rights and public freedoms from a fascist dictatorship. We are ready to sacrifice everything in order to prevent France from falling victim to a regime of bellicose oppression and misery. We will fight against corruption; we will also fight against deception. We will never allow virtue to be invoked by the corrupted and the corrupters. We will never allow the banks, trusts, and arms dealers to deflect the anger that money scandals have raised against the Republic—the true Republic of the people who work, suffer, think, and act for its emancipation. We will never let the financial oligarchy exploit, as in Germany, the discontent of the masses, whom it has demoralized or ruined. Comrades, under the guise of national revolution, a new Middle Ages is being prepared for us. We must not preserve the world as it is; we must transform it, delivering the state from domination by large-scale capital and doing so in close collaboration with the workers. Let those who support our ideas make themselves known![14]

The CVIA, a prototype of left-wing alliances *(rassemblements)*, mobilized union groups to defend their interests—and those of France as whole— against the right. To this end, signatories of the "Aux Travailleurs" manifesto included left-wing politicians, writers, scientists, and academics such as Victor Basch, Julien Benda, André Breton, Jean Cassou, René Crevel, Eugène Dabit, Paul Desjardins, Elie Faure, Lucien Febvre, Ramon Fernandez, André Gide, Jean Guéhenno, Lucien Lévy-Bruhl, Marcel Mauss, Romain Rolland, and Andrée Viollis. Others involved in the CVIA included members of the League of the Rights of Man, local antifascist organizations, war veterans, pacifists, Socialists, and Communists, and other groups ready to collaborate "with one and the same heart in one and the same action."

The Socialist Paul Langevin tried to insist that the term *intellectuel* be barred from the manifesto so that the committee would be identified primarily with the labor-union movement, which he considered better suited to avoiding partisan differences.[15] Nonetheless, an addendum below the signatures of Rivet, Alain, and Langevin contained an explicit call for "intellectuals of every category" to join the Comité Antifasciste et de Vigilance (soon renamed the Comité de Vigilance des Intellectuels Antifascistes) in the struggle against right-wing demagogy. By May 1934, a total of 2,300 scientists, doctors, engineers, lawyers, writers, and artists had endorsed the CVIA's promise to combat the rise of a "new Middle Ages" (as its early brochures characterized fascist ideology), which threatened the rights and freedoms of Republican France. Within less than two years, a rift within the Comité set Communists and their sympathizers, who were eager to fight Hitler, against those who maintained a pacifist stance. Accordingly, though its early phase modeled the unity that created the Popular Front, the CVIA eventually previewed the same kinds of ideological tensions that would break the Popular Front down from within.[16]

The AEAR, Amsterdam-Pleyel, and the CVIA were rallying points for great numbers of malcontents on the left, with intellectuals recasting themselves as "workers of ideas" ready to lend their influence to pacifism and the defense of the Republic.[17] Gide, Barbusse, and others emulated models like Voltaire, Hugo, and Zola, perhaps without realizing the extent to which the role of the committed writer had evolved in light of partisan politics. Meanwhile, this new cohesion on the left was countered on the right by conservative and reactionary groups, many of whom sponsored their own publications. The most notable of these organs—the daily *L'Action Française*, and the weeklies *Gringoire*, *Candide*, and *Je Suis Partout*—denounced "progressive" institutions and values because they allegedly degraded France, whose strength they saw as founded on pre-Revolutionary systems of rule and society.

On neither the left nor the right could writers and artists readily isolate themselves from unresolved political and social struggles. A dilemma facing every writer and artist after February 6, 1934, was the problem of how best to accommodate the codes of their professional worlds (classroom, studio, laboratory, study) with the often opposing imperatives emanating from the streets. This dilemma was also palpable in that other contested public space, the publishing house. How might a *maison d'édition* best function during such a period of heated words? What should happen to the reflective, distanced, even meditative role literature always played in culture when action was on everyone's mind and tongue? And how might a publisher survive when readers, more than ever before, were looking for signs of political leanings in every novel, essay, or book review that came out? Could a publisher afford to play up to one political faction? Could he afford not to? The interactions between literary publishing and journalism were extremely complex during the early phases of the Popular Front movement.

The Pen and the Fist: Writers Respond to February 6

Between the wars, one journal ruled literary discourse in a nation that revered literature: *La Nouvelle Revue Française* (*NRF*). The monthly had been founded in 1909 by a group of writers including André Gide and Jean Schlumberger, both of whom had been marked by the Dreyfus Affair and by the Radical

Party movement that came in its wake under the name of the Défense de la République. Within two years, Gide and Schlumberger had teamed up with the publisher Gaston Gallimard, who systematically broadened the base of the affiliated publishing house, Editions de la Nouvelle Revue Française. (In 1919 the firm changed its name to Editions Gallimard.)

Gide, who was sixty-four at the time of the 1934 demonstrations, had long exuded an aura of austere authority whose basis in what he called *les moeurs littéraires* (literary customs) had expanded over the previous decade to include politics. His denunciation of the colonial system following a 1925–1926 trip to French Equatorial Africa was grounded in moral concerns. But it placed him openly on the political left. By 1931–1932, he had made initial statements in favor of Soviet Russia, yet declined to join the Communist-inspired AEAR. Despite the fact that his contributions to the *NRF* were often of a political nature, Gide made certain to separate his own politics from those of the monthly, so that it could maintain the independence that he saw as essential for its literary mission.

The *NRF* remained widely influential during the interwar period because it served as a point of convergence for important networks that included political parties, the educational system, and the publishing industry.[18] Following World War I, the journal tempered its literary ethos by engaging in political debate. This became clear soon after Jean Paulhan succeeded Jacques Rivière as editor in 1925, when the *NRF*'s three contributing columnists— Alain, Julien Benda, and Albert Thibaudet—openly questioned several Radical Party doctrines to which they had formerly subscribed. A half-dozen years later, Gaston Gallimard, eager to draw attention to the journal, pushed Paulhan to run a series of position papers by young writers committed to political involvement. The result was the *NRF*'s important December 1932 issue, featuring a dossier organized by Denis de Rougemont under the rubric *Cahier de revendications* (Dossier of Demands).

Thus primed to comment on political happenings, the *NRF*'s March 1934 issue responded at length to the February 6 demonstrations that had occurred only weeks earlier. In his contribution, Benjamin Crémieux described the left's dilemma as stemming from a drama in which a minority alliance of Radical and Socialist parties had failed to connect with a middle- and lower-class liberal majority concerned less with workers and antifascism than with defending abstract notions of individual freedom. Crémieux chided the left for invoking fascism too quickly: "What the left should have said right away—because this would have been to its advantage, and also true—was that the demonstration had not been fascist, despite the efforts of some of its leaders. The important thing was that the demonstration was *prefascist.*[19] Crémieux called on the left to counter a neo-Socialist party movement that he saw as a logical extension of prefascism.

Elsewhere in the same issue, Ramon Fernandez called on the left to organize quickly against the right, which would inevitably retain an immediate advantage by crassly appealing to the self-interest (and material desires) of most ordinary citizens. Georges Altman sketched a series of street scenes that took place February 6–12. Julien Benda reflected on conflicts between various groups of demonstrators and the authority of the state, represented by the French army and the Parisian police. Finally, Pierre Drieu La Rochelle exulted in the upheaval of the February 6 crowd rushing down the rue Royale toward the Place de la Concorde amid strains of the "Marseillaise" and the "Internationale": "I'd have liked this moment to last forever" ("J'aurais voulu que ce moment durât toujours").[20]

Drieu added a note in the *NRF*'s May 1934 issue, stating that what attracted him to fascism was a virile disposition linked to courage and a spirit of war in the form of revolution: "For me, therefore, the dilemma, sufficiently tragic, is the following: either an antiparliamentary revolution that will gradually become anticapitalist—and turn into a war—or peace and Stavisky. It seems to me that the gods have already chosen."[21] Later the same year, he recast the February 6 demonstrations as a momentary breakdown of balance between the left and the right, a balance that soon reasserted itself, after the general strike of February 12: "Thus, this enormous world vaguely stirred up on the twelfth has gone no further than the world of the sixth."[22] For Drieu, true and lasting change was possible only if the balance between left and right were replaced with a fusion of forces, in the form of a new party that was both socialist and nationalist. It was this belief that led him to espouse fascism and to collaborate with the Germans during his 1940–1943 tenure as director of the *NRF.*

Coverage of the February 1934 events in other literary journals was varied and often ambivalent. Georges Bataille shared Drieu's fascination with the crowd when he used terms such as *effervescence, contagion,* and *orage* ("storm") to describe a fusion that was affective and physical rather than partisan, as it mainly was for Drieu. Asserting that there was more to learn in the streets of great cities than in political newspapers or books, Bataille wanted to tap into the agitation of men who had nothing going for them except their passions: "What we are interested in above all—now that the analysis of the economic bases of society has been accomplished, and its results have proved to be limited—are the emotions that give the human masses the surges of power which tear them away from the domination of those who know only how to lead them to poverty and the slaughterhouse."[23] Two years later, the significance of February 6 was still being debated. Maurice Blanchot wrote in the February 1936 issue of *Combat* that the magnificence of the demonstrations was undermined by the mediocrity of their results. February 6, he said, was "simultaneously painful and great," becoming a mere symbol whose pious commemoration did nothing to counter the ongoing decline of France.[24] Writing in a progressive American weekly on the eve of the 1936 national elections that would bring the Popular Front to power, the leftist Henri Lefebvre likewise invoked February 6 in his account of the election's importance for all of Europe.[25]

On February 6, 1945, the collaborationist intellectual Robert Brasillach was executed by firing squad at Fort Montrouge. As Alice Kaplan notes, this occurred "eleven years to the day after the riots in the Place de la Concorde that he and the German press had dreamed would be the dawn of fascism for all of France."[26] For the demonstrations and their aftermath raised the stakes among writers and others committed to direct action all along the political spectrum. In April 1934, the group surrounding *Esprit* (organ of the Catholic "personalist" movement), under Emmanuel Mounier, signed a collective text entitled "Pour le bien commun" ("For the Common Good"). The document stressed that Christians had a responsibility to refuse to take sides between the antiparliamentary right and the antifascist left. Increasingly, however, the commitment that Mounier and his group initially thought should be reserved for spiritual matters evolved into out-and-out politics.

Mobilizing Editions Gallimard

In October 1932, two months before the *NRF* published its "Dossier of Demands," Gaston Gallimard launched *Marianne*, an illustrated weekly whose sixteen-page format featured reviews of literature, theater, and film by writers and literary critics such as Jean-Richard Bloch, Ramon Fernandez, and Pierre Mac Orlan. Social and political commentary appeared under column headings such as "Le Monde comme il va" (As the World Goes) and "Les Caprices de Marianne" (The Caprices of Marianne). The latter was a witty reference to current events embodied by the allegorical representation of the French Republic—a female figure known as Marianne—with a wink at Alfred de Musset's 1833 play of the same title. Other contributors to the new weekly included Julien Benda, Colette, Eugène Dabit, Jean Giraudoux, Emmanuel Mounier, and Roger Vitrac. In the tradition of a marketing strategy of the nineteenth-century daily, a substantial part of each issue featured work in progress by established Gallimard writers such as Marcel Aymé, Roger Martin du Gard, Antoine de Saint-Exupéry, and Georges Duhamel.

Marianne exuded the literary aura of the *NRF*, even while its director, Emmanuel Berl, exploited the weekly's topical format to commercial and editorial advantage, covering breaking events in a way that biweeklies and monthlies could not match. The periodical's success was rapid and singular: "Through the quality and diversity of its contributors, and a format in which literature and the arts hold their own against politics, *Marianne* from the outset was on a separate plane from that of militant journalism."[27] Gallimard created *Marianne* to compete with *Candide*, *Je Suis Partout*, and *Gringoire*, weeklies with a similar news-and-opinion format whose hefty readership naturally included members of Action Française and other groups on the political right. In short, Gallimard wanted *Marianne* to do for his publishing house what *Candide* and *Je Suis Partout* had done for Editions Fayard and *Gringoire* for Editions de France.

Marianne was not the first of Gallimard's attempts to compensate for losses incurred by less profitable properties. As early as 1922, journalism *(la presse)* had become the third component in the *NRF*'s mixture of journal and book publishing *(revue et édition mêlées)* when Gallimard had launched a literary weekly. *Les Nouvelles Littéraires*—"the journal for witty people"—was primarily a commercial venture providing visibility for Gallimard's writers, advertising space for his books, and a venue in which to lobby for the numerous prizes that could establish or ruin the reputations of writers and publishers. In 1922, Maurice Martin du Gard (cousin of novelist Roger) was chosen by Gallimard to head this new venture. He would subsequently contribute to *Je Suis Partout*.

Six years later, Gallimard consolidated the journalistic dimension of his publishing house when he established ZED Publications as a corporate umbrella covering his financial interests in publishing, printing, and advertising. ZED gave Gallimard the freedom to pursue additional projects in popular journalism without jeopardizing the *NRF*'s finances or reputation. Through

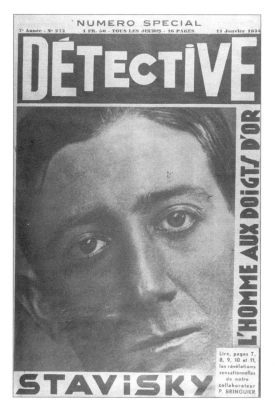

NUMERO SPECIAL
7ᵉ Année - Nᵒ 272   1 FR. 50 - TOUS LES JEUDIS - 16 PAGES   11 Janvier 1934

DÉTECTIVE

L'HOMME AUX DOIGTS D'OR

Lire, pages 7,
8, 9, 10 et 11,
les révélations
sensationnelles
de notre
collaborateur
P. BRINGUIER

STAViSKY

24. Gallimard's tabloid weekly: exploiting big history (January 11, 1934).

ZED, Gallimard soon launched two tabloid weeklies, *Détective* and *Voilà*. The former featured sensational coverage of crime and the minor news items known as *faits divers*. The latter billed itself as "the reporters' weekly" and followed the example of *Détective* by running pinups on its back page to illustrate the memoirs of *femmes fatales* (actually written by reputable authors using pseudonyms). At a remove from both the *NRF* and the literary high end of Gallimard's book publishing, the extensive circulations of both tabloids—as high as 350,000 for *Détective* by 1936—balanced the company's losses on lower-circulation journals such as *La Revue Juive* and *La Revue Musicale*.

Building on his program to diversify a commercial base anchored by the *NRF*'s prestige, Gaston Gallimard's launching of *Marianne* in November 1932 placed it immediately a cut above the rightist weeklies with which it competed. Between 1932 and 1934, the weekly's openness to writers of various ideologies made it a de facto point of reference among a broad range of

25. Gallimard's tasteful weekly: satirizing the Stavisky Affair (February 28, 1934).

readers from the center to the left. By 1934, Berl's pacifism had set him at odds with leftist colleagues on *Marianne*'s editorial board, who broke with him to start up a new weekly, *Vendredi*. Even its peak circulation of 120,000 amounted to less than half of *Gringoire*'s 350,000 and *Candide*'s 250,000.[28] A core of 60,000 regular subscribers failed to keep the journal afloat or compensate for the growing editorial differences between director and publisher. Berl stayed on board until January 1937, when Gallimard sold *Marianne* to Raymond Patenôtre, who adopted a news-and-photo format in hopes of creating another *Paris-Match*. By 1939, Patenôtre's wish had come true, as *Marianne* evolved into *Marianne-Magazine*, a glossy weekly devoid of serious political content. Two months after Paris fell to Nazi Germany in June 1940, Patenôtre set up shop in Lyon and began supporting the Pétain government, which he described as "revolutionary." Later the same month, *Marianne-Magazine* ceased publication after its editorial section was censored.

Marianne showed the capacities as well as the inabilities of mainstream literary institutions to evolve in the face of a cultural environment that became increasingly politicized. Despite Berl's politics on the pacifist left, *Marianne* served as a literary no-man's-land where loners and internal exiles on both right and left—such as Marcel Jouhandeau, Henry de Montherlant, Paul Léautaud, and Georges Bernanos—were able to "rest their swords."[29] When Bernanos broke noisily with Action Française, he did so in *Marianne*. In 1933 and 1934, André Malraux chose *Marianne* as the site for important articles on France's 1931 military actions in Indochina. It was also here that he recorded the late-night meeting with Leon Trotsky that Resnais took care to include in *Stavisky . . . .*[30]

The ethos and fate of *Marianne* coincided in large part with that of Emmanuel Berl. Born in Paris in 1892, Berl grew up in the upper middle-class neighborhood of Passy, the son of assimilated Jews whose relatives included Marcel Proust and Henri Bergson. In 1920, he befriended Pierre Drieu La Rochelle, with whom he later edited *Les Derniers Jours* (The Final Days), a journal that ran for only six issues, from February to July of 1927. Two years later, he published *Mort de la pensée bourgeoise* (The Death of Middle-Class Thought), the first in a projected series of works whose critique of decadent values explicitly recalled Julien Benda's *La Trahison des clercs* (The Betrayal of the Intellectuals) and Albert Thibaudet's *La République des professeurs* (The Republic of Professors), both of which had appeared in 1927. *Mort de la pensée bourgeoise* typified the erudite polemical tract of the late 1920s. Berl divided his argument into opposing camps (*écoles*) and began by invoking Benda's figure of the intellectual who abandoned the pursuit of spiritual matters in favor of the worldly ends of politics. Whereas Benda valued the intellectual's removal from politics, Berl saw it as ineffectual conformity: "The worst danger for the mind is not in the intellectuals' excessive leaning toward the marketplace. On the contrary, I fear that politics may well become something that the mind shies away from, a sealed-off area where the worst offenses might become possible, if they have not already done so."[31]

Whereas elitist writers such as Gide and Anatole France disparaged Zola for his vulgarity, Berl admired his fictional portraits of industry and the working class: "Does anyone notice the extreme rarity of novels on the lives of workers and industries? There is no link between the place of the factory within a country and its place in literature. No one has continued Zola's efforts."[32] Looking at his contemporaries, Berl noted with varying degrees of approval Louis Aragon's mix of love and anarchy, as well as Drieu La Rochelle's attempts to overcome the Surrealists' tendency to romanticize revolution. Ultimately, it was the character of Garine in Malraux's *Les Conquérants* (The Conquerors) whom Berl saw as personifying a commitment to moral action and thus countering the conformity of bourgeois thought. An emphasis on moral action likewise characterized Berl's pacifist stance while he directed *Marianne*.

Like Thibaudet's and Benda's polemical monographs, *Mort de la pensée bourgeoise* was published by Gallimard's major rival, Bernard Grasset. In the intrigues between these two major publishing houses, defections and crossovers between camps occurred regularly as various parties feuded or sought to profit from an opportune turn of events. Berl moved to Gallimard at the instigation of André Malraux, who did the same after publishing *Les Conquérants* at Grasset. But Berl did so with misgivings that returned to plague him once he assumed the directorship of *Marianne:*

> My relations with the *NRF* have always been complicated. At first, I was one hundred percent *NRF.* . . . Later on, my family ties with Proust led me to distance myself from the *NRF*, because Proust used to tell me the worst kinds of things. He liked Rivière, but felt that Gide's cape lent him a false air of honesty. The *NRF* always retained its prestige for me, but I was always annoyed by the puritanical, "Left Bank" side of people like Gide, Martin du Gard, and Schlumberger, and by this form of Protestant pseudo-homosexuality.[33]

Aware of Gide's displeasure with *Mort de la pensée bourgeoise*, Berl agreed to direct *Marianne* despite his sense of removal from the *NRF*'s inner circle. Differences with Gallimard surfaced almost immediately: "Personally, I wanted to edit the journal by myself, the way I had edited *Les Derniers Jours* with Drieu. I wanted to edit a *Cahiers de la Quinzaine* that Gaston Gallimard would publish and distribute for me."[34] As his differences with Gallimard and colleagues at the company increased, Berl commissioned others to edit the journal in his stead.

The November 16, 1932, issue was typical of *Marianne*'s early content and editorial vision under Berl. Covering the entire page under the heading "Vient de paraître" ("Just Released") were a review of Louis-Ferdinand Céline's *Voyage au bout de la nuit* (Journey to the End of the Night), billed by Ramon Fernandez as the "book of the week," and a column by Josette Clotis on Jean Giono. The same page carried a long editorial by Jean Prévost on the divorce between literature and the people. Prévost began by citing post-Revolutionary attempts, notably on the part of Lamartine and Hugo, to write a truly popular prose that communicated with the general public rather than with a more restricted circle of educated, elite, or partisan readers. In contrast to what he saw in France, Prévost pointed to the situation in Spain, where writers such as García Lorca considered journalism integral to popular memory. Prévost ended with a warning to his readers: "The divorce between French literature and the French people (aggravated not by schoolteachers, but by primary-level textbooks full of platitudes passing for simple truths, or inanities trying to pass for morality) derives not from a difference of levels, but from an incompatibility of temperaments. Foreigners, beware: our literature explains us no better than our diplomats."[35]

Prévost's editorial is typical of the mixture of erudition and social consciousness that Berl brought to *Marianne*'s literary pages. Explicit political content was always more of a problem, because Berl's personal commitment to France's neutrality weakened *Marianne*'s market position among politico-cultural weeklies. Forty years later, Berl recalled that the predicament proved fatal for *Marianne:* "It was the rhythm of the period, of the decade, that was pushing us toward catastrophe. I did what I could. I tried to say what the dangers were, at least where I thought I could make them out. The perspective of war repelled me. It was my strongest feeling during those years: the visceral horror of war. Not everyone was like me."[36]

Marianne's isolation grew steadily after the Stavisky Affair and the riots of February 6, 1934, despite the fact that Berl's support for pacifism and neutrality was the culmination of positions taken a decade earlier by Henri Barbusse and Romain Rolland in journals such as *Clarté* and *Europe. Marianne*'s survival was jeopardized after the union of leftist factions gave rise to the Popular Front, with its more activist ideology. In April 1934 a nucleus of writers, including occasional contributors to *Marianne* such as André Chamson and Jean Guéhenno, set out to establish an activist weekly. Their efforts would bear fruit eighteen months later, in November 1935, with the first issue of *Vendredi,* which described itself as "a literary, political, and satirical weekly founded and directed by writers and journalists."

Vendredi was conceived as an independent antifascist weekly, a more militant alternative to *Marianne.* "Independence" here was understood as editorial and financial. Accordingly, its committee of directors—Chamson, Guéhenno, and Andrée Viollis—was chosen to sustain an editorial balance among proponents of Radical, Socialist, and Communist policies. Much like its predecessor, *Vendredi* featured a mix of reports on literature and the arts, extracts of fiction in progress, and political editorials. And in the satirical tradition of *Le Canard Enchaîné*, it enlivened its tone with sharp commentary and cartoons.

Vendredi developed directly in reaction to the events and aftermath of February 1934—events that Chamson's widow, Lucie Mazauric, recalled as being so complex that immediate understanding was impossible: "In order to form a precise notion of the events and their causes, I used to read tons of newspapers every day, from *L'Action Française* to *L'Humanité*, going through articles with a fine-toothed comb, following strict rules of close reading, like a paleographer."[37] By the time Chamson had become a leading force behind *Vendredi*, he was already in the AEAR, whose membership included practicing or one-time Surrealists Breton, Eluard, Aragon, Luis Buñuel, René Crevel, and Man Ray, as well as the elder statesmen of international pacifism, Barbusse and Rolland. In July 1935, Chamson helped to write the Bastille Day oath that was read at an arena in Paris known as the Stade Buffalo: "In the name of the French people brought together today throughout the country, . . . we solemnly swear to remain united in order to disarm and dissolve factitious leagues, with the aim of defending and developing democratic freedoms and ensuring human peace."[38] Four months later, *Vendredi* appeared as a major voice supporting the principles of the Popular Front. For many, this was a cause for great celebration, a moment of elation and release colored by expectation of imminent change. Few foresaw how brief this elation was to be.

Whereas *Marianne* had heralded a transition from the rarefied literary milieu of the *NRF* toward the activist culture of the mid-1930s, the history of *Vendredi* from 1934 to 1938 illustrates the passage from elation ("an immense hope") to disaffection. Shortly before the Popular Front's 1936 electoral victory, Chamson reminisced: "*Vendredi* was born specifically out of the humiliation that writers who had come from the people and were faithful to the people felt when they saw how greatly the people had been duped. It seemed that some of the mud that was covering so many of the writers, journalists, contributors to reactionary weeklies, and policemen who had organized the riot was splashing back onto them."[39] In terms of editorial tone, *Vendredi* soon broadened its antifascism into a stance against the entire political right. It also displayed an openness toward the Catholic church, in contrast to a republican tradition equating opposition to the political right with anticlericalism. The enemy was no longer the priest, the church, the Jesuits, but capitalism and fascism.[40] To this end, *Vendredi* brought together elements all along the political left: from pacifists to planists, from Trotskyites to labor unionists, from Christian leftists to militants from the League for the Rights of Man.[41]

The front page of *Vendredi*'s first issue featured an opening presentation by Chamson, a short polemic on the "three Stavisky Affairs," and a table of contents listing contributions by Gide, Jacques Maritain, Julien Benda, Jean Giono, Paul Nizan, Jean Schlumberger, and Louis Martin-Chauffier. Of special interest was an editorial cartoon showing an armor-clad Death trampling and throwing water on everything in its path. The cartoon was titled "Manifesto for the Defense of the West" and claimed to have taken its caption ("All the things which the West has until now considered superior and to which it owes its historic grandeur and creative virtues") from a "Manifesto of the 64." The cartoon's meaning was less than self-evident. Indeed, the figuration of a violent defense of Western values lent itself at least as much to an ironic comment on nonviolence as to any partisan militancy.

Within sixteen months, *Vendredi*'s support of the Popular Front movement turned to open criticism when its editorials denounced Blum's economic reforms of March 1937. As André Wurmser wrote, the period was becoming fertile in cynicism. On the international front, an excerpt from Gide's "Return from the USSR" (January 29, 1937) and coverage of the Moscow Trials by Jean Guéhenno (February 5, 1937) illustrated growing disenchantment with the Soviet government. Such criticism contrasted with the positive tone that characterized the ongoing coverage of the civil war in Spain. The February 26, 1937, issue featured two human-interest articles, "Faces of the Spanish Revolution: Barcelona" and "Superintendents of War," as well as calls for support of the Spanish Republican cause on behalf of various left-wing organizations.

Less than two months later, Paul Nizan denounced French nonintervention as ineffective. Responding to those who favored negotiating a peaceful protection of Catalonia in exchange for ceding the rest of Spain to the Nationalists, Nizan doubted that even such a concession could cool the ambitions of Franco and his cohorts: "The Italian and German officers who get together at the Hotel Cristina in Seville have a special affection for the phrase 'Next year in Toulouse . . .' I wonder if giving them the means to accomplish this desire really promotes peace."[42] Nizan openly expressed the impatience of hard-line Communists militating within *Vendredi* for a more aggressive foreign policy. Today, his article reads as a chillingly accurate warning against

26. An uneasy Christmas Eve for the left (December 24, 1937).

the mentality of conciliation that was to produce the Munich agreement in September of the following year.

Vendredi came out strongly for the Republican cause in Spain. An August 1937 issue included pieces by Corpus Braga and Chamson, capped by a boxed editorial whose meaning was unambiguous: "Here are two studies on the character of the war in Spain, one written by a Spaniard and the other by a Frenchman. We offer them as a contribution to the history of this conflict, which has no analogue in the history of Europe and which threatens to impose tight limits on our own future."[43] Three months later, a passage from Malraux's *L'Espoir* (Man's Hope) added a literary dimension to *Vendredi's* partisan reportage and editorials devoted to the Spanish conflict.

Through the end of 1937, *Vendredi* followed the marketing formula of the cultural weekly by mixing reportage, feature columns, editorials, and previously unpublished literary texts *(inédits)*. Its editorial tone continued to harden. The front page of the December 24, 1937, issue features an editorial by Andrée Viollis entitled "Peace on Earth," a short piece entitled "Cinema and the State," by Jean Renoir, and a polemical exchange between Gide and Guéhenno. At the bottom, a cartoon entitled "Christmas Night" portrays three Magi equipped with military weaponry hovering over an infant while a protective Liberty extends her hand toward them. The caption reads, "Will the divine child live or die?" ("Vivra-t-il, le divin enfant?") Strapped for funding like many similar publications, *Vendredi* was not above supporting itself with revenue from advertisers whose values it presumably failed to share. An ad by Editions Denoël in the weekly's December 24, 1937, issue announced the publication of Céline's scandalous pamphlet *Bagatelles pour un massacre*, whose anti-Semitic virulence it attempted to tone down with the words: "Pour bien rire dans les tranchées" ("For a good laugh in the trenches"). Did *Vendredi's* editors fail to catch this inclusion? Or did financial necessity force an unfortunate compromise?

By 1938, *Vendredi's* differences with the Blum government's foreign policies precipitated a change within the weekly. Chamson faced what he saw as yet another examination of conscience: "We were the journal carrying the hopes of the Popular Front, the journal of its coming into being. We regret today that we have to be the journal of its disappointments."[44] In the spring, the three directors announced that *Vendredi* would join forces with the *Nouvelle Revue Française* so as to promote all forms of free and creative thought. In fact, given *Vendredi's* circulation woes, the change was an evasive action to preclude attempts from outside the journal to relocate it on the side of right-wing militants. Thus, rather than risk being appropriated by opposition on the right, *Vendredi* opted for a more disengaged stance: "We do not wish to see our face in any shards of a broken mirror. We do not wish to fight against any of our friends. None of us can find it within himself to nourish fraternal hatreds. . . . We will continue the same struggle on a different level. We are certain that the friendships formed in battle will remain true. We and our readers will prepare together the reserves of energy and hope that will make new human victories possible."[45] Four and a half months later, the Munich agreements further undermined the viability of *Vendredi*'s newly adopted position, and the weekly's circulation dropped below 5,000 copies per issue. On November 17, *Vendredi* appeared under the new name *Reflets* (Reflections) and dropped political commentary. *Reflets* ceased publication in mid-December after only five issues.

The histories of *Marianne* and *Vendredi* illustrate the problems of independent leftist journalism during and immediately surrounding the Popular Front period. From 1932 to 1939, both publications sought to balance commercial and editorial concerns. *Marianne* was launched as an open forum in which political content supplemented a primary focus on literature and culture. *Vendredi* was more openly engaged. Neither weekly was a party organ. But to the extent that *Vendredi* claimed to speak for the ideals of the Popular Front movement, its cultural content was secondary to coverage of domestic, foreign, and international politics. In the case of *Marianne*, Berl's position typified the fate of pacifism during a period of growing militancy. Much like Berl, Chamson was unable to exert the control needed to keep *Vendredi* from collapsing under a critical rift between pacifist and militant attitudes toward Nazi Germany. His commitment to collective action grew to the point where he agreed with the editorial board to cease publication in November 1938, rather than allow the weekly to fall into the wrong hands. It was the final gesture of a collective venture whose ambitions and failures paralleled the rise and fall of the Popular Front movement.

Writing in the Arena

On Friday, June 21, 1935, André Gide greeted 2,500 to 3,000 delegates at the opening session of the First International Congress for the Defense of Culture at the Palais de la Mutualité in Paris. Antifascism linked the attendees who had come to Paris from England, Germany, Czechoslovakia, Italy,

27. Barbusse, Malraux, and Gide listen to Magdaleine Paz in June 1935.

Spain, Holland, Austria, and the United States to defend an international culture of free expression which they saw as increasingly at risk. Several months
earlier, Gide and Malraux had agreed to organize the congress in response
to a request from Ilya Ehrenburg, a correspondent for the Moscow daily
Izvestia, who had asked that they provide a platform for leading Soviet writers
to set forth their views to an international audience.[46] Here, in part, is what
Gide saw as being at stake in the five days of speeches and debates at the
congress: "Literature has never been more alive. Never has so much been
written and printed, in France and in all civilized countries. Why, then, do
we keep hearing that our culture is in danger?"[47] While there was every reason to believe that Gide's statement was sincere and without irony, Roger
Shattuck cites the June 1935 congress as a prime example of the specious
politics of cultural activism. Shattuck is especially hard on Gide, Malraux,
and the Surrealist-turned-Communist Louis Aragon, all of whom, he writes,
should have known better. With regard to Trotsky, Shattuck is even more direct: "He was wrong."

What Shattuck calls the shame of the 1930s is the obverse of his assertion that "politically and intellectually, the three years from the February 1934 riots to the initial decline of the Popular Front in the spring of 1937 form the heartland of the decade, the unreal interval during which it seemed still possible to save European culture from totalitarianism without war, and even to assimilate the Soviet revolution into the Western intellectual tradition without more bloodshed."[48] Between the wars, activism among writers, artists, and other intellectuals all along the political spectrum occurred increasingly at a remove from doctrines of established political parties.[49] On the conservative and reactionary right, it took form in the neo-royalist Action Française movement and more militant leagues such as the Croix-de-Feu. On the left, this independence was visible in the anarchist Groupe Octobre and among proponents of the Catholic *Esprit* movement, and it flourished most famously among Surrealists tempted by international Communism. Through the late 1920s, Surrealism evolved under André Breton into a laboratory of innovation and self-styled revolution among educated French youth discontented with a cultural legacy whose values they saw as resulting in the catastrophe of World War I. Most interwar readers of the Surrealists' manifestos, pamphlets, and journals remained at a comfortable distance from class struggles and the revolutionary ambitions that the movement soon espoused. Perhaps part of the reason that the high Surrealism of the 1920s took so long to transform its militancy into serious political expression was that Breton's personal views on revolution were less than consistent. When Breton joined the French Communist Party in 1927, the brevity of his affiliation was more telling than any declaration of solidarity or good faith.[50] Three years later he was unapologetic when, in the "Second Manifesto of Surrealism," he referred to the "uninterrupted series of lapses and failures, zigzags and defections," that characterized the noncoincidence of Surrealist and revolutionary efforts.[51]

The social, indeed political function of the intellectual has been fostered by common usage in the French language. The noun *intellectuel* refers in current usage to writers, philosophers, artists, and scientists who militate, speak, or write on political and social issues in the public sphere. The nature of this shift toward the public sphere is well conveyed in French by the verb *intervenir* ("to intervene"). Accordingly, intellectuals are those whose words and deeds allow them to intervene in public debate. A founding instance of such intervention is "J'Accuse," the 1898 letter to the president of the French Republic that Zola published in the Paris daily *L'Aurore* to protest the government's ongoing indictment of Captain Alfred Dreyfus. As with writers, artists, and others between the wars who spoke out in word and in print, professional distinction was the means to broader recognition. The term *engagement* likewise adds semantic force to the decision to take a stand in public on the basis of an imperative that often evolves from politics toward ethics. Following World War II, the model of the intellectual closely followed Jean-Paul Sartre's definition (in his essay "What Is Literature?") of the committed writer as the bad conscience of society who speaks out against oppression on behalf of its victims.[52] For Sartre, the intellectual is a spokesman who directs or redirects language. The French term for such a figure is *porte-parole*. Translating it literally into English as "word carrier" conveys the material sense of language within a process of communication—*parole*, meaning the spoken word, being distinct from the generic term *mot*, referring to the written word. Sartre's model of committed writing ranked transparent prose far above any poetic attitude that set language between the writer and the world. At the same time, his advocacy of writer and prose revealed the ambivalent status of the *porte-parole* as one whose ability to speak on behalf of others may carry assumptions of paternalism or hierarchy that demean those on behalf of whom the *porte-parole* claims to speak. A series of French verbs promotes the sense of word as material object. Thus, one who, like Gide in June 1935, presides at a meeting gives (*donne*), yields (*cède*), or passes (*passe*) the word (*la parole*)—the spoken word, as distinct from the written word (*le mot*). To have or receive the word is thus to exercise control over the symbolic and material commodity of language. Furthermore, inclusion in discourse always implies exclusion: those who "have" or "hold" the word are distinguished from those who do not.

Régis Debray extends Sartre's conception of the power of the written word in his suggestive synthesis *Teachers, Writers, Celebrities*, which sketches the shifting sites and functions of intellectual labor from the Third Republic to the present. According to Debray, book publishing enjoyed tremendous influence from 1920 to 1960.[53] The period constitutes what he calls the "publishing cycle," as distinguished from the "university cycle" that dominated French cultural institutions from the start of the Third Republic to 1920, and a post-1968 "media cycle" from which, he contends, we have not yet emerged. The 1930s mark a highpoint of engaged and consequential writing which Debray tracks through the ascendant figure of the publisher and the institution of the publishing house. To put it briefly, anyone wishing to contribute to the intellectual culture of this epoch should look first to the bookstores and their suppliers rather than to university lecture halls or the institutes.

No one fretted more than Julien Benda over this shift of influence from the university to the publishing arena. His anxiety is betrayed in the title of his famous 1927 book *La Trahison des clercs*, a flashpoint for debate about "engaged" and "committed" intellectual labor. Even before World War I, Benda had cautioned against putting ideas into the marketplace. Henri Bergson was Benda's special target, primarily for the character of his ideas. Benda found "intuition" to be a soft and muddled notion on which to build an entire philosophy. It seemed "feminine" to him, in comparison to the rigor of logic and dialectic. Benda also felt that Bergson should be ashamed to see his ideas taken up by laymen (and above all by laywomen), sentimentalizing daily life with his charade of philosophy. "Bergsonism" was all the rage in religion and aesthetics when Benda wrote his book. If the most revered thinkers in the land (Bergson held the chair in philosophy at the Collège de France) peddled their ideas in the thoroughfares, it should shock no one that tendentious thinking would corrupt disinterested thought. He worried that editorial journalism, sparked on one side by the cult of Charles Maurras and on the other by the cult of Karl Marx, would become the norm of the intellectual. The betrayal of the sacred search for truth and justice would soon be complete.[54]

Benda's classic style—spare, sharp, and direct—jabbed like a rapier into the miasma of the intellectual milieu around him. Although he might have struck everyone or no one in particular, in fact he pricked turncoat "intellectuals" across the spectrum. In the pages of *L'Action Française*, Léon Daudet scoffed at the bloodless complaints of this "meager" man whose own body had withered under the tyranny of his spirit.[55] In the *NRF*, Gabriel Marcel, whose recent "Bergsonism and Music" made him one of those soft philosophers Benda had in mind, reiterated the same point by claiming that Benda's peculiar Spinozism separated the eternal principles of philosophy from the realms of history and daily life, rendering the human condition as mere abstraction. Two books on the left answered Benda. Emmanuel Berl, as we have seen, shot back in 1929 with *Mort de la pensée bourgeoise*. It took Paul Nizan three years to marshal his broader argument in *Les Chiens de garde* (The Watchdogs). Nizan—a star of the Ecole Normale Supérieure's remarkable 1929 *promotion* (entering class), which included Jean-Paul Sartre, Simone de Beauvoir, and Raymond Aron—broadcast a direct and more virulent attack,

insisting that traditional philosophy could never be "disinterested" and certainly never innocuous. Every philosophy is useful to those in power or to
those desiring power, including the airy, abstract philosophy that sustains
bourgeois indifference to the needs of those around them and that winds up
trampling those it colonizes in the name of progress and enlightenment.

Benda felt especially wounded by this final point because he failed to understand how his pursuit of the unselfish life of the mind could be turned to
anyone's nefarious advantage.[56] Moreover, Nizan seemingly neglected the
moments in Benda's treatise where absolute injustice (the Dreyfus Affair is
once again a touchstone) required the intellectual to take sides. This slight
nod in the direction of history and social life permitted Benda to involve himself in the increasingly politicized world that was reading *Les Chiens du garde.*
Even Gide was affected by it.[57] Benda and Nizan soon became sparring partners in the pages of the *NRF.* Both were featured at the June 1935 Paris Congress of Writers for the Defense of Culture. Benda, according to Shattuck,
was "mousetrapped" into giving another of his anodyne speeches promoting
justice but retreating from the materialism that everyone else in the audito-
rium accepted as dogma.[58] Still, his presence alone belied the distance of the
intellectual that his famous book had preached. Two years later, Benda would
go so far as to write: "I say that the clerk must now take sides," siding with the
Communists and thereby with Nizan, though never abandoning his idealist
view of philosophy.[59] For his part, Nizan not only spoke at the congress; he
manipulated its consequence in the pages of *Commune,* which he coedited
with Louis Aragon.

The nearly touching byplay between Nizan and Benda is less important
for what was said than for where it was said: in short books, in weekly magazines, in daily political reviews, and at rallies and congresses. Of course, there
remained an ensconced corps of philosophers at the Sorbonne and in the
lycées. Yet something had changed even in the more rarefied world of high
ideas. Bergson published his immensely popular *Deux sources de la religion et de
la moralité* in 1932, in part to confront practical life head-on. A year later, the
émigré philosopher Alexandre Kojève (born Kojevnikoff) was lecturing at the
Ecole Pratique des Hautes Etudes, where his theses concerning negativity
and the master-slave dialectic in Hegel's 1807 *Phenomenology of Mind* influenced an entire generation of interwar and postwar intellectuals in attendance, such as Raymond Aron, Breton, Bataille, Roger Caillois, Jacques
Lacan, Maurice Merleau-Ponty, and Raymond Queneau.[60] Philosophy would

go down into the streets or would be forgotten. Thus, the most widely read and quoted French philosopher of the 1930s, Emile Chartier—known simply as Alain—eschewed sustained treatises for brief essays, even aphorisms. Thousands of these appeared in weekly newspaper installments. Alain, too, was at the 1935 Paris congress. The "official" philosopher of the Radical Party, he brought it into the Popular Front, a political phenomenon spawned less in the universities than in the cafés and editorial offices where writers gathered in this grand era of publishing.

Forces larger than intelligence and more powerful than politics determined the activities, functions, and effects of the intellectuals who debated so furiously in the 1930s. The economy of the printed word as commodity lies beyond the control of those who speak or write. As for the ascendancy of the "publishing cycle," its origins can be found in a commodification of the verbal that extends back to nineteenth-century periodicals and newspapers.

> The daily paper was arguably the *first* consumer commodity: made to be perishable, purchased to be thrown away. It became the most ubiquitous example of the habits of consciousness and of socioeconomic practice which, in more explicit, thematic forms it sought to impart to its audience—or, as we might say, within its market. In selling a transformed perception of its culture, it sold itself first of all. The disenchanted intelligentsia, the alienated writers, reacted predictably. For them, the newspaper became the quintessential figure for the discourse of their middle-class enemy, the *name* of writing against which they sought to counterpose their own.[61]

The emergence and evolution of the daily paper pitted high forms against low. It forced literary culture to recognize popular media. As Richard Terdiman notes, what counts as literary is often asserted in terms of difference: "Much of 'literature' defines its conditions of existence as counter-discursive. Its status as 'literary' *marks* it as oppositional. For this reason, any attempt to seize dominant discourse leads *outside* the high cultural realm and into areas which might almost seem drearily down to earth."[62] A similar motivation is evident among those who, a century after Balzac, refused to isolate literature from daily life. From Guillaume Apollinaire to the early Parisian Surrealists under Breton and Aragon, the literary avant-garde drew regularly on mass print culture for inspiration, using sources that included fantastic popular fiction and sensationalist journalism.[63] Even Paul Valéry, who modeled his early poetry on a Symbolist aesthetic in which politics played no part, published a 1931 volume of essays called *Regards sur le monde actuel* (Reflections on the World Today).

While the *NRF* was helping Gaston Gallimard stabilize his publishing ventures on the eve of World War I, *Le Petit Parisien* and *Le Petit Journal* led the French dailies, with respective circulations of 1,550,000 and 600,000. Both were creations of the mid-nineteenth century and both had survived as victors in the stiff competition among the consortium of five Parisian daily newspapers created around the turn of the century. Of the two, *Le Petit Journal* was the older. Appearing in 1865, it was soon directed by Emile de Girardin, who had founded the first mass-circulation Parisian daily, *La Presse*, in 1836. Girardin had a shrewd sense of the market, using the serialized novel *(roman-feuilleton)* to boost circulation and advertising income. By the turn of the century, *Le Petit Journal* boasted that it had five million readers.[64]

By the mid-1920s, competition from technical, trade, and specialty periodicals had pushed the major Parisian dailies to create their own specialty sections—known as *pages magazines*—which always appeared on the same day each week. These sections, often highlighted by splashy layouts and column headings, ranged in topic from sports to theater, fashion, and home improvements. At their inception, the new *pages magazines* entered fully within the cultural orbit of high capitalism and maximum profits. But since they inevitably reflect the society in which they circulated, they expose for us the illusion of what might otherwise pass for disinterested and politically neutral discourse. A similar mix of cultural and commercial concerns motivated even so high-flown a publisher as Gaston Gallimard when he diversified his publishing operations during a period of political and social upheaval.

This chapter has dealt with the response of publishing houses to the grave events of the time, but we will shortly see the extent to which Gallimard became involved in specialized and tabloid publications. He was not alone. Politics in 1930s France was growing more populist than ever, and publishing had to become so as well. The newspaper must be our guide, in its format and variety even more than in its "news." The daily leads us to the decade.

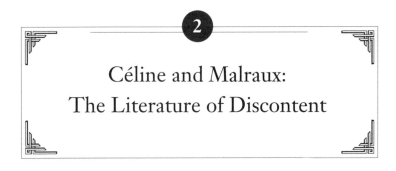

2

Céline and Malraux:
The Literature of Discontent

> Basically, only the street counts. Why deny it? It's waiting for us.
> One of these days we'll have to make up our minds and go down
> into the street, not one or two or three of us, but all.
> —Louis-Ferdinand Céline, *Journey to the End of the Night* (1932)

Throughout the 1930s André Gide stood at the moral center of Gallimard's publishing empire, his authority having long since been established by his authorship. For even when he ratified Gallimard's decision to expand into strata of popular culture that he cared little about, he knew that literature—the novel above all—still reigned as the prestige cultural product in this era that Régis Debray later dubbed the "publishing cycle."[1] True, Gide was finished as a novelist after *Les Faux-Monnayeurs* (1926), but he retained his power because more than once he had so masterfully demonstrated sovereign command over a complex literary universe of characters, themes, and ideas. Descending from the universe of fiction, he felt compelled to make a difference in the social world beyond it. At the outset of the thirties, making a difference in culture was also on the minds of most of the aspiring writers who gathered in offices of journals and newspapers where Gide's force was palpable, as a strong paternal presence to draw on or contend with.

"How old must you be to get your 'cultural driver's license'?" Denis Hollier asked whimsically with reference to the intellectuals of interwar France.[2] Gide was fifty-five before he took his political ideas out for a trial spin on the streets of Paris. By contrast, Nizan dared to drive straight into political action while still writing his first novels. Others thought they could forgo the apprenticeship of fiction altogether. Nevertheless, the literary field remained the prototype of the cultural terrain, and prowess in literature

28. Back from Africa: Alexandre Iacovleff, *Portrait of André Gide* (1927).

meant a sure advantage in mastering the political grid later on. Even Julien Benda's very long career as cultural gadfly began when his impressive novel had been scandalously denied the Prix Goncourt in 1912, a case of blatant prejudice. Those who for the next forty years were pricked or deflated by his severely judgmental pen had to admit that, Jew though he was, no Frenchman wrote purer French.

Politics is surely endemic to literature—although, amid the hushed halls of the academy, the elegance of libraries, and the bright optimism of bookshops where literature has its say, politics generally has the good manners to remain smartly disguised, at least most of the time. Yet in Paris each December the mask comes off when the literary prizes are adjudicated, the Prix Goncourt above all. In editorial offices, in cafés and bars, and in theater lobbies all around the capital, writers and activists weigh the chances as well as the merits of that year's block of books. For novelists are supposed to imagine, not merely follow, cultural destiny.

In the early thirties, bookstores displayed works by stalwart novelists at the higher echelons of "literature," like François Mauriac and Roger Martin

29. Gallimard's *Marianne* covers the 1932 Prix Goncourt: Céline as blind spot.

du Gard; and the shelves were full of popular storytellers of slightly lesser rank, such as Colette, C. F. Ramuz, Pierre Mac Orlan, and so on. Many writers were read, enjoyed, and debated, but when it came to novelists of profound ambition, novelists boasting styles muscular enough to act out those ambitions, two men commanded attention: Louis-Ferdinand Céline and André Malraux. If the novel lent profundity and gravity to the politics of culture in the era of the Popular Front, these two authors provided most of the mass. Their imposing works and personalities, whether vaunted or excoriated, simply could not be avoided by anyone preparing to have a hand in fashioning culture.

The weight of their accomplishments could really be felt at the tail end of 1932 and the beginning of 1933. First came Céline's moment. The front page of the December 7 issue of *Marianne* is bordered by head shots of ten authors, contenders for the 1932 Prix Goncourt. Strangely, the center position—that of the eleventh candidate—is empty, and the name under the blank space is that of Céline. *Voyage au bout de la nuit* had just been published by Denoël and talk of it was everywhere, although somewhat muted in Gallimard's publications.[3] Days later, Céline would be denied the prize under circumstances as scandalous as the novel in question (key votes peremptorily reversed, allegations of bribes, then a libel suit).

All this was in the air when the *NRF*, the very next month, began to serialize Malraux's novel *La Condition humaine*, with its unforgettable opening scene: the Communist revolutionary Tchen, stealing into a moonlit bedroom, lifts a mosquito net and plunges his knife into the body of a sleeping official. In their unabashed presumption, these two daring novelists measured up to the political passion of a new generation of "nonconformists" who themselves had just been singled out by Jean Paulhan, editor of the *NRF*, as "the ones to watch." For, as noted in Chapter 1, the group had made its formal debut in December 1932, when Paulhan consigned the bulk of that month's *NRF* to Denis de Rougemont, charging him to provide a forum for a range of pent-up young voices under the overall title *Cahier de revendications*.

Despite the huge ideological rifts separating factions of the dozen intellectuals who were given space in this issue of the *NRF*, they must all have taken Malraux to be something like an older brother and Gide's adopted son. Indeed, the "Two Andrés," as they came to be called, were increasingly seen together around this time, particularly after Malraux's brother Roland became Gide's private secretary. Gide depended on Malraux to lead him into

30. Malraux in the 1930s: between East and West, between art and activism.

the heart of politics (in fact, Malraux did coax Gide to accompany him on a flight to Berlin in early 1934 for a meeting with Joseph Goebbels, and the two Andrés sat together at the head table of the June 1935 Revolutionary Writers Congress). For his part, Gide had invited Malraux into the inner sanctum of the *NRF*, assuring his lasting influence.

No matter what their opinion of Malraux's novels or politics, the young firebrands whose opinions Paulhan and the *NRF* solicited must have felt inspired by his elevation. Scarcely older than they, Malraux was experienced, like an older—and prodigal—brother who had left home looking for adventure when sick of the squabbles (literary and political) at the dinner table. Malraux's adventures took him to India and then to Saigon, where he founded the progressive newspaper *Indochine* and where his efforts to "recover" local art treasures near Angkor Wat had run afoul of the law. Jailed, then put on trial, he was released after his wife, Clara, aided by André Breton, collected appeals from the potentates of the Parisian literary establishment. He returned to Paris in 1926 with a certain cachet and with the manuscript of his novel *La Tentation de l'Occident* (The Temptation of the West) nearly complete—he had written it on the ship home. And so while Mounier, de Rougemont, Nizan, and Thierry Maulnier were still on the sidelines watching the literary and political power struggles—indeed, while they were still in school—Malraux, already acting the grownup, found himself in the midst of those struggles.

Gaston Gallimard's personal nemesis, the publisher Bernard Grasset, was putting his money on Malraux. Through his chief editor, Daniel Halévy, he had signed Malraux the wunderkind to write three novels (Malraux was just twenty-five when *La Tentation de l'Occident* was published). While this slim first effort develops a familiar thesis (the dynamic West expending itself fruitlessly in its endeavors to penetrate the eternal East—as in, for example, E. M. Forster's *Passage to India*, published two years earlier),[4] it came cleverly disguised as an exchange of letters between a Parisian intellectual and a wise Chinese thinker. But the epistolary format seemed to blunt the excitement of discovery and the immediacy of drama. And so the novel proved too reflective and too cerebral to be a popular success, though it garnered modest notoriety and had critics on the lookout for this promising author's next book.

Grasset, who had primed the critics, now pushed Malraux into public view on every occasion. Never timid, Malraux filled as many doorways as he could; by force of personality, aggressive and always dashing, he quickly became someone to watch. When Julien Benda's book *La Trahison des clercs* came out in 1927, Malraux confronted him at one of Halévy's weekly literary discussions. He had been invited by Halévy, who was eager to give him a forum; and there he was sure to meet François Mauriac and Henry de Montherlant—both likewise Grasset authors—as well as Gabriel Marcel, Jean Guéhenno, and other opinion makers. They all took note.

The year 1928 brought Malraux completely into his own. In the spring, *Les Conquérants* appeared in installments in the *NRF* and then, published in one volume by Grasset, vied for the Prix Goncourt. Meanwhile, seduced by the electric atmosphere in the editorial offices of the *NRF*, Malraux decided to abandon Grasset and sign on with Gallimard, where he was named arts editor and soon a member of the overall editorial committee. When Gide formally and decidedly invited him to lunch in his fabled apartment on the rue de Varenne, Malraux knew his consecration had come. In August he was asked to attend one of the retreats for intellectuals sponsored in Pontigny. There Martin du Gard and a phalanx of illustrious intellectuals found Malraux's verve and style utterly compelling. Evidently he dominated the discussion. This is one case where personal style and literary style genuinely reinforce one another. As Paul Morand and others believed, Malraux lived his ideas and so was worth getting to know; for only someone who had seen history in the making—right there in the Far East—could have produced the passion and the sensations that make *Les Conquérants* exceptional.

Unquestionably, Malraux felt himself following in the line of Kipling, Conrad, and Dostoyevsky; he had traveled in order to experience the rush of events going on around him and he was ready on the instant to travel again, the more obscure the location the better.[5] Persia would be next. Gallimard warned him not to take himself for one of the brash heroes he had invented. Apparently, Gallimard personally scotched a daring scheme Malraux concocted to enter the Soviet Union with other adventuresome writers (Pierre Mac Orlan, Joseph Kessel, and Francis Carco were mentioned, as was Blaise Cendrars) to try to liberate Trotsky, just then exiled in Kazakhstan.[6]

But Trotsky freed himself and moved to Turkey, where he read *Les Conquérants* and reviewed it in the *NRF* exactly three years after the book had been serialized there. Though impressed by the energy and tactility of its writing, he found the book dangerous for the way it misrepresented the script of social revolution. At one point in his review, he likens it to a painting: "By little touches of color, in the manner of the pointillists, Malraux paints an unforgettable picture of the general strike." But at another point, he says: "The book is called a novel. What in fact we have before us is a fictionalized chronicle of the Chinese revolution during its first period, the Canton period. The chronicle is incomplete. It is in some cases deficient in its grasp of the social reality. By contrast, the reader sees not only luminous episodes of the revolution but also clearly delineated silhouettes that etch themselves in one's memory like social symbols."[7]

Whether chronicler or painter, Malraux, says Trotsky, retains too European a perspective, using the revolution, despite his sympathy for it, as an opportunity for "excesses of individualism and of aesthetic caprice." Trotsky chided him for his arrogance: only "a solid inoculation of Marxism might have protected the author from fatal mistakes," particularly in his characterization of professional revolutionaries and in his belief that the revolution depends on those European professionals rather than on the strengths of the oppressed society. Trotsky used his inside knowledge of Moscow's international policies to question Malraux's fanciful speculations.

In a spirited reply published alongside Trotsky's review, Malraux defends

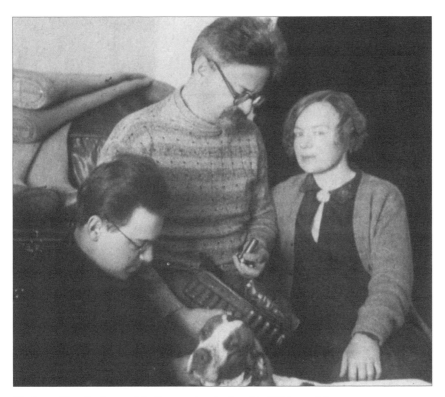

31. Leon Trotsky (center) in France, just before his 1934 expulsion.

his focus on the character Garine, a Swiss anarchist of Dostoyevskian descent: "Revolutions do not make themselves, but neither do novels. This book is not a 'fictionalized chronicle,' because the main stress is placed on the relationship between the individual and collective action, not on collective action alone."[8] Always believing the novel to be a dialectical form, Malraux was proud to have advanced beyond the alternating reflections of *La Tentation de l'Occident*, this time concatenating perspective (principally Garine's) with the forces of history that operate beyond any perspective.

Trotsky was right to seize on the privileged position of the narrator: in *Les Conquérants*, the general strike is "not seen from below, as it is carried on, but seen from above." One can imagine Malraux apprenticing to write this novel while working out of his first-class hotel suite in Saigon, where he edited *Indochine*. He memorized the smells and especially the sounds of Saigon, and of its Chinese district, verifying their validity with one quick trip to Hong

Kong. He had no need to see Shanghai till after his novels were written; he simply expanded judiciously on what he knew from Saigon.[9] From this post he collected information coming from all over Southeast Asia, as well as from parts of China, not to mention Europe. *Les Conquérants* emulates the "news flash" quality of a daily paper: sections begin with datelines, and uppercase headlines broadcast the starkest facts. Some of the sections emulate background stories, extended reportage, and in one case a travel diary. Without fanfare, the style of *Les Conquérants* reflects the style of Garine, a character who saw himself this way: "My life is action and I'm indifferent to everything that isn't action, including its results. . . . Essentially, I'm a gambler." Malraux described him as having "an aptitude for action, culture, and lucidity, values that were indirectly tied to those of Europe at the time."[10]

How could this novel not impress the new generation who would form the ranks of the Popular Front? A very young Denis de Rougemont proclaimed that Malraux had moved into the front ranks of fiction with this novel. He reviewed it as he was about to leave his native Switzerland and come to Paris, where he was sure that history was likely to be made. "Culture," "lucidity," and "action" became his watchwords too. Emmanuel Berl went so far as to dedicate his *Mort de la pensée bourgeoise:* "To André Malraux. This book is surely nothing other than a long defense of Garine." An instinct for moral action is what Berl, like Denis de Rougemont, fervently threw in the face of sedentary, academic philosophy and political thought.

At the outset of 1933, when Céline and Malraux dominated successive issues of the *NRF,* the latter had more than come into his own. *La Condition humaine* would become a bestseller and be canonized with the Prix Goncourt the next year; throughout the decade, it would remain the only novel to rival in significance *Voyage au bout de la nuit.* In composing it, Malraux seems to have listened to Trotsky. Like Tchen, he knifed his way into the flesh of history and felt its resistance.

More certainly, Malraux listened to those who urged him to break with traditional novelistic structure and narration, for he abandoned the emotional security that the single hero provides both the novelist and his readers. Instead, *La Condition humaine* is peppered with breaks and ellipses so that its shape emerges only when one steps back.[11] The novel's drama of political destiny comes clear after the particular quality of its myriad, scattered vignettes register their discrete effects. Intermittently illuminating one character and situation after another, Malraux coordinated a complex representation of revolution. He pressed its inexorable movement up against the varying temporalities lived by a spectrum of passionate characters drawn to Shanghai at a moment when the force of history could not fail to precipitate drama. The revolution in Shanghai may have failed, but the real revolution of *La Condition humaine* lay in its style, which was based on multiple centers of attraction. This aesthetic, which Malraux deemed political at heart, he associated with the Soviet films that he championed, and that he praised outright when he met Trotsky just weeks after his novel was out. Less than a year later, he and the director Sergei Eisenstein met in Moscow to dream of an adaptation of *La Condition humaine*. It would have been memorable, for both men thought of art and politics as inseparable, and both believed in revolutionizing the world.

In the meantime—between Malraux's meetings with Trotsky and with Eisenstein, and just weeks after his Prix Goncourt—politics exploded in France. In January 1934, when Malraux and Gide flew back from Berlin (they had gone there to help liberate the individuals falsely accused of torching the Reichstag), the Paris papers were full of the consequences of Stavisky's "suicide." Scarcely a week later, while Gide went south to sunny Sicily, Malraux and Clara found themselves caught up in the street marches and riots of February 6. The revolutionary fervor of Shanghai had spread to Paris.

Malraux's signature stands out on a series of manifestos, including the initial "Appel à la lutte" that Breton drafted on February 11, and of course he figures on the roster of the CVIA. Young as he was, Malraux was deemed a veteran of revolutions, a real authority. That summer, he went to Moscow, where he was first honored and then commissioned to help organize the Paris Congress of Revolutionary Artists in June 1935. In 1936 he returned to Moscow and then exported a scaled-down version of the congress to Madrid, where he watched (and got drawn into) the fever of the civil war there. Nearly too large a figure, and too nervous, to remain with any single enterprise, he took himself for a knight errant. During the Paris strikes of June and July 1936, he correctly understood that unless France committed itself to intervention on behalf of Spain, its own Popular Front would lose credibility and would fall. Raising money in the United States and England, recklessly putting together an international air brigade, he threw himself once more into direct action; and once more the agony and suffering of a failed political struggle would help him produce an extraordinary work, *L'Espoir*.

Because Malraux was young, optimistic, and revolutionary, he was close kin to the restless nonconformists of 1932. And he was everywhere visible. By comparison, Céline was like a fascinating but jaded uncle, who drops in from unknown pursuits every so often to spoil family occasions with his world-weary and contemptuous remarks. He was proud to have caused a scandal with *Voyage au bout de la nuit*. And its rejection by the Goncourt committee was just what he expected. It proved him right, as he would say over and over in ever more inventively nasty ways.

No one better gauged the corrosive power of this acid novel than Leon Trotsky, who wrote about it just after coming to France from his initial exile in Istanbul. In a review that would wind up in the *Atlantic Monthly* in 1935, Trotsky zeroed in on the "pessimism, even resignation" of Céline, a man "who hates lies yet has no belief in truth."[12] Trotsky was instantly drawn to Céline's thick materialism, linking him to Rabelais, another medical doctor unafraid to plunge his hands into the guts of life. But as much as Céline may have exposed the innards of a diseased culture, Trotsky deemed his indignation to be ultimately self-gratifying. Though Céline caustically mocked the fraudulent clichés that upheld the bogus "Cartesian lucidity" of bourgeois nationalism, his indignation wound up in the gutter that so fascinated him. Trotsky could not understand why it didn't instead lead to direct "action and to hope" for a renewed society. Writing during the moment of the very Stavisky scandals that would lead to his own expulsion from France, Trotsky actually identified Stavisky as the fruit of the diseased republic that Céline mercilessly and deliciously dissected. But since Céline rejected both the present and the possibility of a future, his resignation ultimately allied him with the system he abhorred.

Trotsky felt more comfortable with André Breton's righteous invective, which likewise targeted the inane nationalism of a crass bourgeoisie. Breton, who would visit Trotsky in Mexico later in the decade, had recently issued the "Second Manifesto of Surrealism" and launched the explicitly Marxist review *Le Surréalisme au Service de la Révolution*. Like Céline, his experiences in World War I and afterward in medicine had soured him on "culture" as it is conventionally conceived; in contrast, however, he could imagine another culture, a society of spontaneous filiations, driven by liberated desire and uplifted by collective imagination. The "delirium" often recognized as the chief effect of Céline's incantatory prose has its counterpart in the automatic writing of the Surrealists and in the oneiric logic of Buñuel and Dalí's aggressive films. Freud stands behind the audacity of these expressions of fissured subjectivity. The special Surrealist manifesto published to support the belea-

32. Céline in 1920: a shady ID.

guered *L'Age d'or* against the censors proclaimed the film's magnitude in terms that apply just as easily to *Voyage au bout de la nuit*, explicitly invoking the conjunction of death drive and sexual urge.[13] In fact, Buñuel and Dalí satirize colonialism, empire, religion and the grandeur of art, just as Céline would two years later; as for "love," in *L'Age d'or* it amounts either to masturbation or to bodies squirming one atop the other in the mud. Like Buñuel and Dalí, Céline's hero, Bardamu, peeks behind the ludicrous trappings of culture to locate cruelty and insatiable desire; yet far from deploring these instincts, he (and they) luxuriate in them as the fecund source of their excretions, a term they would surely prefer to "expressions" or to "art." Trotsky, on the other hand, believed in art and in reason. He took Céline and Breton seriously because they went to the very end of the night; his dream, however, was meant to usher in a new day, one in which such terms as "politics" and "the people" might be spoken without derision. He would be a hero and martyr to many of those who built the Popular Front. Céline would not.

Within the encyclopedia of horrors that constitute *Voyage au bout de la nuit*, two scenes stand out: Bardamu's penetration into the African bush and his participation in the ritual slaughter of a pig in a working-class neighborhood where Céline once lived. The African episode crystallizes the entire novel, being a voyage into "blank darkness" that begins aboard a ship called the *Admiral Bragueton*.[14] Bardamu, exiled from the corrupt aftermath of war-shattered Europe, harbors visions of a certain clichéd grandeur associated with the colonies. Yet his trip soon takes on a sinister and then an absurd and nightmarish air once the boat drifts past the Canary Islands. Loathing his aggressive shipmates, a paranoid Bardamu feels his energy sapped along with that of the boat: "The *Admiral Bragueton* began to go slower still; she slowed down in her own juice. Not a breath of air stirred about us; we were hugging the coast and doing it so slowly that we seemed to be shifting through molasses. Syrupy too was the sky above the decks, nothing but a black deep paste which I gazed at hungrily. To get back into the night was what I wanted most of all, to get back there, sweating and groaning or any way, it didn't matter how."[15] Bardamu finds the night soon enough, after he works his way upriver as part of a colonial company exploiting the continent's resources. "There are two ways you can go about penetrating a forest; one is by tunneling your way through it, like rats through a hayrick. It is the suffocating method. Or you can face going up the river bundled up in the bottom of a hollow tree trunk, paddled along from bend to wooded clump, glimpsing an end of endless days, surrendering yourself entirely to the glare, without respite. And so, dazed by these squawking blacks, you get to whatever place you are going to in whatever state you can" (*Journey*, 161). Once at the furthest outpost, he meets the white man whom he is meant to replace, his double. He spies the man just after sunset:

> Night then opened the ball with all its prowling beasts and myriad croaking noises. . . . I saw Robinson's face once more, veiled by this haze of insects before I put the light out. . . . He went on talking to me in the dark while I searched through the past, . . . wondering where I could possibly have met this man before. No voice answered me. You can lose yourself groping among these twirling forms of memory. It's terrifying how many people and how many things no longer stir in one's past. . . . I couldn't help being seized by a terrible fear that he might start to murder me there, on my camp bed, before going off with what was left in the cash box. . . . The idea petrified me. But what should I do? Call out? But to whom? Those cannibals in the village? . . . Was I lost? Surely I was, already. . . . Hours passed in fits and starts. He didn't snore. All those forest calls and noises made it impossible for me to hear him breathing. (*Journey*, 168–169)

After realizing—or coming to believe—that this man is his companion from the war, "I called out gaily, as if I had a piece of good news for him. 'I say, Robinson! Hey there!' . . . There was no answer. My heart beat fast. I got up, expecting an ugly jab in the face. Nothing happened. Then, greatly daring, I ventured, groping my way, to the other end of the hut where his bed was. He had gone. I waited for the dawn, striking matches at intervals."

The revulsion at unchecked jungle growth, at a nature so fecund it destabilizes structures, invades Bardamu's little hut, latches onto his skin, nauseates him even before he falls ill with a fever. "We slipped further into the mud after each downpour, thicker, soupier than the last. What yesterday had looked like a rock was today a treacly mess. From down-hanging branches tepid rain water pursued and drenched you wherever you went; it lay about the hut and everywhere around like a dried-up river bed. Everything was melting away in a welter of trashy goods, hopes and accounts, together with the fever, itself moist too" (*Journey*, 175). Bardamu suffers classic symptoms of *le cafard*, the heat-induced hysteria common to the heroes of *le cinéma colonial* (Jean Gabin suffers from it in *La Bandera*, as does Pierre Richard-Willm in *Le Grand Jeu*). Africa threatens one's integrity, dissolving the personality as the body's temperature rises with fever. Its merciless sun blanches distinctions; its fathomless nights utterly disorient. In the end, the debilitated colonizer Bardamu finds the tables turned: sold by the natives to a galley ship, he is bound for the New World. A slave chained to his oar, Céline's hero, unlike Sartre's in *La Nausée*, achieves no secure realization as the world melts at his touch. Language alone—that is, invective—compensates for the humiliations of existence. Bardamu's language overflows the banks of sentence structure, breaking down French just as Bardamu's self breaks down when he came to face utter isolation in the hut at the end of a trail in Central Africa.

There is a society for which Céline's language is its poetry, but it is neither the society of academicians nor that of literary journals like the *NRF*. As many scholars have pointed out, Céline's characters speak the tongue of the lower middle class, the disenfranchised shopkeepers eking out their petty lives on the outskirts of Paris. One of the most emblematic social scenes of the novel (early in the "Rancy" section) celebrates this society, as Bardamu returns from a day in downtown Paris. Passing the Place Blanche on his way to the outskirts just beyond Montmartre, he notices

a lot of people in the rue Lepic, more people than usual. So I went up too, to see what was happening. There was a crowd outside a butcher's shop. You had to squeeze your way into the circle to see what was going on. It was a pig, a large, an enormous pig. He was grunting away in the middle of the circle like a man who's been disturbed, grunting like hell. He was being damnably treated all the time. People were tweaking his ears to make him squeal. He twisted and turned, trying to escape, tugging at the rope that held him: other people teased him and he squealed all the louder in pain. And every one laughed all the more. . . .

He didn't know how to get away from these humans. He realized that. He piddled at the same time as much as he could, but that didn't do any good, either. Grunting and squealing did no good. There *was* no way out. Everyone laughed a lot. The butcher behind in his shop made signs and jokes to his customers and waved a great knife in the air. He was pleased as Punch, himself. He had bought the pig and tied it up out there as an advertisement. He couldn't have enjoyed himself more at his daughter's wedding.

More and more people kept arriving in front of the shop to see the pig wallowing in great pink folds of flesh each time he tried to get away. But that wasn't enough. They put a small, excitable little dog on his back and made it skip about and snap at the pig's exuberant mound of flesh. That was so extremely funny that now you couldn't get through the crowd. The police arrived and moved people on. (*Journey*, 288–289)

For this brief moment, Bardamu finds himself unexpectedly swept out of his isolation and into the spirit of a crowd, experiencing cohesion and heightened existence in what can only be described as the ritual sacrifice of a pig in the middle of Montmartre. The irrationality and cruelty that provoke contagious laughter are short-lived, as the police come to disperse this concentration of popular energy. "People moved on," Bardamu among them—on into the night. Alone he saunters homeward:

When at that time of the evening you come out on to the Pont Caulaincourt, you can see the first lights of Rancy beyond the great lake of night which covers the cemetery. Rancy's on the other side. You have to go all the way round to get there. It's the devil of a long way. You'd say you were walking all round night itself, it takes such a time, and so much walking round the cemetery to reach the outer walls of the town.

And then when you get to the gates, you pass by the damp toll office where the little green official sits. Then you're quite close. The dogs of the neighborhood are all at their posts, barking. There are some flowers in the gaslight though, on the stall of a flower seller who is always sitting there, waiting for the dead to come by from day to day, from hour to hour. The cemetery, another cemetery, comes next, and then the boulevard de la Révolte. It goes off broad and straight into the night with all its lamps. You keep up it on the left. That was my street. You never meet anyone on it. (*Journey*, 289–290)

One could hardly ask for a more precise example of the principle laid out in Emile Durkheim's *Les Formes élémentaires de la vie religieuse* (1912; Elementary Forms of Religious Life) concerning the alternation of ecstasy (effervescent assemblies) and anomie (the solitary walk by the cemetery). This book became crucial to Bataille at just the moment (1929–1931) when he was editing the eclectic avant-garde journal *Documents* and sitting in on Marcel Mauss's courses that transmitted Durkheim's thesis.[16] Together with Caillois and Leiris, Bataille made plans to promote a sacred sociology in contemporary life. Céline's sociology is hardly sacred: he renders here the degraded secular form of such an assembly, a brief collective incandescence quickly dimming as individuals separate, Bardamu taking empty roads lit intermittently by streetlamps into the zone beyond the city walls.

Where was Céline on February 6, 1934, just sixteen months after his novel was published? Shouldn't he have felt called out onto the streets as crowds gathered at the Place de la Concorde and then marched randomly in search of sacrificial victims? The police had quite a time getting them to "move on." In fact, that very month Céline put the finishing touches on *Mort à credit* (Death on the Installment Plan), and then looked for ways to exploit *Voyage au bout de la nuit* internationally. He wound up going to London for the English translation, and in the late spring of 1934 would travel to the United States in a failed attempt to interest Hollywood. Although self-absorbed, he could hardly avoid the aftermath of the February 6 riots. Indeed, he was recruited immediately by leftists who associated his novel with the populist fiction of his friend Eugène Dabit. Henri Barbusse got him to sign a petition to free the scapegoats of the Reichstag fire, but Céline explicitly declined to go further than lending his name. Even to appear at a rally was unthinkable to a man who had no faith in politics and negotiation.

Elie Faure befriended him at this time. The great art historian had been overwhelmed by *Voyage au bout de la nuit*, and Céline was only too glad to learn even more about painting from a professional theorist.[17] Faure did his best to bring Céline into the CVIA during the spring of 1934, but by this time Céline had learned how much he enjoyed digging in his heels. He was appalled by the self-righteousness of the left, as if one could expect workers to be any less greedy or cruel than professional people or the aristocracy. Utterly misanthropic, Céline predicted the victory of fascism on the strength of its base appeal. The lowest form of politics was bound to dominate in a base world, he thought. Soon he found that his writings, particularly his paranoid dithyrambs, were valued by the virulent right. But Céline was so consistently negative as to make a rather useless ally. He was uncontrollable.

Céline's friend Pierre Drieu La Rochelle, on the other hand, was certainly in the streets on February 6 and would never forget the effervescence he experienced there. The epic novel he published in 1939, *Gilles*, concludes with the exhilarating days of the Stavisky riots: the bodies pressed together, moving on waves of undirected energy, lashing out unpredictably and satisfyingly in bloody violence. France had finally shown itself capable of virile action in the face of an aging bureaucracy no longer fit to govern.[18]

Voyage au bout de la nuit may appear to be an excremental dirge on existence in general, or a pessimistic anthropology of human beings as lone agents, as vying for space in crowds, and as taken up in societies (military, colonial, labor, institutional). But it opens at a precise political moment, the recruitment of soldiers for World War I; and President Poincaré is targeted for satire on its very first page via a newspaper, *Le Temps*, which is also satirized ("Now there's a really great paper for you. . . . There isn't another paper like it for defending the interests of the French race"). When published in 1932, the novel found itself enmeshed in the political turmoil of that year, and discussed by papers not so different from *Le Temps*. It was an "actionable" novel, one might say. And it was precisely in the discourses of politics, newspapers, and the courts that the remainder of Céline's career would be conducted. Though he would write more fiction, *Voyage au bout de la nuit* marked the last stage of the novel as privileged site of deep cultural investment and critique. For how could anyone go further in outrage, except in the form of the direct action of pamphleteering?

Painful to digest, this novel lay like a rat inside the distended python of French politics throughout the decade. Everyone seemed to have read it, but no one knew how to make it nourish new ideas. A veteran of the Great War,

Céline was half a generation older than the nonconformists, many of whom emulated his bilious rhetoric while lambasting the gerontocracy and mediocrity of the Third Republic or bickering with one other. Yet Uncle Céline took pleasure in demoralizing from the outset the revolutionary and utopian visions of this younger group, including people whose rightist politics he was later associated with. His own journalism, if we can so label *Bagatelles pour un massacre* and his other pamphlets, placed itself effectively outside the field of debate. He relished his uselessness to the times.

As useless as it arranged for itself to be, *Voyage au bout de la nuit* set an inimitable and anxious tone for the decade. It disturbed everyone, including Paul Nizan, the young Communist firebrand just returned from a voyage of disenchantment with the manuscript for his book *Aden, Arabie*. Writing in *L'Humanité* on December 9, 1932, Nizan preempted Trotsky's combination of infatuation and frustration with the book. Céline "tears off all the masks, all disguises, knocks down the props of illusion." Yet "he is not one of us; it is impossible to accept his profound anarchy, his contempt, his general revulsion that doesn't even spare the working class. For such pure revolt can lead him anywhere—to our side, against us, or nowhere. He is missing the revolution, the true explanation of the miseries that he denounces and the cancers he strips bare, the very hope that carries us forward."

Nizan's review appeared at just the moment of his contribution to the *Cahier de revendications*. A great many French people must have simultaneously read this incendiary issue of the *NRF* alongside a newly purchased copy of Céline's book—"this enormous novel," as Nizan called it in his review, this novel "of a force and breadth to which the well-groomed dwarves of bourgeois literature do not accustom us." While de Rougemont's dozen writers vented their disgust with bourgeois life in France, Céline went further. He must have both approved their hostility and scoffed at their ingenuous humanism, their program for a future which he, experienced as he was, knew for a fact had been foreclosed. His book had preempted them, deflating their hopes. In Céline's view, there is no future to look forward to, for neither God, nor France, nor Communist Utopia, nor spiritual revolution can save humanity from itself. Let no one try to outdo him in rhetoric of rant or in bleakness of vision.

Malraux and Céline were the novelists of the decade. They admired each other. Or at least Céline claims to have loved *Les Conquérants*, and Malraux asked Céline to contribute a preface to a book that Clara was translating.[19] Brazen, aiming to shock with their topics and their style, they both presumed to stand above or beside other writers of the time. While desperate for recognition in France, they made it clear that their concerns and vision were international. Scorning the universities, they claimed an unspoken privilege that in France permits writers to speak on any topic whatever. Literature for them was an anteroom to politics, and politics fed their writing. Other writers certainly competed in this arena (such as Paul Claudel, Georges Bernanos, Paul Morand), but Malraux and Céline—in their daring, in the way their novels carried them into action—marked the generation of nonconformists who wanted above all for France to become dynamic. If this spelled the end of the influence of the classic French novel (in particular, the irrelevance of Mauriac, whom Céline dismissed irreverently),[20] then classicism had ceded to something vibrant and new. Unafraid to emulate the dynamism of newspapers and even of the cinema, this new generation thought of literature as a field of action, a field that had been completely changed and renewed by the novels and the personalities of Malraux and Céline. Both men embraced these popular forms of expression, and both of them traveled the world within their fiction and on behalf of it. Couldn't the same thing happen to the larger field of culture? Couldn't forceful action make France a place where history was lived, rather than endured or merely watched? A younger generation wanted exactly this, though, as we shall see, they differed radically in their hopes for what that history would bring to the nation and to the world.

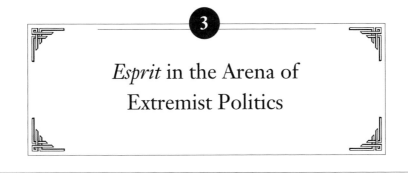

3

Esprit in the Arena of Extremist Politics

Faith and Politics

Eugène Ionesco opens the preface to his 1959 play *Rhinoceros* by recounting an anecdote in which an intellectual visiting Nuremberg as a tourist finds himself irresistibly tempted to partake in the mass frenzy during a Hitler rally he haphazardly attends in September 1938. This was the crucial rally that gave Hitler the confidence to walk into the Munich meetings later in the month and announce the annexation of the Sudetenland. Ionesco applauds that intellectual, Denis de Rougemont, for managing at the last moment to muster what he describes as "total moral revulsion"—something arising not from argued principles or ethical judgment but from the animal depths of his being to combat what was essentially an animal instinct: the pulse of some repressed tribal feeling that surfaced within him to greet the approaching Führer.

If Denis de Rougemont remains in public memory, he most likely does so through his most famous book, *L'Amour et l'Occident* (1939), translated as *Love in the Western World* (1940). What is generally taken to be an engaging but academic composition, an early exercise in comparative literature, changes complexion in the light of Ionesco's anecdote. De Rougemont, it turns out, wrote the entire intricate book in a concentrated period of inspiration during the spring of 1938, not long before his encounter with Hitler. Moreover, he presented one of his most controversial chapters—on modern warfare—in May of that year (just after the March 11 annexation of Austria to the Third Reich) at a gathering of the Collège de Sociologie, a loose association of dissident intellectuals and former Surrealists, chaired by Georges Bataille, Michel Leiris, and Roger Caillois. We can imagine, then, that de Rougemont didn't merely happen on the Hitler crowd, but sought it out so as to test the ideas about "transpersonal ecstasy" that he and the members of the Collège had been entertaining at their meetings.

In fact, this was not de Rougemont's first Hitler rally. According to his diary, he saw Hitler in March 1936 and then took Emmanuel Mounier, founder of the journal *Esprit*, to a rally in June of that year. Despite the fervor these outsiders could sense all around them, de Rougemont coolly compared such rallies to something very familiar and very conventional: Protestant liturgy.[1] His sang-froid in the face of this momentous political tide appears even more surprising in view of the dates of the diary entries, indicating that they were written at the very moment of the Popular Front's ascendancy under Léon Blum. De Rougemont's quite different reactions to the Hitler rallies mark extremes on the scale of French *esprit* in the final years of the Third Republic, for between spring 1936 and autumn 1938 the Popular Front had faltered, Hitler had expanded his German base, and de Rougemont had understandably lost his composure.

De Rougemont serves as a particularly apt index not just to the brief moment of the Popular Front but to so-called nonconformist thought and action throughout the 1930s, because he was, relative to those around him and despite his intelligence and talent, unexceptional. Nondogmatic, he could associate himself, as we have just seen, both with Mounier's *Esprit* group and with Bataille's Collège, as well as with other groups, scarcely known today, such as the one allied with the journal *L'Ordre Nouveau*. Dispassionate ("gloomy," Mounier would label him in a less friendly moment), de Rougemont was nevertheless obsessed by the workings and effects of passion—by crowds at rallies, for example, or by suicidal lovers. Without any recognizable personal pathologies, without any compelling allegiances to militant ideologies (whether French or Catholic or Marxist), he was merely a young, socially committed intellectual who, like many in his generation, had given up on standard politics and announced a stance against the inertia of the Third Republic as a nonconformist.

While other figures may better exhibit the fanaticism the era seemed to incubate, de Rougemont sought to encourage in a quiet way the *révolution nécessaire*, as it was famously dubbed by Robert Aron and Arnaud Dandieu, and by Maurice Blanchot. De Rougemont's function was to bring together young malcontents across a spectrum of positions and then broker the accumulated outrage of this generation in the general market of ideas, explaining

to the culture at large why radical change was in the air and why it was something to be welcomed and shepherded into the future rather than repressed.
De Rougemont labored behind the scenes, going to the Ile de Ré (off
France's Atlantic coast) on a year-long retreat during the Popular Front's gestation. There he wrote *Penser avec les mains* (Thinking with Your Hands), a
text that appeared in early 1936 just in time to encourage intellectuals to get
out on the street and bring about a populist politics. Yet because he stayed off
the front lines (he was out of the country when Blum took over the reins of
government), de Rougemont's role has receded in accounts of the decade, focused as they are precisely on the Front. Tracking de Rougemont's activities
lets us look behind the leading edge, where agitated air masses produce a variety of local conditions. De Rougemont's temperament and placement make
him a sensitive barometer that senses and measures much of the turbulence in
the political atmosphere of the decade.

De Rougement entered the Parisian cultural scene from a cool distance,
unlike his French *confrères*. He was a Swiss Protestant, first of all, and the son
of a pastor. Educated in Geneva, moreover, he was deeply marked by the
German theological tradition, or rather by the contest in the 1920s to reform
that tradition. Indeed, his spiritual autobiography begins with a debt to his
countryman Karl Barth, whose writings and social commitment brought him
back to a faith he had briefly abandoned in a dark moment. Barth's early years
and ideas form a template de Rougemont applied to his own experience.
Barth had interrupted an academic career to work as a pastor and community
organizer in a small farming canton. Out of this local experience, and to rebuke the liberal Protestant church for its failure during World War I, Barth
joined the Religious Socialist movement, organizing workers in his district.
In the evenings he composed *Der Römerbrief* (The Epistle to the Romans;
1933), shocking the Protestant establishment with a brand of existential
theology at odds with their rational, comforting liberalism. God's complete
"Otherness," his mystery and obscurity, would become the cornerstone of the
formidable dogmatic reconstruction that occupied the rest of Barth's career.
In these first years of his fame, Barth must have seemed, in de Rougemont's
eyes, to be a modern-day Kierkegaard for the way he rebuked the cocky intellectual establishment. Was it with Barth in mind that de Rougemont advocated a return to Kierkegaard in the early 1930s—a time when he was urging
intellectuals to work in socialist communities just as Barth had?

The religious and ethical issues that Barth spearheaded turned de Rougemont into an engaged intellectual. Indeed, he would coin the term *engagé* in *Penser avec les mains*.[2] Barth also turned him toward a vibrant German philosophical arena where Martin Heidegger had transformed his theological preoccupations into the *Existenz Philosophie* of *Sein und Zeit* (Being and Time; 1927). When de Rougemont arrived in Paris in 1931, his knowledge of Husserl and Heidegger made him feel at home in the intellectual circles where he found that these thinkers, just then being translated, were essential to the school of phenomenology that was forming.

But de Rougemont would always require a philosophy that ushered immediately into social action. And so his deepest intellectual influence came from Alexandre Marc, a Russian Jew who converted to Catholicism in 1933. The two first met at the home of the eminent Christian literary critic Charles Du Bos (Gabriel Marcel was also present). By all accounts brilliant and deeply committed to social revolution, Marc was one of the forces, along with Aron and Dandieu, behind *L'Ordre Nouveau*. Given such acquaintances and such an education, and given his perfect fluency in the key languages of the day, de Rougemont moved quickly into the circles that permitted him to try out his ideas in print. Once he had published some of this work, editors were quick to call on him because of his levelheaded and conciliatory nature. They appreciated his ability to convey sensitive issues while attracting and holding an audience.

De Rougemont solidified this reputation when, after he contributed a particularly lucid article to *Présences* (July 1932), Jean Paulhan invited him to put together a survey of the grievances of his generation. This became the issue of the *NRF* entitled *Cahier de revendications*. At age twenty-six, de Rougemont represented a generation that was coming into its own by pushing up through the cracks in the entrenched institutions of the Third Republic. This situation went far beyond the bounds of a conventional Oedipal struggle for power. First of all, none of these nonconformists had experienced combat in World War I. They felt little need to bow before the political and military establishment that could claim to have saved the nation through great sacrifice. Second, a worldwide economic depression indicated that massive readjustment of resources was immediately called for. Relying on the political and economic theories of Hendrik de Man, leader of the Belgian Socialist Party, de Rougemont took this to be a crisis of culture with economic consequences, rather than an economic crisis with social consequences. For de Man defined "culture" as the general pattern of consumption within a society. From this perspective, French, European, and world cultures were patently out of sync with the older forces of capital that continued to produce goods (and values) superfluous or deleterious to life in the twentieth century, which de Man believed to be socialist in orientation and, in comparison with life in the nineteenth century, far more mobile and efficient.

The preceding generation of malcontents (for instance, those affiliated with the journal *Clarté*, or those who called themselves Dadaists, or the first wave of Surrealists) kept the agony of the war in mind as they railed against the mindless proliferation of material goods during a period justly known as *les années folles*. The nonconformists of the 1930s, by contrast, felt a responsibility to enact not an adolescent rebellion in their father's grand château, but the complete takeover of a decaying estate. "Decadence" was precisely the word used by the left, the right, and those adhering to a middle way that they termed the "Third Force."

In late 1932, when de Rougemont assembled contributors for his *Cahier de revendications*, the urgency of the world situation was fueling the stridency of everyone's rhetoric. Mussolini's regime had sent more than a million Italians fleeing across the border into France for refuge. Germany, as it likewise fought its decadent Weimar past with a youth movement, was clearly a country to keep an eye on—a hopeful eye, in the opinion of several contributors. Those with friends in Spain heard talk about radically new political options for that country.

De Rougemont would later lament that only the French were governed by aged men, who were clearly out of touch with modern conditions and altogether out of energy. Mussolini was not yet fifty, and Hitler, about to be appointed chancellor, was just forty-three. Even Stalin looked youthful when you compared his picture in the newspaper with photographs of the French ministers. Members of France's young, educated, eager generation must have felt exasperated when they realized that their leaders were propped up not just by outdated traditions, but by an alliance between business and government that foreclosed all hope for major change. This was the "established disorder" that *Esprit* hammered at, beginning with its first issue late in 1932. De Rougemont would claim that disorder is the condition capitalists love to exploit as they cleverly shift material resources toward themselves, while workers, farmers, and artisans are at the mercy of market forces and flows they neither comprehend nor control. Nevertheless, de Rougemont, unlike so many others of his generation, refrained from taking the leap of faith to Marxism. He considered the options of a completely planned state economy to be crude, obvious, and ultimately unreflective. Marxism, like capitalism, he would argue, had fallen prey to the "occult dictatorship of economics" without considering the human values that the materials of the world ought to serve and not control.

De Rougemont was not alone in seeking an alternative to capitalism and Marxism—the "Third Force"—which would reintroduce values that had been abandoned in the Renaissance. The Action Française movement had been preaching something like this ever since 1908, in the wake of the Dreyfus Affair. Of course the values that Charles Maurras and his followers preached were those of the monarchy, and few of the nonconformists considered them an option. Nevertheless, under his leadership Action Française had demonstrated that ideas spawned outside the conventional political arena were viable and could galvanize a sizable following, even when they advocated violent revolution. Ironically, however, its most direct impact on the young nonconformists occurred in 1926, when Action Française was officially censured by Pope Pius XI. Since so many figures connected with this monarchist organization—both members and sympathizers—were practicing Catholics (though not Maurras, an atheist), the pope's censure caused a massive realignment. In the hollow crater that remained after the pope's bomb had exploded, many young intellectuals rushed to join—or found— new organizations and journals. De Rougemont may have abhorred the programs advocated by Maurras, but he could only be glad that for more than two decades Action Française had paraded a cultural agenda leading to direct political action. For this is precisely what de Rougemont and his *confrères* had in mind.

As the 1930s dawned, de Rougemont's search for a sympathetic setting brought him to Paris to work for Editions Je Sers, where he oversaw the publication of texts by Ortega y Gasset, Kierkegaard, Barth, and Nicolas Berdiaeff. Then, under the force of Alexandre Marc's social vision, he founded an aggressive periodical that he dubbed *Hic et Nunc*. All his projects explicitly linked spiritual piety to utopian social thought, the formula that Mounier would bring to prominence at *Esprit*. De Rougemont had yet to join up with *Esprit* (indeed *Esprit* was just beginning to coalesce) when he was given the singular assignment by Paulhan. He did not let the *NRF* down: the *Cahier de revendications* instantly attracted interest and has remained a rich source for scholars ever since. Collected in one place were the beliefs and

21ᵉ ANNÉE Nº 231 — 1ᵉʳ DÉCEMBRE 1932

LA NOUVELLE
REVUE FRANÇAISE

Cahier de Revendications

Onze témoignages

nrf

FRANCE : 6 FR. — ÉTRANGER : 7.50

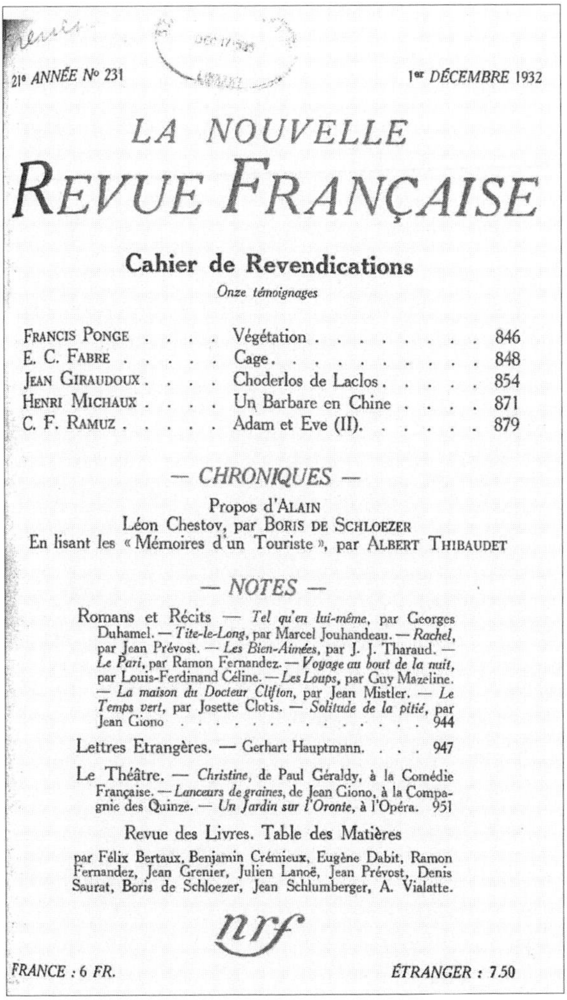

33. De Rougemont's *Cahier* heads an issue replete with familiar names.

commitments, as well as the hatreds, of a dozen of France's most promising young thinkers. De Rougemont selected a spectrum of opinions, loading its center with what had become his own position, recently dubbed "personalism" by Marc.[3] From the far right he cajoled fiery remarks from Thierry Maulnier, who represented two groups, Réaction and the Jeune Droite. At the other end of the spectrum, he could count on powerful and undisguised Marxist invective from Paul Nizan, who had just published his scathing attack on Julien Benda, *Les Chiens de garde*. The brilliant essayist Henri Lefebvre

joined Philippe Lamour in supporting Nizan's views.[4] The remaining eight contributions all came from the budding Personalist movement: three from *Esprit* (Emmanuel Mounier, Georges Izard, and Jean Sylveire) and five from *L'Ordre Nouveau* (Robert Aron, Arnaud Dandieu, Alexandre Marc, Claude Chevalley, and René Dupuis).

De Rougemont's preface to the *Cahier* expresses "solidarity in the face of danger, creating in us a . . . united protest at the dismaying misery of our times."[5] He goes on to claim that this constellation of forces, strategically prepared to stand together at least for the moment, "defines a single front." This front, sustained mainly by Personalist rhetoric with all the bravura of youth, would last until a more genuine Popular Front coalesced after the Stavisky riots of February 1934. For in 1932 the Marxists were less inclined to "extend a hand" toward fellow travelers of any stripe.

The first section of the *Cahier de revendications*, given over to Lefebvre, Nizan, and Lamour, makes that plain enough. While Lamour's piece is a schematic outline of standard Marxist dogma, the other two writers, especially Nizan, understand the peculiar forum in which they are participating. Nizan strikes out, with more force than any other contributor, at "the scandal of a civilization . . . where people are on their way to total deterioration," insisting that in the face of this scandal all the niceties of culture must be "swept away."[6] He then insists that this menace is in no way "spiritual" but concerns the material realities of unemployment, famine, and war preparations. He finds his contemporary historical situation remarkably simple, likening it to a "brutal crime." And while he applauds his coauthors for recognizing the absolute necessity of revolution, he insists on the difference between revolution and the halfway measures advocated by those lacking the full historical understanding provided by Marxism. No doubt with de Rougemont in mind, he says: "The revolutionary struggle takes place not between Capitalism and the Spirit, but between Capitalism and the Proletariat"—suggesting that every revolt against the current order not tied to the struggle of the proletariat is self-indulgent and historically insignificant. "Whoever would fight today can fight only within the ranks [of the proletariat]," he concludes. In the months following, Nizan would work to distance himself even further from the "single front" by directly attacking the "spiritualist" deceptions of *Esprit*, *L'Ordre Nouveau*, and the Jeune Droite group and doing so with the hammer of the Parti Communiste Français in his hand and the authority of Moscow behind him.[7] This effort was needed, however, because the center and the right used a vocabulary sufficiently similar to that of the PCF that a degree of unity among them was imaginable.

Chief among the factors that might homogenize all contributors to the *Cahier* was their across-the-board effort to set themselves apart from traditional political categories such as "liberal" and "conservative." Both of those terms were explicitly repudiated. Maulnier, whose Jeune Droite opinion was placed just after that of the Marxist triumvirate, preempted the standard stereotypes by leveling his attack at tradition rather than at Marxism. He writes with exquisite irony, "'Conservative'—now there's a word that's bad from the start. We are not the splendid younger generation . . . that the traditional right hopes will arise to defend Tradition, Property, Family, Morality, so that it will be able to prolong the age of horses and carriages . . . and the period when people still had servants."[8]

Maulnier's sympathies lay with the turn-of-the-century revolutionary right born of the Boulangists, the anti-Dreyfusards, Georges Sorel, the Cercle Proudhon, and Action Française. Antidemocratic and anticapitalist, this line propounded a vision of a heroic nationalism in which a virile minority would lead the country in a decisive way. In this light, Maurras' monarchism should be taken less as a form of nostalgia for the age of aristocracy than as pure disdain for the values of the 1789 revolution that had ousted the monarch—values leading to universal suffrage and rule by what Maulnier termed the "unconscious majority." After the church banned Action Française, several rightists drifted toward an alliance with a splinter group of socialists around the journal *La Vie Socialiste*, creating a "fascist left" that would not be drummed out of the official French Socialist Party (the SFIO, or Section Française de l'Internationale Ouvrière) until 1933. Convinced that parliamentary government had been invented to serve the bourgeoisie and international financial interests, men such as Gaston Bergery and Marcel Déat proposed to overthrow democratic processes because they stood in the way of the powerful conjunction of nationalism and socialism. In 1932 National Socialism may have appealed to Maulnier, but it appeared dangerously volatile to the Personalists and the Marxists, whose eyes were on ominous political developments in Belgium and especially in Germany.[9]

The rightist quest for a "spiritualization of materialism" had its inverse counterpart in Nizan's program to "materialize the spirit" through a revolutionary Communist takeover.[10] Both extremes saw capitalism as the enemy, American capitalism above all. Both believed that a vanguard needed to bludgeon the old order with youthful force. Both ridiculed the passivity and senti-mentality of democratic humanism. Both believed that violence was not just necessary to produce a new order but was a valuable expression of the life force currently suffocating under bourgeois paternalism.

Yet aside from those who confidently relied on Karl Marx and Lenin, the nonconformists had few models on which to base their aspirations. This is what concerned Nizan, who was certain that undirected revolutionary enthu-siasm was more dangerous than mere conformity to tradition. De Rouge-mont could feature a range of political positions in his *Cahier* because he was putting together his own ideas on the spot, as it were, in the heat of debate. His adulation of Hendrik de Man is symptomatic in this regard, for although de Man may have been the longtime leader of the Socialist Party in Belgium who eventually came to power, he also held many ideas that could be termed protofascist. Sternhell documents de Man's correspondence with Mussolini at the very moment de Rougemont found his ideas so attractive. And he goes on to argue that de Man was the most powerful and perhaps the most brilliant of a band of radical thinkers whose socialism would nevertheless align them with Hitler's New Europe after 1940.

De Rougemont would never be tempted to subscribe to the "National Revolution"[11] after the fall of the Third Republic (as Mounier was, at least for a time). But many of his associates in those heady days of 1932–1934 would find themselves without a political anchor when the winds of history gusted so strongly later in the decade. The group Ordre Nouveau sought to provide such an anchor as early as 1930, when Alexandre Marc wrote his "Manifeste d'un ordre nouveau" and organized meetings of dissident students from the various academies of higher learning in Paris. Marc's international connec-tions, particularly his acquaintance with intellectual circles in Germany, gave him the authority to set an agenda that would help orient the energetic peo-ple who came to him. He initially joined forces with Philippe Lamour, whose journal *Plans* was selling well and publishing some of the most visionary fig-ures in the arts: Fernand Léger, René Clair, Arthur Honneger, and Le Cor-busier. One could also find idealized pictures of Mussolini and Hitler in its pages.

It was while organizing issues of *Plans* and of a spin-off journal, *Mouve-ments*, that Mounier sought Marc's advice concerning a new publication and a new organization he wanted to head: *Esprit*. De Rougemont was a familiar figure in the *Esprit* offices from very early on, having already been recruited

by Marc for *L'Ordre Nouveau*. At the time, it must have been difficult to separate the numerous Personalist groups that were sprouting up annually. But
those separations were nonetheless important. Mounier, for instance, distanced himself quite early from all forms of fascism and never allowed himself
to write in support of Mussolini. *L'Ordre Nouveau*, by contrast, presumptu-
ously composed a lengthy "Letter to Hitler," praising his programs and his
spirit in paragraph after paragraph, then offering a brief critique at the end
urging him not to fall into "mass politics" and a new form of crass materialism. While members of *L'Ordre Nouveau* had impeccable records during the
Occupation, refusing all support for the Vichy regime, in 1933 they gave
the appearance of young elitists. Nietzsche's thought explicitly excited them,
for instance, and they promulgated virtues that today are associated with
fascism.[12]

De Rougemont was able to float on this wash of ideas in part because of
the eclectic nature of his own philosophy and in part because politics had not
yet forced the kinds of cleavages between groups that would come soon
enough. Reminiscing about de Rougemont in the preface to a collection of
the Swiss thinker's unpublished essays, Alexandre Marc distills the era into a
formula that is tantalizingly clear: after 1789, conflict and revolution, endemic in the history of the species, seemed to move humanity toward greater
autonomy. Yet in the nineteenth and twentieth centuries, the salutary tran-
scendence of mythology by science and of monarchy by democracy resulted
in a crucial casualty—namely, "the person."[13] De Rougemont put his hopes in
personalism as the only viable program to resuscitate humanity once it became clear, after a decade's worth of Soviet rule in Russia, that Karl Marx had
merely replaced one totalizing system with another, thereby replicating the
injustices of what he termed "the established (dis)order." The basic element
of every encompassing system (feudal, religious, or collectivist), the element
these seem so ready to sacrifice in the interests of private or public power, is
the individual—not the alienated individual produced by mass culture, but
the individual in search of personhood, the individual willing his or her humanity into social existence as person.

Marc does not hesitate to draw the theological analogy of the three-per-
son God whom de Rougemont worshiped—the God who underwrites revolution as a general social "conversion" of the person away from the illusions
of materialism on the one hand, or from those of Marxist or fascist collectivism on the other. The values of the person de Rougemont preached were

ratified and modeled by the person of Jesus Christ. While few of the *L'Ordre Nouveau* cadre were Christian (Robert Aron, for instance, was militantly atheist), de Rougemont's Protestantism, because of its existential orientation, mapped itself as "protest" across the full contour of the group. No one complained. Mounier would later state that religious differences only strengthened the rhetorical power of *L'Ordre Nouveau*'s position. That position was simple enough: the individual becomes a person only by participating in larger human orders, specifically family and community, both of which exist to foster persons. Disorder can be attributed to an imbalance caused by the hypertrophy of community and the diminution of the person. In the modern era, persons no longer participate in community. Under capitalism they are alienated from it, while under Communism they are dependent upon it. In the "New Order" the social world would be adjusted to the scale of the person, not vice versa. Matter would serve humans, not the reverse. This was Christ's message, and this was exactly the message that *L'Ordre Nouveau* conveyed to the Christians and non-Christians who joined the group.

Robert Aron and Arnaud Dandieu spelled out that message most clearly in the conclusion of *La Revolution nécessaire*, surely the most influential Personalist volume ever published. To the critics who objected to their harping on the "primacy of the spiritual," calling it flimsy and sentimental, they replied with an elaborate biological conceit. A germ, they said, is always harder to notice than an aging body or the skeleton that the body will soon become; nevertheless, anyone interested in life rather than etiology will examine the nearly invisible germ, not the grossly visible body. The revolution that history has made so necessary must, in their view, overturn the conditions that have produced the codependent poles which dominate political thought in the West—poles characterized as the right and the left, or as capitalism and Communism. These political options, opposed though they claim to be, both preach the accumulation of power, whether in the form of resources and capital or in the form of masses of people collectively organized. To reestablish the priority of the human over that of the system, any truly new order must put scale ahead of growth and quantity. For Dandieu and Aron, this meant that Personalist politics and economics should attend above all to the local needs of people, fostering their natural proclivity to live and work within families and small communities. Otherwise, as experience has shown, both politics and economics (whether free enterprise or state-dominated) inflate themselves to an impersonal scale where they determine and rule human beings, rather than serve them.

34. Emmanuel Mounier with the inaugural issue of *Esprit* (October 1932).

The *Esprit* group, whose journal had just been launched, was represented by Emmanuel Mounier and Georges Izard, who apparently coordinated their responses. Mounier asserted the primacy of action even in the so-called spiritual life, stressing the purifying power of action, which forces the fullness of personality to emerge from the individual expressing it. "Discretion, patience, and taste," virtues of restraint associated with private life, must give way to more declarative virtues as the spirit becomes visible through public action. And since action takes place in public, Mounier could write that it amounts to "the superabundance of soul in the service of humanity."[14]

By intimating that spirituality depends upon social action, Mounier offended *Esprit*'s more conservative backers, particularly Jacques Maritain, who once argued with Henri Bergson precisely over the latter's suggestion that truth is something brought into the world rather than discovered there. Mounier's Catholicism didn't subordinate piety to social action in the world, but found the former through the latter.

Mounier left it to Izard to specify how action ought best to take place—or rather, where it should take place. For Izard was always concerned with locus and locality. World War I had grotesquely discredited the great ideologies of

Fatherland and Nation, he cried, yet they had, if anything, only strengthened themselves since. Nations turn citizens into statistics (numbers of soldiers, numbers of casualties, numbers of workers and consumers) as they calculate growth and exploit the autonomous movement of capital. Izard challenges his readers to imagine a world composed of small communities to which the inhabitants feel sensual rather than ideological bonds, communities that they see and smell and are nourished by every day. He is certain that every Frenchman is attached first to his or her region and only secondarily to something called France. It is one's neighborhood, the land one traverses routinely, to which one becomes devoted. As for urban civilization and the modernity it has brought, Izard says, "We want the city to be the projection of the person, so that the source of power might lie quite close to those under its sway, and servitude to a central power would be unheard of. . . . Political activity should be limited to those places one loves. . . . This would avoid the danger of economic hypertrophy, which is the error of communism and capitalism alike."[15] The city, he implies, serves as the hub of the region, for "the region is the natural organ of ordinary life, based as it is on a climate that is both physical and psychological."[16] National culture should be nothing other than an accretion of daily social behaviors played out in contiguous locales by people with "quasi-instinctive affection" for their regions. National culture is authentic and human insofar as it retains this natural scale.

Next in the *Cahier*, Alexandre Marc and René Dupuis of *L'Ordre Nouveau* isolate the politics such regionalism might require, advocating federalism as a healthy and radical alternative to nationalism. Federalism, because it is founded on economic relations among local groups, remains free of the vices of political power. The nation, if needed at all, would emerge as the negotiated synthesis of communities, supple enough to be inflected by the history of local concerns rather than enslaved by the state, with its hunger for centralization and homogenization. Robert Aron summed up *L'Ordre Nouveau*'s position in a sentence: "The new revolution will be essentially the revenge of the concrete on the abstract, of personal human factors on artificial and collective mechanisms, whether born from sheer idealism [Marxism] or from the inverse idealism that makes up materialism: banks, Fordism, rationalization."[17]

De Rougemont felt authorized to make explicit his own views in his afterword to the *Cahier*. He immediately sided with the Personalists against the Marxists, because of what he described as his fear of determinism and his skepticism about proletarian "reason." Revolutions had all been made by intellectuals, he reminded Nizan, including that of the Bolsheviks in 1917. Moreover, a complete revolution had to do more than perpetuate the demeaning struggle for material resources. Literature, art, and religion could revolutionize the spirit, making life more than merely comfortable and risk-free; life could become an adventure and a project, the spirit giving direction and force to the material revolution that had been the sole focus of the Marxists.

Despite taking sides in this way, de Rougemont maintained solidarity with the anger of all serious young thinkers who for so many different reasons had given up on parliamentary solutions to the national and international problems of the day. When Aron and Dandieu published *La Révolution nécessaire* the next year, he would issue his *Politique de la personne*. Meanwhile a vibrant young priest, Henri Daniel-Rops, contributed *Eléments de notre destin*, the three books consolidating in an ecumenical way the "single front" proclaimed in the first pages of the *Cahier de revendications*. All these publications, editorials, and essays by Personalists and Marxists of the day identified the United States with a crude capitalism they found intolerable.

This rather academic picture of the world political and economic drama changed in February 1934, when the Stavisky Affair brought the fascists out of the coffeehouses to assail those marching against the current government. The enemy now had a face. While the riots of February 6 may have produced the Popular Front by softening Marxist positions and creating such groups as the Comité de Vigilance Antifasciste, they simultaneously strained relations among many of these publications and groups. Mounier, as we have seen, was quick to take an antifascist position, which alienated him from Thierry Maulnier, Robert Brasillach, Maurice Blanchot, and other young intellectuals affiliated with the Jeune Droite, *Réaction*, and *Combat* and even from his former friends at *L'Ordre Nouveau*, who were still waiting to see if the adventure of National Socialism in Germany might not be applicable to France in some radically revised form. By 1934 more than one hundred groups allied with the journal *Esprit* had already sprung up around Europe, and keeping them together required increased attention to the distinctive political and religious orientation Mounier had worked out with his associates. De Rougemont, along with film critic Roger Leenhardt, served as the Protestant voice in the *Esprit* think tank. *L'Ordre Nouveau*'s notorious "Letter to Hitler" gave Mounier the opportunity to define *Esprit* against this related Personalist group.[18] The Communists began to court Mounier as he moved toward the left. The diaries of the individuals involved allow us to imagine the extraordinary evening of July 3, 1936, when, freshly back from his Frankfurt rendezvous with de Rougemont, Mounier talked through the night with Nizan and Malraux concerning the differences between Communism and Christianity as foundations for a new society. For traditional Catholic intellectuals such as Maritain, it was time to part ways with Mounier, who now appeared more concerned with social effects than with philosophical or theological principles.

The Popular Front period marked the end of ideological incubation for all these nonconformists—the "doctrinaire period," as Mounier called it—after which explicit political engagement became the norm. Mounier felt that February 6 had curtailed reflection several years too early; it forced everyone to take sides and to engage in parliamentary politics when politics was in question.[19] *Esprit* would try to stand above even the elections of 1936 by claiming, as always, that the current democratic system was part of a problem that could not be solved by a plebiscite. Still, as the fortunes of the country declined and the dangers posed by the Nazis grew, Mounier and his journal had to take sides, if only to denounce regimes where discussion could no longer take place. Discussions in *Esprit* were increasingly directed at political rather than spiritual affairs.

De Rougemont participated faithfully throughout, even while he was in Frankfurt. He projected a coolly intelligent demeanor, and was even haughty in the breadth of his personal culture, yet his prose grew exasperated and short-tempered when confronting the affairs of the day. His tone followed, or led, that of *Esprit* itself. Consider, for example, his contribution to the October 1935 issue. This long essay launches itself as a satiric response to a piece that had just appeared in the mass market periodical *Le Journal*, promoting the idea of a "Palais de l'Esprit" ("Palace of the Spirit" or "Palace of the Mind"). One of the Deputies of the Chamber, Hippolyte Ducos, writing with great sententiousness, reported the government's plan for still another magnificent public building as part of the upcoming 1937 Paris Exposition, this one devoted to the international history of ideas since the Renaissance. Amused and horrified by the proposal, de Rougemont realized immediately that one ought to expect nothing international whatsoever about this temple of genius, for it would display what its proponents believed—namely, that French genius had for half a millennium led civilization in the sciences, social sciences, and humanities.[20] Ducos had in mind as models the recently de-signed Trocadéro and the Palais de Tokyo when he insisted that this monument to thought would remain a permanent foyer to welcome intellectuals ever after and to inspire them to contribute to the brilliant French intellectual tradition.

Finding this a characteristic mockery of the life of the mind, de Rougemont mocked it in turn. How apt, he wrote, that this government should consider bottling up thought and displaying it in a museum during certain hours each day. Like the Bibliothèque Nationale, it would represent the idea of thought even if no one were thinking. Most of all, it would segregate thought, keeping it safely off the streets where it might become meddlesome. Citing Hendrik de Man, he demonstrated how empty such a building was destined to be, for *l'esprit* must be in the world or not be at all. Here he conflated the vulgar Marxist, who demeans the culture of the intelligentsia as a parasitic superstructure, with the traditional bourgeois, perfectly represented by Deputy Ducos, for whom thinking was treated as an accoutrement of culture, not an essential part of social movement and life. De Rougemont blamed this attitude on Descartes and on those like Julien Benda who maintained a strict separation of mind and body. The mind, to Benda and to official intellectuals like him, was a container of ideas, each of which could be pigeonholed or in some cases honored. Real thinkers—Nietzsche was de Rougemont's example—were repudiated for failing to be useful "technicians of thought."

De Rougemont's Bergsonian revulsion in the face of the literal "monumentalizing" of intellectual activity led him to offer a counterproposal to the commission in charge of the exposition—a proposal whose satiric form only underscores the catechism of points it presents. Laid out like an official request, it states:

In view of the general disorder; in view of a cultural situation created by the decree separating body and soul, a decree pronounced by Descartes in 1637, attenuated by Romantic idealism, exploited by the bourgeois elite in a way that makes the intellectual class useless in view of the economic crisis brought on by the crash of Wall Street; in view of the commercialization of *esprit* brought on by said crisis; in view of the existence of the press and the power of advertising; in view of the unemployment of intellectuals; in view of the nationalistic panic that the culture of the nineteenth century is responsible for . . . ; in view of the demands [*revendications*] of the young, who reject any life of the spirit that has become complicit with the general criminality of our times—

we state: that the problem of culture is the chief problem of our time, culture being responsible for concentrating, humanizing, and transmitting the doctrines of intellectuals at all levels who should be directing the Republic but who, out of lack of interest, sell themselves;

that this problem is today posed only by thinkers who have no audience and carry no prestige in the state;

that the construction of a Palais de l'Esprit should be undertaken, designed to serve as a club for all those who discuss in public the following questions:

a) The definition of culture, including its means and final goal.

b) What has happened to culture in theory and in practice under today's regimes? Does culture retain any force today, or does the world rest on another sort of foundation altogether?

c) What is the intellectual class now good for? What role should it play in the Republic, and whom should it address?

d) What is the source of the authority of intellectuals, and what means should they adopt?[21]

De Rougemont concludes brazenly: "Insofar as thinking strives to pose serious questions, it is inconceivable under official patronage. To show off the newest of mechanical gadgets, or to open another library, or to spin grandiloquent speeches into a microphone before an elegantly dressed and utterly silent throng—this is what they know how to do. But it is an entirely different thing to invite the public to reflect on the role of the mind and spirit. . . . One can hardly imagine our officials inaugurating such a subversive venture, a genuine Estates-General of culture. But so what? Do we need the state to take up this agenda?"

The particulars of de Rougemont's agenda, and its rationale, were published soon enough in *Penser avec les mains*, whose title answers Benda's *La Trahison des clercs* by insisting on engaged rather than contemplative philosophy. Ironically, as we have seen, he penned all this in solitude, on an island off the Atlantic coast. When he returned to public life, in 1936, he did so in Germany, where, thanks to the German cultural minister in Paris, he was given a year's appointment to teach French literature at the University of Frankfurt. As his meeting with Mounier that June testifies, he had in no way discarded personalism since his withdrawal from Paris after the Stavisky riots; unquestionably, however, the solidarity he had felt with other nonconformists prior to 1934 had been lost and, like youth itself, could never be reclaimed. He could not deny that he was now a member of the establishment, a professor of French.

In 1937, de Rougemont was back in France. Indeed, he was all over France, stumping for *Esprit* groups. He helped to organize cadres of "Friends of *Esprit*," and he participated in symposia with such allies as Ramon Fernandez, Maurice Merleau-Ponty, Jacques Ellul, Robert Aron, and Marc Chagall. Hundreds of people in the provinces, in Belgium, and in Switzerland would turn out for these *Esprit* evenings. But the era of experimenting with ideas was over and Mounier found it necessary to inject discipline into his growing ranks, lest doctrinal heterodoxy dilute his mission at this precarious moment in European history. Ellul and Merleau-Ponty were immediate casualties, needing more independence; but at the same time, *Esprit* gained key supporters (one was Simone Weil) and held onto others, such as de Rougemont.

Passion and War: The Collège de Sociologie

With so much energy devoted to public debate about the organization of society within world systems, where did de Rougemont gather the resources for *L'Amour et l'Occident*, his book-length meditation on romantic love and the fate of marriage? Was it because he found himself teaching in the German city of Frankfurt that he began thinking about Tristan and Iseult? And did he conjugate this study of desire and coupling with the sociopolitical ideas that had consumed him for so long? The preface he added to the 1956 edition employs a familiar vocabulary: "If our civilization is to endure, it will have to carry out a great revolution."[22] Yet the revolution he has in mind here is of the most intimate sort, involving the soul as it reaches out to bond with another soul. Hardly radical, he concludes that "marriage, upon which the social structure stands, is more serious than the love which it cultivates, and marriage cannot be founded on a fine ardor."

Just as de Rougemont had used a rhetoric of absolute reform in the early 1930s to demand that something as tame as federalism be built to the modest measure of the person, so here he calls for a revolutionary return to the ideals of marriage, that bourgeois institution which the Surrealists, espousing *l'amour fou*, declared dead because it was deadly boring.[23] De Rougemont's own marriage was breaking up at this time. And when he left Europe for the United States in 1940, he left alone. But if there is a personal explanation for the fever of critique in his treatise, his writing never takes on a confessional tone; instead, he moralizes about the cultural consequences of emotions and their artistic representation in Western civilization.

But why, first of all, the "Western" mind? Because, he says immediately, Western civilization alone has made passion an ingredient in its most basic institution, marriage, where, at least according to the mythology of eroticism, it so often exacerbates a scenario of self-destructive adultery.[24] No doubt certain universal factors are at play in adultery (sexual attraction, above all), yet only in the West has sexual longing been written into the commitment of marriage, so that the inevitable variability of the former must necessarily weaken the latter. De Rougemont's concerns, though not his attitude, coincide here with Bataille's sociology of marriage: unquestioned in the West, this sanctioned institution of reproduction contains *la part maudite* ("the accursed share")—the perverse expenditure of eros.

Although not personally drawn to Bataille (Caillois, on the other hand, was a good friend), de Rougemont adopted a cultural and literary approach that shared something with Bataille's vision, in which erudite analyses of literary themes lead to immense psychosocial consequences. De Rougemont was certain that he had found the historical origins of his century's rampant epidemic of divorces and unhappy marriages. He audaciously concludes that such moral and psychological degradation goes beyond households and can be located on Europe's military battlefields, where its horrific results are evident. The Swiss Personalist may have preached modesty, but he maintained the most extravagant expectations for the reach of his ideas.

The Tristan myth (and it is a myth, since it stems from an anonymous source and expresses the universal but unthinkable scandal of death in the heart of love) produces "an exquisite anguish" because it establishes a sacred goal whose realization would desacralize and trivialize it.[25] "Tristan and Iseult don't love one another. . . . They love being in love"—something they can feel only when obstructions produce the friction of suffering. As friction inevitably wears away suffering's causes, new difficulties must be compounded until the lovers reach the ultimate obstruction, which they themselves devise and which brings them to the deepest, most delicious suffering: that of death. In death, lovers can sense that they are transfigured into something otherworldly.[26] Part I of *L'Amour et l'Occident* ends with the thunder provided by Hegel: the quest for sublime intensity experienced as the pure self-consciousness of knowledge (the Faustian quest) can be realized only in death, in the final "privation, when one feels more alive than ever . . . living dangerously and magnificently."[27]

But what kind of love can this be, de Rougemont asks, especially if its goal is sublime self-transcendence? "The love which 'dominates' [Tristan, Iseult, and all who follow their lead] is not a love of each for the other as the other really is. They love one another, but each loves the other *from the standpoint of self and not from the other's standpoint.* Their unhappiness thus originates in a false reciprocity, which disguises a twin narcissism."[28] To this he opposes the standard Christian alternative, Agape over Eros, a love for the other in his or her own difference and limitation, rather than a love that consumes the participants in a flame of unity.[29]

De Rougemont develops this rather conventional set of moral oppositions from a historical and theological analysis that is quite extraordinary, even if the stereotypes he deploys strike us today as ludicrous. He begins by establishing that the Western problematic linking marriage to passion actually derives from an Eastern conception of the erotic mystery of woman (coming through Iranian and Orphic antecedents of Platonism that spread with the migration of the Celts). Later, Manichaeism contributed its dramatistic conception of the world as a battleground between opposing forces of light and dark, and then of the person torn between soul and body. The "woeful" body, it taught, restrains the soul as the latter strives to leave the earth and join the sun, where it would brighten before losing itself in measureless light.

These two pagan antecedents converged in the Tristan myth during the twelfth century, and did so with such force as to alter not just literature and music but behavior (chivalry) and religion (the cult of Mary, a mysterious, nearly divine woman sheathed in light). De Rougemont's ingenious thesis (which remains ingenious whether right or wrong) ties the rise of the Tristan myth directly to the spread of the Cathar sects in southwestern France through the agency of a new breed of poets, the troubadours. Far from being profligate wanderers, the troubadours constituted a priesthood devoted to the philosophy of the Cathars, an ascetic but mystical doctrine that countered the degraded worldliness of the thirteenth-century Roman Catholic church. The troubadours' anguished hymns to untouchable ladies are in fact allegories for the heretical doctrine of the Cathars. And their fullest achievement, the Tristan myth, effectively promulgated the Manichaean desire for escape from the world into the oblivion of transfiguration by death. The values the troubadours praised in their songs and the forms of poetry that shaped those songs were Arabian in source, coming across the Alps on one side and across the Pyrenees on the other to incubate in southern France. De Rougemont concludes: "Thus it was that from the final confluence of the 'heresies' of the spirit and those of desire, which had both come from the East, . . . there was born the great Western model of the language of passion-love."[30]

De Rougemont may have elaborated this arcane scholarly argument to contribute to the understanding of literature—yet he was far more interested in social psychology on a grand scale, edging up on what today is known as the history of *mentalités;* and he certainly felt himself engaged in moral polemics. His tone makes that evident enough, as in this characteristic passage:

> Courtly love came into existence in the twelfth century during a complete revolution of the Western *psyche.* . . . It shared in the epiphany of the *Anima,* which, to my mind, marked the reappearance in Western man of a symbolical East. What makes it intelligible to us today are its historical signs or marks—its literally congenital connection with the Heresy of the Cathars, and both its surreptitious opposition and its overt opposition to the Christian conception of marriage. But it would leave us now indifferent had it not, after many avatars, . . . preserved in our own lives an intimate and ever renewed virulence.[31]

De Rougemont wants to maintain the singularity of Christianity as the West's great contribution to human civilization. Christian ideas incubated in Rome but were immediately menaced in the fourth and fifth centuries by Neoplatonism and Manichaeism coming from Eastern thought. Hundreds of years later a disguised version of Manichaeism again infected Christianity, producing heretics like the Cathars in southern France. Although the heresy was brutally stamped out, the literary form it gave birth to, the romance, especially as rarefied in versions of the Tristan myth, infected Western culture at its core. Indeed, de Rougemont claims it has enervated the Christian experiment ever since and doomed millions of marriages to a hopeless conflict between an official doctrine of fidelity and an inculcated ideology of eros and sublimation.

De Rougemont treats the myth as the preconscious and anonymous representation of a feeling so general that only religion can account for its power.³² Whereas the Tristan *myth* makes full sense only in a religious context, the Tristan *theme*—as literary expression—has shed its religious connection, has become authored (Petrarch, Shakespeare, Milton, Racine, Chateaubriand, Goethe) and has replaced its desperate longing for a distant God with a yearning for the unavailable woman. In her various literary avatars, the "figure" of woman no longer embodies the divine; instead, her role is to instigate desire with no hope of fulfilling it. In 1938, when de Rougemont wrote his book, the Wagner cult fostered by the Third Reich was reaching its apogee. A poetics of spiritual *sehnsucht* ("longing") had become part of a German rhetoric that appealed to loss of self in a higher, mystical union. De Rougemont, sensing, like so many others, the immanence of international conflagration, concluded his study with a meditation on the aesthetics of immolation—the ultimate consequence of the Tristan *Liebestod*.

"Love and War" is the title of the lecture he gave at the Collège de Sociologie and then included as Part V of his book. A highly schematic rundown of the "morality of war making" from the Middle Ages to the twentieth century, it sustains an analogy between the conquest of woman and that of an opponent by examining the evolving technology and vocabulary of war. This erudition prepares the way for the polemics of the book's last three sections, titled, respectively, "Revolutionary War," "National War," and "Total War." Although Napoleon is the example he employs, de Rougemont writes covertly of Hitler in describing the inculcation of "nationalist ardor as a self-elevation, a narcissistic love on the part of the collective Self. . . . Passion requires that the *self* become greater than all things, as solitary and powerful as God."³³ In order for a people to believe in their spiritual union, they must suffer danger, including ultimately the danger of annihilation, for which they volunteer. This parallels the "obstructions" sought by lovers, who sense the reality of their state only when it pains them. Boundless nationalism must end in wars "fought under no restraint whatever." Chivalry and its demise have led Europe to the brink of a catastrophe whose scale de Rougemont predicts will be incalculable.

De Rougemont surely knew he would receive a sympathetic hearing in speaking to the Collège de Sociologie on a topic that involved eroticism and violence. After all, he was not just stating that religious problems were more crucial to modern Europe than the political and social issues that usually received attention; he was also giving a detailed account of the function of a degraded myth in Western literature and society. This conformed to the ethnographic profile which the Collège flattered itself by cultivating. Denis Hollier, in his introduction to the anthology of writings titled *The College of Sociology, 1937–1939*, makes the members of the Collège into quite extreme thinkers, interested not at all in reform or even revolution but in a negative collectivity that the anonymity of the group represents. Hollier includes de Rougemont as a key ally of the Collège, even though de Rougemont was finally concerned with hygienic social relations rather than abject ones. The final paragraph of *Love in the Western World* opens most revealingly: "A last time, however, I shall side with moderation." De Rougemont unequivocally sides with marriage and limitation against passion and the straining for the limitless. Marriage issues onto a "happiness on the hither side of tragedy." Bataille, in contrast, was preoccupied with tragedy. Evidently, there was room in the Collège for both orientations.

Many dissident Surrealists, no longer capable of following Breton "in the service of the revolution," felt free to pursue the extra-moral, passionate experiments with life encouraged by the Collège. As James Clifford and Michèle Richman have amply demonstrated, the Collège's peculiar form of ethnography siphoned off the power of whatever it found attractive in the lives and dreams of the peoples it studied.[34] One might say that the Collège took an aesthetic rather than an ethical view of even the most political questions. Yet its members stood eager to exploit the political consequences of aesthetic issues like the ones de Rougemont raised, particularly the issue of "participation" in a national endeavor involving violence. Indeed, they thought of their stance as going beyond aesthetics (always something individual) and beyond politics (always something negotiated) into the zone of the sacred (collective by definition). De Rougemont, an avid proponent of Kierkegaard, would surely have seen these stages as "either/or" possibilities, even if the Collège's ethnographic understanding of the sacred did not quite match Kierkegaard's "religious" stage.

As to their social commitment, the now famous essays "L'Apprenti sorcier" (The Sorcerer's Apprentice) and "Vent d'hiver" (Winter Wind), published in the July 1938 *NRF* by Bataille and Caillois, respectively, cry out for a sociology that would be collective and effervescent rather than academic.[35] True, de Rougemont's *Penser avec les mains* had likewise insisted on engaged thinking, but his title makes the thinker an artisan of ideas, a modest tinkerer whose efforts contribute to social life. Bataille and Caillois, by contrast, aimed to raise the virility of intellectual life through rituals and through the investigation of dangerous phenomena. Perhaps this is what Bataille meant when he wrote that, unlike Breton's Surrealist group, the Collège provided no political orientation; its members were free to expound their own quite idiosyncratic opinions, so long as they did so passionately. There was plenty of room for Bataille's extremism and de Rougemont's fiery moderation within the Collège's mission of an engaged anthropology of modern civilization.

The Collège de Sociologie stood as a warning to later scholars that nationalist sentiments were not the sole property of right-wing groups or of anxious, uneducated citizens looking for an anchor amid the storms created by economic depression at home and hostile foreign powers nearby. The phenomenon of nationalism appealed also to those intellectuals who had declared themselves to be post-Enlightenment—that is, to have gone beyond the reassurances of Kant's *Critique of Practical Reason*. The recovery of Hegel, notably through the Collège's guru, Alexandre Kojève, and the fascination with the post-philosophy of Nietzsche and Heidegger, tempted intellectuals to calculate the importance of ideas on the basis of their power more than their truth. Hence, nationalism became an acceptable sentiment once it was shown to be a contemporary expression of elemental group feelings. And the rituals of nationalism, including the bombastic rallies being held in Germany, could be taken as the sign of a rejuvenation of experience in a Europe grown stodgy with advanced, liberal ideas.

None of these men were fools. De Rougemont made certain that his fascinating descriptions of engrossing Nazi rallies contained his unequivocal disapprobation; and Bataille dedicated an entire issue of his journal *Acéphale* to salvaging Nietzsche from those who would misappropriate him.[36] He complained that when the Nazis used Nietzsche, they assimilated him, lifted him into a grand project; whereas Nietzsche's value, and the values he proclaimed, were those of uselessness. Both de Rougemont and Bataille honored Nietzsche for his rejection of received ideas; Bataille applauded everything in him that could be considered abject. This was not, however, de Rougemont's Nietzsche, whom he coupled with Kierkegaard (the philosopher he preferred above all), seeing both as nineteenth-century prophets accused of madness while they forcefully and brilliantly decried the state of things.

Nationalism must surely be counted among the most flagrant of modern excesses, a false god to whom the masses around the world were bowing so uncritically in the 1930s. But the Collège had declared its interest in false gods that carried such impact. Nationalism permits individuals to feel attached to a primordial life force. It poses an alternative to the bankrupt individualism of Enlightenment democracies, healing in a trice the sickness of alienation. The members of the Collège wrote extensively about "elective affiliations," using a vocabulary they picked up from the group Ordre Nouveau. Caillois, in particular, was drawn to bivalent organic structures that supersede the primacy of the individual or the state. He was sensitive to the intervening factors that make every organism already a participant in something larger. The nation turns out to have been the most dynamic intervening organism at play in the pre–World War II era. Although he supported the Popular Front, Caillois wondered if the nation, conceived as a democratic agglomeration of multiple regions and cities, was viable. The Collège understood that Hitler and Mussolini had injected a vital nationalist fluid into the rejuvenated citizens of Germany and Italy.

While leftists made their customary effort to internationalize the concerns of their fellow citizens, pressures felt on the borders with Germany, Italy, and Spain contributed to the decade's hypertrophic nationalism. By the time of the 1937 Exposition Internationale, the adjective "international" must have seemed ironic to most people close to the industries of culture. We have already seen de Rougemont's incensed response to the proposed Palais de l'Esprit, which would, he knew, be dominated by the great tree of French philosophy that would throw everything else into the shade. Given his views on regionalism and federated politics, he must have been even more incensed by the way the national bureaucracy organized and arranged the "provincial exhibits" exercising its control over each region of the country. The layout of the 1937 Expo replicated for the geography of France what the plan of the 1931 Colonial Exposition had projected as Greater France (la plus grande France).

What kind of resistance could be offered to the overwhelming ideology of nationalism? At the outset of the 1930s, Surrealism had served as a noisy brake; indeed, the movement had become international in the extreme, Breton himself traveling to Prague and Mexico, while Surrealist groups spontaneously sprouted everywhere. Yet Surrealism lost much of its ethical edge as the decade progressed. The radical fringe in Paris was migrating to the Collège de Sociologie, which could point with disdain to the 1938 International Exposition of Surrealism—a retrospective organized at the Galerie Beaux-Arts by Breton and Eluard with the help of Dalí and Ernst. Surely this was a sign of the commodification of the avant-garde.

For its part, the Collège welcomed de Rougemont's lecture "Love and War," which implied that Europe's dangerous obsession with national borders had tapped hidden wellsprings of psychic power within ordinary citizens. Leaders marshaled that power by pointing to threats outside a nation's borders in nameable places like Germany or Italy or England and, more compellingly, in what lay beyond the notion of border altogether in the charged, mysterious, and unnameable colonial space.

De Rougemont relied on a crude psychoanalytic explanation for the attraction of nationalism. He adopted the vocabulary of thermodynamics, by which Freud had taught an earlier generation to calculate the energy of psychic life as a function of the difference between elements in a system, between Ego and Id just as between a cold air mass and a warm one. Under the Marxian version of Hegel that Kojève preached, the same sort of entropy might be seen in the history of ideas, and in history generally. The greater the level of difference at play in any system, the more energy can be released across the borders that mark that difference. In this way, the Tristan myth was fueled by the electricity sparking between man and woman, eros and friendship, private obsession and civic duty, vast differences figured by the sea journey which opens the Tristan tale and the country of death into which the lovers depart once they abandon civilized life. De Rougemont might have pointed to the final scenes of such enormously popular films as *Le Grand Jeu* (Jacques Feyder, 1933), *La Bandera* (Julien Duvivier, 1934), and *Pépé le Moko* (Duvivier, 1936) to illustrate the displacement of the Tristan theme to the exotic setting of North Africa. Here France's anxiety about its borders and its identity was compulsively dramatized.

De Rougemont engaged love, war, nation, and otherness, as did the Collège, but he did so through a moralizing lens. Their view of the sacred and its components has been characterized as negative or inverted, particularly when set alongside the always positive tone of de Rougemont. For instance, whereas Bataille's "heterology" gives special place to useless and abject erotic practices, de Rougemont finds homosexuality and masturbation to be the pitiable consequences of unnatural, uncivil psychosocial relations. He specifically adulates chivalric war—and its epitome, the joust—as a natural, even healthy displacement of the struggles and conquests of heterosexual love; whereas modern mass warfare has so obliterated the image of the individual that today's soldiers compensate by engaging in sexual vices that are essentially narcissistic.[37] Narcissism, de Rougemont argues, provokes engulfment whereby one loses oneself in something that claims to be a larger self. Culminating in totalitarian politics and in massive military display, the temptation of narcissism has been tendered by what might be termed the "culture of engulfment" evident since the French Revolution in romantic poetry, Wagnerian opera, and subsequent popular representations like the cinema. De Rougemont might have compared the conditions of cinema spectatorship to those of massive political rallies such as the ones he attended in Germany. In both situations, anonymous viewers by the thousands are mesmerized in front of images of larger-than-life spectacles organized around the body of a magnificent yet vulnerable figure, a Führer or a star. In French cinema of the late 1930s, those stars frequently fall into tragic love with one another, to the point of self-immolation.

To seal his characterization of the popular culture of narcissism, de Rougemont could have turned to Anatol Litvak's *Mayerling*, a perfect example of the mapping of nationalism onto melodrama and the second most successful French film of 1936. Starring Charles Boyer and Danielle Darrieux as the doomed lovers, *Mayerling*, set in a milieu of declining aristocracy and belligerent politics, tells of the abject suicides of Crown Prince Rudolf of Austria and his lover in 1889. Forced into a political marriage devoid of feeling, Rudolf whispers to his mother in the wedding procession near the opening of the film: "Pray God that I never know a great love." But on the fairgrounds of Vienna's famous park, the Prater, he discovers such a love in the person of Maria Vetsera. Separated by inflexible class hierarchies and scarcely able to exchange words, Rudolf and Maria meet furtively at spectacles where they can let their imaginations loose. At a puppet show, they understand the thrill and danger of their situation; then, at a ballet, their beings come together through their eyes; and finally, in church, gazing straight ahead at the image of God, they secretly touch hands to sanctify their adulterous desire.

The climax that brings the lovers into complete intimacy occurs in the most public and hostile of spaces, a state ball, where the scandalized guests gape at the pair. Rudolf asks the young Maria if she would follow him on the farthest of journeys; she comprehends his meaning, as does the camera, which dissolves from a two-shot of the couple to an extreme close up of her serene face as she answers: "Avec toi, oui" ("With you, yes"). Before we dissolve back to public time, Maria has visibly let go of her soul, joining it to the prince's in their destiny.

Mayerling moves forward less on plot and intrigue than on the increasing anguish of its lovers, whose passion mounts with each separation. After the

35–36. *Liebestod*: Danielle Darrieux dissolving into destiny with Charles Boyer in Anatol Litvak's *Mayerling* (1936).

ball, Rudolf gathers his beloved in his arms and leaves for Mayerling, the isolated hunting estate already hushed by an early snowfall. Accompanied by a *Liebestod* musical motif, the couple retire for their final night. Then the trusting Maria falls asleep, secure in the knowledge that her prince will take them into oblivious union. "A grief-bowed Romeo," wrote a critic in the *New York Times*, "before the still form of his Viennese Juliet. . . . They are the only people in their world; the rest are shadows; and when the shadows grow too black, they leave it." A gunshot follows, with a tasteful cutaway. And then the second shot as their fingers intertwine. The critic claimed to have been dragged into the world of the film—"carried breathlessly," he says, "along an emotional millrace, exalted and made abject as the dramatist directed."[38] Such is the lure, and such the pleasures, of engulfment.

Mayerling was hailed in the United States as "the best film yet turned out in France." It was followed by other grand tragedies of love and death, such as *Katia* and *Le Quai des brumes*, which topped all French films at the box office in 1938, and by Max Ophuls' *Le Roman de Werther*, which de Rougemont surely saw on the Champs-Elysées, where it premièred that spring when he was writing on Goethe. The title of Ophuls' next film, *De Mayerling à Sarajevo* (From Mayerling to Sarajevo), and its opening title shot, superimpose the legend of the love suicides of 1889 over a map of the empire, a national body ready to be pierced in the Great War of 1914. Production of this film was delayed by the onset of the second total war, which Ophuls' predicts in a prescient epilogue. Then, during the German Occupation, came yet another Tristan wave—this one led by Jean Cocteau's apotheosis of the Tristan phenomenon, *L'Eternel Retour* (The Eternal Return; 1943), the single most popular film of the entire Occupation period.

Epilogue: Postwar, Postfront

De Rougemont's contempt for the degeneration of the Tristan theme into mere movies may stem from a repressed elitism. Since a mass audience took this theme to heart in the twentieth century, its beauty was soiled, anguished literary expression having devolved into trivial images served up by the industries of culture. Ostensibly, however, his objections were more high-minded. His defense of marriage was meant to protect a more humane politics in a period of totalitarianism. At a time of escalating rhetoric glorifying grandeur of one sort or another, de Rougemont never appealed to grandeur. He argued instead for the virtue of what Bataille and Caillois, satirizing democracy, considered merely middle-class values. Even his friend Mounier seemed to have given up on the ordinary politics of citizenship when he wrote to Catholics in the United States that in the shadow of world war democratic individualism should give way for a time to collective ideals, implying that, as in the Renaissance, citizens should accept those proposed by enlightened authorities.[39] While intellectuals all around de Rougemont were thus tempted by aspects of collectivism, including blatant nationalism, he focused his gaze on a larger Europe and, beyond Europe, on the Kingdom of Heaven. In tune with the paradoxes of Christianity, for him the larger view meant fidelity to smaller ideals; his was a democratic, Protestant, Swiss view, unlikely to be heard in the din of war preparations, but emerging all the stronger on war's other side.

Had de Rougemont looked for a cinematic alternative to *Mayerling* and the degraded Wagnerianism it purveyed, he might have pointed to Jean Renoir's witty and understated film *Le Crime de Monsieur Lange*, which played concurrently with *Mayerling* in the winter of 1936 and which represented a modern cinema sharing his federalist view in politics and his personalism in ethics. Renoir's fable of workers who transform their little publishing company into a "cooperative" hinges on a love story where, refreshingly, passion is replaced by elective affinities—that is, by friendship, humor, and respect. No "grand illusion" hovers over the central couple; no spotlight keeps them perpetually in focus. Their allegiance is less to their romance than to the community whose collective life they help establish in the courtyard. Renoir's set design and camerawork emphasize the circularity of social relations in this public space (the film was originally titled *Sur la cour*, or "In the Courtyard"), and the courtyard, with its inclusive populism, becomes an apt term for *arrondissement* (district), Paris being an oval federation of *arrondissements*.

In 1937 Renoir released his most famous film, explicitly called *La Grande Illusion*. Set in military prisons far behind the front lines of World War I, Renoir avoids all-consuming battles. Instead he focuses on the shared interests of ordinary people who find themselves thrown together in prison camps. The cooperative societies that the prisoners of war spontaneously establish and, when dispersed to other prisons, establish all over again, express Renoir's belief in self-governance and in the federated coexistence of neighboring groups, even groups that have been told they are at war. Belligerence, which de Rougemont links to eros, rules at the front; elsewhere, consideration and cooperation stand a chance of springing up, even on inhospitable soil. This is the myth of a different form of love; in de Rougemont's vocabulary, this is Agape.

In place of a passion that consumes a couple in an ecstatic or fatal union,

La Grande Illusion treats the love of Frenchman Maréchal (Jean Gabin) and the German woman Elsa (Dita Parlo) as accommodation to difference: difference of nationality, language, occupation, even marital state. Dependent on the Jew Rosenthal as their interpreter, they come to the fullness of love aware that their separate lives have been brought together in affection for a time. With Rosenthal and Elsa's young daughter, they form a makeshift rural family. This is the family unit Renoir espouses, one based on respect, limited demands, and an unlimited concern for the welfare of others. In the final shot, Maréchal and Rosenthal strike out across the frontier, whose invisible border keeps the Germans from following them. They reach safety in the haven of de Rougemont's native Switzerland. As a multilingual federation of semi-autonomous cantons, Switzerland, an oasis in the inhuman drama of opposing nationalisms, was for de Rougemont the historical model of the Europe he wanted to build on the other side of the war.

When Sartre and de Rougemont met in New York in 1944, Sartre famously declared that "you Personalists are the victors; in France now everyone is a Personalist."[40] After the war, many of those associated with *L'Ordre Nouveau* and *Esprit* would spearhead the Mouvement Fedéraliste Français, described by *Esprit* in November 1948 as "not just a particular mode of international relations, but a complete doctrine born out of personalism, a full conception of man and society." Summarizing the history of the group just before he died in 1950, Mounier included de Rougemont among the key architects of personalism and of the federalism it had spawned, and he was proud to note that his friend had become an eminent and politically influential man of letters. The war having exhausted extreme views, Europe seemed ripe for the kind of moderation de Rougemont had stood for all along.

In his 1986 eulogy for de Rougemont, Alexandre Marc gloats that history seems to have vindicated his friend and the views he developed back in the turbulent 1930s. The breakdown of the Soviet system, like that of colonialism in the 1950s, has allowed us to imagine politics on a human scale, a Popular Front without frontiers. This vision, which came out of the 1930s, was not de Rougemont's alone. He was proud to have been part of a movement—call it nonconformist—that, as he said as early as 1932, pursued "a deeply French tradition of revolutionary force. This revolt of the person is a Jacobin revolt, the revolt of 1789, from which it takes whatever is valuable and dynamic; from here on out, this is the emergence of the French Revolution."[41]

The Popular Front movement, at least among its most radical dreamers, was meant to instigate the emergence of that original French Revolution within all classes. Joining de Rougemont among such dreamers was Jean Renoir, who orchestrated a film, *La Marseillaise*, in which the memory of 1789–1792 was meant to provoke a revolutionary emergence (and emergency) in the 1930s.

Jean Renoir's *La Marseillaise:*
The Arc of Revolution

Bastille Days

The decade of the 1930s, like any other period, changes character according to the size of whatever lens brings it into focus. A traditional scholar like Jean-Baptiste Duroselle, who keeps politics in the foreground, calls the years 1932–1939 "La Décadence."[1] For when placed in the sweep of an overall project that outlines the fate of France from the mid-nineteenth century on, these seven years mark an unmistakable national decline. In contrast, Julian Jackson's excellent *Popular Front in France, 1934–38*, traces an ascent—indeed the *ascendancy*—of the people in a march toward self-determination, even if economic and military factors beyond their control soon doomed this dream. Jackson's social history narrates four years of genuine change for France's citizens.

Whether taken as political or social dramas, such histories of the end of the Third Republic make room for the "cultural" dimension only as super-structure or as epiphenomenon. Although marginal to the engine of history, culture nevertheless takes its place at the very center of both Duroselle's and Jackson's books. In Part VI of his twelve-part history, Duroselle paints the "atmosphere" of France within which politicians conducted their business in the 1930s. Mere background, atmosphere can be represented in brief brushstrokes. Duroselle takes care of it in forty of his seven hundred pages. For his part, Jackson describes "the cultural explosion" as a way to elaborate the daily consequences of the "social explosion" that saw new ideas come briefly into prominence in mid-1936, altering policies that governed the lives of forty million citizens. Weighing in as denser—and more directed—than mere atmosphere, "culture" for Jackson nevertheless remains at best a sign of shifts in social institutions which are themselves dependent on political and economic realities (the base-structure of history).

Whether represented as rising or falling action, and whether seen through a political or social lens, the period's historical development reaches the apex of its arc in mid-1936. This explains the placement of culture at the very center of both Duroselle's and Jackson's accounts, for at just this time an increasing effervescence can be felt in journals, in the arts, and in newly established cultural institutions. The exclusively cultural focus of our book in fact enables us to discern two arcs—one popular (mass-market films like *Mayerling*), the other elite (exclusive coteries of intellectuals, like the Surrealists or the Collège de Sociologie)—which abut to form the shape of an hour-glass. The year 1936 would be the compressed point where the popular and the elite come closest to each other, and where the individual grains of sand passing through the neck of the glass—grains that represent ideas, images, and practices—are constricted in the pressure zone of those intense months. The circulation of viewpoints in all media (print, radio, newsreels) had never been so concerted. Or if we look at the circulation of atmosphere in 1936, we see the pressure gradients—the isobars of the meteorologists—narrowing to a limit as the front passes through. Or again, if we look at the circulation in the streets, we see—on July 14, 1936—the largest demonstration Paris had ever known. By every measure, it seems that the diffuse opinions and wildly disparate styles characterizing the arts and ideas at the beginning of the decade braided themselves into filiations and associations until 1937, when sheer entropy, as much as political and economic disappointment, led to a listless dispersion of groups and their members, culminating in the demoralizing months of the phony war and then the Occupation.

Let us zero in on 1936, the moment of sharpest definition, when culture, street noise though it may be, found its direction—found itself directed—in a massive choral outpouring. Jackson chronicles the increasingly coordinated and concerted popular activities by noting the change in tone of Paris' largely spontaneous public gatherings. Whereas early in the decade individuals and small groups (the various nonconformists, for instance) railed against an indifferent establishment or against one another, progressively they joined forces and voices.

Gradually there was a transition from demonstration as protest to demonstration as celebration. Demonstrations became family outings:

the number of women and children participants increased. The work-ing class inhabited the street, as it was to inhabit the factories—as much to assert a presence as to make specific demands. Politics became a pageant. The most famous of these popular *journées* took place in Paris. Estimates of the number of participants vary, but there is no doubting the orders of magnitude: 12 February 1934: between 30,000 and 100,000 marched from the Porte de Vincennes to the Place de la Nation; 14 July 1935: between 100,000 and 500,000 marched from the Bastille to the Place de la Nation; 16 February 1936: over 500,000 marched from the Pantheon to the Bastille to protest against the attack on Blum; 24 May 1936: possibly 600,000 marched to the Mur des Fédérés.

None of these occasions was more spectacular than the demonstra-tion of 14 July 1936. It was, comments Werth, "the most immense procession Paris had ever seen," with possibly over one million partici-pants. Two columns of marchers set off separately to converge for the first time in the tricolor and flags of the provinces of France. The two cortèges then set off by different routes to meet again in the Place de la Nation, where they were addressed by Blum, Thorez and others. The speeches started at 5 P.M., but when they finished at 7 P.M. there were still demonstrators at the starting point. Many of the demonstra-tors dressed in costumes of the Revolution; they built floats depict-ing events of the Revolution. This popular creativity was mirrored by the contribution of professional artists who contributed gigantic por-traits of Revolutionary heroes—Robespierre, Voltaire, Marat, Rouget de Lisle (composer of "La Marseillaise"), Hugo—which were set up at the base of the July column. Politics, history and art were fused into a massive popular celebration. As the Radical Albert Bayet enthused: "On July 14, 1936, something as momentous has occurred as on July 14, 1789."[2]

Politics, history, and art—to find these "fused" is ever the dream of the cultural historian. Here that dream advanced alongside a million citizens in a pageant conspicuously modeled on the inaugural event of the nation-state: the French Revolution. While not every French citizen celebrated the down-fall of the monarchy (the reactionary *Gringoire* boasted the widest circulation of all political weeklies, topping 650,000), the Popular Front's version of the

37. Bastille Day, 1936: a new revolution on the march.

Revolution was truly "populist" (Danton's ethos rather than Robespierre's), building on the ideal of an inclusive culture, as opposed to the exclusivity of the "200 families" that controlled the nation's economy.

This process of cultural consolidation, as we have seen, began in 1932 with the establishment of the AEAR (a Communist organization that welcomed fellow travelers like Gide) and took shape following the Stavisky riots of February 1934. The heat of those riots forged the tools that hammered together coalitions like the CVIA in an emergency measure. In the summer of 1934, when the PCF offered to join with the Socialists and with certain members of the Radical Party to defend French democracy against fascism within and outside France's borders, "La Marseillaise" was the anthem sung rather than the Communist "Internationale," the French Revolution serving as emblem of the universal Rights of Man. Far from contesting and overturning French values, the Revolution was seen as the event that consolidated all of the gains of Western civilization. It marked the fruition of European culture, not a break with it. Note the rubric under which the June 1935 International Writers Congress was held: "In Defense of Culture." Note, as well, Louis Aragon's goal of fostering "an *indivisible* culture" in the programs he mounted in Paris.[3] Jackson takes the weekly *Commune* as a legible index of this new orientation: formerly a trenchant organ of the PCF, merciless in its critique of French values, by 1936 *Commune* was describing itself as a "French literary review for the defense of culture."

In this conciliatory and expansive mood, and striving to sustain the momentum of the great Bastille Day march of 1936, the PCF decided to support the development of a full-scale feature film on the Revolution, to be called *La Marseillaise*. The idea purportedly came from Noémi Martel, a party member who had worked with Jean Renoir and her husband, Jean-Paul Dreyfus (a.k.a. Le Chanois), on *La Vie est à nous*.[4] All three met frequently on the rue Navarin to publish a radical monthly, *Ciné-Liberté*, the organ of the Alliance de Cinéma Indépendent (ACI), funded by the French Communist Party. At one of their meetings, Martel handed Renoir a book about a battalion from the army of 1792; and as early as December 1936, while Renoir was completing pre-production for *La Grande Illusion*, he told his colleagues at *Ciné-Liberté* that he thought they should launch a Revolutionary film in a revolutionary way. Renoir, the ACI, and the PCF felt they could convince the government (Renoir speaks of a promise of some 50,000 francs) and the labor unions (the Confédération Générale du Travail, or CGT, would advance a small sum, and workers would contribute) to support a nationalist effort of this sort.[5] After all, the Soviet Union in the late 1920s had sponsored cinematic masterpieces, including several films rehearsing the Bolshevik Revolution. In 1937, state-funded films were under way not only in the Soviet Union *(Alexander Nevsky)* but in Italy *(Scipio Africanus)* and Germany *(Olympia)*.

Still, the participation of the French government in feature-film production would have been unprecedented, the relation between the two spheres being informal and suspicious at best.[6] Indeed, successive governments—including Léon Blum's—denied cinema a place within the powerful Ministry of Education, thereby separating it from theater and the other arts. Instead, Blum's bureaucracy identified cinema as a "spectacle" and placed it within the newly created Ministry of Sports and Leisure. Although that ministry, under the dynamic leadership of Léo Lagrange, would become one of the lasting legacies of the Popular Front, only two of its committees—Fresh Air and Tourism—made strides in the brief period before World War II. "Spectacles" abutted entrenched commercial industries, thwarting Lagrange's aspirations for a socially responsive cinema. Recognizing its ingrained status as mere diversion, he complained:

Until now in France nothing has been done to make the cinema a social means of transcending class and educating the people. Without much choice and under the most deplorable conditions, children, workers, and peasants absorb a motley assortment of films, many of which are inspired by the basest feelings. And so the cinema, which might be a marvelous instrument of popular culture if it were used with purpose, must be considered (there's no denying it) one of the countercurrents working against culture. . . . My wish is that the cinema, already an excellent leisure activity, may become an instrument for the intellectual and moral development of the masses.[7]

How far the Blum regime was from treating cinema on a par with theater! Lagrange's sentiments demean the medium and patronize its audience. Powerless or unwilling to take measures to coordinate, support, and perhaps make use of an industry at once large and decentralized, the government appeared rather to undermine it. Indeed, the film industry was specifically targeted by the strikes that immediately followed Blum's election; then came the Matignon Agreements, which settled some issues behind those strikes but also disrupted film production routines.[8] Meanwhile a governmental commission under Jean-Michel Renaitour was collecting information from all sectors of the industry, in an effort to rationalize it. But the government had neither the means nor the will to implement most of the recommendations in the report. And even when the minister of education, Jean Zay, hammered out a comprehensive statute concerning the cinema in national life, it was shunted into subcommittees in the Chamber of Deputies.[9] It would take the muscularity of the Vichy government to organize the industry. Until then, even under the Socialists, no one could expect the government to intervene on behalf of a more responsible cinema. To top it off, the Blum regime horrified its most ardent supporters by pursuing a pattern of censorship that had kept a film like Jean Vigo's *Zéro de conduite* from reaching the screen.[10] Vigo had been an original signatory of the CVIA manifesto, and his own reputation, as well as that of his little masterpiece, made him a saint of the left. When Jean Zay went further by upholding the ban on *La Vie est à nous* from commercial distribution, Henri Jeanson could imply in *Ciné-Liberté* that Popular Front censorship was more stringent than that of the government it had just replaced.[11]

Zay's concern was that movie theaters might become zones of political debate, with an unpredictable and volatile populace caught in the middle. If *La*

Vie est à nous were approved, one could only expect fascist propaganda in reply. This vulnerable government evidently took care not to alienate any fraction of its minuscule majority by promoting itself directly through movies.
And so it left it to political parties and sectarian interests to make and distribute visionary social films. The French Socialist Party evidently saw cinema as
a way to galvanize its constituency. Its 1937 *Almanach Populaire*, for instance,
lists eleven documentaries for rent, ranging between twenty-five minutes and
an hour in length, several portraying recent Bastille Day celebrations.[12] For
its part, the ACI produced as many as fifteen films for the French Communist
Party, including its own newsreel designed to point up the mendacity of established ciné-journalism in the national organ, the *Pathé Journal*. Of course
the *Pathé Journal* could be seen each week in most of France's 5,500 commercial movie theaters, whereas *Ciné-Liberté*'s version, lasting only a couple of installments, played in a few union halls at best. Unquestionably, the ACI's major project was their election-year salvo, the trenchant *La Vie est à nous*. It was
to oversee this project that Louis Aragon recruited Jean Renoir.[13] Though
never a party member, Renoir would stay on with the ACI, contributing regular editorials to *Ciné-Liberté* and later to *Commune* and *Ce Soir*, where he be-
rated the industry and the government week after week.

The party's choice of Renoir was inspired but risky, for he was very late
coming to politics, and although he now dominates our view of the cinema of
the 1930s, his importance prior to his engagement with the PCF was dis-
counted by all but a fringe. For instance, he failed to make the list of France's
ten key directors in the 1935–1936 *Motion Picture Almanac*.[14] Still, Aragon
saw in his films the qualities that would make him the perfect *frontiste*
cinéaste. Even in his rather amateur silent efforts he displayed mastery of a
style equivalent to the democratic, open-arms politics that would be the order of the day in 1936. That style is already visible in the satirical *Tire au flanc*
(1929), whose silly soldiers (particularly the one played by Michel Simon) become more than butts of easy jokes when given room to improvise. Renoir's
spontaneously erratic camera movements expand cinematic space as they follow these lovable, frisky soldiers who joust among themselves and frolic in a
series of cleverly chosen environments.

As André Bazin would note, such a style carried easily across the sound
barrier into the naturalism of *La Chienne* (1931) and *Boudu sauvé des eaux*
(1932)—both vehicles for the rambunctious Michel Simon—and then on to
the proto-neorealist *Toni*, which Renoir shot on location without stars in the

spring and summer of 1934, during the formation of the Popular Front.[15] Although the party's weekly review *Regards* scarcely attended to *Toni*, Renoir received an invitation to screen the film in Moscow at the end of 1935. There, too, the melodrama failed to connect with its audience, despite its condemnation of capitalist exploitation of immigrant workers. Yet even though he could not boast a single box office success since 1930, Renoir attracted the attention of Aragon and the PCF.[16] He worked inexpensively and cooperatively on serious social themes; moreover, he came highly recommended. Aragon's friends in the October Group undoubtedly told him about the magical spirit that prevailed on the set of *Le Crime de Monsieur Lange*, which had just finished shooting in autumn 1935.[17] They could vouch for Renoir's talent, intelligence, and populism; most of all, they could vouch for his sympathy and goodwill.

And so the party was happy to invite this so-called amateur to help them professionalize their growing cinematic aspirations. For his part, Renoir began to pay close attention to politics as he heard about the deterioration of civil life in Germany. Surrounded by radical friends, including his editor and companion, Marguerite, who stayed a diehard party member, he could sense a satisfying convergence of his social art and a socialist France. But perhaps it was his haut bourgeois friend, the producer Pierre Braunberger (with whom he was just then preparing *Une Partie de campagne*), who tipped the balance in Aragon's favor. Braunberger advised that working with the PCF would guarantee Renoir an audience of intellectuals and workers, and that this in turn would bring him bigger stars and budgets. Whatever his motivation, Renoir stepped into the ranks of the ACI and soon enough into the national spotlight. Within a year he had won the first Prix Louis Delluc (for *Les Bas Fonds*) and found himself working with some of France's most esteemed actors and on a grand scale. After 1936, the *Motion Picture Almanac* treated him as a force in national and international cinema.

To the extent that the ACI had helped Renoir reach this coveted status, his ardent leftist sympathies, evident in *Toni, Le Crime de Monsieur Lange, Les Bas Fonds,* and *La Grande Illusion,* pleased Aragon, Vaillant-Couturier, Georges Sadoul, and the other members of the party who backed him and looked on him as a cohort. But in this era of didactic fiction and socialist realism (Aragon's own novels, as well as those of his wife, Elsa Triolet, and of Paul Nizan), the two films Renoir made directly with the ACI, *La Vie est à nous* and *La Marseillaise,* counted most—particularly the latter, because as a big-budget production it had the potential to reach the entire country. An undisguised allegory of leftist solidarity, it could only encourage the faithful.

As we will see, *La Marseillaise* fit neatly into the party's endeavors. *La Vie est à nous*, however, belongs to an earlier, more strident rhetoric, one not customarily thought to be congruent with Renoir. Its sixty-minute length, multiple discrete episodes, and outright declamatory sections are more in line with the ethos of the political avant-garde that goes under the rubric *cinéma engagé*. The confident tone of such radical filmmaking certainly produced some of the most interesting films and commentaries of the decade, but no more than a few thousand individuals seemed to care. Seldom were the screenings of such films reported in the mainstream press; never was this rival genre mentioned by the film industry. The government did not heed it. Uncompromising, it had little effect on social or cinematic history, despite the fact that its lifespan coincided with the ascendancy of a socialist government, on the one hand, and with a seemingly wide-open, unregulated moment in national film production on the other. The existence of *cinéma engagé* marks a limit that indicates both the passions of the time and the inertia of an industry that was at once too powerful for a truly alternative practice to thrive and too weak to direct itself beyond its day-to-day quest for survival in a marketplace that, being undeniably international, it could scarcely control.[18]

La Vie est à nous bucked industry norms in countless ways, but first of all in being a genuinely collaborative project. Renoir may have supervised the final product, but this propaganda film for the May 1936 elections had been decided upon before he came on board. Although he was given certain assurances about creative freedom, he was not yet so renowned that he could shoulder his way to the front of the production and draw it behind him. His commitment to it may even have waned once he saw the limited prospects of a medium-length didactic exercise, to be made for $10,000 in a very short period and by a committee of creative personnel, with various "directors" in charge of shooting individual sections. Still, he assumed responsibility for its completion and for its overall shape in editing, being delicately steered toward the party line by Jean-Paul Dreyfus, who was assigned to direct a sequence and monitor the production. The film brought Renoir into direct contact with the power structure of the PCF (whose secretary-general, Maurice Thorez, even stayed at his home) and it encouraged him to work experimentally. Tough and direct, *La Vie est à nous* stretched the limits of what was then acceptable in cinematic style and topics.

38. Tough and direct: PCF secretary-general Maurice Thorez in Renoir's *La Vie est à nous* (1936).

Jonathan Buchsbaum has elaborated the verdict that favors *La Vie est à nous* over *La Marseillaise*, itemizing their many differences as leftist films—differences that seem best summarized by the terms "revolt" and "revolution," which punctuate the prologue of *La Marseillaise*.[19] At the conclusion of that marvelous sequence, the Marquis de La Rochefoucauld informs the king of the taking of the Bastille. The king, looking up from a repast in bed, asks in genuine surprise: "Alors, c'est une révolte?" ("So it's a revolt?") "Non," replies La Rochefoucauld, "C'est une révolution" ("No, it's a revolution"). Dangerous and potentially lethal, *revolts* were to be expected by a sovereign who ruled twenty million subjects through a complex network of subordinates and protocols. They were like fevers, indicating imbalances and unhealthy practices that needed correction once the fever was reduced. But La Rochefoucauld portends far more in uttering the word *révolution*. He foresees the entire system rolling over, including the meaning of health and balance, of sovereignty and subjects. *Revolts* are willed by heroes and martyrs who make history, but the *Revolution* is a name for history itself, history passing through innumerable and anonymous agents who accept the moral pressure it exerts. Renoir would characterize *La Marseillaise* as a film of the *Revolution* in all senses of the term—while *La Vie est à nous*, shot frantically just before the elections, was a film in *revolt* against the ruling state of affairs. Clumsy and brash, it lashed out against French society and simultaneously against the constraints of standard cinematic form. It opens with a schoolteacher reciting at length to his pupils (and to us) a litany of social inequities. This dictatorial setup is repeated in the finale, when the leaders of the PCF preach from a podium hung with the sacred photographs of Marx, Lenin, and others in the political pantheon. Audacious, to be sure, and agitational, *La Vie est à nous* stands closer to the anti-aesthetic of *revolt* that fueled successive avant-garde movements, from Dada to Antonin Artaud's Theater of Cruelty. Only the political emergency born of the February 1934 riots and of Hitler's ascendancy brought Renoir into working relations with this fringe and led to his coordinating such a propaganda film. Audacious and insolent, *La Vie est à nous* proudly took its place alongside Vigo's *Zéro de conduite* and Buñuel's *L'Age d'or*, censorship confirming its purity and assuring its renown. In Renoir's case, this renown came as credit drawn as an advance on *La Marseillaise*, a mellow film by contrast, and frequently reviled as such.

The opposition of this pair of films, separated by less than a year, points to an overall shift in the rhetoric of political discourse as the trajectory of the Popular Front reached its apex in late June 1936, when the Matignon Agreements provided huge gains for the working class. *La Marseillaise*, then, might be taken as *postrevolutionary*, unrolling in a wholly different register from the confrontational *La Vie est à nous*. Once over the hump of the elections, Renoir readily returned to a style that was by nature accommodating. In the fourth issue of his own journal *Ciné-Liberté*, and just as he was gathering ideas for *La Marseillaise*, Renoir could read Jean Cassou's article "De l'avant-garde à l'art populaire" (From the Avant-Garde to Populist Art). Cassou, a poet and art critic who had just become editor-in-chief of the Marxist journal *Europe*, must have had Renoir in mind as he wrote:

> It is not surprising that the very artists who were in the front ranks of the aesthetic avant-garde are the same we find at the forefront of social demands, the ones most determined to make this epic and collective art of emotion into a popular art to which the masses begin to aspire. This movement toward the popular is more evident in cinema than in

literature or the plastic arts, for here the avant-garde must be more than an intellectual attitude or a search for artistic purity; it is a refusal to accept a financial system [that controls most films and brutalizes both cinema and its audience].[20]

Cassou sees the day when an audience, educated at ciné-clubs such as the one just launched by *Ciné-Liberté*, will at last permit avant-garde artists to address the public they have always sought, but which crass commercial movies have alienated from them. *La Marseillaise* proclaimed faith in this audience and in a new form of grassroots distribution, fanning out from labor unions.

In a way, the progressive diffusion of culture evident over the decade of the 1930s recapitulated a century's worth of transition to modernity, in that the public sphere expanded from the cafés of the educated members of a leisured class to the streets of the populace. As the sphere widened, so the shape and quality of discourse inevitably changed. The ferocity and subtlety that characterized the best articles written by rogue intellectuals at the beginning of the decade became, after 1935, less important than the reach of more official rhetoric. "From argument to propaganda," one might say, except that rhetoric is always both, and by mid-decade this fact was generally accepted.

Recall the shift in the career of André Gide. Not long after World War I, when he was setting the tone for the *NRF*, he claimed to be seeking a reading public of under a thousand. A wider appeal than that would endanger the quality of the journal's prose, he felt certain. Yet in 1932 Gide joined the AEAR. Three years later, he was a keynote speaker at Aragon's Maison de la Culture and at the Congress for the Defense of Culture. After 1935, he penned articles for the many thousands of citizen readers of *Vendredi*. Or take the artists who vied for a place at the 1937 Exposition Internationale. Robert Delaunay and Fernand Léger painted murals that were hymns to the railroads and to electricity, exciting hundreds of thousands of viewers with the audacity of their designs and colors, while preaching confidence in technology and in the institutions that harnessed it. Picasso's *Guernica* shocked these same viewers with the tortured fragmentation of its figures, arousing mass feelings against Franco and his German allies. Seldom have artists and thinkers so readily sensed the political consequences of their work. In mobilizing and coordinating political feelings through their art, formerly isolated or alienated intellectuals could sense themselves at one with an organic left wing that grew larger with each demonstration of solidarity.

La Marseillaise promised to be grand enough to reach an immense public in just this way, but Renoir must have asked himself the same question that struck Gide, Léger, Picasso, and any serious artists working suddenly for direct political ends: How could the radical vision held by a few expand to inspire the throngs of society at large? Specifically, how could beliefs about a populist cinema, promulgated by an elite at *Ciné-Liberté* and in an uncompromising work like *La Vie est à nous*, break out into the commercial cinema so as to revolutionize it? Finally, how could the Popular Front spread throughout the country without losing its shape as a "front"?

These same questions were in the minds of both the new government and the Communist Party, which found themselves immediately at odds in June 1936. The Communists refused to participate in government programs, fomented a flurry of strikes, and assailed policies like censorship; but six months later, conciliation was in the air. Blum's beleaguered government, fearful of deeper conflicts, could support *La Marseillaise* while repressing *La Vie est à nous*. For *La Marseillaise* used history to speak about nationalism, the military threat on the eastern border, and the defection of the upper class. And its main theme could hardly have been more pertinent: the constancy and virtue of a new species of human being, known as the citizen *(le citoyen)*, ready to respond to the call of history in the present.[21] Thus, this costume film recreated not just the summers of 1789 and 1792 but also July 1936, when, as Julian Jackson has shown, Parisians modeled themselves on their patriotic forebears. Far from being a deviation to avoid censorship, as Renoir would later suggest, the clear historical allegory tendered by *La Marseillaise* promoted the cultural agenda of both the government and the PCF.

This was clear when, on March 16, 1937, at the Salle Huyghens in Paris, Renoir announced to an overflow crowd the launching of a great film made "by the people and for the people." Smiling at his side and speaking in turn was Jean Zay, who just months earlier had been the butt of Renoir's ire for his censorship policy. But this time Léon Blum's thirty-two-year-old genius of a minister was there to support a project consistent with Blum's mandate to build the Popular Front on an inherited notion of culture, taken out of the hands of the privileged few and given over to every citizen. Blum, with a formidable background in literary studies, believed deeply in the utility of the arts. He took a personal interest in—indeed, he continually monitored—the 1937 exhibit at the Palais de Tokyo entitled Les Chefs-d'Oeuvre de l'Art Français (Masterpieces of French Art). He also encouraged Zay's initiatives in continuing education, such as the famous Tuesday evenings at the Louvre when admission was free.[22] The government and the PCF alike wanted to transform France into one grand Maison de la Culture.

While such a program claimed to be an Enlightenment idea taken from the Revolution 150 years earlier, it was repugnant to many of the anarchists and radicals who had spurred France toward the left earlier in the decade. For example, the October Group felt its edge blunted, and it disbanded. Jacques Prévert was explicit: "I myself gave up at the time of the Laval Agreements, when, in working-class circles, it became good form to replace the 'Internationale' with the 'Marseillaise.' I didn't like this, because I had known the 'Marseillaise' since I had been a small child, I had seen it in all its guises, and I really liked the 'Internationale,' so that's where it ended."[23] Other members of the group—indeed, unreconstructed radicals of every stripe—resisted the party's reconciliation with the government, with the army, with the great tradition of French culture. As the extremists gave in or gave up, culture after the Popular Front victory was treated less as a war than as a project and an inheritance.

Adapting the Revolution

Like Christ—indeed, in imitation of him—the French Revolution inaugurated a new epoch, and signaled this by instituting a completely new calendar, as though sidereal time had been altered at a historic juncture. And yet, speaking astronomically, a revolution is not a juncture at all—and thus not a revolt—but a cycle. To spin around, to come around, to orbit time and again. Thus, in *La Marseillaise*, when Renoir filmed ordinary citizens ("extras," we call them) who had dressed up in period costumes, as many did on Bastille Day 1936, he figured the Revolution as changeless. What power can remain in an event that has been so repeatedly represented, updated, adapted, and effectively institutionalized? The cliché was Renoir's true enemy, and he fought it using a "revolutionary" way of conceiving history and of making film.

Just as would be depicted in *La Marseillaise*, this mission developed as a genuine experiment in collective action, even if it depended on timely exhortation from a nearly invisible cadre of strategists, Renoir at their head. At the outset, the script included every incident, character, and angle brought up at those organizational meetings on the rue Navarin; assistants led by historians Georges Lefebvre, Jean Bruhat, and fellows of the Sorbonne's Centre d'Etudes sur la Révolution Française collected dossiers of information and constructed a detailed timeline of the events on which any film of the period might draw.[24] Renoir forced himself to imagine as complete a cinematographic treatment of the Revolution as possible, so that all views could be represented. A first outline that he submitted to the Société des Auteurs et Compositeurs Dramatiques in March, then again in April 1937, consists of thirty-two sequences in chronological order, opening in 1787 and concluding with the Battle of Valmy in September 1792.[25] Following an initial sequence involving a destitute peasant family being exploited by the local lord, all subsequent scenes pit key political players against one another. Not until the second half of this preliminary script outline do we encounter another commoner, an artisan; and he serves only as a transition to what is explicitly labeled "la scène principale du film"—an unusually lengthy dialogue between Robespierre and Brissot, to be played by Louis Jouvet and Pierre Renoir, respectively. Jean Renoir estimated that if actually filmed and edited, this first draft would have constituted over twenty hours of screen time.[26] Unfeasible, this design was also unimaginative—merely a set of illustrated flashcards of the events of the Revolution, as commonly laid out. More than this was needed by the flagging Popular Front, and so Renoir and his collaborators began to narrow the focus to pertinent themes.

Next came a June 28, 1937, outline submitted to the Société des Auteurs consisted of 113 scenes grouped into six sections. While the common people now receive far more attention, this outline retains the essentially pedagogic ethos of the first. For instance, a prologue, disguised as a newsreel documentary, lays out the chief causes of popular unrest in the eighteenth century. The formation of the Third Estate dutifully follows, though on the heels of a telling incident in which a peasant is caught and tried for poaching a nobleman's pigeon. (As in the final filmed version, the peasant manages to escape and eventually meets up with a progressive priest.) Next comes the storming of the Bastille. This version concludes with the thwarting of the king's escape at Varennes, an action that shows the people's ratification, in word and deed, of nation over monarch. Despite this rousing populist finale, most of this script pits famous orators against conniving aristocrats or against one another in a conventional, pedagogic manner.

Truly radical by comparison, the final version—the one actually filmed starting September 1937—swept virtually every illustrious politician off-screen. As for the aristocrats, Renoir treats them with bemused detachment, observing the peculiarities of their reactions to their ill fortune rather than

39. Abel Gance's wide-screen vision in *Napoléon* (1927).

tracking their nefarious counterinsurgency measures. This change in Renoir's orientation from politics to everyday life can be glimpsed already in two lengthy sequences of the second script outline (the June 28 version). One takes place in a Parisian beauty salon and the other in a clothing store in Germany. In both cases, details of the political crisis emerge as merchants and clients discuss and bemoan fads, prices, and moral behavior. While the intent of these scenes remains homiletic, they give Renoir room to exploit his vaunted archive of information about daily life. In the final version, such freestanding scenes proliferate within the loose structure modestly evoked by the film's subtitle: "A Chronicle of Some Events Leading to the Fall of the Monarchy."

And so a "chronicle" of the everyday becomes an "anthem" for everyone. This is the flexible design Renoir settled upon and within which he then had great freedom to select and order characters, incidents, and dialogue. Absorbing the new spirit in historiography that was just then coming into existence under the name "Annales," *La Marseillaise* differs in every respect from the two competing film versions of the Revolutionary period available at the time. The first of these, *Napoléon Bonaparte* (Abel Gance, 1927), represents the epic approach, while the second, *Danton* (André Roubaud, 1932), is in the dramatic tradition. Both versions are constrained to repeat a well-known sequence of actions, encounters, and speeches, striving to enliven them with a panoply of media flourishes. For the sonorized version of his inimitable silent film of Napoleon's life, Abel Gance synchronized classical music to add still another layer of homage to the heroic trajectory he never wavers from. This is the sort of national history Renoir's critics pined for when they expressed their disappointment at the clumsiness of *La Marseillaise*. History should soar like Napoleon's eagle in Gance's films, whereas Renoir's history seems pedestrian, content to saunter alongside the common folk. In fact, for the 1935 film, Gance cut from his original the entire sequence of the storming of the Tuileries on August 10, 1792, and the wresting of all traces of authority from the king—the central event that Renoir depicts. But surely the most telling difference between the directors is evident in their renditions of Rouget de Lisle's song, which Gance hands over to Damia, the great *chanteuse* of the day, while Renoir's citizens can scarcely hold the key even as they learn and pass on its infectious melody and words.

The other competitor, *Danton*, is a different story altogether, or rather several stories. Renoir and his countrymen were exposed to a 1932 French remake of a German *Danton* shot in 1930. This, in turn, may have been based on the play *Sprawa Dantona* (The Danton Case), published in 1928 by Stanislawa Przybyszewska, which was explicitly inspired by Georg Büchner's famous play *Dantons Tod* (Danton's Death) of 1835.[27] Whether or not Renoir knew Przybyszewska's play, it is telling to set these works side by side. *The Danton Case* unfolds as a taut duel between the title character (sensualist, libertarian, a figure adored by the people) and Robespierre (intellectual, self-contained, a model for the elite). The few ancillary characters of the play's early scenes disappear behind curtains toward the end of Act 2 during the central confrontation of these two men—representing antithetical interpretations of history—over a superb dinner. They brilliantly uphold their respective positions, each of which seems not just plausible but necessary, Danton drinking beyond his enormous capacity while Robespierre scarcely allowing the wine to touch his lips. Przybyszewska designed her play to fatally interlock two opposing aspects governing human experience; in their mutual destruction, she senses a tragic impasse in the very notion of government. An emperor will be needed to clear the corpses from the stage.

The Danton Case, the first representation of the French Revolution to incorporate clear references to the Soviet Revolution, prudently went underground after its 1933 production in Warsaw, the year of Przybyszewska's death at thirty-one.[28] After waiting out the Stalin era, the play reemerged in 1967 (the same year *La Marseillaise* was reissued), then was discovered by Andrzej Wajda, who staged it to great acclaim in 1975 and again in Gdansk in 1980. His own famous film *Danton*, starring Gérard Depardieu and Wojciech Pszoniak, made under martial law in 1983, tailored the drama as an allegory of the suppression of the workers' rebellion, tilting the balance in favor of

40. The Revolution as a drama of great men: Gérard Depardieu and Wojtek Psoniak in Andrej Wajda's *Danton* (1983).

Danton, who loses his head but wins all sympathy. Adapting Przybyszewska's adaptation, Wajda delivers the kind of French Revolution Renoir scorned as hopelessly clichéd, a Revolution full of edifying speeches by bigger-than-life characters (and actors) caught in a classic dramatic net. Przybyszewska, it is true, had no patience with the masses. Reclusive and anorexic, not so different perhaps from her beloved Robespierre, she believed that the Revolution came from the minds and wills of heroic individuals and only later penetrated society. Minds and wills clarify themselves best in the theatrical crucible she chose: neoclassical tragedy. Renoir, more like Danton in his love of life and his apparent willingness to negotiate and compromise, trusted the people, offering them, in the baggy design of his chronicle and the amiable tone of his anthem, an "everyman's revolution" for their own day.

The battle for control over the French Revolution has been joined most recently by Eric Rohmer, in his idiosyncratic film *L'Anglaise et le duc* (The English Lady and the Duke; 2001). Rohmer has been counted among Renoir's staunchest allies for half a century,[29] yet in this film he puts his political principles ahead of his allegiances, and seems to "relish this opportunity to have it out with French historiography in general and Renoir's *La Marseillaise* in particular."[30] Rohmer's starting point could not be farther from recent

41. The execution of Louis XVI witnessed from afar, in Eric Rohmer's *L'Anglaise et le duc* (2001).

directions in historiography. Not only does he focus on the privileged classes and on the great events of the time (the film being broken into discrete chapters such as "July 14, 1790: The Anniversary of the Storming of the Bastille," "August 10, 1792: The Storming of the Tuileries," and so on), but the source of his work is unique: the memoirs of a foreign eyewitness, the English lady *(Anglaise)* of the film's title. Whereas Renoir combed through a plethora of accounts and facts, striving to bring out the feel of momentous times as they affected countless unnamed citizens, Rohmer's attention and artistry go entirely into adopting the singular perspective of a woman who was in every respect "exceptional." This he does without the irony characteristic of his moral tales, where first-person accounts (think of Frédéric in *L'Amour l'après-midi*, for example) are intermittently held out at arm's length for wry inspection by Rohmer's crystalline camerawork. But Grace Elliott, the Englishwoman, is never second-guessed. From start to finish, her memoirs and their attitude control what is shown, even when, on occasion, her commentary is supplemented by material Rohmer took from the memoirs of the duke.[31] Lucy Russell, who played Lady Grace, appreciated her intelligence and courage, recognizing that her views, so alien and even repugnant to most viewers today, developed in the closed drawing-room world of the aristocracy of the

42. *La Marseillaise*: allegorical shadow play for the masses.

times. She had virtually no contact with the people who make up Renoir's cast of characters. And if Rohmer prefers the drawing room to the streets, it is because, like so many of his characters across four decades, he treasures solitude and reflection.[32]

The film's personal and political climax justly pushes the question of point of view to its limit. On a hillside, some miles from Paris, Grace and her serving woman witness the execution of Louis XVI. In fact, Grace cannot look, refusing the telescope her servant offers. But she hears the cries of the crowd and the retort of the cannon, signaling the fallen head, the fallen monarchy, and a fallen way of life. Her own head bows sadly in response. All this is filmed with the city spread out before her, in *repoussoir*, a painting come partly to life. But only partly, for the film seems detached from its moment, like the characters it observes. "Detachment," Philippe Azoury reminds us, was just the way Michelet spoke of the real "actors in the time of the Revolution." And so Rohmer renders "a silhouette of the Revolution played on a phantasmagoric stage by bodies that seem to have been cast in their roles while dreaming."[33] The bodies that Renoir films, on the contrary, are earthy and have nothing of the phantasmagoric about them, even when attending a gen-

43. The molecular structure of the Popular Front: priest, lawyer, peasant, artisan.

uine shadow play. Practical, pedestrian, and sensual, they seem most at home when chatting and eating. In their mountain hideout, four of them (priest, peasant, artisan, and lawyer) cook a rabbit and consolidate their grievances and their hopes. Like Renoir, they seem closer to Danton than to the coolly intelligent Robespierre, whom Rohmer portrays with sympathy.[34] The incorruptible Robespierre is also, despite his many disquisitions, a man of silence, the one who wanted to clear the stage of politics by shortening debates and trials, and by insisting on the absolute simplicity of judgment. Remaining hidden from the people as much as possible, he inspired the terror that stands sublimely above discourse, like its symbol, the guillotine.

Lady Grace witnesses the king's decapitation in silence and from a sublime, even artistic distance, above Paris in Meudon. Rohmer might have remembered that Renoir lived in Meudon, in a house famous for conviviality where much of *La Marseillaise* was planned. Surely Renoir's privileged upbringing made him equally sensitive to the passing of refinement. In the films just preceding *La Marseillaise*, he registers feelingly the decline of the world of aristocratic sensibilities—that of the Baron in *Les Bas Fonds* and that of von Rauffenstein and Boeldieu in *La Grande Illusion*. But Rohmer boldly accuses Renoir of being "partial" to the lower classes: "They were a violent people, largely manipulated. Let's face it, they weren't amicable." Their excesses, he claims, laid waste to civility. In adapting the memoirs of Grace Elliott, Rohmer has given us something that is precious, a time of trouble reflected in a delicate sensibility. In this case, Rohmer's position is oddly the common one, for the Revolution has generally treated the masses as an unruly and un-differentiated danger against which the private lives of politicians, lovers, or other highly individuated characters must operate. Whereas Renoir particu-larizes the crowd, turns them into human beings one can imagine knowing— or being.[35] With this goal in mind, no character appears irrational or venal. This is a gentle group of revolutionaries, a brotherhood that becomes a na-tion when it recognizes itself. Thus, no character seizes the film's viewpoint; this is reserved for the anthem itself, representing the inevitability of history at a moment of nationalism. In *La Marseillaise*, Renoir is indeed "partial"— partial to history, specifically the history of France.

La Marseillaise, charged with propping up the flagging Popular Front, aimed to forge history even while representing it. Yet how could it do so decisively when decisiveness characterizes historiography in the grand, virile mode (sagas of actions and virtue), which is precisely what Renoir always avoided? Unlike the actual participants in the Revolution, Renoir hesitates to condemn and is seldom judgmental. His harmony with the Popular Front can be felt in their shared tone of reconciliation. Even before he himself, playing Octave in *La Règle du jeu*, uttered the memorable phrase "Everyone has his reasons," he had promoted understanding among rich and poor, Jew and Catholic, even Frenchman and German (as in *Les Bas Fonds* and *La Grande Il-lusion*). Renoir's method and style are characterized by the interplay of inter-ests and values under a guiding rule that might be termed a "unity of concep-tion." *La Marseillaise* carries the tone of the Jacobin meetings it represents— meetings where many individuals have their say, where all react enthusiasti-cally in their own manner, and where a song uniting them seems bound to emerge, sung in various registers but sung together. Spontaneous and general decisiveness occurred in July 1789, August 1792, and on the fields of Valmy, all moments swelled by an upsurge of national feeling that came about not despite differing views, but as a result of debates in the Jacobin clubs, heated exchanges on hastily printed broadsides, and respectful altercations in public

44. Marketing a people's revolution.

squares. Could this unity in diversity be recovered in 1938 to save the Popular Front? Arguments there must be, but the differing voices holding forth in different registers should in the end intone a national anthem; and in moments of genuine crisis, the anthem (or the unity and nation it represents) can carry a people forward into the history they make.

Harsh critics in 1938 and in our own day dismiss *La Marseillaise* for its flaccid politics. To them, Renoir's decentralized aesthetic, ready to adjust to circumstances and to the impulses of the moment, produced a quaint film that disarmed the dynamite within the Revolution of 1792 and compromised it as a model for the Popular Front. Renoir was said to have betrayed the hopes that had made him the key leftist filmmaker of the day.[36] *La Marseillaise* proved unpopular, because avant-garde critics found the film tame, while the larger public was attuned to representations previously monumentalized in official, intellectual, and popular culture. Renoir did not represent heroic events in the heroic style those events were said to demand, a style that most other versions felt authorized and pleased to employ. His film, unlike Roubaud's *Danton* or Gance's *Napoléon*, slides past the personal tragedies that inevitably befall some of his characters. In 1792 the people succumb to a historical moment they sense in the making; in a decision that is both active and passive, they join up so as to be carried along by it. Those participating had little sense of the outcome. They marched to protect the king from false advisors. They wound up executing him and making way for the deeper revolution. Look at the poster that was most frequently used to advertise *La Marseillaise*. Above and to the side shines the medallion of the royal couple.[37] Below, but also on the side, are the shadowy figures of the organizers of the Revolution. Both "powers" find themselves mere witnesses to the color, energy, and outright commotion as the Fédérés march into the carnivalesque capital. Revolution seems neither designed nor willed, Renoir said just a month before the May 1968 uprising, thirty years after his film: "I don't believe the monarchy fell just because of the attacks of the people. It fell because it had to fall, because it had come to its end and something new had to come about. Nevertheless, there are moments like this when nothing comes about. I believe that the greatest merit of revolutionaries is to know when it's time for revolution."[38] Confident that the Popular Front had digested Revolutionary history and that his film had adopted its tone, Renoir was disinclined to retrace each of the steps leading to the Revolution, and thus felt no need to include cornerstone occurrences and obvious characters. Instead, he recorded representative activities from a period of exceptional social awareness, a period he rigorously reimagined from the documents he amassed. Sweeping his mobile camera across the country, he situated and interrelated various events that constitute, in François Truffaut's words, a "montage of newsreel footage of the French Revolution."[39] And so he built up the plot of history from below, with vignettes of marginal relevance, filmed with rare intimacy. In one scene, new recruits are taught to load their muskets step by step, as in a training film. In another, a young man named Bomier receives his mother's blessing to march with the Fédérés. Every principle of filmmaking requires Renoir to follow Bomier, to pick up his energy and his direction, as he joins the band that will be the focus of the narrative. Instead, Renoir lingers with his mother, discreetly tracking from her tear-streaked face along the wall of their modest home, where it notes a pitcher, a platter of potatoes, a coffee grinder, en route to the window, where Bomier's sister looks out in silhouette. As she shutters the window, we glimpse a group of men roofing the building across the way. Only incidentally do we catch sight of Bomier running, whistling through the streets. Such understatement characterizes Renoir's style. While sitting down to eat at a restaurant on the newly laid out Champs-Elysées, the patriots are accosted by members of the king's guards (a confrontation recorded in the "news" of the time). Clumsy swordsmanship and a downpour undercut the epic register we expect of fights such as this.

Among the documents that constitute the film's dossier, one can read three of Robespierre's speeches before the Convention in the first weeks of 1792, all dutifully transcribed from the Bibliothèque Nationale by Renoir's assistant Marc Maurette.[40] Though early on Renoir had thought of giving voice to these discourses of Big History, now he mocks that urge, for in a telling scene his camera follows Bomier and his girlfriend to a shadow play rather than Arnaud, who has gone to hear Robespierre. Not only does this validate our own decision to watch history on a screen; it suggests a new hierarchy in art and politics: "More than the jumps and jolts of history, [Renoir] has chosen the *longue durée* which makes ordinary people into conquerors. This sense of history brings a vision . . . of the quotidian."[41] The "quotidian" means, of course, daily life practices, but it is also a name for the newspaper. Renoir shows the French Revolution traveling on pages of newspapers printed by the people and for the people.

Revolutionary Historiography

Renoir's rather shapeless design serves the texture and tone of *La Marseillaise*. He filmed mainly unremarkable vignettes (a peasant being tried, a scuffle on the Champs-Elysées, a shadow play, and so on) in a style whose integrity and capaciousness are comparable to those of the anthem that gives the film its title. Sung in chorus, "La Marseillaise" expresses a style and an outlook that invites one to scan not just the Revolution's past, but also its still incomplete future. In this, it shares the *parti pris* (though not the content or the structure) of some previous historians of the Revolution. Renoir's sympathy for the lower classes, for instance, can be found nearly a century earlier in Jules Michelet's *Histoire de la Révolution française*, which was republished in Gallimard's prestigious Pléiade series in 1938.[42] But Renoir shares neither Michelet's hero-worship nor his need to be comprehensive. Jean Godechot would likely place Renoir within the Marxist tradition of Albert Mathiez and Georges Lefebvre, the dominant historians of the Revolution of Renoir's period, and men whose viewpoint coincided with that of the people in his circle. But Mathiez's three-volume study, written in the 1920s, was the principal source from which Przybyszewska quarried her characters and their speeches.[43] And her play, as we have seen, stands at the antipodes to *La Mar-*

seillaise. Mathiez (like Michelet) may share Renoir's political predilections, but their historiographic inclinations have nothing in common.

Lefebvre is surely the historian whose leftist but inclusive attitude Renoir best adapts to his film. Remarkably, this man, who ranked among the most prominent historians of the day, actually contributed his personal research to *La Marseillaise*. He was at the time finishing *Quatre-vingt-neuf* for the 150th anniversary of the Revolution, a project taken on at the behest of Jean Zay, the same Popular Front minister of education who sat beside Renoir to announce the production of *La Marseillaise*. Zay might very well have brought the two men together. The structure of Lefebvre's book (with separate chapters on revolutions of the aristocracy, the bourgeoisie, the popular class, and the peasants) scarcely fits *La Marseillaise*. Given his populism (which led him to suppress all signs of scholarly superiority, such as footnotes), he "used the occasion to delineate the revolutionary legacy common to all Frenchmen and to issue a call for its defense."[44] Lefebvre must have found it easy to contribute in a small way to Renoir's Popular Front film, especially since he had only to supply notes on topics about which he had amassed mountains of information. Among the files he submitted is a dossier on the Army of the Coalition that helped turn the tide at Valmy. Just as Renoir no doubt wanted, Lefebvre meticulously establishes the diverse geographic and social backgrounds of the 100,000 men who went out to face the Prussians. Other entries informed Renoir about the wheat famine and the concomitant "great fear" that helped foment the strikes and other actions of 1789. Lefebvre's most arcane entry tells of an entourage of women from Les Halles who approached Louis XVI but were mistreated by the Swiss guards. Lefebvre goes so far as to identify six of these women by name and occupation. Here he shows himself not just a social historian, but one who joined the growing trend toward recounting daily life, something he pursued as editor of the *Annales Historiques de la Révolution Française* without, however, joining the Annales group.

Lefebvre was the most illustrious of a group of consultants who put together an impressive set of notes, hundreds of pages in length, on an amazing array of topics.[45] Renoir cared less about the structure of the Revolution than about the texture of the period's forms of life, insofar as this could be gleaned from the nearly random facts he pored over. From material catalogued under rubrics like "Elegance," "Food," and "Costs of Living," he learned about fashions in wigs, hats, and handkerchiefs, and about social differences in the vocabulary used for these fads. There is much information about military and

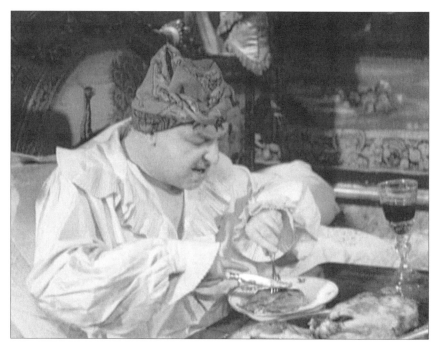

45. Renoir shows off his historical research.

46. Potatoes: a revolution in everyday life.

aristocratic lifestyles. Four full pages detail a banquet of the "Regiment of Flanders," including prices for food and wine. New dietary fads—of special concern for women—included milk and a variety of juices and concentrates. The basis of the prologue sequence jumps out of this section of the archive, in an entry signed by the historian Caron, concerning protocol at the king's table. Louis XVI boasted an enormous appetite. A single meal could consist of twenty separate items. Before going hunting, he was said to eat a breakfast of a *poulet de grain* (small chicken), four cutlets, and poached eggs with ham, washing all this down with a liter of champagne; then he would return from his hunt once again famished. A note in the margin of the file questions the wine service. Did the servant serve the king only after tasting the wine and washing the goblet in front of him? In any case, goblet and carafe were brought in together on a platter—and this is the way it is done in the film.

Information about the middle and lower classes, no doubt harder to come by, helped Renoir imagine the sets he wanted to build. He learned, for instance, that the barricades thrown up by police in Paris were made of logs, not iron; he found out just how much difficulty the new government had in rationalizing Parisian street names, for the people refused to give up their picturesque vocabulary. The price of salt in three different French cities is compared, but the dossier also reminds Renoir that only two million of France's twenty-three million people inhabited the cities. Perhaps the most detailed section of the entire dossier concerns types of entertainment available in Paris, from serious theater to Italian comedy, variety shows, and fairs with circus acts. Included here are the names and reputations of actresses. As for audiences, the documentation indicates that they frequently applauded performances by stamping their feet. Details like this bolster individual scenes, such as the one at the shadow play; they also helped Renoir in countless ways to bring politics into a concrete world. Renoir knew, for instance, that when Camille Desmoulins declaimed against the Brunswick Manifesto, it was in a salon above the Café de Chartres, a notorious gathering spot. This bit of information may not have been lifted from the archive into the film, but having it in his mind could only have helped Renoir solve the cinematic problem of presenting something as abstract as this manifesto. Altogether, Renoir is attentive to the material culture that resulted in a new way of life. Hence his obsession with cooking and eating, as the country welcomes new ingredients (tomatoes) and new culinary habits; hence his inclusion of the shadow play that figures the end of the monarchy in its plot and whose very form of representation would be the popular melodrama, the chief theatrical legacy of the late eighteenth century.

What could Renoir have been thinking when he offered his countrymen a history of the everyday rather than of the exceptional? The king talks one moment about state policy, the next about the hygienic fad of brushing one's teeth in public. As for the heroes of the Revolution—Danton, Robespierre, Marat—they never even appear. Taken at its most abstract, Renoir's idea was to show a transition from monarchy to nation, with the king's sacred head falling at the feet of his anonymous former subjects. But actually these men are not anonymous at all, for Renoir proudly attests that his patriots (Bomier, Arnaud, Moissan) are documented in the registry of Marseilles.[46] Attending to these ordinary people in their extraordinary times, attending to their quotidian activities (their food, their banter, their entertainment, their music), Renoir related the situation of French people in 1938 to that of their counterparts 150 years earlier. Revolution, it seems, comes into one's life not with fanfare but casually; one picks it up like a song, passes it on like a recipe. "There are twenty ways to cook a potato," brags one partisan of this curious *nouveauté*. Soon everyone is eating potatoes or tomatoes (we hear them dubbed *pommes d'amour*, "apples of love") and singing *La Marseillaise*.

But the viability of such a fraternal political order, in 1938 just as in 1792, depends on how this brotherhood responds to enemies both outside and within. Renoir made it rather easy on himself, or rather on France, when he condensed all ill will and treachery onto foreign agents, Marie Antoinette and the Duke of Brunswick. When taking the fort in Marseilles, the ragtag citizen insurgents swiftly overcome soldiers whom they just as quickly befriend. Not so easily persuaded to reconsider his allegiance is the commander, yet his resistance stems from incomprehension, not malevolence. Renoir avoids real bloodshed, including the massacre of prisoners in early September 1792, as well as the victorious but costly battle with the infamous Prussian army at Valmy. And of course we do not see the king's head fall, or any of the thousand other victims of the guillotine. The film takes leave of the Revolution once it has produced out of ordinary citizens a united front for the defense of culture marching east to confront foreign forces of reaction. Renoir proudly gives Goethe the final word: "From this place and this time forth commences a new era in world history. And you can all say you were present at its birth."[47]

Renoir had wanted his film to invoke precisely Goethe's feelings. He wanted all who watched it to feel the rush of being present at the birth of a new social era; but *La Marseillaise* was not understood that way. Indeed, Renoir thought it was not understood at all (except in the USSR, where 250 prints were hurriedly made to meet the demand, and seven million people saw it within two weeks).[48] Still, the most astute and least biased critics of the time, Pierre Bost in *Vendredi* and Roger Leenhardt in *Esprit*, understood its endeavor perfectly well. They recognized that Renoir had put the background of history to the fore. Bost admired the way countless minor strands of action, seemingly independent anecdotes, were woven tightly together by the anthem.[49] Leenhardt found the film fundamentally lax, both as drama and as historiography.[50] It would take a different attitude toward the past, one difficult to imagine prior to 1968—prior to Michel Foucault, the history of *mentalités*, and cultural studies—to prize the raconteur above the grand synthesizer and the simple chronicle above epic History.

Every claim made concerning the exceptional quality of *La Marseillaise* addresses its truly new style of historiography. While the radical social aspirations that surrounded this project began quickly to fade in the downslide of the Popular Front, Renoir maintained, indeed increased, his distinctive manner of evoking the past, challenging France by thrusting in its face a democratic view of the Revolution. He also challenged the common understanding of the "event" of history. Rather than take nameable "events" as solid units, he represents as events what would formerly have been treated as ancillary details or as mere qualifiers, whose variable size and importance depend on the power of the lens we used to isolate them. The Revolution names not an event but a "wave" flowing through myriad happenings that organize it and that are in turn organized by it. Maurice Merleau-Ponty, who surely saw this film during a crucial period of his nascent political engagement, would arrive at a stunning formulation of this radical historiography. He wrote:

> In a sense everything that could have been said and that will be said about the French Revolution has always been and is henceforth within it, in that wave which arched itself out of a roil of discrete facts, with its froth of the past and its crest of the future. And it is always by looking more deeply into how it came about that we give and will go on giving new representations of it. . . . It changes itself and becomes what follows; the interminable reinterpretations to which it is legitimately susceptible change it only in itself.[51]

The final sentence refers at once to the Revolution and to any painting that deserves to be called "art." Here Renoir's upbringing among the Impressionists, and his familiarity with Cézanne's work, allow us to imagine a historiography of small strokes that animate the bulging yet unformed mass of a landscape, a mountain, a face, or an imposing past. His film would indeed paint the Revolution as cresting out of a "roil of discrete facts," each caught up in an unstoppable motion. It may be in this allegedly retrograde, programmatic film that Renoir shows himself a post-Impressionist in his effort to provoke reality by breaking down, first of all, the large blocks by which we routinely organize what we see and know. *La Marseillaise*, docile and amiable, subverts our comfortable view not of the happenings of the past but of the way they in fact happened.

Yet Renoir has been attacked for exploiting rather than exploring the past. And in fact he has hardly abjured the pedagogic heritage of the historical film. Hiding just offstage, he directs this ingratiating shadow play. Listen to the film. A great many of its speeches are bellowed past their diegetic interlocutors and out into the movie theater. Particularly at the Jacobin meetings in Marseilles, anonymous men and women hold forth impressively. In the mountains, priest, peasant, artisan, and lawyer talk without interrupting one another, speaking to posterity (to us) as much as to each other. Moreover, Renoir provides a teacher in the person of *citoyen* Arnaud. An autodidact himself, Arnaud explains the new ideas of the age to the honest men who are his equals and yet follow his advice and (military) leadership.

Is it only personality difference that separates Arnaud, the typical middleman in history—like Jean Zay—from an orchestrator like Napoleon? Or is Arnaud (like his creator, Renoir) a more subtle agent of history? Henri Jeanson dared to accuse Renoir of betraying the democratic pretense of the production. Behind his disingenuous rhetoric, Jeanson fumed, Renoir reserved all decisions (artistic and financial) for himself, benefiting from the goodwill he inspired.[52] Jeanson's comrade Marcel Achard was livid: "Despite the 250 collaborators carefully mentioned in the credits, there was only one man on the site. It was Jean Renoir."[53]

Often deemed innocuous, *La Marseillaise* provokes debate across the parallel domains of pedagogy, narrative style, and historiography. Renoir's control over a production that he envisaged as liberating for the spectator is analogous to the teacher's control over a classroom aimed at the maturation and self-improvement of the student. In addition, the film's plot and rhetoric organize the independent incidents that form its body and discipline the multiple registers that bring that body to life (music, lighting, acting, and so forth),

47. Arnaud's watch interrupts natural time: let the revolution begin.

so that they build a tale with accumulated force. Finally, the historian selects and groups minutiae of all sorts (facts, acts, motivations), until they take shape in hierarchies that can be characterized as events, causes, and perhaps even progress.

To summarize the problem: Renoir's distance from his public might be expressed as the distance of the head from the body. Coordination is required for the organism to put into effect any of its projects. Even the anarchy of free play demands an organism capable of governing its spontaneous responses and whimsical gestures, in which the parts submit to the head. Renoir figures this situation early in his film when he tracks along the men relaxing by the shore of the Mediterranean just before they take the fort by ruse. The camera pauses momentarily at each group, lingering longest before two characters, one a painter, who discuss the mediocre look of the dawn (versus the glorious dawns that conventional artists forever paint). Without a cut, it passes next to Arnaud, who has been just offscreen. His vigilant gaze surveys the lounging group; he looks at his pocketwatch and signals that the moment has come to put the plan into action. Thus, the *longue durée* represented by centuries of "rosy-fingered dawns" is yanked to attention and to a singular event for which the polysemy of the word "momentous" seems appropriate. The pocketwatch Arnaud looks at while the others enjoy the dawn is an apt synecdoche for plot. The question is whether it is equally apt for history. In 1938 critics and spectators alike believed that this film needed rewinding, that its spring had unwound. Renoir saw things differently. It was the Popular Front that needed rewinding; otherwise, there could be neither national cohesion, nor victory in the east. He was soon to be proven right.

La Marseillaise behaves less as a film of plot than of atmosphere, and in this it fits our re-vision of the era. When Duroselle turned to the cultural atmosphere of the '30s, it was merely to bring to life his account of decisive action. Following Renoir, we treat atmosphere as the source of the stormy events that comprise history, a song "in the air," the anthem as "an air." Atmosphere preexists and outlasts the events that precipitate from it. Still, the project of *La Marseillaise*, conceived in the high offices of the PCF, carried out by Jean Renoir, a larger-than-life figure with a most famous name, lays open the dilemma of the Popular Front in relation to the intellectuals who believed in it. Ultimately, such grand tutorial spectacles as the 1937 Exposition or the film we have looked at here result when those who wield cultural power descend into the streets. Despite their best populist intentions, the discourse that results is inevitably patronizing and is unlikely to inspire grassroots movement. At most, it sows the seeds for later generations, which look back fondly at the culture produced in this period, worrying little over how it was generated.

Atmospheres

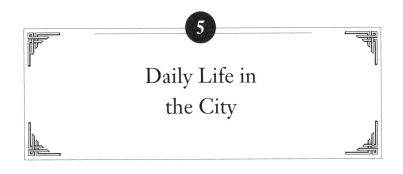

Daily Life in
the City

The Paris evoked thus far in this book has been a city of writers and intellectuals, thus very much a symbolic entity. Those who descended from their
studies into the streets, often drawn by mass-market opportunities, political
emergencies, or social ideals, wrote of Paris knowing that it was considered
France's political capital, the cultural capital of Europe, the city of light, the
site of world-shaking events like the Revolution, the Commune, and the
Dreyfus Affair. Even the nonconformist writers who debunked the master
narratives on which they had been raised thought of themselves as making
history in the streets, thereby creating new landmarks or revitalizing old
ones. Whatever their politics, writers invariably represent Paris—this territory that over the centuries has spread like an organism beyond the Ile de la
Cité, the ancient heart of the city—as bearing a history, a soul. But how did
Popular Front Paris look and sound to the urban populations who spent their
days on its streets? What if we shifted focus from a Paris of landmarks to a
Paris of everyday spaces, considering the form and infrastructure of the city
as these affected the various lives of those who lived and worked in it?[1]

The second part of our book aims to characterize the distinctive atmosphere of Paris during the 1930s. This atmosphere includes elements of physical and geographic spaces: streets, buildings, parks, waterways, and mass
transit above and below ground. It also emanates from novels, films, popular
music, architecture, photography, graphic design, and public exhibitions that
plot the city in different ways. Daily newspapers and illustrated weeklies once
again take on special importance as guides to this urban space, both in their
content (the myriad interests they address) and their format (their manner of
presenting everything all together). For if front-page headlines chronicle the
landmark events of the Popular Front's rise and fall, the back pages hint at

other stories and facts of interest to local readers. Specialized columns, sections, advertisements, and public announcements record a great number of daily concerns, ranging from the arts, sports, and fashion to the weather.[2] Newspapers present daily life in a format that simulates the repetitions and regularities of the everyday. Readers of the five large-circulation Parisian dailies might look at the sports results or fashion columns before turning to the politics and major news on the front page. Whether they bought *Le Matin*, *Le Petit Parisien*, *Le Journal*, *Le Petit Journal*, or *L'Echo de Paris*, these readers surely knew where to find the results of a soccer match or photos of the new collections by Chanel and Schiaparelli.

This shift of emphasis from front page (headlines) to the middle and back pages ("the rest of the news") in no way elides politics, since the newspaper format allows us to explore the permeability of politics and daily life that seldom emerges in the linear presentations of the "straight story." A medium-range shot early in Resnais' *Stavisky* . . . underscores this point: Baron Raoul (Charles Boyer), facing the camera, reads a newspaper article aloud to Stavisky (Jean-Paul Belmondo), but the angle allows the spectator to see a headline about foreigners that the baron does not see. It is this other ("back") side of the page that our subsequent chapters explore.

The newspapers and illustrated weeklies often picture a Paris tinted by the politics of publishers, who also had to represent the interests of their readers, the anonymous masses or solitary pedestrians *(promeneurs solitaires)* who simply inhabit Paris, living and working on its streets. Refocusing on quotidian Paris draws attention to the numerous differences that characterize urban existence. The Parisian readers whom the intellectuals addressed were scattered among myriad subgroups with different desires and concerns based on particularities of gender, sexuality, class, and ethnicity. In the 1930s, these differences were abetted not just by rampant immigration, but by the proliferation of new technologies, by the new modes of entertainment that technology made possible, and—of course—by options in fashion. Paris in the Popular Front period manifested this heterogeneity all at once and in a distinctive way, like an atmosphere full of sounds and smells.

Yet the historical city of Paris, the Paris of monuments and of a certain destiny, does not disappear for all that, since its gravity and magnetism exert a constant force on daily activities. Henri Lefebvre points to an urban dialectic:

In Paris, as in any city worthy of the name, the allied effects of centralism and monumentality have not yet run their course. Each of these trends is based on simultaneous inclusion and exclusion precipitated by a specific spatial factor. The center gathers things together only to the extent that it pushes them away and disperses them, while a monument exercises an attraction only to the degree that it creates distance. It is inevitable, therefore, that the reduction of old particularities, of ethnic groups, "cultures" or nationalities, should produce new differences. It is impossible to bring urban reality to a stop. To do so would kill it—and in any case it puts up far too strong a resistance.[3]

Lefebvre identifies a struggle for the control and management of the city in a "production of space"—a constructive process that he formulates by tracing interconnections between social representations and the observable lives of various types of people who constantly deal in practical terms with architecture and city planning.

City planning brings representation into contact with the lived city, since urban history speaks not only to intellectuals concerned with social relations but also to the average inhabitant preoccupied with just coping. To take a prominent example: What were the long-term consequences of the vast public-works projects undertaken during the mid-nineteenth century? Was Paris in the 1930s still the "urban machine" that Baron Haussmann's transformations had fashioned sixty to eighty years earlier? To what extent had daily life in the streets and neighborhoods of the city evolved in the interim? If demography, urban planning, and mass culture under the sway of Haussmann's template still dictated movement through and around the streets of the French capital even in the mid-1930s, they did so against increasing countercurrents of unofficial and even transgressive popular activity.[4]

We are dealing, then, with Paris as an urban space in which changes were occurring at different rates, even if we put to the side the dramatic tempo of political Paris. The rate and evidence of change for families who traced their roots deep into this space (families like that of Baron Raoul in *Stavisky . . .*) unrolled at a slower pace than they did for immigrants from the Russian Revolution or more recent groups fleeing fascism in Germany and Italy. Change occurred scarcely at all for women of all classes, who were particularly tied to daily life. But, as we shall note immediately, it occurred even among people who saw Paris as "a timeless web of vernacular streetscapes, historic buildings, and monumental stage sets" where nostalgic modernism had achieved a balance between historical continuity and the implementation of progress.[5]

In this chapter and throughout Part II, we register various velocities of urban life coexisting in the single geographic space of Paris. After all, monuments and landmarks each have their place within a *plan de Paris* (city map) that includes boulevards, back streets, and the anonymous zone beyond the fortifications. Tourists, workers, intellectuals, and schoolchildren get around (and along) in this pluri-site called Paris, breathing in and exhaling its peculiar atmosphere.

What were the distinctive features of daily life in Popular Front Paris? In 1931, two-thirds of France's population of 41.3 million lived in towns and cities. Only forty years before, two-thirds had been listed as dwelling in rural areas.[6] This reversal is often explained as a shift from an agrarian to an industrial economy or, in figurative terms of collective identity, as a transition from peasants into Frenchmen.[7] It also involved substantial immigration from outside France. During the decade ending in 1931, the number of foreigners in Ile-de-France (which includes greater Paris and seven surrounding *départements*) doubled to 600,000, or 9.2 percent of the country's population. Census figures for the same year list the three largest groups of foreign nationals in the region as Italians (148,000), Poles (83,000), and Belgians (52,000).[8] Paris also boasted the third-largest Jewish community in the world, surpassed only by those of New York and Warsaw.[9] By the end of 1933, some 55,000 Germans—only a third of them Jews—passed through France following Hitler's accession to power. Six years later, they made up 7 percent of the metropolitan population. As arrivals from the east increased during the decade, political parties on both the right and the left associated the presence of foreign nationals with lost jobs for French workers and the added burden that this influx placed on social services and an economy in the throes of the Great Depression. Following the Munich Agreements of September 1938, the inevitability of renewed war with Germany seemingly added to an anti-Semitism that had festered at least since the Dreyfus Affair.[10]

Many of these "new" Parisians arrived in search of the material benefits that salaried work made possible. (Laws authorizing employers to pay foreign workers less than their French counterparts were seldom applied.) Others came to escape persecution or to enjoy the relative tolerance that the city afforded in terms of politics, religion, and sexuality. While the population of Paris remained largely French-born and Catholic, the presence of immigrant minorities—many from the French colonies—made the city far more ethnically diverse than the rest of the country. Aimé Césaire and Léopold Sédar Senghor arrived from Martinique and Senegal, respectively, to enroll in school before launching reviews that spawned the Négritude movement.[11] Those newly arrived from abroad often moved in with compatriots clustered in certain areas and neighborhoods within the city. Many Jews coming from Germany and eastern Europe gravitated to the Right Bank (around the church of St. Paul, the Place de la Bastille, and the Place de la République), as well as to Belleville to the south and east of Montmartre.[12] North Africans who migrated in large numbers to France after World War I (73,000 from Algeria alone) settled in the ring of northern and northwestern *arrondissements* and suburbs, including Saint-Ouen, Aubervillers, Saint-Denis, Gennevilliers, Asnières, Boulogne, Clichy, and Colombes.[13] This population consisted largely of single men who lived in residential hotels while working in construction and menial jobs. Religious and cultural roots combined with a shared condition of exile to promote solidarity among these foreign workers. The emergent nationalism that resulted was promoted as early as 1926 by such groups as the Etoile Nord-Africaine (North African Star), launched with support from the French Communist Party, which abandoned it a decade later.[14]

These new Parisians soon learned how to make their way with the aid of an interior (cognitive) map that processed urban spaces as zones of danger, enticement, familiarity, and difference.[15] This mental *plan de Paris* configured areas of the city as a spiral of twenty *arrondissements* spinning outward and clockwise from the Louvre, the Tuileries, and the Place de la Concorde just north of the Seine to the one-time village of Ménilmontant (which had become a suburb, or *faubourg*) and Père Lachaise cemetery at the northeastern edge of the city. In the years 1900–1940, these and other peripheral sectors drew recently arrived immigrants as if the newcomers had been tossed by cyclonic movement outward from the city center.

A more tangible dividing point was constructed in the mid-nineteenth century by the belt of fortified masonry walls marking the city limits. Norma Evenson notes that the partition was symbolic as well as geographic:

The fortifications themselves, with their walls and bastions, formed a ring 35 kilometres long and 130 to 135 meters wide. Beyond this lay a military zone averaging from 250 to 300 meters in depth, and subject to a regulation of *non aedificandi*, prohibiting permanent building. The purpose of the zone was to insure that nothing blocked the training of artillery placed on the ramparts and to provide a clear view of enemy approaches. Although owners of land in the zone might erect low wooden structures, they would be compelled to demolish them whenever requested by military authorities. Together the fortifications and zone encompassed an area of 1,200 hectares, equivalent to one quarter of Paris.[16]

Deemed obsolete as early as the 1880s, the walls and surrounding area evolved into a vast shantytown known as *la zone*. In 1926 this area was occupied by some 42,000 *zoniers* and *zonières*, living in filth and squalor.[17] Just outside the city proper, the *zone* was the most notorious of sixteen officially designated slums (known as *îlots insalubres*, literally "unhealthy islets") that housed 200,000 people in 4,200 apartment buildings, mainly in the northern and eastern areas of the city.[18]

These districts served as a figurative dumping ground for what the urban machine of Haussmann's Paris thrust to its periphery in order to facilitate the flow of pedestrians and vehicles along straight thoroughfares that accelerated movement from one part of the city to the other. During his 1853–1870 term as prefect of Paris, Haussmann authorized the construction of some 200 kilometres of new streets, with special attention to horse-drawn and rail traffic.[19] This urban "demolition artist" destroyed old neighborhoods in order to build new ones.[20] The latter included a commercial district of specialty shops and department stores along the *grands boulevards* on the Right Bank, just to the north of the Théâtre National de l'Opéra (known since 1989 as the Opéra-Garnier), in the eighth, ninth, and tenth *arrondissements*.[21] Haussmann also oversaw the construction of some 34,000 new buildings containing 215,000 apartments, but the fact that priority was given to traffic flow meant that the new streets were early instances of transitory nonplaces without significance in themselves.[22] A threefold increase in vehicles during the years 1922–1938 brought the total number of cars registered in the city to 500,000.[23] The removal of trams from service in 1933 marked a final break with spatial and historical continuity based on the mid-nineteenth century model of the city.[24]

The internal division of Paris according to wealth and class has provoked vivid literary characterizations. Few are more pointed than that of Céline, who wrote: "The rich in Paris live all together. Their homes form a wedge, a slice of urban cake whose point touches the Louvre and whose rounded end meets the trees between the Pont d'Auteuil and the Porte des Ternes. There it is, the best part of town. All the rest is wretchedness and rubble."[25]

Yet at the very moment that Céline was decrying the segregation by wealth that shaped the internal geography of Paris, the emergent technology of radio broadcasting was reconfiguring the city and its inhabitants in a way that overcame such divisions, changing how nearly everybody thought about their neighbors. Initial broadcasts from a transmitter atop the Eiffel Tower provided daily weather reports to everyone in Ile-de-France, not just those in the eighth and sixteenth *arrondissements*. In November 1922, the voice of announcer Marcel Laporte introduced a concert organized by the new Radiola station under the aegis of the SFR (Société Française Radio-électrique).[26] Music lovers throughout the city could tune in from their homes, making up an audience that was larger and more diverse than any that clustered in a band shell or hall in some particular district. By 1928, Radiola (renamed Radio-Paris) had been joined by Radio–Tour Eiffel, Radio PTT, and nine public stations in the provinces, as well as by thirteen private stations, from Radio-Fécamp and Poste Parisien to Radio-Béziers and Radio-Nice.[27] Competition meant that entertainment programming became more important, to draw listeners and to secure advertising as revenue. As early as 1926, radio's unknown economic potential led to a minor scandal when the artistic director of Radio–Tour Eiffel, Maurice Privat, agreed to sell the station's advertising concession for three years to none other than Alexandre Stavisky.[28]

This minor episode, which occurred some seven-and-a-half years before Stavisky's death in January 1934, points to the uncertain status of radio throughout the 1920s as a medium of mass communication straddling public service and commercial exploitation. Debate on this issue increased in vehemence during the rise of the Popular Front, when programming became an outlet for political parties as well as for associations representing religious and other interest groups. A flap over skewed coverage of the February 6, 1934, riots led to a restructuring of Radio-Journal de France. Reforms instituted a year later by Georges Mandel, minister of the PTT (Postal, Telephone, and Telegraph Service), created a recording center to monitor all domestic and foreign broadcasts, public as well as private.

In that same year, a Popular Front coalition created the Association Radio-Liberté, whose manifesto on programming called for broadcasts consisting of reports from the Senate and the Chamber of Deputies, live commentary from political rallies, children's shows, and even courses from the Sorbonne.[29] Radio-Liberté hoped to prevent rule of the airwaves by crass commercial interests and by the fascists, whose demagoguery they had heard (or heard about) in Germany and Italy. By 1937 the group claimed more than 50,000 members, mostly in Paris.[30] In times of crisis, listeners received information almost instantly—an immediacy with which newspapers could not compete, even with "extra" editions. More important, radio established a virtual community of city dwellers, diminishing the importance of districts and neighborhoods, and thus of perceived differences in class and wealth. Newspapers, despite their urban or national diffusion, were posted on neighborhood kiosks or sold on street corners. Radio, in contrast, emanated into the atmosphere from a central tower (such as the Tour Eiffel). Everyone in range could listen simultaneously to the same program. This crucial technology altered the physical and mental landscape of cities in the years between the wars.

Radio emerged as a medium of mass culture alongside related technologies—for instance, the sound film and the 78-rpm recording. But it was radio that most rapidly became an indispensable machine of daily life.[31] In 1930, there were around 500,000 radio receivers registered with the government's postal administration. Within nine years this number had increased to more than 5 million, with an estimated 19.5 millions listeners, nearly half of France's total population.[32] This citizenry of "dear listeners" ("cher-zauditeurs," as the announcers said) would begin to rival in size the readership of newspapers. But the functions of these mass media overlapped far less than was first imagined. Radio turned increasingly to entertainment, and especially to song, as an inexpensive way to fill airtime and to recruit advertisers and sponsors. The political tone set by so many newspapers through their editorials, satirical columns, and cartoons was seldom felt in radio broadcasts. As pastime or background, programs of songs were mainly escapist, catering to romantic fantasies, cheap exoticism, and mindless comedy at odds with the ever more somber mood of the decade. "At a time when Franco was slaughtering people in Spain [1938], the big hit of the moment was Rina Ketty's 'Sombreros et mantillas' [Sombreros and Mantillas]. The breakthroughs of Tino Rossi's 'Y'a de la joie' [Everyone's Happy] and Ray Ventura's 'Qu'est-ce qu'on attend pour faire la fête?' [What Are We Waiting For? Let's Party!] coincide with the *Anschluss*, the defeat of the Popular Front, and the threat of war."[33]

Another strain of popular music featured the *chanteuse réaliste*, who parlayed the sufferings of the plaintive street singer *(la goualeuse)* into a character type representative of urban lowlife. Projecting her voice to suggest a certain lifestyle, the *chanteuse réaliste* had to make the transition from live entertainment to the phonograph and sound film. For some singers, this difficult change heightened the personal dramas that were the sources of the songs. This seems to have been the case with Fréhel (1891–1951; née Marguerite Boulc'h). Fréhel was a rising star of live popular song when she left France around the start of World War I, in a self-imposed exile following an unhappy affair with another popular music star, Maurice Chevalier. Over the next two decades, she appeared in fourteen films, most famously in the role of the world-weary prostitute Tania in Julien Duvivier's *Pépé le Moko* (1936). Unlike the lead roles given to one-time music-hall stars Mistinguett, Arletty, and Josephine Baker in early sound films of the 1930s, the supporting roles that Fréhel, Damia, and Lys Gauty played onscreen conveyed the joys and sufferings of women with which urban audiences—especially women—readily identified.[34]

Realist song recast the underside of urban life—which had been depicted in the fiction of Emile Zola in quasi-scientific detail half a century earlier—into an object of nostalgia. At the same time, the figure of the realist singer fostered social anxieties surrounding the modern woman, whose autonomy and sexuality defied conventions of monogamous heterosexuality.[35] Prostitution was a recurrent point of reference that the persona of the *chanteuse réaliste* exploited, highlighting the ambiguous status of the urban woman, whose overt sexuality made her both predatory and vulnerable. This ambiguity extended to children, minorities, and the poor—groups whose marginality likewise forced them to the interstices of the city, where they coped with its contradictions "in their own particular way."[36]

The *chanteuse réaliste* projected a social and sexual ambiguity that in some measure affected all women following World War I. A case in point is the voluble controversy provoked by the 1920 legislation outlawing abortion. This law ostensibly addressed anxiety over depopulation, but it baldly implied government control of women's sexuality.[37] Prewar stereotypes blurred in the figure of the modern woman—single and sexually active—who remained an object of controversy precisely "because she symbolized shifts in the social organization of gender" debated among natalists and feminists throughout the 1920s.[38] The hundreds of thousands who read Victor Margueritte's 1922 bestseller, *La Garçonne*, included many who were also at the core of a mass-market fashion industry for which the urban marketplace was a principal site. "To buy and wear the new styles—at the workplace, on the streets of Paris, wherever social interchange took place—was to participate in a truly social fantasy of liberation. Fashion became a political language of signs used to herald the arrival of a new world."[39]

The politics of women's fashion extended, at the level of daily life, to a sexual division of labor in the domestic chores assigned to women. Doing the weekly laundry for a family of four required no fewer than eight hours of manual activity, which amounted on an annual basis to some forty-nine eight-hour workdays "for housewives or for drudges."[40] New technologies improved the physical conditions under which this labor occurred. The spread of indoor plumbing in apartment buildings meant that women no longer needed to go outside to fetch water for cooking, laundry, and personal hygiene. The fact that by 1938 electric lighting had been installed in more than six out of ten homes eliminated for many women the two to three hours per week previously needed to clean and maintain oil lamps.[41] And the vast majority of city dwellers brought bread home from the local baker rather than making it themselves. Such advances saved time when it came to the routine of daily and weekly chores. But they neither increased men's participation in housework nor altered society's expectations that a woman would prepare two home-cooked meals a day for her family.

The division of labor across classes was sharpened by the relative invisibility of housework within a system that listed a majority of women over the age of twenty-five as "inactive" because they did not engage in an occupation included in national economic statistics. Census figures for 1931 suggest that only about half of all women over the age of twenty-five were "active," in the sense of "employed."[42] For men, the same census recorded rates of 95 percent or higher through age 54. Even the decrease to 48 percent among employed men beyond sixty-five is more than twice the figure listed for women in the same age group. Such figures provide a skewed sense of activities whose official invisibility contrasts with the realities of daily life in a majority of working- and middle-class households. Not until a decade later would models of informal economy begin to account for voluntary, unrecorded, and unpaid domestic labor. Through the end of the 1930s, women's work falls through the cracks of government statistics.[43] Women increasingly held high positions in business and government, but they did not have the right to vote until after World War II.

The sense of daily life conveyed by the hard statistics contrasts with images of Parisian architecture and décor displayed in feature films and the mass-circulation press—images that often serve in retrospect as purveyors of atmosphere and period nostalgia. Yet we should not dismiss these images as irredeemably skewed by ideological factors such as class and gender, for they are undeniably grounded in material conditions of the period. The seventh-floor garret represented in René Clair's *Sous les toits de Paris* was a reality for many Parisians before it was reconstructed in the film studio to convey a distinct urban atmosphere.

> In the 1930s, as they had been ever since 1914, rents were so low that the poor artist or *grisette* could indeed live sparsely, especially in a central *arrondissement*. And the *pneumatique does* arrive within two hours, the post *is* delivered on Sundays, the newspaper *does* come out on Sunday (but not on Monday), taxi-drivers *do* wear peaked caps, *mauvais garçons do* wear checked ones and black-and-white shoes, senators *are* fat and bearded, important personages *do* wear stocks, artists and *instituteurs do* wear *lavallières*, and Parisians of both sexes are more likely to be dark than fair, so that their eyes will dilate in the light and dark of the city night, their brilliantined hair will glisten under the white lights.[44]

The evocative force of films by Clair, Jean Renoir, and Marcel Carné (the furniture of a maid's room, the trace of a regional accent, the gleam of a cigarette holder) drew on details of a reality which filmgoers of the period could confirm. No matter the genre, such representations contain images that thicken the history of life in the 1930s.

Throughout this transitional chapter, cold statistics and fleshy images have supplemented narrative histories of the Popular Front, providing some sense of its specific place and moment. In very different ways, these alternative perspectives reveal pervasive or slowly evolving conditions that affected most Parisians up through the events leading to the June 1940 fall of the Third Republic. Part I of this book focused on the key individuals who made up the dramatis personae of the largely political drama of the streets. Part II, "Atmospheres," takes the temperature of the times, measures the prevailing winds of change, and samples the environment within which *everyone* coexisted.

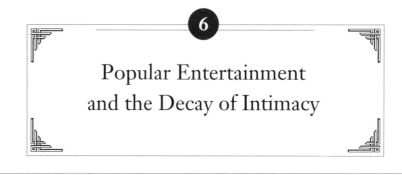

Popular Entertainment and the Decay of Intimacy

René Clair's Canned Music

People have always entertained one another through song, dance, mime, and stunts. Amateurs of the neighborhood, roving troupes of professionals, and constellations of small-time star performers are as universal in human society as are farmers and nurses. But in the first years of the Great Depression, this constant in human culture received a shock: radio, phonography, and sound films arrived. In France, as elsewhere, the crisis in entertainment this produced was much discussed in the press. Curiously, it was also treated obsessively by cinema: scores of films recorded various forms of "live" performance. And why not? Plays, operettas, variety acts, and musical revues provided pretested material that the cinema could disseminate to vast audiences too poor to afford a theater ticket or unable to travel to the limited venues. Naturally the cinema would strive, in varying degrees, to supplement such material with its own particular flare for photographic realism and efficient storytelling. The musical comedy film was—and remains—the epitome of such mixed forms. While many of the first musical comedies dealt with the haute bourgeoisie—the class with enough money to attend live performances in fancy Parisian music halls—the ones that have come down as particularly memorable are, on the contrary, those for whom the "people" were the primary audience as well as the main topic. The tone of popular culture was visibly and audibly altered in the 1930s, and not only because of the populist themes that were in the air. The popularity of the new media, particularly of the sound film, changed entertainment by lowering its target. It did so, as we will see, in full view of traditional modes of entertainment, represented as inadequate to modern times and forced to step aside.

The first European genius of the musical comedy, René Clair, took on a different rival to the cinema in each of his first three films, *Sous les toits de Paris* (1930), *Le Million* (1931), and *À Nous la liberté* (1931). Taken together, these recapitulate the evolution of vocal entertainment, dealing with, respectively, the neighborhood street singer, the large music hall or comic opera, and the phonograph. Each pays tribute to traditional entertainment forms while promoting the cinema as their inevitable heir.

Sous les toits de Paris proved a dramatic insertion into Parisian popular culture and into world film history. It was hailed as the first artistic success of the sound era. Clair directed it unwillingly, he claimed, because of his fear that sound would clumsily upset the aesthetic equilibrium which the silents, at least the kind he promoted, had finally begun to attain. He rejected standard "talkies" as dull, because they were redundant. In no way would any film of his merely reproduce dance, or drama, or the musical theater, although he would explicitly draw on these and other forms. His films, spare and meticulous, aimed to choreograph heterogeneous elements until a pattern emerged above the minimal dialogue required by the plot. After drawing enthusiastic audiences internationally, *Sous les toits de Paris* returned triumphant to a Paris that had received it coolly at its première. Now, in the spring of 1930—at the Moulin Rouge, of all places—"*Sous les toits de Paris* unrolled every ninety minutes, displaying itself as a symbolic event to mark the conquest of Montmartre by the 'film parlant et sonore.'"[1] Conquest indeed! One after another the immense music halls on the north end of Paris were converted into movie palaces: La Cigale, La Gaîté-Rochechouart, Le Fourmi, L'Apollo. Simultaneously, new movie theaters were constructed, most prominent among them the Gaumont-Palace and then the Rex, which was the largest and most impressive in the world. Although live acts were often interspersed with screenings at these theaters, one could sense that the dancers, musicians, and acrobats were being edged to the "preliminaries" of programs whose main event was definitively the feature film.

Ironically, *Sous les toits de Paris* evokes with unabashed nostalgia a simpler Paris, one not yet taken over by mass entertainment. Specifically, it evokes a neighborhood much like Montmartre, where people amused themselves in the local cafés and dance halls and on the streets. In the marvelous opening sequence, the camera tracks across a line of smokestacks, then cranes down to the narrow street where a small group gathers around one of the film's heroes. He sings the song that the film has already begun to bring to life:

48. Place Clichy, 1931: the largest movie theater in the world.

49. A street singer validates the talkies in René Clair's *Sous les toits de Paris* (1930).

"Sous les toits de Paris." By 1930 such street singers had begun to disappear, or they had degenerated from choral leaders to buskers. But in the mythology of the cinema (which is to say, in the popular imagination), Paris' street corners have always been capable of erupting into communal song. And from the street corners, songs were moving into the cafés, and from the cafés into the music halls. After the conversion to sound, movie theaters (whether local corner cinemas or converted music halls, like the Moulin Rouge) would bill themselves as the place to hear the songs that once filled the streets.

While performers now could reach a far wider audience, they were undeniably changed in the process of being filmed. In *Sous les toits de Paris*, the street singer and the café-concert world to which the singer is linked become subordinated to a Parisian symphony, shaped by innovative photography and editing. *Le Million* more blatantly satirizes live entertainment by setting its climactic scene at the Paris Opéra Lyrique, where the "real" cinematographic drama (the love story between the film's central characters, and the search for a missing lottery ticket) makes a shambles of the "live" performance attended by well-dressed patrons. This performance begins with a romantic duet between two grotesque and antagonistic singers, while behind the props the film's attractive genuine lovers mime their true feelings. Next, the chorus is infiltrated by ruffians and the show is interrupted by an all-out chase, one in which Clair himself participates by laying sounds of a rugby match over syncopated images. *Le Million* celebrates the cinema as the art of movement and of common people who literally displace the static singers and props of the lyric opera. To Clair, everyone is potentially a star of the cinema, insofar as all gestures and actions can be incorporated or channeled into a kind of democratic ballet of life.[2] No stars dominate any of Clair's films; no single element bears significance or meaning. Instead, coordinated heterogeneity offers a utopian vision of popular culture.

This vision is on full exhibit in *A Nous la liberté*, an overtly populist comedy whose political allegory travels along the trajectory of a song. Genuine song, we are meant to believe, erupts spontaneously: in the opening scene, it bursts from the camaraderie of the two main characters, Emile and Louis; in the film's finale, from workers on holiday. Such unmediated joyous expression in the outdoors contrasts with the siren song of the lovely girl at her balcony—a melody that seduces the imprisoned Emile midway through the film. Here a timely pan of the camera reveals that the girl is not singing at all, but lip-synching to a gramophone record. Are the flowers she tends real, we must ask?

Clair's satire is doubly self-reflexive. In the first place, it is set in a factory where assembly-line workers under close surveillance produce gramophones meant for leisure and entertainment. In the second place, by exposing the ersatz appeal of recorded song, Clair's cinema exposes itself, for France's leading cinema magnate, Charles Pathé, got his start selling and then mass-producing gramophones in the 1880s and 1890s. Whereas *Le Million* spoofed the rituals of live entertainment in which spectators dress up to watch performers simulate the feelings of a song, *A Nous la liberté* goes further, attacking the industrial and technological underpinnings of modern culture altogether.

The solution embedded in the lyrics of its theme song is a return to nature:

> Mon vieux copain, la vie est belle
> Quand on connaît la liberté!

50–51. From street peddling to assembly line: the growth of mass entertainment in René Clair's *A Nous la liberté* (1931).

N'attendons pas, partons vers elle!
L'air pur est bon pour la santé.

[My friend, life is grand
When you have known freedom!
Let's not wait—let's head toward it!
Pure air is so good for the health.]

But this is a solution that depends on the imagined benevolence of automation. Even the song smirks at such a fantasy:

Partout, si on en croit l'histoire,
Partout on peut vivre et chanter,
Partout on peut aimer et boire.
A nous, à nous la liberté!

[Everywhere, if you believe the tale,
Everywhere you can live and sing,
Everywhere you can love and carouse.
Freedom belongs to us—to us!]

Since the promise of automation is a ruse held out to grumbling workers by exploitative capitalists and politicians, Clair's workers can expect to be called back to the grind even if they're on holiday. The gramophones they mass-produce will distract them in their few evening hours of lonely leisure (if one assumes the workers can afford what they build).

Clair's style may be more rigorously mechanical and dehumanizing than the world he satirizes. His actors are hardly characters; his cityscapes are painted backdrops. He polishes everything to a smooth surface without mystery or depth, so that all elements can interact according to a rhythm. Thus, his own films, as well as the cinema industry he works for, partake of that inauthenticity which the gramophone represents.

The case of René Clair makes one wonder to what extent cinema had the potential to be a truly "popular" art, let alone sustain a genuinely populist vision. Posing as the inheritor of the street song and live theater, Clair's films play out cinema's presumption as the chief industry of popular entertainment. Cinema offered to provide public access to the extraordinary, but on the scale of the ordinary. Differing from theater and music hall, which brought the spectator into contact with talent, the cinema photographed such talent out in the streets, or backstage in the dressing room, as belonging to daily life. For Walter Benjamin, the cinema thus dispersed the aura associated with sacred art, an aura that until the age of technological reproduction still hovered over popular as well as elite art, particularly in the adulation given to the persons of singers. The projected image of Maurice Chevalier or of Mistinguett neither signs autographs nor blows kisses. Nevertheless, Clair banned such overwhelming personalities from his work. He even argued for the suppression of credits. By drawing attention to this or that singular talent or independent element, credits stand in the way both of the "ordinariness" and of the ensemble that together produce the sublimity of cinema at its best, the *ciné-ballet*. Clair retained an affection for the simple street singer who could transform a dull *quartier*, with people trudging to or from work and errands, into a community animated by music.

Sites of Song

Street performers present themselves as self-contained sources of emotion; but alongside them one usually finds the businessman, who maximizes their economic value, and the critic, who establishes their cultural value. This larger entertainment complex tends to evaporate quickly with time. Only the striking melodies of the past continue to reverberate, and they do so without the noise of promotion or contestation that the historian listens for. This is particularly true of the earliest examples of popular expression. For instance, the *chanson* is generally taken to be a ubiquitous expression of the popular classes of modern France; yet its development is tied to the café, a thoroughly middle-class institution. Nevertheless, its growth in modern urban society provides striking evidence about the values and tastes of people whose feelings are otherwise underrepresented in the usual political histories of the nation. No matter what kind of songs previously entertained aristocrats in their manors, or delighted peasants around their hearths, urban song acquired its own characteristics in the eighteenth century. The standard chronology has it that coffee was introduced to France in 1663, followed soon by coffeehouses, especially after chicory arrived in 1707.[3] Diaries report singers present in cafés in the late eighteenth century. These same diaries also make it clear that as quintessential public spaces, cafés were sites of the ideas, intrigues, exchanges, solidarity, and camaraderie necessary to the volcanic years during and surrounding the Revolution.

Understandably, the authorities began to control cafés through licensing and censorship. On June 8, 1806, a notorious Napoleonic decree reduced the number of legal theaters operating in the capital to eight, instantly dooming many cafés that had developed their own revues. The monarchies of the Bourbon Restoration (1814–1830) were equally suspicious of unauthorized or spontaneous expressions, so that the few illegitimate entertainment clubs presenting performances had to be sanctioned by someone powerful in the aristocracy. This was the case, for instance, with the club known as Le Gymnase, protected for years by the Duchess of Berry.[4] Meanwhile, with theater closely monitored (and effectively eliminated for all but the wealthy), singing clubs grew into a popular form of social diversion. Groups of *goguettes* (tipplers) would gather regularly from eight to midnight at a wine bar or café to drink and sing. By the 1840s, the stage at these *cafés-chantants* was set for the development of the kind of professional entertainment that had already sprouted in Great Britain.

The enterprise of the *café-concert* grew steadily but sporadically in the nineteenth century, at the mercy of the political and military events of 1848, 1851, and 1870, but taking advantage of the demographic changes wrought by Haussmann's newly laid-out boulevards. Paris' overall economic growth in the second half of the century produced a sizable class of bureaucrats and salesmen—literate but generally uncultured men—whose leisure hours in the evening required filling. A ceaseless supply of footloose males frequented the new establishments along the boulevards or on the Champs-Elysées.

Successive governmental agencies policed—when they could not utterly repress—such unregulated social gatherings, where inevitably the limits of propriety were tested. There were regulations enjoining singers from interacting dramatically with others onstage, for example, and costumes were only gradually permitted. Yet neither gentle nor severe censorship could keep up with the volume of the new music-theater industry. By century's end, nearly 15,000 songs were being produced annually; the police simply hadn't the staff to bottle up the insatiable public taste for risqué or seditious lyrics.[5] Even when steps were taken to ban certain songs, the sheer number of performers and clubs was such that they were performed anyway. T. J. Clark's magnificent essay "A Bar at the Folies Bergère" catalogues such concurrent factors as the industry of songbook production; the proliferation of drugstores, spectator sports, tobacconists, sweepstakes, and the *roman-feuilleton*; and everything that catered to the new anonymous functionaries of the metropolis.[6]

The *café-concert*, or *caf'conc'* (pronounced "kahf-KOHNCE"), took off with the Second Empire, when stars like Thérésa (née Emma Valadon) and Rigolboche (née Marguerite Badel) became known across the city, attracting patrons to larger halls that were specifically built or remodeled for performance.[7] Accounts tell of the crush of people at the Ambassadeurs (designed by Haussmann's chief architect, Gabriel Davioud, to hold more than 3,000), at the Eldorado, and at the Alcazar. This last, constructed in 1850 on a grand scale, thrived right up to the moment of the Prussian invasion, with Thérésa singing a repertoire that included several numbers by Jean-Baptiste Clément, who would become famous during the Commune for his song "Le Temps des cerises." So successful was her cycle of Austrian songs (complete with Tyrolean costume) that other singers began to develop exotic personae. Rossini and Gounod were known to sit at the table closest to her act, sometimes alongside the literary critic Champfleury.[8] For the Eldorado, the first big theater to term itself a *café-concert*, the literary lion Théophile Gautier even scripted a revue. The *caf'conc'* had obviously become respectable, and the public entertainments given there, at least up to the Dreyfus Affair, helped to define the confident sensibility of a middle-class society flush with the prospects of its ascendancy.

For later generations, the famous *cafés-concerts* of this era expressed in dance, mime, and particularly in song, an edenic urban naturalness that could not survive the century. Jaunty or morose songs celebrated the lovers, buffoons, drunkards, and civil officials who walked the streets. On those streets one could also find another corps of singers, many who dreamed of gaining access to the limited stages; they hawked sheet music in the working-class *quartiers*, just as we see in the opening sequence of *Sous les toits de Paris*. Most of those who gathered around such singers couldn't afford to toss away money at the Alcazar, nor did they feel themselves to be part of an urban utopia. One only has to read *L'Assommoir*, Zola's novel of the urban working class, to sense the limited vision most Parisians commanded from their overpopulated tenements.

Yet it was during the second half of the nineteenth century that the term *populaire* (meaning not just "popular" but equated with "populist," pertaining to the masses) took on its attractive, though ambiguous connotations. People of all classes rubbed shoulders on the new boulevards and, increasingly, inside these eating and drinking establishments. While certain cafés and some areas (notably Montmartre) were considered physically and morally unhygienic, if not dangerous, families and "respectable women" made up an important part of their clientele. This was true even for those cafés where prostitutes were known to ply their trade. In what has always been thought of as the golden age of the *caf'conc'*, contagious melodies managed to harmonize the dissonances that surely could be felt between café and street, between *quartiers*, between classes. Although the lyrics sung there so often concern the poor, in reality "the songs of the *café-concert* . . . represented the middle class, the perfect echo of its aspirations, or of its least secret thoughts, and, up to a certain point, of its good sense."[9]

Perhaps this "perfect echo" is exactly what makes this period and this form a vanishing point of nostalgia for later generations contending with the undisguisable cultural and political dissonance of the twentieth century. In 1933, a reviewer of the music-hall circuit could ruefully proclaim that Manet's painting *Le Bar aux Folies Bergère* "shows a simple world of pleasure and entertainment that is gone now."[10] Of course the "popular" was never uncomplicated; nor was there ever a simple world of pleasure, since the pleasures of modernity stand propped up by business and by ideology, both of which are conflicted by definition. The *caf'conc'* meant to the 1930s what the "good old days when movies were movies" signify for many of today's adults, living amid streams of electronic images emanating from televisions and computers. One critic wrote that the *caf'conc'* was, "in a word, our national spectacle, that of the half-century extending from the Second Empire to 1914, before it ceded to the music hall and before it was chased from the popular venues by an art that was even more exciting, but one that soon would likewise present itself in sound and song . . . the cinematographe."[11]

In fact, however, even in this prelapsarian era before World War I and before Dreyfus, class differences and class conflict affected the conditions and the content of entertainment. A disproportionate number of *cafés-concerts* sprang up in the poorer *arrondissements*, where rents were low. Certainly these served a portion of the local masses, but many also set out to attract well-heeled revelers in search of thrills and novelty. Jacques Becker vividly portrays this phenomenon in his film *Casque d'Or* (1951) when a quartet of very well-dressed daredevils strut into a working-class *bal populaire* called the Ange Gabriel, only to be systematically humiliated and terrified, presumably getting exactly what they were seeking when they set out for that nightspot. Less dramatic but equally revealing is the simultaneous appropriation of "Le Temps des cerises" (Cherry-Blossom Time) by those who took it as a sentimental love song and by those for whom it was a reminder of the revolutionary furor of the Commune. Popular performance, which in the context of the nineteenth century has frequently been misconstrued as some form of homogenous folk ritual, has always provoked varied, even conflicted responses.

Adopted immediately by left-wing groups, Clément's famous song might have served as an anthem for a daring avatar of the *caf'conc'*, the so-called *café-artistique*, which sprang up in Montmartre. Scholars argue today about the political tenor of the standard *caf'conc'*, some holding it to be naturally subversive while most tag it as innocuously middlebrow; but there is no questioning the radical aspirations of the *café-artistique*. This institution dates from 1878, the period following the relaxation of post-Commune censorship and the establishment of bohemian drinking groups in the Latin Quarter. Such groups would regularly gather at their favorite cafés, where they could ostentatiously proclaim their dispensation from the mores of the middle class. Their notoriety stems from their annual *Walpurgisnacht*, invariably written up with gusto in the papers.

In 1881, when one of these clubs accepted an invitation to move its rendezvous to a new café called Le Chat Noir (The Black Cat), the Parisian *café-artistique*, or cabaret, was born. Much has been written about the rowdy, blasphemous, and wonderfully imaginative evenings concocted by Rodolphe Salis, owner of Le Chat Noir. Much also has been written about his acute business sense—about the way he enticed poets, painters, and singers to perform gratis, using them to lure middle- and upper-class patrons in search of creativity and excitement.[12] While the majority of *cafés-concerts* were content to deliver the patriotic, sentimental, and moderately licentious ditties that so reassured the Third Republic, Le Chat Noir outlasted them all by insulting a masochistic clientele ready to play along.[13] Curiously, this cabaret became equally well-known for the shadow-play theater installed on its third floor. At the moment of the birth of the movies, more than a hundred people nightly were attending spectacular shadow plays lasting up to three hours and costing as much as 20,000 francs to produce. It was precisely this conjunction of disingenuously primitive spectacle and trenchant social satire that the October Group would revive with their politicized burlesques in the 1930s.

Le Chat Noir and its plentiful rivals in Montmartre maintained a countercultural tradition that assaulted middle-class values right up to the German invasion. Between the wars, its most notorious genius was Georgius (né Georges Guibourg), who managed to appeal both to a mainstream audience and to the anarchists and socialists who otherwise tended to scorn professional singing. Michel Leiris placed Georgius in a Rabelaisian lineage of atheistic comics who could always cut beneath their audiences' foundations.[14] And Robert Desnos remarked, "It is the infinitesimal margin of difference separating the excessive and the unacceptable that gives Georgius' performances all of their power of hilarity."[15] Eugène Dabit ridiculed Félix Mayol and Maurice Chevalier—the most famous music-hall stars of the day—for the inanity of their acts, but he praised Georgius for shocking audiences into questioning the nostalgia and simple-mindedness of this entertainment form. Dabit describes how Georgius, in the first half of his show, would re-create the comfortable and innocent tone of the *café-concert*'s hallowed era (before Dreyfus), only to wake up his audience with a second half loaded with biting and crude satire aimed at contemporary Paris.[16]

Although, broadly speaking, Georgius belonged to the same entertainment world as Chevalier, Mistinguett, Dranem, and the other stars whose names crop up each week in *Comoedia* or *Paris Music-Hall*, his irony cracks the veneer of good humor that live entertainment liberally applied to the tablet of middle-class values. In his songs and routines he evoked the lives of sailors, prostitutes, and petty gangsters, some of whom could be glimpsed by the clientele once they left his Montmartre cabaret. The Surrealists and the October Group adored this celebration of the underside of Paris, while Dabit gloated that his "rapid, modern, and very Parisian" satire did not require the audience to come prepared, as though this were the Ballets Russes.[17] The naturalness and spontaneity of the *caf'conc'* were meant to attract everyone. In Georgius' version it first attracted, then shocked them.

When the October Group (Jacques and Pierre Prévert, Marcel Duhamel, Max Morise, and others) came to stage their own satirical skits, in the years when the Popular Front was taking shape, they deployed a style that derived from Georgius' destructive form of vaudeville. The films these skits grew into—*L'Affaire est dans le sac* (1932), *Ciboulette* (1933), and *L'Hôtel du libre échange* (1934)—exemplify an acerbic conjunction of burlesque and radical politics, a mix of "Marx and the Marx Brothers," it was said. Flaunting their amateurism at a time when all forms of mass entertainment promised spectacle, these films went unappreciated by the larger public.

Overall, the street performer, the local *caf'conc'*, and the traveling vaudeville troupe swiftly lost popularity in the 1930s. Intellectuals may have been drawn to the quaint atmosphere of these popular forms, but fashion passed them by. Jacques Prévert would shift registers in the mid- to late 1930s, moving (like Georgius)[18] from the broad humor of his satirical farces to the darker poetic realist tone that brought him fame. "The *caf'conc'* disappeared in 1934. Tastes had changed. Those singers were too histrionic, like silent actors. The 1930s constitutes the capital turning point for French song, with the advent of radio and the talking film and with the influence of American jazz."[19]

In fact, it was less the cinema than the hugely successful music hall that broke the back of the *caf'conc'*. A contemporary journalist realized this right away: "The *caf'conc'* fell to the music hall because of the richness of the latter's mise-en-scène and the variety of its presentations. In Paris, there were well over a hundred *café-concerts* in 1886 but fewer than twenty in 1933."[20] Recent research makes the decline even more dramatic by putting the peak number at more than 250.[21] Indispensable though it was in the genesis of all forms of live entertainment in France, and attractive though it remains for anyone who likes to imagine a form that is at once humane and popular, the *caf'conc'* had lost its force by the time the Popular Front rolled through. Its best performers had gone over to the music hall; its audience now went to the movies, which in many cases had usurped its very premises. But since its overfed and spoiled rivals needed to draw on the subject matter it had pioneered, the *caf'conc'* was explicitly recognized as the incubator and nourisher of virtually every form of popular French entertainment up to the Second World War.

Some music halls like the Eldorado made sure to promote themselves as though they were merely large *cafés-concerts*. Founded in 1858 as a theater, and destined to become a movie palace in 1932, the Eldorado "maintained a legitimate café at its entrance. This was the first Parisian theater to become a large *caf'conc'*. In such places, especially in the cheap seats, you could smell bottles of wine being passed around, and sausages too, just as though it were a picnic ground at the Longchamp races."[22] Food, drink, and of course song were the essence of the *caf'conc'*, an essence that the music halls tried to retain no matter how large and impersonal they grew.

Yet spectacle, together with the technology that amplified and disseminated it, took popular culture out of the hands of the people. For the *caf'conc'* in its original conception can be said to have approached its audience seductively, by thrusting its ramped stage out among the tables, while the music hall seduced at a distance, using the artifices of light, the veils of costume, and above all the raised stage to excite its patrons with the unknown, and with an "image of presence" rather than presence itself.

Up to World War I, the *caf'conc'* and the music hall were allies. Did it matter that the Eldorado, despite its grandeur, called itself a *caf'conc'* while the Olympia, an establishment of the same proportions, was baptized a music hall when it opened its doors in 1893?[23] For that matter, the Moulin Rouge, soon to become more famous than either of these, started in 1887 as a dance hall. At all three, and at the scores of other pleasure halls of the *Belle Epoque*, people spent money eating and drinking, drawn by the songs, routines, and novelties, and occasionally by the chance to participate.

In his study of this period of entertainment, Charles Rearick attributes the stunning success of the huge and gaudy music halls to their policy of charging quite reasonable entrance fees. Moreover, compared to the hierarchized ticket structure of theater and opera, they "democratized" entertainment by leveling prices. As a contemporary journalist put it: "The public at a music hall should be treated as much as possible on an equal footing. That is to say, the series of seating areas should show as little differentiation as possible, and should not form separate spheres. Hence the fewest number of loges."[24] Since everyone, no matter what their means, could be counted on to eat and drink, the music halls thrived on crowds. The variegated diversions they provided not only on their stages but in their bars, in their sumptuous *promenoirs*, and in their foyers (unofficially sanctioned for prostitutes), made these places a hubbub of excitement.

Music halls bet on size over intimacy at just the moment when the increasing scale and impersonality of Paris could no longer be hidden. The construction of the Métro, for instance, dealt a blow to the autonomy and distinctiveness of Paris' *quartiers*. Then came the post–World War I tourist industry, which encouraged music halls to attract a well-heeled cosmopolitan audience, rather than to direct their shows at Parisians. Music halls vied to be listed in guides to the city; their notoriety for eroticism, particularly exploited at the Folies Bergère and the Casino de Paris, brought visitors from around the world who ate and drank in grand style. Obviously, the romantic period portrayed in Puccini's *La Bohème* had come to a close, and members of the Parisian avant-garde, which had so identified with Montmartre, were now ambivalent about its live entertainment. Excited by the explosive power of lower-class, physical spectacle, they were put off by any pandering to a supercilious and now international bourgeoisie. Many concluded that after World War I the candor and freshness of the French *chanson* had been commercialized beyond recognition.

Yet virtually all music-hall performers had begun on the smaller stage, and it was on these hundreds of stages that audiences had made known their tastes and weaknesses. Thus, the values and styles promoted in the songs and dances of the music hall had been pretested, so to speak. But something was different: "democratization" had given way to the "massification" of entertainment. The rapport between the Parisian music hall of the 1920s and the turn-of-the-century *caf'conc'* approximates that between the rationalized Hollywood studio system (a 1920s assembly line for the making and distribution of feature films) and the earlier "cinema of attractions," where variety was the rule both onscreen and in the wildcat business milieu of cinema's first two decades.[25]

An essential shift in the function rather than the content of entertainment is visible in the increased concern about the cumulative effect of "variety." As late as 1924 Pathé constructed the enormous Empire, complete with the most sophisticated machinery, a partly rounded stage, and even a circus top, so that it could hold every sort of act imaginable; and some postwar entrepreneurs enlarged the *caf'conc'* variety model to suit the grandeur of their music halls. Yet a new generation of producers stood ready to risk their fortunes in the *music-hall de grand spectacle*. Sequencing a dozen acts into a kind of narrative, they promised "to plunge the spectator into a vague stupor, an agreeable overwhelming intoxication."[26] By arranging for top-rated talent throughout, and by using the breaks between acts as an opportunity to display the hall's resources in music, lighting, and scenery, producers varied the elements in each sequence to deliver an accumulated effect, whereas at the *caf'conc'* and at the circus, multiple acts were offered so as to satisfy spectators intermittently. The professionalism of the increasingly well-organized music-hall evenings outclassed the Montmartre cafés and drew large audiences in search of a good value for their money. By 1930 the most important music-hall revues were offering those audiences thematically motivated proto-narratives with names like "The Sins of Paris" and "The Extravagant Queen." The "single overall effect" would be achieved in the extravagant *tableaux vivants* with which many revues concluded, freezing the audience in an otherworldly trance, the kind of trance more often thought to be the effect of the cinema.[27]

One indicative casualty of this aesthetic inflation was the "satirical revue," whose original significance didn't survive World War I. The revue had been conceived for the *caf'conc'* as a series of related scenes that satirized the events of the year: politics, scandals, and the like. But when the big houses adapted revues to the large stage, topicality lost out to general sentiment. Instead of introducing subjects of common concern, to initiate at least the pretense of a dialogue with the public, performers had to keep spectators enthralled, rendering them mute. Not that the public complained. Indeed, during the 1920s they opted for the music hall of grand spectacle over that of variety. The *chanson* was submerged beneath the splendor of its setting.

But worse days were in store for the traditional *chanson*, as a 1933 elegy to the *caf'conc'* ruefully declares: "Sites of song gave way to sites of images, until the images learned to sing as well. Still, one can't help lamenting the end of an era in which music and the human voice were not disfigured by loudspeakers. And in stark contrast to those bothersome distractions [movies] invented by the peculiar genius of the fancy-free Americans, one can still prefer another form of gaiety, forever French: *la chanson*."[28]

Usurping the very venues and materials of musical theater, the cinema began competing for top personnel once sound arrived in 1929. One has to wonder how much the music hall learned from the even more prodigious success of the cinema. Until 1928 both forms could work to enthrall their huge audiences, using different methods. But with the introduction of sound, the cinema suddenly became a direct rival to the music hall at just the moment when the latter was attaining mastery of its form. Clearly these forms shared business concerns: they both engaged stars, maintained large theaters, rotated programs, provided food concessions, and deployed a panoply of advertising techniques. Meanwhile, the *caf'conc'* and the circus failed to develop in line with modern business practices. Modeled as they most often were on the personal charisma of their directors, only a few of these could coexist with the immense publicity machinery of mass entertainment. This was particularly true of circuses, whose performers and management formed an integrated unit—often a family—as opposed to the rapidly changing slate of acts and actors put before the public at the big music halls or in the cinema.

The gradual diminution of ribald comedy at the music hall is another indication of its drift toward unified entertainment and, some would say, toward the cinema. Clowns fared badly on the stage, their irreverence, parody, and spontaneity being far more suitable to the discontinuous and decentered experience offered by the circus. But standup comedians were integral to the *caf'conc'* and to the variety form of the music hall. As the grand spectacle outdistanced the variety show at the larger music halls, comedy had to soften itself and work within the limits of the evening's overall theme. In stressing

52. Visirova: luxury and
sensuality at the Folies-
Bergère (1935).

atmosphere, sensuality, luxury, and entrancement, the music hall found dis-
ruptive comedy difficult to integrate.

Dancing girls, in contrast, became central to displays of luxury and sensuality. In addition to masking transitions between acts, a new breed of chorus
lines and dance troupes worked with choreographers to motivate their routines according to the themes and tales of the revues. From the advertising,
one would guess that most of these routines managed to show the girls partly
disrobed. While semi-nudity had long been an attraction of Parisian cafés,
cabarets, and music halls, the level of nudity—its art and daring—increased in
the 1920s and particularly after 1927.

The developing sophistication of the music hall during the twenties, and
then its panic in the face of cinema in the thirties, can be tracked concurrently
in the magazines and newspapers that covered entertainment. For instance,
in the first years after *Paris Music-Hall* was launched in 1920, this weekly provided not only advertising and standard gossip, but sophisticated features
about the aesthetics and sociology of live and mass entertainment, including a
knowledgeable column that kept abreast of the culturally significant films in
Paris. Early on, for example, it ran a piece praising the subjective camera
techniques in Marcel L'Herbier's *Eldorado;* a later column enumerates stylistic possibilities that were cinema-specific, cautioning music-hall producers

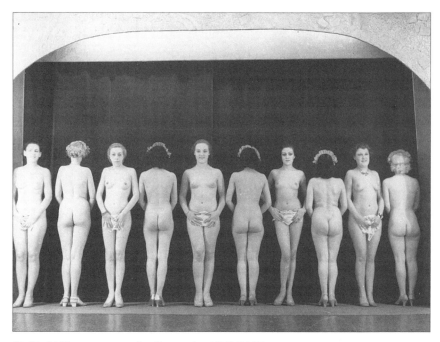

53. Forbidden on screen, but live at the ABC (1937).

against trying to aim at such psychological "impressions." In 1925 a front-page column predicted, with only slight regret, the victory of cinema as the popular art of the future. "One must learn to respect the cinema, which has become virtually a religion."[29] For the editors of *Paris Music-Hall*, this meant that the two media should share exhibition space, talent, and popular subjects. The music hall for a time could count itself indispensable because it presented what the cinema could not: the human voice talking and singing. Up to 1927, then, the journal included reflections on the cultural and aesthetic impact of popular entertainment, goading it on to newer, higher ambitions.

This focus changed drastically in 1928. The cinema column was reduced and the gossip expanded. More apparent, however—apparent on every cover and throughout the interior—was the journal's display of the beautiful girls of the stage. By 1930 *Paris Music-Hall* had blatantly succumbed to visual pornography. Other reports of the time confirm that this was more than an isolated publishing strategy, and that music halls, in their competition with the sound cinema, were striving to offer what the screen was forbidden to show.

At the better halls, the nude dancers were "artistically" incorporated into the show—for example, as the embodiment of a "South Seas" or "African" motif. Nudity of body fit in well with what one might call nudity of soul, the music hall's notorious sentimentality. "Sentimentality is one of the bases of the music hall. Everyone comes to weep, whether they be adolescent boys or old men seeking to recapture lost memories. The music hall is full of magnificent and unabashed dreams."[30]

Unabashed, indeed. The music hall promised to provide whatever might arouse the spectator's senses or feelings. With only moderate accommodations to decency and taste, nudity of one form or another was what this industry sold—along with wine, beer, and tobacco, of course. It shouldn't surprise us, then, that libraries today refuse to lend out (and few archives preserve) scenarios of music-hall programs, for no matter how thematically unified these programs may have been, the texts (lyrics, scores, monologues) were never more than pretexts for sensual stimulation. Opera and theater, on the other hand, can point, perhaps pretentiously, to the dramatic texts and scores that outlast any given performance or audience. The event that transpires on the other side of the footlights is meaningful with or without the spectator, a ritual between actors, singers, and significant texts. In the music hall, meaning resides solely in effect, so that properly speaking it is the audience, not the text or program, that is being played.

These aesthetic factors led quickly to sociological consequences. Novelist and future screenwriter Pierre Bost was certain that "the music hall succeeds because its songs, though horridly sentimental, appeal to those who are unfamiliar with their own passions and who therefore fall prey to such sentiments. Either they are manipulated without knowing it (uneducated reaction) or they enjoy the manipulation while being fully aware of it (effete reaction)."[31] Bost's judgment may seem irredeemably elitist, but his allegiance, we soon learn, is not with the higher arts of theater and opera, but with the much-maligned circus. At the circus, one watches feats and displays that stand out unprotected in the 360-degree ring. Talent rather than mystique draws the attention and admiration of even the least-educated viewer: "Much music-hall performance seems such a falling away from the frankness of the circus. Huge spectacles appealing to eye and ear have been represented, including storm-tossed ships and raging forest fires. Luxurious costumes aim to satisfy spectators paying to enter these pavilions of luxury."[32]

Whether one denigrates or applauds this kind of appeal to eye and ear, it is easy to see why the editors of *Paris Music-Hall* should proclaim the sound cinema and the music hall close kin in the entertainment world (much closer than they are to their distant cousin, the theater, about which, we are told, one hears far more than it deserves).[33] One commentator preferred to see the relation as filial: "The cinema, insofar as it is a spectacle, could exist only because the music hall existed and flourished. For the cinema creates nothing itself but requires a preexisting reality, even a fictional one, to make an image of. This reality it very often finds at the music hall. Thus, the music hall is the basis for, and works together with, the cinema. . . . So why should the cinema want to kill the music hall?"[34] Offering, rather pathetically, this strategy of mutual support, the music hall did make use of cinema, while inevitably succumbing to it.[35]

A graph in *La Cinématographie Française* charting the fate of various "spectacles" in Paris from 1926 to 1936 shows the cinema overtaking all competitors, especially the music hall. In 1926 their receipts were nearly equal, whereas a decade later the cinema was taking in eight times as much money as the music hall (and five times as much as the boulevard theater). Most of the damage was done in the years 1930 to 1933, as might be expected. And "damage" is the proper word, for counter to what the live entertainment industry had hoped, and counter to what some historians have suggested, the sound cinema did not attract a significantly new audience. It seems to have drawn its revenue straight from the coffers of theater and music hall. In fact, the amount of money spent on these three forms of spectacle decreased slightly over the entire decade, making cinema's 150 percent growth factor even more devastating to its rivals.[36]

The situation in Paris hardly differed from what was occurring in London, Berlin, and New York. Everywhere, the cinema was colonizing the audiences and the venues formerly ruled by the theater and music hall. Individual performers tended to benefit from this, as did the state, especially in France, which taxed cinemas far more heavily than it did other spectacles.[37] But the public, many believed, lost out. Gone were the *cafés-concerts*. Gone also were the circuses, which drifted completely off the bottom of the graph around 1934. As for theaters of various sorts, their number and variety declined. What remained of the music hall were a few magisterial sites—the Folies Bergère and the Alhambra, chief among them—playing to increasingly touristic and well-heeled audiences. The cinema had indeed become Paris' one truly popular art.

Allegories of Entertainment

After seventy years, Renoir's film *Le Crime de Monsieur Lange* remains in focus as an extraordinarily telling picture of the sociocultural struggles of the Popular Front period. Featuring urban laborers in their fight against exploitation and corruption, this film contrives the solution of its social drama by invoking the power of popular art itself. For the central event of its plot—the overthrow of the immoral manager of a publishing house by a workers' cooperative—is, in the film, modeled on the exploits of a fictional hero named "Arizona Jim," a legendary cowboy whose exploits, appearing serially and read by throngs in Paris, brings the enterprise out of bankruptcy.

Because of the lightness of Jacques Prévert's script, the serious political issues that this film raises (issues about the legitimate use of violence, including assassination, in the formation of a just society) bubble up in laughter. The film's hero is a would-be writer whose imagination sets aflame the imaginations of his *confrères* at the publishing house and soon the imaginations of a whole class of society—the workers of Paris, who each week await the next installment of Arizona Jim's adventures. Through the deepening awareness of Amédée Lange, the *feuilleton*'s creator, art and life converge in a directly political act: his shooting of the corrupt manager, Batala, representative of the ruling class. Thus, everyday life is mythologized through fiction until fiction provides the model for politics. *Le Crime de Monsieur Lange*, as unpretentious and effective as its hero, deserves to be seen at the front of the Popular Front, the movement whose official program was published just days before the film premièred in January 1936.[38] Yet its own popularity was slight. On its first run it played only a few weeks, received limited critical attention, and disappeared from the screen before the Popular Front slate acceded to power in June. Renoir did receive the first Prix Louis Delluc, in 1936, but he was awarded the prize for *Les Bas Fonds*, not for *Le Crime de Monsieur Lange*, whose political clairvoyance and artistic ingenuity evidently hold more appeal for us than for the people it was meant to inspire.

Also premiering in 1936 was Christian-Jaque's *Rigolboche*, whose star, Mistinguett, commanded genuine as opposed to represented or imagined popularity. The opposite of *Le Crime de Monsieur Lange* in technique and ideology, *Rigolboche* likewise concerns an exploited natural artist who becomes famous and who is pursued for a crime. Jules Berry plays nearly identical roles in both films. In *Rigolboche* he incarnates a cardsharp named "Mr. Bobby," us-

54. Pulp fiction as political allegory.

ing the same inimitable hand gestures, practiced improvisation, and uncon-
cealed cunning that gave such verve to his portrayal of the magnificently impeccable swindler Batala. In each film, that cunning snares an unsuspecting
innocent. In Renoir's film, it is Amédée Lange, who is but a closet novelist
until Batala gives him a chance; in Christian-Jaque's, it is the naive cabaret
singer just arrived from Dakar, to whom Mr. Bobby gives the antique name
"Rigolboche." Managing their careers, the characters played by Jules Berry
use the grateful artists as shields to protect themselves from the irate victims
of their failed scams.

In what must have appeared as references to Stavisky and the scandals of
1934, the Berry characters duck out of Paris because of their financial mis-
dealing and illegality. In Renoir's film, the scoundrel's disappearance is balanced by Lange's rising fame as author; similarly, the character Rigolboche
moves progressively up in the nightclub world until she owns a major music
hall, just as Lange's serial magazine stories underwrite the publishing house
that prints them. Thus, these popular artists jettison their managers and take

over the means of production.[39] Ultimately, Mr. Bobby and his pals are edged to the side of an enterprise that has outgrown them, and Batala, in trying to reclaim command of the cooperative, is dropped by Lange's bullet amid the garbage cans of his building's courtyard.

Despite the similarities in their personal charm, Berry's Batala and his Mr. Bobby are quite distinct morally. Because Renoir and Prévert provide no authority figure able to sort out the authentic from the sham, Batala's charm, delightful as it may be, proves genuinely dangerous, indeed evil. Against his wiles and power, the people must become their own saviors. They do so, first, by banding together and, second, by risking a necessary act of violence. In *Rigolboche*, the police, a detective, and a powerful count (as well as midlevel cabaret managers) keep Mr. Bobby in check and ultimately form an umbrella over Rigolboche herself, even though for a time she must live in hiding. Thus, Mr. Bobby's efforts can be appreciated as those of an attractive but ultimately harmless, even pathetic seducer. Working the system from many angles—including shady ones—he seems a savvy big brother to Rigolboche, rather than her evil seducer.

Unlike Lange, Rigolboche cannot really protect herself; she would be ruined financially were it not for her adoring count, the man who ultimately buys her the music hall that crowns her success. The count plays a role seemingly analogous to that of the daft publishing-house magnate in *Le Crime de Monsieur Lange*—a benevolent capitalist who, after Batala jumps ship, renounces his authority and agrees magnanimously to the adventurous idea of a workers' cooperative. But the count renounces nothing, ultimately laying claim to Rigolboche, bringing her through marriage into the social system where his class reigns. In Renoir's film, Lange's fate is determined by his peers, a hastily constituted jury of locals at the border café who can aid or prevent his escape. Urban society is the new Wild West, where violence is required and where justice belongs to the people. A lone ranger, Lange understands that he must retire from the fledgling community which he has audaciously protected with his gun and which must now govern itself.

Rigolboche, on the other hand, knows nothing about community. A survivor, she is at the mercy of forces beneath her (a blackmailer from Dakar) and above her (the count). Her success depends upon her winning ways, her smile, and her goodness of heart. Even if she is exploited by Mr. Bobby and others, guilelessness protects her. The contagious spirit of song, of singing itself, ultimately extricates her from the traps that in Paris are too numerous to

55. *Monsieur Lange* and the triumph of the cooperative.

avoid. Taken under the wing of smitten older men, Rigolboche treads unfal-
teringly up the ramp from club to cabaret to magnificent music hall, a ramp
of money and power. But she treads alone, without community, and in the
final shot she has reason to smile broadly as she gazes at a huge billboard displaying her own smiling face.

Compared to the vibrant courtyard that Amédée Lange shares with laun-
dresses, workers, and an old concierge, a courtyard that no amount of financial success can make him abandon, *Rigolboche* presents a social climber's fantasy of rugged individualism.

Anyone looking at the French cinema of 1936 and hoping to find either aesthetic or political sophistication should be discouraged by the relative success
of *Rigolboche* over *Le Crime de Monsieur Lange*. Evidently, the people (or at
least most people) prefer the puerile dream of rising to the top of a system
that Prévert and Renoir had dreamed of reshaping altogether. In fact, the
comparison shows something more symptomatic: the triumph of a music-hall

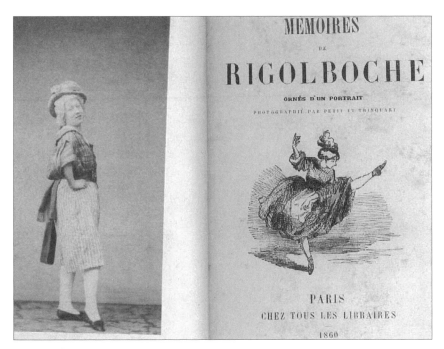

56. Frontispiece and title page of an authentic source.

57. The music hall's lineage: Lina Bourget (a.k.a. Mistinguett) rebaptized as Rigolboche in Christian-Jaque's 1936 feature.

aesthetic that could hardly promote any but conservative values. Not only does *Rigolboche* concern a singing star (whereas Amédée Lange scribbles pulp fiction), but its title character is played by unquestionably the most famous music-hall performer of the era—Mistinguett—in her only sound-film role.

An imaginary autobiography, *Rigolboche* asks us to accept Mistinguett (whom Colette called a "national treasure") as a reincarnation of one of France's original rags-to-riches entertainers. At the same time, the over-whelmingly sumptuous décor and intricate technological precision of the music-hall sequence that concludes the film asks to be taken as the natural celebration of the expressive human voice, a voice that might be heard in the street or singing a lullaby behind a curtained window.

Thus, the film is reactionary in justifying power through an appeal to "natural origins." Those origins lie in the title of the film, *Rigolboche*, a name that the eponymous heroine promises never to relinquish even after her mar-riage to a count. But in fact it's not her name at all, for Mistinguett's character is baptized Rigolboche when, pressed by a nightclub owner to promote his "discovery," Mr. Bobby scans the walls of the room and lights on an antique poster that says "Rigolboche." The name remains a rich but unexploited allu-sion. The original singer Rigolboche had been a beggar named Marguerite Badel. In 1841 she found her way onto the stage of the Chartreuse, later to become the Closerie des Lilas. This coffeehouse, according to a contempo-rary report by Théodore de Banville, "allowed onstage whoever wanted to sing or recite, especially students who felt they had musical or poetic genius. They would execute their compositions to great effect before a crowd recep-tive to free-spirited and instinctive performances. I heard things there that were amusing and of an unusual and bizarre originality."[40] The most remark-able thing de Banville heard there was Rigolboche before she gained her fame. Hardly beautiful, indeed thin and pale, she spent her days in an attic darning the castoff clothes she had gathered. "In the evening, having ob-tained with her fairy's needle something resembling the appearance of a dress, she sang at the Chartreuse! She hadn't been trained in composition or verse, but she understood both instinctively, and her couplets often had the ingenious and primitive grace of popular songs."[41]

Thus, Jeanne Bourgeois, the flesh-and-blood girl who became Mistin-guett, adopts in this film the name and role of an earlier singer with authentic popular origins and appeal. Yet Mistinguett was known not for rags magically stitched together but for splendid costumes of feathers and jewels weighing kilos. In this film, such sumptuousness is represented as the amplification of a natural style visible in the character's humble origins and private lullabies.

The spectacular career of Mistinguett summarizes that of the music hall itself. She made her debut in 1885 at the age of twelve, blossoming at the Eldorado in the first years of the twentieth century, performing regularly at the Folies Bergère during the heyday of the medium, and continuing to appear onstage even after World War II. From 1910 to 1940, she was unquestionably France's dominant performing artist. A host of younger stars, from Maurice Chevalier in 1912 to Fernandel (né Fernand Contandin) in 1933, would be fortunate enough to trail behind her into the spotlight. One virtually needed her blessing in order to succeed.

Mistinguett was destined to run up against the cinema. A woman of extraordinary presence whose personal vibrancy counted far more toward her success than her mediocre voice and dancing, more even than her fabled legs and costumes, she was bound to be attracted to the silent cinema. In fact, she played in nearly a dozen silents, which she treated as a lucrative respite from her live acts. But sound film troubled her deeply, as it did the entertainment form of which she was the queen. For here a recording would replace her most prized quality, her "presence." In 1932, when her colleague Georges Tabet began making records, she felt disappointed, certain that the spontaneity of his performance would be lost.[42] She understood instinctively that her own success depended on the way she could measure and play an audience, seducing them each night anew. But the camera and the microphone refused to respond, and so she refused them, at least until 1936 and *Rigolboche*.

For her sound-film première, Mistinguett demanded a script in which cinema could show off the particular possibilities of music hall. She insisted that the story allow her to change station (and costume) over and over; this way, audiences could ride with her from poverty and anonymity to the heights of wealth and glory. She called for a melodrama in which she could be both a doting mother and a seductive woman of the cabarets. Naturally, her shifts in fortune would be marked by the mise-en-scène of the production numbers, which were the true reason for the film in the first place. For three weeks she worked closely with Christian-Jaque, until she was satisfied that the film would overwhelm neither her nor the music-hall world that was its subject.

The moral superiority she exerts as Rigolboche comes from her status as a

58–59. *Rigolboche*: a mother's lullaby (top) seals a star's connection to her mass audience.

60. Posing for *Arizona Jim:* the visual culture of democracy.

61. Florelle, as the self-assured Valentine, flirts with Lange.

devoted though indigent mother alone in Paris with a young son. Her tender lullaby to him guarantees the authenticity of song as the medium of pure communication, and it establishes the family as the natural source of its outpouring. Mistinguett—we, the audience, may now go on to believe—cares about us, tucks us into our seats in the movie theater, as she performs at the nightclub and finally on the ornate staircase of the music hall she owns.

Le Crime de Monsieur Lange puts this fairy tale of rugged individualism in perspective. When his writing attains the summit of popularity, Amédée Lange can think of no better enterprise than to make a movie version of "Arizona Jim," effectively bringing his public (hordes of readers are shown storming the magazine vendor) to the medium that we, the true public, have already chosen: the cinema. Unlike the histrionic Rigolboche, whose art is her self-display, Lange hides behind his words and seems more concerned with the society of his courtyard than with himself or his future. In fact, he has no domestic life whatever in the proper sense of the term, though he ultimately accepts the affection of Valentine, the tough-minded owner of the laundry who once had an affair with Batala. In a bit of casting that deepens the opposition between the two films, Valentine is played by Odette Florelle, a singer who moved from the *caf'conc'* to the music hall after World War I, replacing Mistinguett at the Casino de Paris and Moulin Rouge in 1928. Her one song in the film, "Au jour le jour" (From Day to Day), written by Jacques Prévert and Joseph Kosma, tells of the hard urban life of a woman of the world. Florelle belongs to everyone because she belongs first to herself. In contrast, Mistinguett gives her song to everyone because she has sung it first to her child. Florelle's sexuality is as open as the windows that unite the spaces of the courtyard, whereas Mistinguett's is hidden in a secret past in the colonies, and in the little house where she raises her child and retains her privacy.

Opening in the same year, these two films vividly contrast social and aesthetic values, yet both indicate how all media (including live performance, cinema, radio, journalism, and pulp fiction) maintained a fertile collaboration by incorporating references to one another in the ample circus ring of French entertainment. French cinema could claim a patriotic rapport with its dramatic and novelistic intertexts: it deployed them to counter Hollywood's international reach. In addition, sound cinema brought the studios a great deal of work in the early years of the Depression, employing French actors and technicians, if only for voice dubbing. The healthy jump in the number of French films produced—from 59 to 150 films annually over the course of the first four years of sound—exhausted the supply of experienced film personnel, inviting those from other media and arts to come to cinema's aid.

And so the cinema worked (or pretended to work) in tandem with its putative rival, the music hall. After the defection of a large segment of the public from live performance to cinema in the first years of sound (Paris nearly doubled its number of cinemas in the years 1928–1935), a stable bourgeois clientele allowed the boulevard theaters and the (now far fewer) music halls to function at capacity right up to World War II. An effect of audience "accumulation" benefited both cinema and theater.[43] This helps to explain the generally conservative, even regressive aesthetic of French films in the 1930s—an aesthetic based on a limited number of actors famous also for their live appearances. Performance values held sway over every other concern; French audiences were attuned to acting, including song and dance, more than to story and certainly more than to "cinematic" values like camerawork and editing. Thus, French cinema was in the business of adapting entertainment by reshaping popular forms. And so, *Rigolboche* is far more representative than *Le Crime de Monsieur Lange*, if only because it more forthrightly squeezes the sentiments of the day into the genres that were best loved: melodrama and the musical.

Yet Mistinguett had been a vocal opponent of cinema. Looking past the agreeable face of "popular entertainment" (epitomized in her famous smile), we can observe a frantic search for secure footing, a search that involved serious infighting among the arts.[44] The so-called system of entertainment maintained itself as a network of counterbalanced forces pushing against one another, competition among media and texts being the norm. Through the filter of economics, the amiable *Rigolboche* takes on a strategic demeanor. Contemporary interviews with Mistinguett do not reveal why it was that she turned at last to movies in 1936. By then, the reign of sound cinema had been recognized and entertainers of all sorts had adjusted to that fact. Perhaps this aging star (Mistinguett was in her sixties) had scrutinized the reviews of her sumptuous return to the Folies Bergère in 1935. They hailed her performance as remarkable "for her age" but no longer magical. Mistinguett also watched her most recent partner, Fernandel, gain fame onscreen before moving to the Folies Bergère, while her current rival for popularity, Josephine Baker, had just expanded her reputation and her wealth in *Zou Zou* (1934) and *Princess Tam Tam* (1935).[45]

In this debilitating war between forms of entertainment, Mistinguett deployed *Rigolboche* as a Trojan horse. She could appear to capitulate to an overconfident cinema industry that had no qualms about serving up ersatz music-hall fare. But Mistinguett meant to emerge from this film to grab movie audiences through her alluring performance and draw them to defect to live entertainment. She didn't require much of an opening. The "Chantez" number sung early in *Rigolboche* makes this plain. There, under the eye of Mr. Bobby and the *caf'conc'* owner, she seduces a cynical audience into singing along. How could the cinema spectator resist her? After all, dazzled by the fabled smile that her carefully designed costumes so perfectly set off, she had often conquered audiences at immense distances in music halls seating 3,000; somehow, each seat was within range of her charisma. At the high point of her routine, she could rouse the crowd into sharing her song—a duet performed with thousands of partners.

A rhetoric of "intimacy" and "contact" has always fashioned the manner in which theatrical personalities speak of themselves as performers. Actors tell of experiencing a different feeling with each successive audience during the run of a stage play. Dancers and singers go further, since it is their very persons (their voices and bodies) that constitute the site of attention, rather than a drama played through them. Over and over, music-hall singers decried the impersonality of the cinema. Just a year before *Rigolboche*, Maurice Chevalier declared that performing live was "the best *métier* in the world" because it provided true contact with the public, contact he never felt before the camera.[46]

Of course, what Chevalier truly craved was the public's love cascading down on him from the balcony, a love he soon learned to exchange for the cascading money that film producers were ready to shower on him. After all, in entertainment, money serves as the best measure of popularity. If Chevalier felt the need to return from time to time to the music hall, it may have been to reconfirm this abstract relation, like a miser who must tally his worth by running real currency through his hands or, better, touching the gold such currency and calculations represent. Stars like Chevalier were the public's point of personal contact with an entertainment industry. Just as Mistinguett advertised the music hall in *Rigolboche*, so Georges Milton's revue at the Alhambra Theater in 1936 consisted of a run of sketches pulled from his hit film comedies. Those privileged enough to be there in person could see, hear, and nearly touch Georges Milton himself, not his image. Thus, music hall anchored the cinema.

More often, music-hall fare celebrated the idea of live entertainment. A typical revue, which premièred at the Alhambra in September 1935, was titled *Boîtes de Nuits* (Nightclubs). It featured four separate nightclubs, including the "Collegiate American Bar," each illustrating the social need for places where individuals could gather, drawn by the lights, the people, and the food and drink. The act integrated all these sensations into an overriding musical rhythm that became slightly demonic. The music hall here represented itself as satisfying a universal need for community, conviviality, and partially controlled emotional release.[47] In its advertising, the Alhambra followed other music halls by touting both its opulence (color, live music, formidable acts) and its hominess. The Alhambra proudly announced that its beverage service would make you think you were at your corner café. It even promised to have you paged in case your babysitter or business partner phoned. Such attention one could never find at the cinema, impersonal site of lonely viewers hypnotized by the cold images of stars.

Survival of the Fittest

The music hall was obliged to purvey extraordinary entertainment in an atmosphere comfortable and familiar enough to make its middle-class patrons feel at home. As the decade wore on, public relations targeted wealthier and more cultured patrons. *Music-Hall* magazine ran interviews with high-art figures whose testimonials praised their close contact with live audiences. Its issue for November 22, 1935, featured a cover picture of opera diva Yvonne Gall in her role as Marguerite from Gounod's *Faust*. Inside, Gall declared her love for the atmosphere of the music hall. She eventually showed up on an Alhambra program in January 1937. Similarly, Edna Covey described how her earnest study of ballet was redirected when she accidentally fell during a performance, causing a roar of laughter. She so liked the experience that she began to bring dance parody to a large public. The Alhambra's most daring high-art attraction, though, was surely Maurice Rostand, the popular versifier, son of playwright Edmond Rostand and the poet and playwright Rosemonde Gérard, "whose spirits and genius are united in him, giving life to this poet who thinks in alexandrines, dreams in sonnets, and expresses himself in hemistichs. He sings of grand ideas for people who hope for a better future." And so the music hall recruited the arts to uplift its audience and to attract new devotees from the educated classes, justifying increased ticket prices. As for personalities from the movies, many worked at music halls between jobs.

Le Music-Hall ran features about Chevalier, Noël-Noël, and others. It was particularly attentive to Albert Préjean, since he had begun his career in the music hall and at one point was shooting a film at the Alhambra in the morning while playing there live at night.

Though any art promotes itself in as many ways as possible, these examples show that the music hall exerted appeal both up and down the social scale. It considered itself lodged somewhere between live theater (at the high end of culture) and cinema (the low end). Costing ten to twenty-five francs for seats (depending on their location) at a time when a movie cost five,[48] an evening at a music hall was within reach of a sizable percentage of Parisians. Of course, one was then tempted with food and drink, crucial to the self-definition and financial success of the institution. Theatergoers, accustomed to spending 50 francs a ticket, found the music hall a bargain and could splurge on refreshments.

With so many venues converted to movie theaters and so many stars gone over to the screen, the music hall was unsure how to retain its faithful followers. In an all out barrage, it tried to attract both those in search of the exotic (via acts and dancers) and those looking for a comfortable evening in a familiar and personal setting. This latter impulse accounts for the music hall's increasing reliance on nostalgia, always a sign of the illness of a form as it rummages in its past glories for reasons people might want to attend.

In the case of the music hall, those reasons and that glory rested on the myth that live performance was equivalent to local and personal values, as opposed to the international and homogenized appeal of the cinema on one side and high art on the other. Here the music hall was apt to fall back on its evolution from the *caf'conc'* and the *café-chantant*, where performers would sit down with patrons and simply come onstage to take a turn. No matter what claims it made, the music hall could only fabricate this homey atmosphere as one of its many illusions. For as we have seen, the economics of entertainment were transformed after World War I. This was the era of the cigar-smoking entrepreneur, whether film producer or music-hall manager. Such men cut deals with stars (or rather, with their agents), arranged tours, redecorated their buildings to follow or start a fad, and so on. While each house would become known for one or another of its attractions (the Folies Bergère for its chorus line, the Hippodrome for its variety acts, the Eldorado for its *tour de chant*, the ABC for its risqué acts), all depended on novelty and increasingly on size to outdo one another and outdo competing forms.

In what amounted to an entertainment war, the first casualties were those promoting a traditional ethos. The music hall survived the *caf'conc'* because its scale and business methods were commensurate with those of the cinema. For the same reasons, it overtook the circus, which had consistently attracted larger audiences well into the 1920s. The circus was old-fashioned in both its institutional structure and in its fare; it was bound to fall. Before the Depression, circuses were organized and advertised as family enterprises. Seldom did a key performer dominate the ensemble. More rarely did any performer flit from circus to circus in search of more money or a better position on the program. The circus was truly a concerted form, symbolized best by the concept of multiple rings, which came into vogue at just this time. It is impossible to imagine Mistinguett or Maurice Chevalier strutting before an audience whose eyes were being encouraged to flit to other sites of attention. The music hall thrived on "staging" such individual stars, even if this meant (as it soon came to mean) changing programs every other week. In the coordinated family ring of the circus, however, programs changed far less often. Yet spectators returned, to be thrilled by the prodigious acts of a consistent group of performers.

The image of the circus ring also helps us to recognize how the circus differed from, and ultimately lost out to, the music hall. Central to the former are clowns and animal pageantry, while the music hall found its soul in the *tour de chant*. Although the music hall engaged numerous acrobats and jugglers, interest in clowns and animals was severed by the proscenium separating audience and performer. The circus dares to present itself in the round, exposing whatever artifice it relies upon. Clowns cavort about in the ellipse of the arena and occasionally climb into the seats. Performers sometimes assist in rigging their own equipment. Everything remains in view.

The music hall masks its performers behind curtains so as to present them dramatically or mysteriously. A hidden technology of lighting, décor, and music assists the performers from a world beyond, and suffuses the spectator in an ambience of the marvelous. In many respects the kind of Brechtian devices advocated by post-1968 film theorists (devices that break the illusions cinema has always traded on), invoke the aesthetics of the circus, including multiple sites of action, visible technology, direct solicitation (by clowns and ringmasters), and communal rather than individual appeal. In the circus the audience looks at itself across a ring that becomes a space of community valor, parody, or ritual.

In Europe, the modern circus developed from the Renaissance fair, and, in France, specifically from the traditional fairground attractions known as *la fête foraine*. Performers emerged from the community they entertained; for its part, the audience participated by walking through the fair. Pierre Bost stressed just this in his clairvoyant 1930 monograph *Le Cirque et le music-hall*.[49] He regrets the defection of the circus public to the music hall (and implicitly to the cinema) not out of nostalgia but because of the loss of authenticity in entertainment. Whereas in the cinema or on the music-hall stage, the acrobat defies us with miraculous wizardry and cultivates an image of escape from our everyday world, circus acrobats relate casually to those they entertain, almost like neighbors. We cheer them to greater feats as a way of congratulating ourselves on what the human body is capable of.

Effectively, circus performers play frankly right in our midst, counting on our friendliness and indulgence. Such an open ambience attracts families to the circus, just as fairs do. Children are welcome, to be impressed by what the world has to offer: feats and freaks, and animals brought from afar. One might venture to say that the circus depends on its virile presentation (on prowess and broad humor), whereas the nude or erotically clad female serves as the central lure of the music hall. This lure is enhanced by décor designed to excite and seduce through its mystery.

In fact, we have seen that the music hall was promiscuous in its appeal, testing out every conceivable sort of act. Crude comedians would alternate with torch singers; flamboyant bicyclists would follow exotic dancers draped in chiffon. Nevertheless, as Bost so clearly understood, the music hall, despite its historical link to the *caf'conc'* and its recruitment of selected circus material, had thrown in its lot with modern practices of entertainment, practices the cinema knew best how to exploit. In the 1920s one music hall advertised a spectacular South Seas theme, established through music, songs, story, and décor, culminating in an exotic dance with nude or topless girls.[50] And so, spectacle may have given the music hall its years of glory around World War I, but spectacle, especially bolstered by narrative, was the genius of sound cinema. And as it felt itself losing ground, the music hall thought to trump cinema with something it alone could provide: nostalgia for intimate contact.[51]

The bad faith of an industry's appeal to authentic entertainment brings *Rigolboche* back for a final appearance. The blatant fabrications of *Rigolboche*—a spectacle about the values of intimacy and a hymn to the future of nostalgia—epitomize the conflicted entertainment complex that existed throughout the

Third Republic. In each of the four numbers carefully punctuating the plot of this movie, Mistinguett gives value to personal and social experience simply by putting such experience into song. Isolation, exploitation, and tragedy find their fulfillment and justification when they become the subject of the music hall, and especially when they are presented in the form of song by a star before a worldwide audience. The sins of society, including the small privations of daily life, are thus expiated on stage by a heroine whose fitness for her role is registered by the distance she has put between herself and her audience, through her exceptional success and wealth. No wonder Mistinguett celebrates the act of singing so jauntily and with such sincerity; song has literally transformed her life into glitter. There is no "outside" once the music hall has grown to the size of the egos of its producers and performers. Rather, the audience is invited inside to partake of their glory.

Florelle sings otherwise in *Le Crime de Monsieur Lange*. With only Amédée Lange to listen, and us to overhear, she invokes the "outside" of the streets of Paris:

> Boulevard de la Chapelle, where the Métro soars by,
> There are some pretty girls and boys who aren't shy,
> Starving bums soak up canned heat
> And dolls at sixty-five
> Still walk the street.
> Day to day,
> Night to night,
> Under the stars—
> That's how it is.
> But where are the stars?
> I've never seen them,
> Though I roam forgotten streets at night,
> Day after day,
> Night after night,
> Under the stars—
> That's how I live.
> And never a lucky star—
> That's how I live.

This *chanson réaliste* returns to a guttural style of singing which had dominated the *cafés-concerts* of the nineteenth century but which, with a few exceptions, was definitely out of favor at music halls in the sophisticated 1930s.[52]

Those exceptions include Damia, Fréhel, and a rising phenomenon named Edith Piaf. While a great many French films of the 1930s incorporated popular song into their dramas, the specifically tawdry quality of the *chanson réaliste* makes it an index to the ideological difference of the most important style of film of the decade, poetic realism—the style Jacques Prévert is credited with founding.

The appearance of such a song at the very center of *Le Crime de Monsieur Lange* evokes the milieu of the small cafés where such songs originated and the shady milieu about which its lyrics invariably spoke. Damia sings a similar song in Duvivier's *La Tête d'un homme* (1932) and Fréhel sings like this in several of the half-dozen key films in which she played a part, *Pépé le Moko* (1936) being the most famous. In the complex ecology of textual borrowings and influences, we find the cinema propelled forward stylistically by songs that were out of fashion if heard at a music hall. Paradoxically, the music hall appealed to nostalgia for an older form of entertainment, yet excluded sentimental songs like these because they made so little use of elaborate mise-en-scène. The cinema—at least that portion of it known as naturalist, realist, or poetic realist—eagerly indulged such sentiment, coming in for close-ups of pathetic faces, spreading feeling across the screen.[53] And so, although the *chanson réaliste* was nearly an anachronism at the music halls of the 1930s, it helped to establish the most daring sensibility produced by the cinema of the time.

Prévert's realist lyrics and dialogue can be taken as an angry reaction against the brilliant artifice of both the music hall and the conventional cinema that he so loathed. Like many politicized intellectuals of his day, he retained a deep affection for the small *cafés-concerts* displaced by music halls, for the street singers displaced by radio, and for the silent serials (like Louis Feuillade's *Fantômas* and *Les Vampires*) displaced by extravagant sound films. What his generation of malcontents approved was the down-and-out world of social marginals with whom they could unashamedly identify. With this in mind, Florelle's song is not an homage to music-hall performance but rather a paean to life on the boulevard de la Chapelle, in the eighteenth *arrondissement*. Many poetic realist films celebrate this *quartier* as one of the last Parisian neighborhoods untouched by modernization and sanitation. And they celebrate the *bal populaire*, the indigenous entertainment site still thriving in the alleys behind the Moulin Rouge and other music halls which had long since bartered away their connection to the people living there.[54]

Insignificant as an attraction, scarcely ever mentioned in histories of entertainment, the *bal populaire* was the only live amusement form to register significant gains in revenue during the 1930s. The *bal* stands opposite the music hall in every respect. It had no use for illusion, technology, grandeur, and passive spectacle, but instead promoted participation (the clients danced, talked, and even sang). Like the *café-concert* of the nineteenth century, it fostered a family atmosphere, only this time the "family" could include the Mafia, or its Marseillais and Corsican counterparts.[55] Prévert claims to have felt truly alive at the *bal populaire*, and so did artists like Utrillo, photographers like Brassaï, and writers like Francis Carco and Pierre Mac Orlan.[56]

Le Crime de Monsieur Lange was shot at the Paris-Studios-Cinéma in Billancourt, but it consciously mythologizes the milieu of working-class Paris, which it evokes into an extended and utopian family. The film was produced in just such an atmosphere by an *équipe* (team) of artisans whose dedication and mutual respect lifted their labor out of the alienating conditions that new technologies and studio business practices had made the norm. Renoir's productions of the thirties—particularly this one—were fabled for their camaraderie, for the inventive horseplay on the set, and for the meals shared after each day's shooting was in the can. Renoir seemed intent on reasserting the intimacy of the neighborhood *café-concert* and spontaneous energy of the circus, which were losing out to the impersonal industry that the music hall had become. The family unit celebrated in *Le Crime de Monsieur Lange* and other poetic realist films such as Marcel Carné's *Hôtel du Nord* and Julien Duvivier's *La Belle Equipe* is definitely not a product of a middle class grounded on conservative "family values." It resembles instead a *bande à part* (gang of outsiders) like the October Group, for whom the local *bal populaire*—rather than the gaudy music hall—was the natural place to gather.

Curiously, although *Rigolboche* aims to simulate the lush music-hall experience, its opening sequence is set in a dingy *bal*, as if Mistinguett needed to return to her own origins so as to recapitulate her rise to stardom.[57] In 1918, while in search of a showcase number to anchor her act, she came upon an early novel written by Francis Carco. Working with his images and prose, she and her writers composed what would ever after be her signature song, "Mon Homme." And so Carco, who prior to World War I had liked to slum by taking in life at the *café-concert*, inspired its greatest star at just the moment when she would take the music hall into the realm of mass art and he would desert her for the back-alley *bals* of Montmartre. Though a Parisian could shuttle among all these entertainments in the 1930s, it was at the movies and onscreen that their interconnection and competition were, and remain, most visible by far.

The Look of Paris
in the Age of Art Deco

At once grand and neighborly, Paris must be the most photographed, drawn, painted, and filmed city in the world. Grandeur emanates from its historical monuments, churches, august official buildings, and luxurious *maisons particulières* (private mansions). Around and among these memorable structures—and interrupted only by the Seine and relatively few parks—a dense network of districts spreads out in agreeable harmony. From a distance, this homogeneity results from the ubiquitous seven-story buildings—a norm enforced through the late 1960s—which formed an even more continuous skyline in the years between the wars. Up close, Paris breaks not only into *arrondissements*, but into distinct neighborhoods where entire lives may be spent. We know all this because we have seen it endlessly pictured in advertisements and artworks, in movies, magazines, and newspapers. This chapter surveys the city's visual surround, stopping to look at the way scriptwriters, artists, photographers, and designers presented Paris to itself and to the world.

Compared to citizens elsewhere, Parisians must live a most self-conscious existence, as they walk down streets and past buildings that are on display to the world. A city of fashion and daring modernity that is also devoted to its past, Paris has developed a visual environment comprising a discourse of styles and values. The intellectuals who argued over Popular Front politics, the writers and artists who expressed interwar anxieties, all did so with the city unavoidably in view. Their discourse had to be inflected by the discourse of the look of Paris. In the 1930s, genuine discussions of Paris' appearance—not to mention tendentious displays in exhibitions, galleries, journal spreads, photographic essays, and the like—were customarily organized as dramas between notions of tradition and those of modernity. Whether unrolling as battles among competing styles or as their coordination, such dramas played each week in the era's biggest, most popular arenas: movie theaters, many of which had been built as bold stylistic statements in themselves.

Playing at the Rex: *En Exclusivité*

Coffee-table books presenting Paris in the 1930s (and they would make a lofty stack) generally feature either fashionable Art Deco architecture and design or somber working-class quarters, most of which have since been razed or relegated to the suburbs. Such books invariably signal the powerful presence of the cinema, and just as invariably they feature Jean Gabin—the sturdiest movie icon of that decade. Under a mantle of earnest authenticity, Gabin lured audiences to identify with him as he pursued his forthright urges. What he desired (a woman, justice, a chance at a better life) often drove him to cross into a sophisticated part of town, graphically set off from his own dowdy, if picturesque, milieu. Through Gabin's unforgettable gaze, we confront the looks of Paris.

In his first-ever appearance on the movie screen, Gabin plays a young department store clerk who decorates display windows with the latest fashions, catering to the whims of wealthy customers and selling apparel that he himself could never afford. The film, *Chacun sa chance* (Everyone Gets a Break; 1930), shows Gabin, as both character and actor, quite prepared to take his chances. After work one evening, he happens to walk past a magnificent music hall, where the lights and the attractions of the building beckon him to enter. Greeted by a team of short-skirted *vendeuses* rehearsing their routines (all customers are made to feel personally welcome), he is led along by a ticket-taker who ushers patrons to their proper seats once they have checked their coats. Such amenities puff the vanity of pampered customers, provoking fantasies of adventure and luxury. Gabin finds his fantasy immediately realized when he inadvertently becomes involved in the double duplicity of a baron and baroness, each of whom has shown up at the theater for a tryst with a lover. Available for an adventure, Gabin is whisked off to the couple's townhouse and recruited for a real-life drama of deception hardly distinguishable from the kind of play-acting one expects on stage. The townhouse resembles the music hall in its opulent bad taste; in both places, Gabin sings his way jauntily into the exclusive Paris he dreams about all day at work. Spectators who identified with this actor's frank, working-class persona—and they were soon legion—followed him in this and later films in making momentary contact with a Paris quite outside their experience. "Chacun sa chance," indeed!

Six years later, in the depths of the Depression, spectators once again locked their destinies to Gabin's in his desperate pursuit of a bejeweled woman. Playing the title character in *Gueule d'amour* (Lady Killer; Jean Grémillon, 1937), he was never more confident in his candor and charm; surely he must win Madeleine, the Parisian *mondaine* (Mireille Balin). This time, however, he finds his sexual and social aspirations rudely flummoxed. In a powerful scene, her wealthy protector throws him out of the classy apartment where she is a kept woman. Excluded from the highlife he has glimpsed, Gabin retreats to his shabby room in a proletarian district, and eventually falls back to the undistinguished outskirts of the town of Orange, where he grew up and where echoes of his reputation as a ladykiller (hence his name) might still reverberate. At a seedy bistro attached to a gas station—with his cap cocked resignedly on his head—he supplies food, drink, and fuel to travelers passing through in their fancy cars. Madeleine passes by one day, and he strangles her.

These two quite different fairy tales mark the distance traveled by French cinema in the 1930s: from jaunty theatrical presentations of *la vie en rose* to grim novelistic portrayals of sexual and class anxiety. But how great a distance was this? Both sorts of films depend on the gap between the life and the aspirations of the ordinary, honest wage earner, who pays for two hours of unattainable cinematic expressions that tie eroticism to splendor. So, despite its political edge, *Gueule d'Amour* engages and exploits the same audience desire as does *Chacun sa chance*.

That desire lured audiences from all over Paris to downtown picture palaces like the Grand Rex or the Ciné-Opéra (where Grémillon's film premièred), all of them advertising inordinate luxury to prop up their film fantasies. Middle- and lower-class spectators shared with Gabin's characters the urge to enter, if only provisionally, oases of opulence, fashion, and sensuality. The Grand Rex in particular, like so many of the films that played on its screen, was a travesty of life, an architectural scam; but it nevertheless represented quite directly the "representation of life" at a particular moment. How did the Rex fit the city's self-image in the 1930s? Did it affect the way its cross-section of spectators looked at Paris when the show had ended and they filed out of this jewel-box onto the boulevard Poissonnière to return home?

Picture palaces became a gaudy feature of the urban landscape in the late twenties, as commercial promoters engineered a crass bid to buy their way into the artistic nobility. Among these fabulous structures (in 1932, twenty-three of Paris' 260 movie theaters contained the word "palace" in their names) the Grand Rex stands out to this day as the realization of a dream world with regal ambience. Built in 1932 by André Bluysen and his American colleague, John Eberson, it served as both music hall and cinema.[1] Its Moorish motifs, unabashedly borrowed from the Moroccan Pavilion of the Colonial Exposition, are set off incongruously alongside elements taken from the 1925 Exposition des Arts Décoratifs.[2] The largest cinema in Paris, with a capacity of 3,300, the Grand Rex sported (and still sports, having been declared a "historic monument" in 1982) Art Deco's ziggurat patterns. With its projected and encased light sources, its grand organ, its army of uniformed personnel, its loges, and its myriad amenities, it was made in the image of aristocratic grandeur to be enjoyed by all the people of Paris.[3] The Rex aimed to sell a vision of wealth for a pittance to Parisians, many of whom could scarcely afford even a pittance in the Depression. Streaming toward the boulevard Poissonnière from the shadows of the brilliant city whose energy their labor generated, the poor would be led by the *ouvreuse* (usherette) to their place inside this plaster synecdoche of de luxe Paris, to gaze their fill on urbane or exotic images. "Once inside the entryway, the spectator is lifted out of everyday life. The décor transports him magically into a stupendous ideal world. At the Rex, the spectator is king."[4] Its regal name advertised its own distinction, as well as the distinctiveness of the films it played *en exclusivité*— that is, films in their first run that could be seen only in select theaters on the boulevards. *Exclusivité*, certainly an odd term for a mass-market product, captures the relation of the spectators to the fashionable world they pay to watch, a world from which they are precisely "excluded."

The designation of the Rex as a "picture palace" distinguishes it, albeit slightly, from the other film-exhibition spaces in the capital, known variously as "theaters," "studios," or just plain "cinemas." The connotations of these three terms sort out the multiple ways cinema was conceived at the time by those who produced and consumed it. The English language has extended the term "theater" from stage to film exhibition, since in both cases spectators buy tickets to watch actors from a seat in front of a representation. But since the full enterprise of cinema, from production through consumption, might just as well be modeled on painting and handicrafts, the French reserved the term "studio" for select *salles de cinéma*. In the art world, the public might be invited occasionally to visit an artist's "studio" for a close inspection of new creations. This fine-art practice resonates in the names of such famed Parisian cinemas as the Studio des Ursulines or Studio 28, both of

62–63. The Grand Rex, built in 1932.

which had hosted avant-garde productions in the late twenties. The kind of evenings they offered and the clientele they cultivated evoked a sense of intimacy.

Yet the intimacy of the "studio" suppresses the machinery and the business required for the arts of mechanical reproduction, and indeed for art in

general in the modern era. After the French Revolution and the demise of ec-
clesiastical and court patronage, most visual works in France were turned out
in organized ateliers and schools, where they were designed and produced in
various media through a calculated division of labor. Subjects and genres, as
well as the styles and techniques needed to render them, were all aspects of
artistic "speculation" in an increasingly organized art market.[5] Only intensive
specialized labor, often carefully calculated, could produce, as if out of thin
air, the limited number of fine-art images that appeared so radiantly exhibited
in galleries, salons, and museums. In short, a system of image production
linked lionized artist to artisan, technician, and supplier.

In the area of applied art, the system became more visible. Studios, ateliers, and undisguised factories produced decorative art, porcelain, glass, and
other craft items through rationalized processes. An administrative cadre
oversaw the successive labor of personnel in planning, design, materials,
technology, and fabrication. The results showed up most often in the display
windows of exclusive shops and department stores. This is the model echoed
by the small, elite *salles de cinéma* ("art houses") operating under the name
"studio." The name implies that such theaters produced the films they exhibited—and this was sometimes the case, as with Jean Renoir's first work, sponsored by the Vieux Colombier, where it was shot and screened. Given this
analogy, a flagship commercial cinema like the Rex must be considered the
opposite of a studio-cinema—more like a midtown department store, let's say,
than a boutique. Its screen, a gigantic display window, offered the type of
manufactured luxury product that was fabricated by workers at an image-
factory in the suburbs for mass visual consumption.

In the 1930s, producers could rent eight major film studios in Ile-de-
France.[6] By definition, studios such as Eclair, Apollo, and Pathé Cinéma were
empty boxes ready to be transformed into any epoch or place. Still, located as
they were in or near Paris and serving so many productions destined to appeal to the capital's inhabitants, these studios equipped themselves with store-
rooms full of costumes, backdrops, and props that could reproduce Paris, effectively folding it into a suitcase.

In their hierarchical organization, these studios and the production companies that rented them also replicated the class system apparent in the city.
There were those in charge and those taking orders. The pyramid was immutable: anonymous laborers below guilds of artisans, creative personnel, actors,
directors, and *vedettes* (stars). Above these were line producers and general
producers whose authority could never be bucked. In sum, a fully organized

subsociety kept the film factories running so that they could supply images to the Rex and the other movie theaters in Paris, all 300 of them.

Yet while picture palaces displayed week after week whatever wares came off the industry assembly line, they promoted the intimacy of the experience they provided. In this they emulated not so much the artist's studio as the music hall, which, as we have seen mimicked the cozier feel of the nineteenth-century *café-concert*. Given the technological advances of the period, someone as unreachable as Mistinguett could give the impression of singing exclusively to each of her paying cinema customers. The Rex was in the business of selling, to thousands of people at a time, an experience of intimacy with the stars they read about in *Pour Vous* and other fan magazines. In its first years, it booked several films starring the immensely popular music-hall comedian Bach, who might on certain nights appear live on its stage.[7] The Rex claimed to concentrate the essence of Paris' charm and wit; it was a grand palace, but nevertheless a miniature of a grander city.

In designing their picture palace, Bluysen and Eberson naturally took inspiration from the Art Deco Exposition and the Colonial Exposition, which had recently attracted millions of spectators to gape at the fashionable and the exotic. Such miniature utopias promised to fascinate all sorts of spectators equally. Of course, differences reappeared once the audience was ushered out of the exposition's gates or the theater's doors. Some would leave by chauffeur for swanky districts like Passy; others, more numerous, took the Métro to working-class Belleville and beyond. The Rex and the expositions were constructed as autonomous zones of perfection within a very imperfect city. Politically, Paris would be polarized by the Stavisky riots a little more than a year after the Rex opened its doors. Culturally, Paris had long since parsed itself into distinct zones that, except for the monuments and the tourist areas, scarcely communicated with one another.

All films require class and gender divisions to drive their dramas; most, like our two Jean Gabin examples, take these divisions for granted. The French Communist Party produced an exception in 1937. *Le Temps des cerises* (Cherry-Blossom Time) explicitly refused the ideology of universal cohesiveness held out by the standard cinema and by the state-sponsored expositions. Its title alone is ironic and divisive, taken from a song that, along with the "Internationale," was a sort of anthem for the radical left.[8]

As it happens, the film opens just outside the Exposition Internationale

64. Politics at the 1937 Exposition: the Nazi pavilion.

des Arts et Techniques Appliqués à la Vie Moderne, which was on the verge of opening when the film was in production. Two working-class lovers huddle next to the new Palais de Chaillot and look out onto the pavilions being constructed for the summer events that were meant to bring prestige to the capital. Pointing across the Seine to the Eiffel Tower looming above the German and Soviet pavilions, the young man recounts the misery of his grandfather, who worked on the tower and was injured in a construction accident before the turn of the century. The allegory is clear: the poor build the modern city, which the bourgeoisie enjoys. When the poor age, they are discarded, kept out of sight. Their children and grandchildren then take up the yoke of their class. This tale is an object lesson for the Third Republic, an era of rationalization and modernization whose greatest monument remains the 1889 tower that looks across at the Palais de Chaillot. The Exposition Internationale, spreading out in the shadow of the tower, aimed to show off a Paris whose advances in technology after the Great War were boldly continuing despite the Depression.

Le Temps des cerises challenged such claims to progress in its subject and mode of production. Jean-Paul Le Chanois' rough documentary style thumbs its nose at the more professional and often pretentious French cinema of the time. The implicit contrast in *Le Temps des cerises* between rough and fine art follows from its explicit way of representing class: a Paris of the ascendant bourgeoisie (a city that is modern, light, clean, convenient, and luxurious), set off against that of the working class (a maze of dark alleys, still medieval). The lovers in the film's opening sequence are literally overshadowed by the new Palais de Chaillot, later to be a Mecca for film students everywhere as the home of the Cinémathèque Française, founded by Henri Langlois in 1936. Thus, even the cinema, the working-class entertainment par excellence, harbored upscale illusions when it successfully lobbied to install itself in a *palais*.[9]

The Petit Palais and the Independence of French Art

A steady stream of French movies kept Paris informally in the public eye all decade long. The city's official self-presentation—its preening glamour shot—was the International Exposition of 1937. Not everyone fawned over this pose. Le Chanois, adopting the role of coarse artisan, was joined by truculent artists suspicious of the exposition as a whole and of its alleged "modernity" in particular. Like the lovers in *Le Temps des cerises*, these artists hovered outside its aureole, excluded from it or refusing its universal appeal. In the first place, the exposition had the inevitable effect of institutionalizing art. From 1934 on, hundreds of painters and sculptors vied for invitations to contribute. Robert Delaunay, Fernand Léger, and Raoul Dufy won the most coveted commissions and eagerly filled up the French pavilions with gigantic lines, forms, and colors as audaciously modern as the railroads, airplanes, and electricity they celebrated.

In his examination of Parisian visual culture in 1937, James Herbert points to an anomaly: the fact that the technocratic International Exposition would carve out a place for the fine arts. Aiming to resuscitate a moribund global economy by encouraging the worldwide exchange of the latest technologies, the expo's directors naturally commissioned art that reinforced a progressivist ideology. One pavilion was given over completely to the *beaux-arts*. While it focused on up-to-date trends from the 1925–1932 period, its notion of "up-to-date" was something quite other than "avant-garde." Indeed, the Beaux-Arts Pavilion mainly consolidated the gains that had made the Art Deco Exposition and the Colonial Exposition so memorable and that informed the décor of the Rex, not to mention that of a good many hotels and

65. Progressivist ideology commissioned for the 1937 Expo.

ocean liners. The pavilion likewise aimed to please rather than challenge the average passer-by, albeit in a sophisticated manner.

The 1937 International Exposition proclaimed that art in an increasingly rationalized and modern world should migrate from arid museums and from the attic studios of bohemians onto the streets, so as to play a direct, visible, and progressive social role. Lionized painters lent their illustrious names to public institutions and utilities (electricity, railroads) or public causes (the war victims of Guernica); and fine art commingled with applied design, since the Pavillon des Beaux-Arts was subsumed under the Centre des Métiers (*métiers* meaning "trades" or "professions").

This celebration through painting, drawing, and design of a highly commercial modernity left hundreds of artists out in the cold or jealous, including Matisse, Picasso, and Edouard Vuillard. Intent only on eye-catching appeal, the state committee that selected works for the Pavillon des Beaux-Arts completely neglected the complex aesthetic debates and advances of the recent past. Scandalized, Raymond Escholier, the forward-looking head curator at one of the capital's major exhibition venues, the Petit Palais, saw the tunnel vision of the International Exposition as his chance to display the twentieth-century French paintings that he had been collecting under a metropolitan mandate.[10] Employed not by the national government but by the city itself, he mounted a challenge that is proclaimed by the last word of the title he chose: Maîtres de l'Art Indépendant (Masters of Independent Art).

Just when the notion of a "modern art collection" was taking form, and right after a museum specifically set aside to house it had been commissioned (the Palais de Tokyo), Escholier turned the Petit Palais into an unrivaled mansion of the modern, hosting 1,500 works by 120 artists "whom he took to be the 'Masters of Independent Art,' meaning what today we call modern art," rather than academic or decorative work.[11] Herbert suggests that Escholier deliberately set out to humiliate the Pavillon des Beaux-Arts, which had already been judged weak and decorative because its sponsors were the staid groups formerly associated with two of Paris' academic salons: Artistes Français and the Société Nationale.[12] At the Petit Palais, on the other hand, art's "independence" was guaranteed by the names of individual artists, posted at the entryway of each of its many rooms.

Herbert argues that if the International Exposition displayed the advances of commerce, then the Petit Palais served to shore up the decidedly noncommercial zones of culture. The obsession with efficiency and exchange that constituted what might be seen as the nave of the International Exposition needed to be propped up by the flying buttresses of traditional aesthetic values. One such buttress was the out-and-out nationalist exhibition entitled Chefs d'Oeuvre de l'Art Français (Masterpieces of French Art), which inaugurated the Palais de Tokyo in 1938, while its modern counterpart at the Petit Palais formed the other. Taken together, these two museums demonstrated a continuity that gave substance to the flimsy offerings at the Pavillon des Beaux-Arts. In effect, masterpieces by Poussin and Watteau (at the Palais de Tokyo) constituted a fulcrum leveraging hundreds of years of French genius, right up to works by the likes of Derain and Bonnard at the Petit Palais. Forging the crucial link back to this tradition via Poussin was Cézanne, who ushered in the modern period that, according to this scheme, has maintained unbroken ties with the past.

What nearly did break this tradition after Cézanne was a notorious 1919 auction where more than 2,000 post-Impressionist and Cubist works were sold off by Paul Léon, briefly and disastrously head of the Académie des Beaux-Arts.[13] Escholier made it his mission to retrieve much of this French art that had been circulating around the world, gathering into his "little pal-ace" all these "independent" spirits now roaming Germany, the United States, and even Asia. In this way, he could assert simultaneously the univer-sality of French painting (it was desired and emulated everywhere it went) and its national character (its source was Paris). He also stamped modernity with the seal of French genius, of genius *tout court,* and thereby opposed two grievous maladies, decorativeness and functionality, passed down respectively from the Art Deco Exposition and the International Exposition, still visible in 1937 on the Champ de Mars.

Assembled under the rubric of "independence" was a phalanx of artists led by Henri Matisse, whose sixty-one works filled a room devoted exclusively to him.[14] Roger de La Fresnaye and Georges Rouault had more than forty works on display; Maurice de Vlaminck thirty-nine; Maurice Utrillo and Raoul Dufy thirty-six each; André Lhote and Pierre Bonnard thirty-three; Pablo Picasso, Edouard Vuillard, André Derain, Georges Braque, Fernand Léger, and Juan Gris somewhat fewer. Marc Chagall had seventeen pieces and Marie Laurencin sixteen. There were a dozen late Robert Delaunays and as many Modiglianis. Only one painting by Pierre-Auguste Renoir appeared, but it was hung on a "stairway of honor." As the catalogue of a 1987 restag-ing of this show makes clear, Escholier's orientation promoted the "percep-tualist" mission of French art—a view that was based in Impressionism and that excluded the historical avant-garde. Nothing by Marcel Duchamp was selected, and the Surrealists were present via a few works by Giorgio de Chirico, one by Francis Picabia, and one by Max Ernst.

Escholier meant to celebrate the most prized French artists up to 1925—after which things became murky, with so many aesthetic values being put to the test. The art market had to absorb the impact of new technologies, incipi-ent globalization, and especially the fickle tastes of the middle class, whose role in the market had been openly acknowledged ever since the Art Deco Exposition. Although insisting on the priority of individual approaches (con-veyed both by the word "independent" and by the clustering of works), one reviewer in 1937 praised Escholier for restricting the exhibit to artists who clearly inherited one or the other of the two main traits of traditional French aesthetics: intelligence and sensuality. These were represented, respectively, by the superstars of the exhibit, Picasso and Matisse.[15]

This aesthetic duel between the Petit Palais and the International Exposi-tion did not cover all positions, since both derived from an upper-crust cultural tier. The International Exposition stood for recent culture as seen from the seat of French political power, while the Maîtres de l'Art Indépendant represented the viewpoint of Paris' traditional arbiters of taste. In both cases, their official stature insulated them from the ferment of some of the most vibrant artistic developments in the metropolis. Escholier buffered his selection against the turbulent winds of fashion and change by insisting on a 1925 cutoff date, for he couldn't be confident in his choice of works from the years 1925–1937.[16] And so, how "modern" could his selection have been?

Parisian art museums thought of themselves as institutions equivalent in their own domain to the Sorbonne in the world of ideas. And like the Sorbonne, the museums felt their impact on culture drop in the 1930s. Among intellectuals, it was the publishing houses and their upstart political reviews that recruited the dynamic young talent in the 1930s. Similarly, several schools of artists opposed the aesthetics of the reigning schools of "modern art." Force Nouvelle explicitly set itself against Surrealism, Cubism, and Impressionism, claiming to rejuvenate the French realist tradition by emphasizing patient techniques of formal design. But as with the nonconformists, no unified position could be established. Tal-Coat joined Force Nouvelle for their inaugural exposition of 1935 at the Galerie Billiet, contributing mainly portraits, but then went his own way. Boris Taslitzky, a committed Communist (he directed one of Aragon's Maisons de la Culture), may have been inspired, like Force Nouvelle, by a major 1934 exhibition called Les Peintres de la Réalité en France au XVIIe Siècle (Georges de La Tour to Le Nain), but his large paintings were hardly contemplative in the classical manner. He was after something with more immediate impact, as in his Popular Front celebration *Les Grèves de juin 1936* (The Strikes of June 1936) and his vibrant and inflammatory *La Grève chez Renault après le dictat de Munich en 1938* (The Strike at the Renault Factory after the Munich Accords in 1938). Taslitzky reminds us that a great many painters (and gallery owners) set agendas in art without worrying over what Monsieur Escholier might think or what the throngs at the Petit Palais might be discussing.[17] As the famous 1951 retrospective on the Ecole de Paris pointed out, in the first half of the century the city of Paris boasted "130 galleries, as opposed to thirty in any other capital."[18] To register the tenor of the quotidian practices of unofficial culture— their aesthetic drift and social valence—one must access and compare a variety of visual expressions as they could be seen in these galleries, in illustrated magazines, on posters, and elsewhere around the city. Only a few images bear anything like the direct ideological weight of a state commission or museum selection, but in their cumulative impact they determined the overall look of the capital.

Art historians have grouped one informal collection of artists of the period under the rubric l'Ecole de Paris (the School of Paris). Romy Golan sets off this group against the set of painters known as the French School. Suggesting that progressive ideas are inevitably urban, galvanized by social mix, social desire, and social energy, she holds out hopes for the Ecole de Paris after being disappointed in the interwar return toward rural and traditional subjects by formerly progressive artists like Derain, Vlaminck, and the old masters who inspired them (Matisse, Picasso, and Braque). Golan sketches an incriminating picture of a nation that, following World War I, relinquished the avant-garde drive that had made Paris such an aesthetic and cultural utopia during the Belle Epoque.[19] The Ecole de Paris, whose very name connotes the avant-garde, in fact fell into a nostalgia of its own. Mainly immigrant painters (Chagall, Chaïm Soutine, Pavel Tchelitchew, Ossip Lubitch), they turned to memories and visions of prewar life, transforming the Montparnasse district they haunted into an organic village of sorts, one of the most common subjects associated with members of this school.[20] The vibrancy of Paris and its inhabitants did not inspire them the way it had so many of the Impressionists fifty years earlier.

The nostalgia of the Ecole de Paris is corroborated by the catalogue of the recently established Musée des Années Trente (Museum of the 1930s).[21] As this collection displays, the interwar period saw a revival of sacred themes, alongside two other prominent aesthetic tendencies: Art Deco and Orientalism, which derive directly from the 1925 and 1931 expositions. The existence of this new museum displaying lesser-known artists encourages one to imagine the day-to-day discourse alive in cafés, galleries, and the journals that disputed the "Great French Tradition."

Given that painting in this decade fell back from modern art's progressive mission, we should expect a full retreat in the popular arts, including the most popular of all, the cinema. Nostalgia was the principal fuel for the entertainment engine that drove the first decade of sound film in France.[22] The provocative title of one social history, *De Blum à Pétain* (From Blum to Pétain), locates in the cinema of the 1930s an unmistakable predisposition for a return to the old values of "fatherland, family, and work" that Maréchal Pétain would preach from Vichy.[23] Yet the entertainment cinema proudly advertised itself as "modern" in spirit and certainly in design. Evidently, the cinema could be a popular art only by asserting nostalgia and modernity simultaneously—that is, by reassuring a mass public that comfortable feelings of a harmonized French tradition permitted a daring but confident approach to the future. The same doubtless held true in many popular songs of the day whose lyrics called on a repertoire of shared values, although many were sung in the syncopated, often frenetic tempos of modernity, and although they came to the public through such new technologies as radio and the phonograph.

These conflicting feelings are intertwined in a film like René Clair's *A Nous la liberté*, as we saw in Chapter 6. In the finale, the two buddies kick their way down a dusty road à la Chaplin, after passing workers on vacation who fish near jaunty riverside cafés. When they sing a song of leisure and solidarity in the rural outdoors, both the moral and the irony of the film are clear: they have adopted a carefree life by abandoning the urban factory that had made their fortune. The deeper irony is that these are nothing other than mass-marketed movie characters, artifacts of a modern film industry ready to cash in on such sentiments.[24] The futurist lines of Lazare Meerson's factory set could be found in many of the Parisian movie theaters where the film would be likely to play. Audiences were thus drawn to the up-to-date look of a film that nevertheless offered them a sensibility with which they really felt at home: old-fashioned France, rather than modern Paris. What Clair would never show, and what the movie theaters functioned explicitly to repress, were the decidedly regressive effects of modernity on a huge part of the city and its population. While *Sous les toits de Paris* (1930) was set in the poorer districts, Clair's poetic realist mise-en-scène transmuted danger and decrepitude into the fine feelings of populism. The most important of 1930s genres, poetic realism, is known for the nostalgia and regret on which it capitalized, and for evoking (on carefully lit studio sets) the dark atmosphere of Paris' back alleys.[25]

Le Temps des cerises aimed to correct this tailored and poeticized image of the working-class *quartier*s, while also countering the bright postcard images of the capital seen in standard entertainment films. It took a third way, and its difference was noted: "You can immediately appreciate the documentary perspective in which the action is immersed—shots of factories and fields, of working-class streets and carnivals, of elderly faces. These deliver an authentic, genuinely popular atmosphere to the whole film, something quite distant from 'studio reconstructions.'"[26] Meanwhile, programming at a theater like the Rex thrived on such reconstructions, mainly "vapid melodramas, which were the staple of the French industry, an industry which manifested remarkable indifference in their films to the lives of working people."[27] *Le Temps des cerises* attacked this indifference in both its subject matter and its documentary production methods. A tough film, relegated to union halls and anonymous *cinémas du quartier*, it challenged the urbanity—and apathy—of the regular fare at the Rex, especially those films pretending to depict Paris.

Why should the documentary shots of Paris in *Le Temps des cerises* appear so remarkable in the late 1930s? Wasn't Le Chanois simply answering Marcel Carné's clarion call from 1933: "When will the cinema go down into the street?"[28] So great were the pressures to film in a studio setting—given the primacy of actors and of standard photographic values during the period—that even Carné, when he finally earned the chance to shoot a feature, *Jenny*, in 1936, made an about-face and thereafter kept primarily to the studios, where he had better control over the look of the image.[29] In fact, *Jenny* can best be read as a struggle between two types of décor: a couple of scenes filmed on location in the poorer *quartiers* are meant to stand out as authentic, while the main action takes place in the studio-built brothel, apartment, and bar, which are all very much in the modern style—a style that signifies falseness and duplicity in the script.[30] As our next chapter will show in detail, Carné, more than any other director of his time, would come to picture Paris, including its poorer sections, by rebuilding it in miniature, then fussing over it until it was ready to be projected on a grand scale at a cinema like the Rex.[31]

Carné's fame points to the curious fact that the most prestigious and memorable films coming from France in the 1930s—those that dominated critical attention at that time and thereafter—belong to the high-budget poetic realist strain, which featured lower-class subjects. From Clair and Pierre Chenal to Carné and Duvivier, these populist films achieved distinction as fine products despite their grim subject matter. The irony is that the more popular and ostentatious genres (the comedies, musicals, and "vapid melodramas" of the middle class) were by and large flimsier in their production values. Apparently, the ordinary moviegoer was satisfied to follow familiar actors in familiar highlife dramas even when these were played out on recycled sets and props. The key was that those sets had to signify splendor and comfort, representing an elite lifestyle that spectators would in fact pay to dream of. Paris at the cinema was evidently supposed to look stunning, no matter what the genre or the theme of the film. *Le Temps des cerises* was a scandalous film because both its subject and its shoestring production mocked this image, shaming the entertainment business *in toto*.

Humanism and Fashion in Parisian Photography
Bohemians Haunting the City

Among photos from the 1930s most coveted today are those of hidden Paris, of Paris by night. Photography here took upon itself Zola's mission of illuminating the dark corners of the city where life both incubates and festers. These populist images were the creation of a number of bohemian artists (Brassaï, André Kertész, François Kollar, Bill Brandt, and more) who have since become famous but who at the time worked with little institutional support and attracted less critical attention than more upscale fashion and art photographers mainly forgotten today except by art historians specializing in the period.[32] Working out of high-tech studios, often in teams or groups, the more commercial photographers dominated the pages of the illustrated journals, produced ads for consumer products, and received commissions to document the art and architecture of the city. Their images were displayed in official exhibitions of photography, including several rooms at the 1937 International Exposition.

The bohemian photographers have eclipsed their officially sanctioned rivals because, while both partake in the history of taste, whoever appeals to current fashion must by definition fade in popularity and relevance as fashions change. On the other hand, the avant-gardism of the bohemians resisted fashion and appealed to a timeless spirit of revolt, associated with those parts of Paris not yet touched by modernization.[33] Brassaï, for example, bridges several decades, from the historical avant-garde through existentialism, having been close to the famous Picasso and the scarcely known Henry Miller. The Paris of such durable painters and writers holds its appeal. It may have helped that Brassaï was originally a novelist, and that his photographs attached themselves to a successful book of poems: Paul Eluard's *Capitale de la douleur* (Capital of Sorrow). Brassaï and André Kertész shared an aesthetic of urban discovery, hard and poetic, like the tough-minded American prose brandished by Miller. They collaborated with novelists Pierre Mac Orlan and Francis Carco, notorious for their evocation of the mystery and danger of Paris and particularly of Montmartre.

Montmartre deliberately stood out as a denial of urban modernity. Already by the 1930s, the village-like *quartier* of Montmartre had come to signify more than its romantic past. Tour guides shepherded visitors through its dank alleys, scheduling pauses for drinks at one or another café formerly of low repute. Painters, poets, and novelists kept its spirit alive, representing an ever quainter neighborhood, while numerous films (invariably shot in the studio) banked on its notoriety to establish mood and setting, as well as attract audiences. One self-conscious film, *Prisons de femmes* (Marked Girls; Roger Richebé, 1938), even features Francis Carco playing under his own name, as a famous novelist who gets involved with exploited women while frequenting Montmartre clubs. Brassaï was close to Carco and closer still to Mac Orlan, known as the Montmartre writer par excellence. Brassaï would accompany his literary friends to their haunts, then begin taking shots of the streets, of the haunts themselves, and of their clientele. In trying to cut into the murky ambience of the nocturnal underworld, did he know that his tripod stood in the soft landfill of what had already become nostalgia?

Photography has always been drawn to the terrain of nostalgia. A direct line leads back to 1855 and to Charles Marville, the official photographer chosen to document Baron Haussmann's projects so as to preserve in some manner a Paris crumbling under the pressures of modernization.[34] Marville's empty streets were meant to suggest a future in the making, but, because of the nature of the medium, they first of all mourn the passing of what they depict. Eugène Atget's immense output in the first quarter of the twentieth century was allegedly documentary in inspiration, yet it increased the mystery associated with uninhabited Paris; Man Ray included several of Atget's prints in a 1929 issue of the periodical *La Révolution Surréaliste*. Kertész and Brassaï were openly indebted to Atget. Both were intent on exposing an authentic Paris characterized by the immutable look of poverty, pleasure, and crime—a genuine Paris increasingly pushed into the shadows by technical and architectural progress and standardization. Alexandre Trauner, Carné's esteemed set designer, recounts his evenings with Brassaï and Prévert exploring the dark side-streets redolent of Paris' literary past. Each imagined—and then would later represent—the city in his own respective medium.[35]

The romanticism of photographers smitten by the timeless dramas of Paris rather than by its modern look dominates one important section of Dominique Baqué's *Documents de la modernité: Anthologie de textes sur la photographie de 1919 à 1939*. Baqué sets this picturesque, populist imagery against the quest for photographic modernism that publications as varied as *L'Illustration* and *Vu* championed in the 1930s. This opposition arises almost naturally in Paris because of the "ambivalence of the modern city—too alive, too

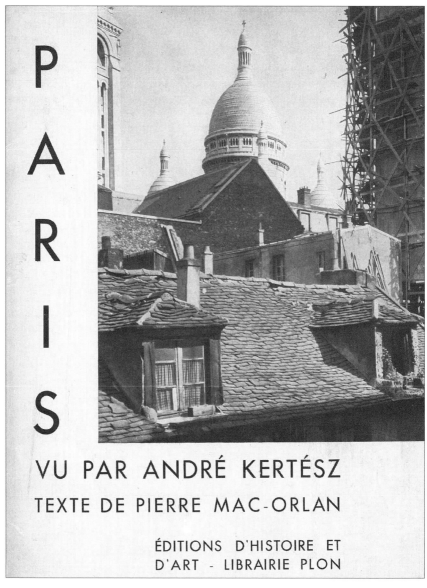

66. The bohemian capital.

disquieting to be reduced to a geometric tableau, yet too rational, too structured to be only picturesque."[36]

In the early part of the decade the humanist photographer behaved like a "*flâneur* and Surrealist rambler tied to a certain French literary tradition," ignoring the architecture and public aspect of the city to focus on "the human and living spaces of the market, the promenade, the chance encounter." A 1934 article on Brassaï, aptly titled "La Ville photogénique," opens with what now sounds like a familiar litany: "Blacks, whites, grays, simple surfaces, reflections, rain, mist, chimneys, posters, depressing suburbs, avenues, windows, . . . the haughty desert of the fashionable areas, the sad dereliction of certain streets, the picturesque desolation of the outlying districts."[37] One can hear echoes of Baudelaire and Poe in Mac Orlan's preface to *Paris vu par André Kertész:* this is a city that is visibly "becoming criminal"—a "theater of crime," as people said of Atget's empty cityscapes.[38] Mac Orlan loved these photographers. In the hands of the bohemians, photography took risks, insinuating itself in the crevices between the seen and the unseen, preparing for unprepared encounters, and even intervening in situations so as to produce the unexpected in order to capture it.

Photography joined and encouraged a literary sensibility going back to Zola, himself an avid amateur of the new technology. Francis Carco had *Nana* and *L'Assommoir* explicitly in mind during his habitual peregrinations through neighborhoods whose literary image overwhelmed his sense perceptions. He speaks of his afternoon walks on the rue de la Gaïté, which were guided by his reading of Zola and by his memories of Charles-Louis Philippe's *Bubu de Montparnasse* (reprinted in 1929 with evocative graphics by André Dunoyer de Segonzac).[39] Breton found it obvious that *Nadja*'s descriptions of Parisian encounters could best be amplified with photographic insertions. And it was just as plain to a critic of the time that Germaine Krull's photographs could be aptly described as extensions of *Nadja*'s effort to capture the mysteries of the capital.[40] An article in 1938 summed up this impulse, so different from that of the monumental and fashion photography dominating the era, as a "return to subjectivity, emotion, and the picturesque."[41] Such a return was supremely evident in the visual style as well as the melodramatic plots of the celebrated films of the time. In 1938 audiences saw the premières of *La Bête humaine, Le Puritain, Hôtel du Nord,* and *Le Quai des brumes* (taken from Mac Orlan's masterpiece set in Montmartre). This was the apex of the poetic realist sensibility, which came from and contributed to the romantic visage of Paris.

The risk of cliché in this conjunction of nostalgia and sophistication has lowered the status of artistic bohemian photography in the eyes of some critics. Robert Short favors instead the unheralded political photographic journalism that emerged in the wake of the Stavisky Affair.[42] Drawing inspiration from initiatives in Moscow, Berlin, and New York (the Film and Photo League), a coterie of French photographers tied their agenda to that of the Popular Front, producing eyewitness exposés, views of demonstrations, reportage of troubling states of affairs, and heroic shots of workers. An equivalent effort at *Ciné-Liberté* turned out Communist newsreels over the course of a few months in 1936. These were shown in union halls and at PCF meetings in an endeavor to counteract the standard weekly news digests that were shown before every feature-film screening at cinemas throughout the country.[43]

Romy Golan's disdain for elegiac images in the interwar period doesn't include cinema but does touch on photography. She recognizes Kertész as a cosmopolitan and progressive artist, yet associates his photographs (especially the sequence called "L'Elégance du métier," depicting the shopkeepers at Paris' central market, Les Halles) with urban nostalgia, since his Paris is "seen again and again through the screen of memory, that of a pre-modern past."[44] Kertész, like Chaïm Soutine, was Jewish and thus inevitably an outsider with respect to modern Paris. These men could rhapsodize about the city's past, since that past belonged to them as much as to anyone.

The lure of the old was pervasive. According to *La Revue Française de la Photographie*, 1938 saw an unprecedented number of retrospectives consecrated to nineteenth-century street photos, which were at the origin of the urban-nostalgia genre.[45] Was this a reaction to the massive rebuilding around the Place d'Alma and the Trocadéro, and to the veneer of modernity slapped onto the Champ de Mars during the 1937 exposition? The tension between an aggressively modern Paris and its nearly medieval substrate was apparent in such retrospectives; it was also available to any creative pedestrian (*promeneur*) strolling around the city. The Surrealists had pioneered such promenades in the late twenties, when Walter Benjamin resurrected the figure of the *flâneur*. His *Arcades Project* can be read as an album of mental snapshots.

Benjamin, Surrealism and photography converged around 1929, the year Germaine Krull published a collection of photographs bearing the wonderful title, *100 x Paris*. Although Krull was associated with Weimar modernism (she had just made her name with a collection called *Metal*), she evidently saw Paris in softer terms. One reviewer expressed what was becoming a familiar mélange of sentiments, including regret and mystery, yet also Surrealist modernity: "I find Paris again—the Paris of France, of autumn. The smell of roasted chestnuts on the street corners reminds me of my childhood. The tradition of Atget lives on in *A Grocery* (a streetlamp stands motionless, like a *flâneur*,[46] before a display of fruit), in several shots of Les Halles, in the portrait of five homeless men sitting on a bench. Let's not forget that the boulevard Bonne-Nouvelle is one of the central characters in *Nadja*. Germaine Krull's lens is sensitive to poetry."[47] Krull—like Kertész, an immigrant and a Jew—had become famous for her aggressive and sharply geometric shots of buildings. Yet this modernity could blend with nostalgia to produce *100 x Paris*.

Fashion Photography: Paris in Hollywood

Bohemian and Surrealist photography—epitomized in Brassaï's *Paris secret des années 30* (Secret Paris of the '30s)—may be central to our feeling for interwar French culture, but it was only an epiphenomenon of the industry of commercial and fashion photography burgeoning in Paris and other metropolises between the wars.[48] Among the most successful French enterprises, and surely the most indicative for us, was the company known as Séeberger Frères. Between 1923 and 1931 their studio assembled a magnificent dossier of Parisian photographs, working on commission at the behest of a Hollywood agency, International Kinema Research. One of many agencies and suppliers in Hollywood, International Kinema served as a middleman to funnel accurate models of various foreign settings to studio set designers.[49] When first approached by Hollywood, the Séebergers were firmly established as fashion and portrait photographers. The commission from International Kinema soon grew to overwhelming proportions, as they shot hundreds of photos, some following specific instructions but many that they themselves composed. Month after month, they shipped the look of Paris to the United States by boat. Their itemized collection, arranged by *arrondissement*, amounts to a visual index of Paris as it appeared in the cinema.[50]

Just how did the three Séeberger brothers represent their city with Hollywood films in mind? Perhaps most telling and least surprising is the sheer quantity of images taken in the inner ring of *arrondissements* (the 1st to the 7th). This, after all, is the monumental Paris—Notre Dame, the Conci-

67. The rue de Lappe, in a photo by Séeberger Frères (1930).

68. A frame from Rouben Mamoulian's *Love Me Tonight* (1932).

ergerie, the Tuileries, the Latin Quarter—and thus incorporates a great deal of what foreign audiences had heard of, read about, or glimpsed in pictures. Beyond the core of the capital, the Séebergers predictably focused more on the fancy 8th and 16th *arrondissements*, while virtually ignoring the undistinguished working-class 12th and 13th. A thematic résumé that serves as an alphabetized table of contents reveals more than this quantitative assessment. Of the twenty headings in this table, by far the greatest number involve entertainment: dance halls, cabarets, café-bars, the Concert Mayol (a music hall), the circus, and the Samaritaine baths, as well as restaurants, theaters, and hotels. Another grouping of photos consists of typical Parisian locales such as work sites, the Canal Saint-Martin, the Cour du Dragon, and the Passage Jouffroy. Even large buildings, such as major department stores and a three-story garage, receive specific attention.

This is upscale Paris, not really so different from the one described in the Thomas Cook guidebooks of the time, though it would be given an ultramodern twist by Hollywood in movies like *Blonde Venus* (1932), *The Worst Woman in Paris* (1936), and *Ninotchka* (1939).[51] Of more "ordinary" Paris, there are far fewer shots. The rubric "trades" (*métiers*) includes clichés—the word means not only "stereotyped views" but also "snapshots"—of particularly Parisian shops (a haberdashery that could have been used for *Love Me Tonight*, a film made in 1932), a shoe repair shop, a hairdresser's, and of course a bakery, including a shot of a shirtless baker pulling bread from an immense oven). For some reason, a stone-cutting factory specializing in marble funerary items gets attention. The city streets are photographed with various vehicles and street-cleaners at work. The latter are not individuated, for the lower classes are given slight attention overall. There are three shots of a cheerless rue du Départ near the Gare Montparnasse, and then—unexpectedly—a truly evocative series on the rue de Lappe, behind the Place de la Bastille. Little passages, with wet cobblestones glistening below peeling posters glued to the stone walls; a sinister courtyard entry, partly blocked by a heap of coal; an aging woman whose face reports a hard biography. In one photo a concierge stands rather proudly by the seedy building she tends. Coincidentally, Kertész also photographed the rue de Lappe in 1931, and in so visceral a manner that Pierre Mac Orlan claimed he could feel the blood running into the gutters.[52] Even Henry Miller deemed this a chancy street—because of its homosexuals.[53]

The Séebergers were told to shoot this street from all angles, and to include its customary denizens.[54] As far as Hollywood was concerned, fewer than a dozen shots of the rue de Lappe were enough from which to design Paris' teeming *quartiers populaires*. Poverty in these carefully chosen documentary photos, and in the studio sets that would be modeled on them, is associated with the unmistakable titillation of immorality. There was no need to calculate the variety of the poor; the masses scarcely count, because in any case their lives are incalculable. Hollywood followed the Séebergers, who in turn followed stereotypes with literary roots in the melodramas of Hugo, Zola, Eugène Sue, and their less celebrated descendants.

Séeberger Frères made an ideal partner for Hollywood. Having established a name for themselves photographing cityscapes and landscapes for the booming postcard industry early in the century, the brothers pioneered a type of less formal outdoor fashion photography in the 1920s, capturing models who appear to be on the move while ever so slightly posing (several next to the Longchamp racetrack in the Bois de Boulogne).[55] They sold this product to department stores in Paris and in the United States (Macy's, for one), and to illustrated magazines such as *Harper's Bazaar* and *Vogue*, which launched its French edition in 1920. Their spruced-up "natural" photographs meshed well with a classic Hollywood style that became increasingly well defined in the 1920s. Hollywood, intent on purveying fashion, looked to these brothers, who had mastered the look of the city that claimed to be the world's fashion capital—a status confirmed at the 1925 Exposition des Arts Décoratifs.

Film and the Internationalism of French Fashion
Art Deco as Vernacular Modernism

The sensational 1925 Paris exposition changed fashion throughout the Western world, bringing Art Deco into popular magazines and into the movies, where consumers grew to admire and crave it. Pure Art Deco films are rare and include few titles beyond *L'Inhumaine* (1924, by Marcel L'Herbier, with Fernand Léger, Robert Mallet-Stevens, Alberto Cavalcanti, and Claude Autant-Lara all contributing to the design) and *Le Mystère du Château de Dés* (filmed by Man Ray in 1927 at the Count de Noailles' new mansion in Hyères, designed by Mallet-Stevens).[56] But as a tendency and a look, "Film Deco" swelled from its hand-tailored origins in France in the 1920s to its assembly-line (Taylorized) versions in Hollywood studios and New York magazines like *Harper's Bazaar*. Through transatlantic exchanges, Paris was represented to the world as the capital of Art Deco.

Strangely, Hollywood was perhaps the major source for purveying the look of Paris, and certainly for determining the way movies everywhere looked, including French movies, which couldn't help imitating Hollywood's success.[57] Yet the Hollywood look derived from Parisian fashion, specifically from the resonance of the 1925 exposition. We must imagine that French cinema and French illustrated magazines felt the full impact of the native Art Deco, as well as the indirect impact of the American version of this style as promulgated in the media.

Just as cinema was crucial to Art Deco, so Art Deco helped to push cinema across the sound barrier by stabilizing the look of the movies.[58] Hollywood has never hidden its fascination with Parisian design (and with Paris itself). Evident in the typeface of the credits introducing so many early talkies from both France and Hollywood, Art Deco is even figured in the logos by which several studios signed all their films, as a guarantee of how up-to-date they were. Credits and logos—the first thing seen in a movie—strike the dominant key that orients the entire film experience. Hollywood promised from the outset of each of its productions to drop the spectator into a world so modern it wouldn't be forgotten.

Although Hollywood may have been the capital of modernity, it looked abroad for inspiration, and not only to France. A powerful cohort of German émigré filmmakers, designers, and cameramen would shape the look of Hollywood's more fantastic genres, particularly musicals, horror films, and science fiction. Hans Dreier, a Viennese with a Bauhaus background, crossed the Atlantic with the great German director Ernst Lubitsch, bringing to Paramount Studios a restrained version of what was often called, in shorthand, "the Modern style." In contrast to MGM, which could be accused of rudely plagiarizing and distorting its sources, Paramount made an effort to imitate European decorative style. This may have been due to the fact that Paramount produced more films with European subject matter. For a time, their Hollywood lot included a Paris set, though in 1930, when MGM was importing Parisian talent to Los Angeles, Paramount built its own studio outside Paris, where it employed French artisans as crew members. Naturally, the style that incubated there appears closer to the French origins of Art Deco.[59]

In taking on contemporary French subjects, Hollywood usually featured nouveaux riches, especially highlife criminals and entertainers. Occasionally, a film might be set in a working-class neighborhood (an example is Frank Borzage's *Seventh Heaven;* 1927). But Paris as imaged by Hollywood was gen-

69. An upscale hotel bath, in a photo by Séeberger Frères (1931).

70. A frame from Ernst Lubitsch's *Trouble in Paradise* (1932).

erally the Paris of monuments, chic restaurants, nightclubs, luxurious apartments, and picturesque boutiques (*Love me Tonight;* 1932). The telegraph messages sent to Séeberger Frères demanding photographic documentation of such sites establish this outright. Hollywood's Paris was the Paris of *Harper's Bazaar* with "just a touch of reality" about it.[60]

Two great names in Hollywood were mainly responsible for bringing French advances in style back to the United States: Cedric Gibbons and Cecil B. De Mille. Though already considered "a style unto himself," De Mille was still on the lookout for something new; in 1926 he enticed to America the eminent Paul Iribe, a designer in the tradition of French elegance.[61] De Mille also prominently displayed a Jean Dupas panel from the 1925 Exposition in a scene in *Dynamite* (1928), an MGM film influential in the development of "Hollywood Modern." MGM maintained a special relation to Art Deco. In 1926, the studio imported at great expense one of France's most eminent designers, Erté (born Romain de Tirtoff), only to reject as too radical his conception for a film entitled *Paris.* They substituted their more acceptable version of Art Deco Paris, inflated and faddish.[62]

"Inflation" was the operative word at MGM, where Cedric Gibbons became director of design sometime after personally attending the great exposition of 1925. Gibbons was completely marked by the tactility, lightness, innovation, and luxury he encountered there, all of which he introduced into the MGM studio style, where it is evident in sets, costumes, even coiffures. This *style moderne* would affect all MGM productions, though it seemed particularly apt for certain popular subjects: films about the nouveaux riches in their flashy lives of entertainment, travel, and consumerism, and about wealthy men in their commerce with women and with the underworld.[63] In the era of Prohibition, Hollywood gave American audiences frequent glimpses through the keyholes of speakeasies and nightclubs, where excesses of every sort could be expected.

Gibbons gratified this American penchant for excess, in both the scale and the luxury of his designs. He enlarged his sets and their fantasy elements to extraordinary proportions, developing MGM's "Big White Style" in films such as *Private Lives* (1931) and *Grand Hotel* (1932), with expansive rooms bathed in the high-key light that the new panchromatic stock could handle especially well. This MGM look was disseminated not just through its films but in ads, posters, and other media, including magazine stories about its productions and stars. Fantasy soon became reality when Gibbons' set designs served as the plans for more than one private mansion constructed during this period. He personally supervised the decoration of the home that Frank Lloyd Wright designed for screen idol Ramon Navarro.[64]

Even in its first emanations, Art Deco aimed to be both distinguished and widely appealing; most of those responsible for its birth were pleased to watch it spread rapidly via the popular media that drew on, disseminated, and contributed to it. Annual salons became attention-getting contests among jewelers, glassmakers, and other artisans grouped under the label *ébénistes* (cabinetmakers). Art Deco must be considered one of the first truly consumer-oriented art movements. Naturally, department stores had been trafficking in mass-consumption items since the 1880s, but with this difference: after 1925, emphasis shifted toward the look of the product rather than the product itself. When department stores, sometimes even in advance of the mass media, showed off the "modern" in windows, cases, and display rooms that were often designed by exposition artists, they were selling appearances rather than objects.[65]

And those appearances traveled abroad. They were diffused in photographs and in an increasing number of *objets* bearing the style. But Art Deco was also literally carried around the world in conspicuous ways. The liner *Ile-de-France*, launched in 1926, was "France's floating emissary of modern decorative art," with wood, glass, and wrought iron fashioned by luminaries from the exposition.[66] The new style made a formidable impression in the United States, when the Metropolitan Museum of Art in New York arranged for more than 400 of the pieces it had bought in Paris to tour the nation.[67] The same year, Le Corbusier built a home and studio in Boulogne-Billancourt, just outside Paris, making use of a great many streamlining motifs. Refashioned in 1936 by Georges-Henri Pingusson, it even sports a first-story terrace "prow" that juts well in front of its five-story "hull."[68]

Though perhaps reaching its creative peak at the 1925 exposition, Art Deco really took off in the 1930s, when it became synonymous the world over with the idea of what was "acceptably modern."[69] Modernists such as Proust, T. S. Eliot, the Cubists, and Igor Stravinsky generally exasperated a public that felt if not scandalized, then simply left behind. Nevertheless, after World War I the media were full of the "modern" as a ubiquitous fact of urban life, often celebrated as such in film and architecture. In the early 1930s, a "new look" is evident in films from places as distant as Shanghai and Japan. Works by the Japanese directors Yasujiro Ozu (*Days of Youth;* 1929) and Kenji

71. Ocean-liner style in the model of an Art Deco building (5 Allée des Pins, Boulogne-Billancourt), by Le Corbusier and Georges-Henri Pingusson (1920s).

Mizoguchi (*Osaka Elegy;* 1936) feature department stores and *mogos* ("modern girls").[70] In Germany, the Bauhaus aimed to find peaceful applications for the mass-production and engineering techniques developed during World War I. The Soviet Union went so far as to imagine redesigning its entire society on Constructivist principles. And the United States was always deemed the modern nation par excellence. In this international ambience, Art Deco was commonly understood to be *le style moderne*, the name by which it was known at the time. It was not actually baptized "Art Deco" until a museum retrospective in 1966.

The French government sponsored the 1925 exposition as a calculated advertising campaign to increase French exports at a moment of economic stagnation.[71] Ideologically, the French wanted to distinguish themselves as inheritors and legislators of a culture they claimed to have successfully defended in the Great War, a culture they were proud to disseminate to their colonies and to their neighbors. The concentration of artists—and, even more, of artisans—in Paris made it the capital of fashion, particularly given the prestige of its centuries-old guilds and fine-arts traditions. The exposition proclaimed this combination of the new and the old, and of the "modern" with the "modish." It did so by warming the cool Cubism of the previous generation with more tactile products destined for the wealthy—products that nevertheless retained Cubist wit and geometry. With a chic twist, it resurrected luxury and comfort, values that had been disparaged by sophisticates ever since the ascendancy of the bourgeoisie in 1850.[72]

Art Deco in its first, defining phase emphasized ornament and surface

72. A 1929 Mallet-Stevens design for his breakaway group.

nearly to the exclusion of structure. Surface sheen and movement caught and held the viewer's eye, not in order to express an idea or highlight the purpose or substance of the artifact, but just for the sake of visual pleasure. The roots of Art Deco can be traced to Art Nouveau (with solid colors now replacing pastels, and vapid swirls rectified and ordered). Its appeal was congruent with postwar directions in the other arts—with the Ballets Russes, for instance, and with the music of Les Six (the Group of Six), who confidently abandoned German symphonic structure for effects of rhythm and tone.[73] On the other hand, a rival aesthetic—international rather than French—thrived under the name "Bauhaus," involving Le Corbusier and, to a lesser extent, Mallet-Stevens in Paris. Functionalist through and through, the Bauhaus artists invested all in clever but rational architectural design. The 1925 exposition brought these two styles of modern design into conflict when the French organizers refused their German rivals a pavilion of their own[74] and consigned Le Corbusier to what is said to have been the worst location on the exposition grounds, a site originally blocked from view by a fence. His design was considered too radical, too international, and too industrial.[75]

In France, the fissure evident at the exposition continued to widen for the next fifteen years. When the powerful and traditional Société des Artistes Décoratifs (S.A.D.) squeezed Mallet-Stevens and his school completely out of their 1928 salon, a countergroup, l'Union des Artistes Modernes, was formed.[76] Invoking science as an ally, these political leftists proclaimed an end to luxury just in time to greet the world economic crisis. The Depression seemed to rebuke Art Deco; ads for luxury items in magazines like *L'Illustration* declined precipitously in number in the early 1930s. And wakeup calls were sounded to bring designers down from their flighty reveries of the twenties. These came frequently from the United States, where the Depression was felt first and strongest. An editorial from *Interior Architecture and Decoration* is typical: "The Fantastic days of 1929 are gone, with their ideals of night clubs, theaters, restaurants and other amusements. The emphasis has come back to the home, . . . from spurious to genuine. . . . Cost is now an element . . . and there is a great premium on good taste, good counsel, and expert buying."[77]

Still, prudence and reason changed the tone but not the spread of modern design. Jacques-Emile Ruhlmann, to take an illustrious example, was known for using precious wood and ivory in the limited-edition furniture he designed for the rich bourgeoisie, but by 1928 he had allowed metal to enter his arsenal of materials after seeing the vogue for Le Corbusier. Ruhlmann, more than anyone else, brought Art Deco into a space of the imagination. He created a great many objects for the *Ile-de-France*; he designed spectacular interiors for the Empire Theater before Stavisky took it over; and he fashioned sections of the Colonial Exposition of 1931. Ruhlmann's luxurious vision was resisted by a concerted opposition, especially the Groupe Espace (comprising Mallet-Stevens, Le Corbusier, and Francis Jourdain). They supported André Bloc, who declared in *L'Architecture Aujourd'hui* that Ruhlmann's decadence had to give way to "modern techniques and methods for renewed goals in real space aiming at functional necessities, . . . from the simplest to the most complex. Constructed according to the needs of private and public life, participating in direct action with a community of human beings."[78]

Popular graphics, advertisements, and above all movies from the early 1930s indicate a general consensus that the solution to the Depression lay in the universal adoption of a streamlined mentality. An American journalist at the 1931 Paris Salon reported the spread of this conception: "Offices, hotels, new shops on the boulevards, new theaters, and modern apartments are all at least partly or entirely decorated in Modern. The style is recognized by the public, and modern interior decoration is apparently becoming crystallized."[79]

But what is this style? Howell Cresswell, the Paris correspondent for *Interior Architecture and Design,* instructed his readers: "The present school of French decorators seems to fall into two classes, according to their first initiatives in Modern. Some took up the absolute straight-line idea, based on our own American architecture and certain German attempts, while others sought to modernize the graceful models of French tradition."[80] Curving lines, always an index of elegance, had become a trademark that French designers marketed during the rage for Art Nouveau. Under the weight of the money crisis, effete taste and excessive ornamentation went into retreat, without, however, utterly eclipsing the craving for distinction: "We have had an enormous amount of straight-line Modern. . . . Since this model is easy to execute and cheaply produced by machine labor and unskilled workmen, it therefore follows that the more complex and handmade types must be sought. The Modern, to remain modern, must not be produced *en série* but must limit itself to single pieces." Cresswell goes on to provide a good example of distinguished yet practical and affordable furniture appropriate for the Depression:

> It is now realized that the use of chromium metal has given chairs and certain other pieces of furniture the advantage of new lines not even practiced in Period furniture. The material itself if used with sharp edges becomes intolerable and by force of circumstances has led the decorators to this new phase of a more friendly appearing chair or table. . . . In addition we find that the "softening down" process is solved by the use of other materials than chromium metal such as wood, wood plus fabrics, leather, and cushioned materials. These not only take away the hardness of the metal but lend other color effects.[81]

And so, while the definitive victory of the modern over retrogressive forces was proclaimed, the modern itself was taken to be a synthesis of decorative and functional impulses. The straight line may have chastened the Art Nouveau influence on Deco, but many French designers continued to round, if ever so little, even their most functional lines. In effect, the visible attention that any amount of curvature lends to an industrial product provides a signature at once personal and national, to humanize life in a period of austerity.

The elegant French twist to Art Deco could not dominate the interna-

73. The height of Art Deco fashion aboard *Le Normandie*.

tional marketplace. Continuing to look backward by referencing period models, much Art Deco found itself out-produced and out-classed by the low-line industrial design demanded of the Depression era. This would be evident at the 1937 exposition—so close to the 1925 event in name, but so much more concerned with the democratization of comfort, with art in the service of industry, which, in turn, was in the service of progress. Bauhaus metal tubing had replaced the hand-carved wood of the cabinetmakers. Yet the original French impulse in Art Deco was still deployed in prominent sites, most famously covering the luxury liner *Normandie* from stem to stern as it floated off on its brief career in 1935, at twice the tonnage of the *Ile-de-France*. While one might expect the international style of streamlined functionalism to dominate the look of a liner such as this or the *Queen Mary*, exoticism and luxury won out.[82] Motifs from the Colonial Exposition were incorporated into a pastiche of elegance on the *Normandie*, a dream ship that, "excepting two suites in eighteenth-century style, . . . was drenched in contemporary design."[83] With glass by René Lalique, bronzes by Louis Dejean, furniture by Jean Dupas, and rooms laid out by Ruhlmann and Raymond Subes, it was the most fashionable transport in the world.

Other arenas still permitting Art Deco to exercise its fancies have come down to us under the rubric of "kitsch," a word invented by the Germans for the peculiar conjunction of industrial mass production, mass taste, and ornate but retro imitation of hollow forms whose historical content has been evacuated. Walter Benjamin prophetically recognized the dangers of kitsch, part of the aestheticization of politics. No wonder decorators in Italy and Germany adopted such a sentimental, degraded, popularized form of *le style moderne*. It disarmed the spirit of criticism and bathed a mass audience in a fog of feeling. The same would hold true for movie palaces like the Rex. The increasing popularization and vulgarization of Art Deco leading up to World War II inevitably tell a story of decline: "The Depression, rampant chauvinism, and nationalistically based art forms ought to have killed off the style were it not for the narcosis of Hollywood, which perpetrated a decorous classicizing version of the hard geometry of the 1920s upon a yielding public. Hollywood ultra-modern became a swan-song style to which the Paris International Exposition of 1937 and the New York World's Fair of 1939 subscribed, but only insofar as they addressed themselves to a new audience of urban white-collar workers."[84]

Everyday Elegance: Paris in the Illustrated Press

While Art Deco's international proliferation depended less and less on its Parisian origins, in France the style retained its national—and occasionally nationalist—prestige. A domesticated version of the "modern look" circulated and recirculated through French movies, newspapers, radio, and illustrated magazines. For instance, a tacit connivance developed between French cinema and the glossy "week in review" magazine *L'Illustration*. Beyond reviewing films and tracking stars (often with glamour shots), *L'Illustration* presented a middle-class version of Paris very much like the one conveyed by many of the 120 feature films that France produced annually.

Dating back to 1843, *L'Illustration* greatly increased its ratio of photos to drawings and sketches after 1926. That was the year in which editor René Baschet hired Emmanuel Sougez, whose photographs had made a tremendous impact at the 1925 Art Deco Exposition. Sougez, who would lead the magazine into its heyday, made no secret of his mission to promote French photography and French style against the disturbing influx of foreign artists, particularly eastern European photographers.[85] With Sougez at the helm, *L'Illustration* focused increasingly on Paris rather than on the provinces and the colonies. Clever, stylish advertisements flourished as the journal grew to a circulation of over 300,000 mostly affluent readers.[86]

74. High-fashion shop in Sacha Guitry's *Bonne Chance* (1936).

Like *Life* magazine, launched in the United States in 1936, *L'Illustration* was known primarily for its photography, which was shown to optimal effect through the exploitation of the most advanced technical forms of reproduction available. Sougez monitored every aspect of the "look of *L'Illustration*," and he did so with a single goal: "To eliminate chance as much in taking pictures as in processing them." Under his direction, the photographs in *L'Illustration* seldom pretended to capture life on the run, even when they covered current events. An article characterizing Sougez's approach stressed the picturesque quality of his own famous shots of Paris, particularly one in which "the spire of the Sainte-Chapelle pierces the fog."[87]

Given *L'Illustration*'s mass circulation, its characteristic approach to images provides a reliable index to the era's self-conception, or, more properly, to the pictorial conception of the era proposed by a forward-looking middle class. For *L'Illustration* was, like *Life*, hardly a magazine intellectuals would pay attention to even if they did find themselves browsing through it. But neither was it a forum for stodgy opinion, or for explicit opinion at all. It took its mission from its title, believing it could shed light on the people, the events, and the trends worth illustrating (with an emphasis on "luster"). No matter what its content, this magazine essentially tried to unify France, for it sold the news in the style of the "new," and it sold it to a broad middle spectrum of the nation.

With such a readership and advertising base, *L'Illustration* projected week after week a vision of modernization and transformation; yet, given its nationalist outlook, it also purveyed the pride of French tradition, evident in its many photo essays about older architecture and current national events. It treated the premodern *quartiers* of Paris with patronizing affection, as charming vestiges of an older way of life, which was to be cherished though no longer credited. Photo essays such as "Flânerie dans le Vieux Paris" (September 25, 1928, illustrated entirely with engravings) and "Paris qui Passe" (December 2, 1933, written by Francis Carco) invite readers on leisurely perambulations into the past. Others document demolition projects in progress. One of these (November 6, 1926) laments that Montmartre itself will soon be a modern neighborhood like any other, and invokes Alphonse Daudet's hymn to its "deliciously anachronistic" ambience. But later photo essays such as "Adieux aux fortifications de Paris" (January 14, 1933) and "Adieux au Trocadéro" (September 7, 1935) are more matter-of-fact. While the latter piece adopts the obligatory nostalgic tone for its six-page glossy tribute to the 1878 monument just as it was to be razed, the text still rings with pride in forecasting the replacement of the dowdy Musée d'Ethnographie with the exciting Musée de l'Homme, to be installed in the new Palais de Chaillot.

It was definitely the new-look metropolis that *L'Illustration* most consistently documented. The December 10, 1927, issue compared photographs of prominent intersections and monuments in 1855 (the period of Marville's documentation) with up-to-date shots taken from the same angle, mentioning the simultaneous progress evident both in urban development and in photography. "Paris sous Napoléon et Paris aujourd'hui" (October 7, 1933) set period engravings against photographs taken from precisely the same perspective. Easily the best example of *L'Illustration*'s orientation can be found in an April 1930 essay, "Paris qui s'en va" (Disappearing Paris), which examines the expansion of the produce market known as Les Halles into the quaint Beaubourg neighborhood. A master plan to raze the 1970s Forum des Halles has sparked debate on how best to retain remnants of the medieval neighborhood that the Forum destroyed.

It is simply a matter of rehabilitating a neighborhood that is turning into a cesspool and of replacing insignificant and extremely dilapidated hovels with air and light. These improvements have long been called for. In 1909, the city of Paris was already concerned about the clearing out of the Saint-Merri neighborhood. At the time, a defender of historical Paris had deplored the demolition of these picturesque streets and old houses, most of which had foundations and part of their construction dating as far back as the fourteenth and fifteenth centuries. No one more respects the past more than do we, or more regrets the destruction of very beautiful and significant things of the past—a destruction that occurred at a time when no protective intervention could stop vandalism on the part of speculators. Yet in the admirable concern for preservation that, for the past forty years, has fallen to an elite of artists and archeologists, one must take care not to go too far and allow oneself to be dominated by emotions. A placard can sometimes say as much as an authentic boundary marker or a preserved section of stone wall, and may even say more. As Théophile Gautier justly wrote, "Let us allow civilization, which needs air, sun, space for its unbridled activity, to carve out broad avenues in the dark labyrinth of alleys, crossroads, dead ends of the old city. . . . In order to go on living, cities are often forced to sweep out the dust of their history, much as they sweep the mud from their streets." These words, dating from 1854, seem to have been written yesterday.[88]

In the autumn 1937 afterglow of the ultramodern International Exposition, whose photo section Sougez headed,[89] *L'Illustration* ran a fascinating series of photos on some of the most downtrodden parts of the city.[90] Exceptionally picturesque photographs of an ancient, dark neighborhood were juxtaposed with clean designs for urban renewal projects in the works. Here, as usual, *L'Illustration* was out to preserve the look of the past, whose disappearance under the wheels of progress it nevertheless applauded and even hastened.[91]

L'Illustration was in the business of readying the French for the future, selling them glimpses of things to come or things that had just appeared: photographs of small-scale models of planned buildings or parking garages, shots of chic cafés and brand-new stores or of august structures built to anchor the transformation of formerly dilapidated zones. In the magazine's ads as well as in its feature stories, Paris was made to appear as handsome as pos-

75. Art Deco for the stolid insurance industry: 21 rue Châteaudun, Paris.

sible, a city primping before the camera's mirror. Emblematic of *L'Illustra-tion*'s many photo essays on Paris is one focusing on a new insurance building, La Paternelle, right around the corner from its editorial offices. Adroitly framed low-angle photographs confirm that this building—as well as, by extension, this company—was "sober, well-proportioned, immense, and efficient, just as it should be."[92] And so, in the uncertainty of the Depression, *L'Illustration* went out of its way to stabilize the nation with an image that conveyed solidity, which was simultaneously an image of progress, for La Paternelle was a splendid example of Art Deco architecture.

In this way, week after week, a saturation of photographs and ads in *L'Illustration* circulated an idea of modern French style in buildings, typography, and luxury objects. This style and many of these objects were simultaneously visible at the movies. Take, for example, something as common as eyeglasses. While ads for Leroy spectacles appeared in certain issues of *L'Illustration*, photographs of debonair men wearing them could be found on many of its pages. A product of the Art Deco 1920s, these spectacles were the sort worn by Tsuguharu Foujita and Robert Brasillach in real life, by Louis in *A Nous la liberté* and by Sacha Guitry in his 1935 comedy *Bonne Chance*. (Guitry's life and movie roles—scarcely distinguishable from each other—spilled often into the pages of *L'Illustration*.)[93]

76–78. The Leroy phenomenon: trademark, newspaper ad, and on the face of
Sacha Guitry in *Bonne Chance*.

79–80. A decade of Miss Europe Prize winners and Louise Brooks in Augusto Genina's *Prix de Beauté* (1930).

81. The circulation of fashion in and through *L'Illustration* (1935).

In Paris, as elsewhere, fashion both produced and depended on the "modern woman," whose image circulated at high speed from films and glossy magazines to downtown shopping. In 1938 *L'Illustration* ran a history of the Miss Europe competition, on the occasion of the contest's tenth anniversary.[94] Each of the ten faces displayed was an avatar of the modern look; each was a model aspired to by women, ogled by men. Beauty contests exhibited a look—call it "classic" or "modern"—that magazines and movies marketed in myriad ways, sometimes doing so outright. In 1929, just after the first Miss Europe contest, Augusto Genina arrived in San Sebastián to film René Clair's astoundingly sophisticated script, *Prix de Beauté*. It starred the American actress Louise Brooks, the sensational Art Deco film idol who changed styles of hair, couture, and behavior in France and around the world.

To read *L'Illustration* or to go to the movies was to participate in the evolution of French culture, not just to witness it. Both media consistently put images of style, not to mention the concept of style itself, into the minds of a broad class of consumers. And Paris, it went without saying, was the world center of style. A supplement to the May 28, 1938, issue of *L'Illustration* bore the heading: "Paris: Capitale Moderne." Essays proudly describing the new museums, the freshly scrubbed Opera neighborhood, and the fountains, all of which made the city utterly new while retaining its specific character, culminate in a feature article betraying the magazine's real interest and reason for being: "L'Industrie et le commerce de luxe à Paris" (The Manufacture and Sale of Luxury Goods in Paris). Here, as always, no matter what its subject matter, *L'Illustration* was determined to present itself as both "French" and "modern"; thus, it functioned much like the movies produced in Paris' studios. An article on yachting, for instance, shows an elegant woman lounging on the deck of a boat that is carrying her down the Seine.[95] The image is designed just like a poster for a film—for, say, Philippe de Rothschild's production of *Lac aux dames*, which Marc Allegret directed in 1933. Set at a chic lakeside resort (décor by Lazare Meerson), and with dialogue written by Colette, *Lac aux dames* showed off elegant young women in fashionable swimwear.[96] Movies and press photos often reinforced the fashions that *L'Illustration* promoted in its ads and featurettes (in this case, a sexy outdoors look), contributing to an expanding industry of high fashion. Mannequins in department stores helped turn this modern image of woman into a reality that one could scarcely avoid when in the city.

L'Illustration could satirize luxury and modernity while selling it. A spread on *la vie moderne* (5 June 1937) reads like a series of scenes from a comedy by Sacha Guitry. Accompanied by photographs of men at a fancy bar, at a restaurant, and in a hotel reading room, the author delivers four clever anecdotes set in fashionable Neuilly and Longchamp. Each anecdote ridicules, but nevertheless repeats and displays, the quest to be modern. The brio of the writing—its witty self-consciousness—could be found in the dialogue of Henri Jeanson, Jacques Nathanson, Marcel Achard, and the many other urbane scenarists of the screen. It could be found, as well, in Guitry's *Bonne Chance*. Modernity had arrived when Paris paraded its sophistication and style, even if it remained pure fantasy for the masses.

Whitewashing Paris at the Movies

In 1937, Guitry's name glowed once more from the Rex's marquee. The brilliance of his new sex farce, *Mon père avait raison* (My Father Was Right), was enhanced by that of the Rex itself. Both the film and the theater were thought to be chic, but the fact is that their modernity was belated. Paris may have invented *le style moderne* (aided by the kind of trend-setting décors Mallet-Stevens designed for avant-garde films by Germaine Dulac and Marcel L'Herbier),[97] but standard French movies did not register the effects of the Art Deco movement until well after Hollywood had.[98] This was because at the end of the silent period, the memorable products of Parisian studios were primarily historical epics and literary adaptations (*Napoléon*, the Joan of Arc films, *Thérèse Raquin*, *Nana*, *La Chute de la Maison d'Usher*).[99] It was sound that brought the city of Paris—modern Paris—ubiquitously back into French film, through the many theater adaptations full of dialogue and song set on rigid sound-stages carefully sized for actors. French producers glanced sideways at Hollywood's version of Paris, since the world's movie capital had quickly picked up design tactics at the 1925 Paris exposition. By 1933, a good many of France's creative personnel had made the voyage to MGM and back, Yves Mirande and Jacques Feyder among them.[100] The French films that they produced during the rest of the decade took advantage of what they had learned in Hollywood, while relying on native knowledge of French life and Paris' look. As with *L'Illustration*, French cinema of the 1930s was distinctively national and putatively modern, but its modernity was largely imported from America, and thus far more middle-class than avant-garde.

American tastes found their French counterpart in the many high-society plays featuring ensemble acting which were transferred to, or written directly for, the screen. The backbone of standard filmmaking, these boulevard pieces take us to Parisian restaurants, hotels, shops, and the boudoirs and sitting rooms of grand apartments. Their sparkling dialogue glistens, along with the jewelry, champagne glasses, and chandeliers. Such movies contributed to and circulated an idea of style, whose appearance was visible in stores and on billboards. This self-validating and closed system had the effect of turning reality into image, as wealthier Parisians bought clothes, jewelry, and furniture of the sort pictured in magazines and films.

The essence of this 1930s bourgeois "French modern" is precisely what Alain Resnais was out to bottle in *Stavisky . . . .*[101] The film's locations, first of all, might well have been chosen by the Séeberger brothers, with key scenes taking place at the Hôtel Claridge and the Empire Theater, both of which are decked to the hilt in Art Deco furniture, ashtrays, and posters. Dazzling close-ups of jewelry signify fashion as much as wealth. Most stylish of all are the automobiles, particularly the Hispano-Souza beside which Anny Duperey poses, mimicking a newspaper photo of Stavisky's mistress, Arlette, whom she plays (see Figure 5 in the Introduction).

In *Stavisky . . .*—and, we are meant to believe, in the epoch it evokes—the automobile seals the connection between modernity and women, rather than serving as instrument and symbol of male domination. The look and feel of

82. How to market an alluring equation.

automobiles are coded as feminine. This connection is made in the first sequence of Jacques Feyder's film *Le Grand Jeu*, which premièred in 1933, the year *Stavisky . . .* takes place. Marie Bell and Pierre-Richard Willm careen drunkenly through Paris, streetlights intermittently reflecting off their shiny Delage—a "D 8.5 model," the final credits proudly assert. An extended scene in the garage of Willm's townhouse gives the spectator plenty of time to admire this exquisite car and the fast woman with the white feather stole for whom it has been purchased. Feyder could choose no stronger way to typify an entire way of life, "modern chic." Available only to the wealthy, flashy cars were nevertheless advertised to catch everyone's attention, with alluring women often posing in or beside them. One ad from a 1933 issue of *L'Illustration* blares the slogan "Delage et la femme." A subsequent issue carried a feature article that extended this metaphor indecently: "Delage vehicles, thanks to their powerful and nervous motors, to the sweetness and precision of their steering, to the capaciousness of their bodies, and to their perfect suspension, . . . [are] the most elegant and the most modern."[102]

The couple in *Le Grand Jeu* manages to acquire an apartment designed entirely in Art Deco by the master, Lazare Meerson. The staircase, the divan, and the overwhelming whiteness of the tiered rooms make this a fantasy abode, the kind of home sold in interior-design magazines. In Feyder's film, Art Deco stands for profligacy and irresponsibility, against the staid and somber family estate in St. Cloud from whose stolid location Willm's father and financial advisors reprove him. Later in the film Art Deco will stand in much greater contrast to a seedy North African hotel to which the diffident Willm has fled, avoiding disgrace by signing on with the Foreign Legion. This is the actor about whom an interviewer of the time wrote: "With him, everything is as modern as possible, . . . nothing old-fashioned, nothing out-of-date."[103]

While the relation of women to modern design, and thus to Parisian urbanity, is exploited in a great many films of the period, most striking and most peculiar are those cases where Paris is evoked from the colonies. Featuring seductive actresses who stand in for the life of the capital wherever they pose, these films bank on the explicit rapport of style to desire. The Paris sequence that opens *Le Grand Jeu* occupies less than fifteen minutes of the film, which moves to Morocco and life in the Foreign Legion. Paris nonetheless returns as a kind of desert mirage through minute metonymies of décor. The climactic sequence takes place at a chic hotel in a North African port city. Here, amid Moorish elements incongruously interlaced with Art Deco arabesques (just as at the Rex and on the *Normandie*), Marie Bell once again humiliates Willm: figuratively, she takes him for a ride.

A few years later, at the time of the Popular Front's success, Julien Duvivier's *Pépé le Moko* would provide the locus classicus of desire for Paris. In the love duet at the film's heart, Pépé (Jean Gabin), who is trapped in the Casbah, and Gaby (Mireille Balin), an adventuresome tourist, conjure Paris in an antiphon of Métro stations that converges on the Place Blanche, in the colorful but rough neighborhood they both knew in the past. Yet what drives Pépé to risk his stature and his life is less a Paris that has disappeared than the image of a luxurious Paris for which Gaby serves as synecdoche—Gaby of the jewels and stylish gowns, Gaby who travels first class aboard ship with her sugar daddy, Gaby who stands out in white, personifying Art Deco.[104]

The poetic realist films that follow in the wake of these fatalistic tales of North Africa are, by contrast, uniformly somber in tone, except for the inclu-

sion in each of an alluring woman who offers a shimmering image of pleni-
tude; inevitably, or so it seems, this woman is clothed in or surrounded by
white, the color of "Hollywood Deco"—also the color of the colonizer. In
Gueule d'Amour, Jean Gabin first rides into the frame on a horse, in the dashing white outfit of a *spahi*.[105] Soon he and Madeleine fall into their deadly love
affair. As in *Pépé le Moko*, Gabin approaches this Parisian *mondaine* from the
south, from his native city of Orange and from Africa, where he has served.
The contrast that develops between his authentic world and her frivolous one
is rendered via three Parisian locations: his cheap hotel and workplace, the
Parc des Buttes-Chaumont, where they stroll and dream, and the upscale
apartment where she is "kept" by her sugar daddy. That apartment's most
telling feature is its ornate and spacious bathroom. In 1937 this must have
signaled the ultimate in modernity, with its state-of-the-art plumbing fix-
tures, its large mirrors, and its blindingly white porcelain (see Figure 69). In
an ironic reversal, it is the actor's nudity (rather than that of the female star)
that is tantalizingly hidden beneath clouds of soapsuds. Immersed in these
suds and in this fantasy set (a parody of the glitzy Hollywood bathrooms that
are allotted an entire section of the book *Screen Deco*),[106] Gabin's persona here
comes as close as it ever does to attaining impossible (because finally insub-
stantial) beauty: the modern woman, clothed in white, whom he strangles at
the end.

One more film, Pierre Chenal's *La Maison du Maltais* (1938), measures desire as a distance from North Africa to Paris. Once again, Paris appears as a
woman in white belonging to a wealthy sugar daddy. This time Safia (Viviane
Romance), lifted out of prostitution, lives in an *haut bourgeois* apartment near
the Parc Monceau. Matteo (Marcel Dalio), a Tunisian Muslim who was once
her lover and is the father of her child, tracks her to the park and then barges
into a world from which he is culturally barred. In addition to Safia, this
apartment contains artifacts of his Tunisian homeland, since its owner is an
amateur archeologist. The stylish apartment can serve, then, as an Art Deco
gallery featuring trophies from other lands set off in the best Parisian manner. Matteo is mesmerized by the place, but alienated from it, too, retreating
to Montmartre and the rat's nest he shares with a criminal gang on the rue du
Chevalier de la Barre, in an area that used to be referred to as the Casbah of
Paris.

All four of these films produce a fatal feeling of helplessness when a strong
male from an older tradition (the military, the underworld, Islam) becomes

obsessed by a French woman wearing white, and bearing the look of the modern. The distance between the sexes amounts to a distance between two styles, one coded as authentic but out of date, the other as attractive but empty, or unreachable. Poetic realism saw women and modernity in just this way.

The ubiquity of a female image of brilliant Parisian elegance is confirmed by its appearance in many other types of 1930s films, where, unlike the poetic realist script, the hero and the audience attain what they seek. For example, Sacha Guitry, playing the hero of *Bonne Chance*, manages to win both a beautiful woman and a Pierre-Auguste Renoir painting first glimpsed in a store window (the painting is of Jean Renoir as a boy—an inside joke, no doubt). In the absence of genres such as science fiction, fantasy, or horror, "the modern" in French cinema expressed itself chiefly in dramatic comedies concerned with the smart set, in musicals, and in a few detective films (for instance, Chenal's *L'Alibi* of 1937). For five francs—the cost of an issue of *L'Illustration*—anyone could enter the Rex to gawk at a highlife drama like *Club de Femmes* (1936) or a highlife detective film that might take spectators to Montmartre (*Prisons de Femmes*; 1938).

In sum, many films, from grim poetic realist works to stylish comedies, relied on an image of Paris decked out in Art Deco. That image survives most indelibly from behind a gate—the viewpoint of Pépé le Moko, who dies by his own hand while he watches the ship carrying Gaby steam out of the harbor. All the elegance and all the possibilities of Paris are on board that ship. In fact, *Pépé le Moko* premièred just a year after the maiden voyage (from Le Havre to New York) of the largest, most celebrated liner yet constructed, the *Normandie*, a vessel of Art Deco treasures. It makes perfect sense, then, given what we know of cinema and of the circulation of fashion, that the *Normandie* would soon serve as a film set. Before the decade closed, it was employed by two of the most scintillating figures of Parisian high society, Sacha Guitry and Yves Mirande. The authors of *Screen Deco* write in awe of this conjunction of floating images and floating design on the *Normandie*:

> Sacha Guitry filmed the climax to his comedy *Les Perles de la couronne* [Pearls of the Crown; 1937] in its main dining room. The largest ever on an ocean liner, this enormous space was 305 feet in length, 46 feet wide, and 25 feet high. René Lalique's dazzling lighting scheme comprised thirty-eight wall panels, two huge chandeliers, and twelve wed-

ding-cake decorative standard lights. There were four twenty-foot-high panels of gilded plaster representing Normandy village scenes, and a twice-life-size statue in gilded bronze by Dejean. The soaring walls were encased in hammered glass, and the ceiling was a honeycomb pattern of square cove lighting. The *Normandie* was a movie star again in Yves Mirande's *Paris–New York* (1940), starring Michel Simon and Gaby Morlay. This film featured hijinks and jewel thievery on a westward crossing, and climaxed at the 1939 New York World's Fair.[107]

Just before the Germans entered Paris, Art Deco had once again sailed to America, to still another World's Fair, and to its final resting place. The *Normandie* was destroyed by fire in New York harbor in 1942. Its flaming out surely marked the end of an era, a *temps des cerises*. With the Occupation, the Rex began showing newsreels and documentaries before every feature. Its legendary status as a dream palace made it useful to the Germans, who requisitioned it as a *Soldatenkino*—a moviehouse catering exclusively to soldiers.[108] The feature films showcased there and throughout the nation after 1940 turned against Paris, looking instead to historical or provincial France. For their part, still photographers had far more serious subjects to shoot than Paris fashions.

If the Deco that flamed out on the *Normandie* was by definition an accoutrement, then movie décor (false, by definition) was particularly flimsy in the 1930s, when it ignored the Depression and the looming international conflict. Art Deco projected an image of a brighter time, of a *belle époque* reborn, complete with colonial motifs, but often projected through a "mist of regret."[109] Rather than having no history, then, modernity contains both future and past. Nostalgia is very much a part of modernity. Just visit the Musée d'Orsay—or, better still, go to the Rex.

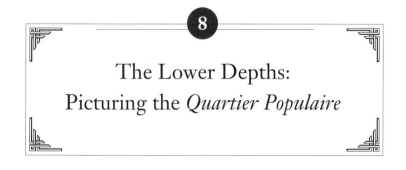

8

The Lower Depths:
Picturing the *Quartier Populaire*

Eugène Dabit's Paris

Balzac concludes *Le Père Goriot* (1834) with his protagonist, Eugène Rastignac, looking down from a hill atop Père Lachaise Cemetery to the area between the Place Vendôme and the dome of Les Invalides, where he plans to
start his social climb that evening. This view from above sums up topographi-
cally what the fates of Goriot and others at the Maison Vauquer (a seedy Left
Bank rooming house) have taught Rastignac about the city. It allegorizes the
loss of innocence that projects his entry into what the narrator calls a buzzing
urban beehive whose honey Rastignac's eyes already seem to be drinking in. A
century later, numerous passages in Céline's *Voyage au bout de la nuit* likewise
pull back from street-level to evoke, from above, the neighborhoods within
and surrounding Paris. Whereas Rastignac's totalizing perspective expresses
his ambition to rise on the social ladder of the city, that of Céline's Bardamu
comes from the lower depths, amid descendants of women and men who had
been drawn to the capital a century earlier by the prospect of employment.

A hundred years after *Goriot*, this urban underclass was the core of a growing population of common folk *(petites gens)* whose identity was grounded in
the street life of neighborhoods that had formerly been separate villages. This
chapter analyzes the depiction of a working-class neighborhood *(quartier populaire)* in Eugène Dabit's novel *L'Hôtel du Nord* (1929), which served as the
point of departure for Marcel Carné's feature film *Hôtel du Nord* (1938). The
novel and film effectively bracket the decade of the Popular Front, offering
two distinct perceptions of Paris' underclass in a Right Bank neighborhood.

"Atmosphère, atmosphère . . ." *Hôtel du Nord* is often reduced to these two
words, uttered in exasperation and with a nasal inflection redolent of lower-

83. "Atmosphère, atmosphère . . ."

class Paris. The words are spoken by the actress Arletty in her role as the streetwalker, Raymonde. Standing on a footbridge with her lover-pimp, Edmond (Louis Jouvet), she tells him off with the unforgettable line: "Atmosphère, atmosphère, est-ce que j'ai une gueule d'atmosphère?" ("Atmosphere, atmosphere. Do I look like an atmosphere kind of girl?")[1] Arletty's inimitable delivery makes the line simultaneously a question and an assertion, part of an outburst whose intensity detaches it from the sequence in which it occurs. Here is Raymonde's response to Edmond in its entirety: "This is the first time anyone ever called me an atmosphere. If I'm an atmosphere, you're a funny hick-town. Oh, give me a break! Guys who only look tough and who boast about what they used to be—they should all be rubbed out! Atmosphere, atmosphere. Do I look like an atmosphere kind of girl? If that's the way it is, go off to La Varenne on your own! Good fishing and good atmosphere."[2] Raymonde's anger comes from the fact that she wants to leave with Edmond for the south of France, whereas he prefers to go fishing on his own.

After she describes the benefits that a trip south might provide, Edmond counters that their life together is suffocating him: "I'm suffocating, do you hear? Suffocating!"[3] When Raymonde suggests that the fresh sea air at Toulon might do him good and that they might even leave together from Toulon for the colonies overseas, he replies that it would be the same everywhere: "I need a change of atmosphere, and my atmosphere is you."[4]

Vocabularies borrowed from geography and physiology give figurative expression to the affective distance between the two characters, both of whom want a break. Raymonde chides Edmond, "You're in a rut, in a rut—it'll just go on making trouble."[5] But they disagree on how and with whom this break should occur. When Edmond invokes the unseemly term *atmosphère*, Raymonde tries to return in kind the insult that she senses. The most she can do is describe Edmond as a funny hick-town (*drôle de bled*).[6] Responding as best she can to Edmond, Raymonde shows herself less than his rhetorical equal. At the same time, her words identify the very divide between the capital and the provinces to which she looks for a temporary "breather." Tensions between the lovers earlier in the film are likewise played out in terms of language usage. When Edmond first agrees to go south, Raymonde is so happy she cannot contain her pleasure: "Ah! You're sweet! . . . You're so swell that sometimes I forget you're my man—to the point of believing you're really my brother [*frangin*]."[7] When Edmond asks her coldly if she couldn't change her vocabulary, she responds, "'Vocabulary'—funny. The only slang word I don't really understand."[8]

Unremarked but visible throughout Raymonde's outburst is the Quai de Jemmapes, which runs along the Canal Saint-Martin between the Gare de l'Est and Belleville. The argument between Raymonde and Edmond occurs while they are standing on the walkway of a lock within sight of what is known as the Chinese Bridge. Surprisingly, neither the argument nor the characters of Raymonde and Edmond appear in Dabit's novel *L'Hôtel du Nord*, which Carné, Jean Aurenche, and Henri Jeanson adapted to screen nine years after its publication. The fact that Carné deleted the definite article when he titled his film is more than a detail. The abstraction it denotes marks a move away from the urban locale whose specific tone Dabit had meant to convey through a composite of character-types, recalling the fiction of Balzac, Maupassant, and Zola.

Apart from two exceptions mentioned below, the character-types Dabit portrays are identifiable as common people whose individual fates are less important than the composite portrait of which they are a part. No single character in the novel emerges as a protagonist; none stands out among individuals within the shared space of the hotel through which they pass. Transience is thus the core principle of Dabit's realism, with which he portrays an underclass urban population marked by the space in and around the residential hotel it inhabits. Carné's film, made almost a decade after the novel was published, frames its perspective on this underclass in dramatic conventions of melodrama and comedy that spectators recognized and in which, presumably, they delighted.[9] This difference results in part from the nature of Carné's film as a form of mass entertainment whose audience of spectators was broader than the readership of Dabit's novel. Yet medium alone fails to account in full for notions of the popular to which Carné gives visual expression. The plotting of urban spaces in Carné's film also departs from Dabit's novel by taking its cue from character-types, much as Marcel Pagnol had done in the 1920s and 1930s, in the plays and films that he set in and near Marseilles.

Eugène Dabit came to literature via the arts. In 1923, he was a twenty-five-year-old World War I veteran studying painting at the Atelier de la Grande-Chaumière in Montparnasse. The same year, his parents, Louise and Emile, bought a residential hotel at 102 Quai de Jemmapes. By the summer of 1926, he had drafted a fictionalized account of everyday life in the hotel, based on his observations while working there as a night clerk. He titled it *L'Hôtel du Nord, ou La Détresse parisienne*.[10] Two years later, Dabit completed it with help from Roger Martin du Gard, whom he had met after contacting André Gide.[11] In December 1929, Editions Denoël printed 3,000 copies of *L'Hôtel du Nord* at Dabit's expense (with help from his parents). Within six months, positive reviews propelled the novel to a third printing. Writing in the *Nouvelle Revue Française*, Jean Prévost praised the sobriety of Dabit's craftsmanship, as well as the honesty with which he portrayed the lives of ordinary people. On the left, Benjamin Crémieux characterized Dabit as a realist storyteller. On the right, Robert Brasillach described the novel in *L'Action Française* as a "little masterpiece."[12] Though Dabit was without pretense concerning literature, he had definite ideas about his political involvement. In the years 1932–1936, he participated regularly in the Association des Ecrivains et des Artistes Révolutionnaires. A short speech that he wrote for the June 1935 International Congress of Writers for the Defense of Culture appeared later the same year in the AEAR's monthly, *Commune*.[13] By the time he died (he succumbed to typhus in July 1936, while visiting the Soviet

84. Eugène Dabit's parents, Emile and Louise, circa 1923.

Union), he had become disillusioned with Communism, finding himself at odds with restrictive Soviet policies, as well as with those people who wanted to appropriate his depictions of Paris and its urban underclass for their own ends.[14]

L'Hôtel du Nord is a composite of minor episodes, arranged in thirty-five brief chapters recounting the purchase, management, and sale of a residential hotel alongside the Canal Saint-Martin in the district of La Villette. Dabit uses profession and gender as descriptive categories to frame his account of the socialized space in the hotel, presenting it as a microcosm of underclass Paris on the edge of destitution. The social milieu and topography depicted in the novel recall those in Balzac's *Père Goriot*. When a couple named Lecouvreur first visit the hotel to consider buying it, the owner reassures them that "with the neighborhood factories here, there's a good clientele of workers, all on the up and up, dependable. . . . With the workers, some single girls, and couples on the fourth floor—without kids, of course—it's a real family."[15] Self-interest motivates the seller to invoke a cohesiveness that the rest of the novel belies. For what Dabit portrays is hardly a real family ("une vraie famille"); whatever the veneer of respectability, it is constantly being worn away by abusive behavior and criminality.

Dabit's social acumen appears in his portraits of outsiders, such as the activist, Bénitaud, and the candymaker, Monsieur Adrien, whose devotion to the cleanliness of his room and to the outfit he wears to the Magic-City dance club mark his homosexuality.[16] Xenophobia and anti-Semitism are likewise present and seemingly acceptable. A mailman has trouble pronouncing a foreign name and adds, "Hez . . . Herzkovitz. . . . You've got some funny names here."[17] Emile Lecouvreur later boasts that he has just sold off a dozen blankets "à un youpin" ("to a Yid").[18] Such details supplement primary determinants of profession and gender with categories of political ideology (leftist, anarchist), ethnicity (central European, Jewish), and sexual orientation (homosexual). The result accommodates difference through variable thresholds of tolerance and exclusion. Dabit's only explicit nod to collective identity is the May 1 Labor Day celebration marked by the singing of the Communist anthem, the "Internationale," and the demonstrations that Bénitaud and his anarchist colleagues hope to spur to violence.

Political activism and homosexuality in Dabit's novel attract surveillance because they threaten norms of acceptable behavior upheld by laws in the name of social order. Heterosexual activity among boarders not married to each other is tolerated until, in the form of implied or actual prostitution, it threatens the appearance of respectability, which must be upheld in order for the hotel to remain in business. Carné, in his film, displaces the novel's social violence onto social vice by treating prostitution as a fact of life, through the sympathetic figure of Raymonde. Monsieur Adrien's homosexuality is accepted by the hotel's occupants, all of whom are marginals of one kind or another. Accordingly, Adrien assumes no stereotypical poses. Neither fey nor rugged, he is what he is.[19]

Carné asserts in his autobiography that *L'Hôtel du Nord* was less a novel in the strict sense than a sensitive painting of a milieu and the characters living in it.[20] Dabit makes plot and character development secondary to the specificity of the urban setting, conveyed by local sites such as the rue des Ecluses-Saint-Martin and La Chope des Singes (The Monkeys' Tankard), the café next door to the hotel. Carné follows Dabit by reverting to recognizable character-types such as the pimp, the whore, and the cuckold. His use of typology mobilizes sympathetic identification to portray kinds and degrees of moral decline with a tone close to that of nostalgia. It engages the film's spectators to savor the picturesque details in their daily lives or imitate the colorful repartees Henri Jeanson had written so "naturally" for the cast.[21]

The warmth evident in the film's early scenes promotes an image of the residents of the hotel as an extended family. This illusory image contrasts with Dabit's character-types: the possibly Jewish foreigner (Herzkovitz), the political activist (Bénitaud), and the homosexual (Adrien). Carné includes no equivalent foreigner, except for the orphan from the Spanish Civil War whose First Communion is celebrated on the ground floor of the rooming house at the start of the film. Carné also replaces the political violence Dabit embodies in Bénitaud with the criminality of Edouard and his former cronies who eventually catch up with him. Dabit portrays Adrien as a mystery whom Madame Lecouvreur fails to fathom. For Carné, he is merely a lodger who happens to be gay.[22] Carné elides the politics of class struggle embodied by May 1 in favor of national identity symbolized by the Bastille Day celebrations. Even so, the film's fatalistic ending suggests that the collective identity celebrated by the neighborhood's outdoor dances may be less than stable.

Dabit's novel greatly revivified working-class literature. The urban milieu evoked is also a product of language marked by class, region, and profession, a staple of middle-class writers, including Victor Hugo, Zola, and the Goncourt brothers. In addition, Dabit's use of slang and colloquial expressions attracted the attention of Léon Lemonnier, André Thérive, and other advocates of the *roman populiste* movement launched in the late 1920s. Yet this middle-class perspective fell short of the ambitions that Henri Poulaille and others promoted in the cause of a proletarian literature emanating from and addressed to the working class. Poulaille (1896–1980) came to journalism and fiction after working at menial jobs such as bottle-washer, newspaper vendor, and railway porter. His 1930 manifesto, "Nouvel Age littéraire," set forth the principles of an activist program that only a proletarian literature by and for workers could provide. "Populism," as Poulaille saw it, was merely a critical label invented by critics "in order to conceal the existence of true proletarian writing" at a time when literature was still dominated by bourgeois ideology.[23]

Dabit rejected overtures from advocates of populism and proletarian literature alike, because he believed that his novel drew on a social environment in which class allegiance and militancy were marginal. He accepted the Prix Populiste in 1931 but never signed the group's manifestos. (He also rejected Poulaille's offer to pay him personally to refuse the prize.)

Because Dabit grounded his fiction on an urban geography that he knew through personal experience, it is no small irony that Alexandre Trauner built

85. Noontime interlude in Marcel Carné's *Hôtel du Nord* (1938): Jouvet on the Chinese bridge.

86. Frame from *Hôtel du Nord:* lock and footbridge on the Canal Saint-Martin.

87. Carné reprises Kertész.

88. André Kertész, "Along the Canal" (1926 or 1927).

the main set for Carné's film at the Billancourt studios after it was decided that shooting scenes in the middle of Paris would be impractical. Trauner (1906–1989) came to Paris from his native Hungary in the late 1920s to study painting. After assisting Lazare Meerson with set designs for René Clair's *Le Quatorze juillet* and Jacques Feyder's *La Kermesse héroïque*, he worked with Carné over the next decade on *Hôtel du Nord, Le Quai des brumes, Le Jour se lève,* and—most famously—*Les Enfants du paradis.*

Carné, Aurenche, and Jeanson framed their adaptation of Dabit's novel within a plot concerning two star-crossed lovers who arrive at the hotel with the intention of killing themselves. To stage this mix of realism and melodrama, Trauner constructed a studio-set in imitation of the actual site along the Canal Saint-Martin, spanned by a footbridge. In the film's last scene, the lovers leave the hotel by crossing this footbridge—just as they had done in the film's first shot, though in the opposite direction. This visual symmetry sets them apart from the film's other characters, especially Louis Jouvet's Edmond, whose attempt to escape a shady past ("for a change of atmosphere") is doomed. As for Dabit's novel, no character manages to leave the neighborhood except by death or by spiraling down to even more marginal and cramped quarters.

A sequence of four shots midway through the film shows the extent to which—even if only briefly—Carné tapped visually into the grittier realism that Dabit had portrayed nine years earlier in his novel. The sequence occurs just after Edmond decides for the first time that he and Raymonde will not go away together. Shot 193 shows the canal, with the footbridge in the background and two barges waiting beside the lock. Shot 194 shows two tramps stretched out on one of the three steps running alongside the canal. Shot 195 is of a worker slumped over and apparently dozing against the backrest at one end of a bench. Shot 196 shows the staircase of the Chinese Bridge framed frontally from below at street-level. This sequence serves as visual interlude between the dramatic scene of estrangement that begins to separate Edmond from Raymonde and the scene of everyday life represented by the lunchtime customers at the hotel. The transition begins by dissolving from Raymonde to a large clock showing 12:15 P.M. It ends by transposing the discord between Raymonde and Edmond onto a heated interaction among staff and clientele. When Edmond flirts with Renée, a libidinal charge precipitates his physical confrontation with Kenel, another resident of the hotel.

The interlude is noteworthy because it strongly recalls two photographs

89. Carné reprises Kertész again.

90. André Kertész, untitled photo (circa 1934).

in the 1934 book *Paris vu par André Kertész*. The first of the two shots was taken along the Canal Saint-Martin, with the three-step border clearly visible in the background. The second represents noonday somnolence in the figure of an inebriated man slumped over on a bench. Carné's eight-shot interlude derives from Pierre Mac Orlan's notion of "le fantastique social" ("the social fantastic"), which combines urban space, romance, and adventure, and in which Mac Orlan, who wrote the preface and captions for the Kertész book, assigns photography a central role. Mac Orlan describes photography as an incomparable source of subtle details and the most accomplished of arts that reveal the fantastic and inhuman elements surrounding human life. The photography that Mac Orlan has in mind is neither that of the postcard nor the sort tinted with watercolors. Instead, it is found in private studios and in the collections of agencies that supply photo documents to the mass-circulation press: "For Kertész, the anxiety generated by a fantastic element of the street, more in line with central European tastes, interprets secret elements of shadow and light, so that others can draw fictional situations from them."[24]

Carné's four-shot scene sets the quay of an urban canal as a boundary or frontier between the melodrama of the lovers' failed suicide attempt and the character-types that inhabit the hotel. It is a visual precedent of the isolation of Edmond, whose fatalistic return to the hotel is fully in line with the interplay of shadow and light that attracts Mac Orlan to certain photographers—the ones he praises for showing humanity in its violence and anonymity. The sequence also marks a brief moment of realist dissonance in a film whose populist atmosphere Carné sustains to a greater degree in the darker visual tones of *Le Quai des brumes* and *Le Jour se lève*, both made within a year of *Hôtel du Nord*.

Mac Orlan's remarks on the social fantastic also complement a realist vision in Dabit that Carné recasts in his adaptation more along the lines of melodrama. When the hotel is torn down at the novel's end to allow a nearby factory to expand, Louise Lecouvreur reflects that it was as if the hotel had never existed: "Nothing remains of it, not even a photograph."[25] This disappearance conveys the reality of transience through understatement. Dabit's sympathy for the underclass of his book derives from what he observed while working at his parents' hotel. Within the novel, transience returns the Lecouvreur couple to their initial anonymity after their purchase of the hotel had transformed them into property owners. Carné's film features individuals who destroy themselves as they try without success to break out from their milieux, both social and physical. Dabit enfolds his characters within an underclass that seldom, if ever, reaches the self-awareness which is central to the poetic realism that Carné's films epitomize through the mid-1940s.[26]

Carné's own self-consciousness was so great that he left the street to build his urban environment in the studio. This fussiness was even more evident after *Hôtel du Nord*, in additional collaborations with set designer Trauner. André Bazin notes that Trauner's 1939 work on Carné's *Le Jour se lève* enhances the fatalist vision in *Hôtel du Nord*:

> Have a look at the suburban square—note the exact fidelity of the setting, the tenement stark against the sky. By rights this dingy suburban backwater ought to be ugly. In fact, one feels that it has a paradoxically poetic atmosphere. Perhaps this setting struck most of you as real. But it is an artificial set, built entirely in a studio. . . . Trauner designed this small suburban square the way a painter composes his canvas. While remaining faithful to the exigencies of reality, he succeeded in giving it a delicately poetic interpretation, so that it appears not as a reproduction of reality, but as a work of art dependent on the artistic economy of the film as a whole.[27]

Let us follow Bazin by looking at how the suburban square designed by Trauner for *Le Jour se lève* (Daybreak) elaborates the mix of realism and poetic atmosphere central to *Hôtel du Nord*. The film opens outside an apartment building in a working-class urban neighborhood in the city of Amiens, about sixty miles north of Paris.[28] First seen from the side, the apartment building stands out against a cloudless sky above a small intersection containing trolley-car tracks, wagons, bicycles, trucks, and pedestrians. The set also contains some small stores and a commercial icon of the period, an advertisement— "Dubo-Dubon-Dubonnet"—painted on a wall, captured by Kertész in his 1934 book. In line with Bazin's remarks above, the opening shot organizes urban space less in terms of specific location than as a setting whose abstraction—the stark outlines of the building against an empty sky—tempers verisimilitude with visual style. The same economy holds for the foundry where Françoise (Jacqueline Laurent) first meets François (Jean Gabin) while delivering flowers, and for the dingy neighborhood to which Jean bicycles when he visits Françoise at her rooming house. The smokestacks visible in both sets tell of an environmental pollution whose adverse physiological effect on

91. Carné's *Le Jour se lève* (1939): in the zone.

François recalls the asphyxiation that leads Edmond in *Hôtel du Nord* to seek a "change of air."

The tenement reaches its full dramatic potential toward the end of the film, during a flashback in which François recalls his encounter and altercation with Valentin (Jules Berry). A shot from above shows François about to throw Valentin out the window; from this perspective, Carné later develops a verbal and visual dialogue between François barricaded in his top-floor room and inhabitants of the neighborhood, who call to him from the square below. As night falls, the streetlights enhance the artifice of the film set during the police stakeout, leading to the violence of capture that François precludes at daybreak—hence the film's title—by shooting himself just as the police throw a canister of tear-gas through the window of his room.

Pairing *Hôtel du Nord* and *Le Jour se lève* displays the heightened sense of fatalism that critics have linked to poetic realism and its offshoots in American and French versions of film noir. Whereas Edmond had craved a change

92. Kertész photographs Paris as *le fantastique social*.

of air, equated with a change of *atmosphère* ("I'm suffocating, do you hear? Suffocating!"), François barricades himself in a room that becomes his tomb. Trauner's sets in these two films of the late 1930s convey a physical isolation in which ties to family, profession, street, and neighborhood yield increasingly to urban expansion. The conjunction of character-type and spatial representation in the two films enhances the instability of an urban environment prone to violence and crime.

Carné's trajectory following *Hôtel du Nord* discloses the extent to which spatial practices associated with poetic realism draw on conventions of drama at odds with the realist depiction of underclass urban spaces in Dabit's novel. The sets designed by Trauner extend the pathos of tragic loners played by Jouvet in *Hôtel du Nord* and by Gabin in *Le Quai des brumes* and *Le Jour se lève*, loners whose demise sets them apart from Dabit's depiction of the underclass as a composite of unremarkable individuals united by the collective spaces they inhabit. Carné's narrative strategy evolves increasingly away from the internal perspective in Dabit's novel that Poulaille considered a primary criterion of proletarian literature. The irony is that the Carné-Trauner collaboration remains a founding reference for a cinematographic vision whose emphasis on pathos and stylized urban spaces implies a bourgeois perspective at a remove from the underclass environment it purports to portray. This vision also serves as an exemplary expression of poetic realism at a remove from the geography and social environment of the urban underclass that Dabit seeks to evoke in *L'Hôtel du Nord*.[29]

More significant in retrospect is the fact that *Hôtel du Nord* failed to meet expectations that Carné had raised in the title of his crucial 1933 article, "When Will the Cinema Go Down into the Street?," where he openly associated populism in literature and film with the "two-faced city" of Paris.[30] In that article, Carné praised the films of Jacques Feyder and René Clair, which captured the hidden, magical nature of the city despite the fact that their sets were constructed at the Epinay studios out of wood and stucco. The keen sensibility of the set designer, Lazare Meerson, protected both directors from the stereotypes that would quickly become the norm in the many films dealing with popular life in the city. Much better, Carné declared, would be films that represented life on the streets by being shot on the streets. He then invoked precedents in novels by Jules Romains, Pierre Mac Orlan, and, especially pertinent, Eugène Dabit, whose vivid depictions of factories, garages, slender footbridges, and freight carts throbbed with the vibrant, restless world of the Canal Saint-Martin. Dabit's novel became the focal point for the manifesto with which Carné ended his article:

> Populism, you say. And after that? Neither the word nor the thing itself frightens us. To describe the simple life of humble people, to depict the atmosphere of hard-working humanity which is theirs—isn't that better than reconstructing the murky and inflated ambience of night clubs, dancing couples, and a nonexistent nobility, which the cinema has kept on doing as long as they've been so abundantly profitable?[31]

When it came time to shoot his own films involving Paris, Carné went into the studios, like Clair and Feyder before him. Yet in *Quai des brumes* and *Le Jour se lève* he came close to attaining the brand of realism he called for, since both capitalized on the fatalistic atmosphere of poetic realism that *Hôtel du Nord* exuded only in the character of Louis Jouvet's Edouard.

Surrealism and the Minor News Item *(Fait Divers)*

Some Métro stations in Paris have maps with colored bulbs along each line of the system. To use the map, passengers push a button with the name of a desired destination, and the bulbs display the recommended itinerary. Like the lines on the palm of a hand, those of the Métro system can be read, especially given the multicolored display of routes whose configuration passengers soon memorize.[32] But what makes an itinerary efficient does not always make it desirable, especially when, in a mode of *flânerie*, movement becomes an end in itself.

Maps show place-names that can be plotted, but they also function in other ways. Michel de Certeau writes that "proper names carve out pockets of hidden and familiar meanings. They 'make sense' as the impetus of movements, like vocations and calls that turn or divert an itinerary by giving it a meaning (or a direction) that was previously unseen. These names create a nowhere in places, they change them into passages."[33] Maps show where the Place des Vosges used to be and how to find the hillside park at Buttes-Chaumont. But it is almost as if, in order to function as formal ensembles of abstract places, maps must erase their genesis. From log to itinerary, the history of maps seems to have evolved in the name of science—from recording a route taken in the past to prescribing one to be followed in the future.

Three years before Dabit's *L'Hôtel du Nord*, Louis Aragon's description of the Passage de l'Opéra in *Le Paysan de Paris* fulfilled this early function of maps by setting the disappearance of a specific urban space within a mythology of the modern that recast it as ephemeral. Two years later, André Breton's *Nadja* likewise plotted an itinerary of urban encounters whose outcome it set in a dark suburban zone.[34] In both texts, "spatial stories" overlay the streets, architecture, and city planning of early twentieth-century Paris. Material fragments such as street signs and advertisements direct attention toward the ephemera of urban spaces and experiences—ephemera that were noted first by Charles Baudelaire and later by Walter Benjamin.[35] They also target locales frequented by an underclass related less to the ambitious protagonists of the *Bildungsroman* than to casual visitors such as Aragon's narrator. Moreover, the narrator's account of the city and its inhabitants drew on character attributes in Balzac's novel *Les Paysans* (which described the lower classes as "drunken, debauched, envious, insolent, cynical, and deviously clever") in the cause of Surrealist provocation against middle-class propriety.[36] Such a perspective is less typical among residents, who are often desensitized to their immediate environment, than among those who are seeing the city for the first time or with an openness that habit tends to foreclose. First-generation Surrealists of the 1920s conceptualized this novelty by cultivating "objective chance" for which the unforeseen encounter was a prime model.

Aragon's and Breton's plotting of the city as a nexus of the everyday and of the exceptional overlaps with urban images in the illustrated press. Between the world wars, techniques of photogravure and halftone reproduction enhanced the quality of photographic images in mainstream weeklies such as *L'Illustration*. These techniques promoted the growth of specialized publications and tabloids that drew heavily on visual materials. In November 1928 the journalist and photographer Lucien Vogel launched *Vu* (the title means "Seen"), an illustrated weekly whose striking layouts were meant to convey the complexity and accelerated pace of the contemporary world. Agency photos and an ethos of committed photojournalism established *Vu*'s reputation as an openly left-wing publication attuned to international politics. Much like Emmanuel Berl at *Marianne* but with a firmer commitment to the political left, Vogel left his mark on the weekly by commissioning special issues on the Soviet Union (issue 192, November 1931) and the Red Army (issue 382, July 1935). He also contributed to *Vendredi* and advised the French Communist Party when it launched its own photographic weekly, *Regards*. After *Vu*'s support of the Spanish Republic in 1936 led many of its advertisers to withdraw, Vogel was forced to sell the magazine. Its next editor, Alfred Maillet, brought out a version of the weekly whose format and politics were more conservative.[37]

Both *L'Illustration* and *Vu* were devoted (though in different ways) to reportage and photojournalism on an international scale. In contrast, the sixteen-page tabloid weekly *Détective*, which billed itself as "the great weekly of minor news items," featured a high degree of visual content, often in the form of lurid photographs linked to the worlds of crime, politics, and entertainment. *Détective* chronicled everyday life from the ground up, with a penchant for sensationalism that ensured its market niche as a lowlife guide to urban modernity "through cities and suburbs, between the *quartiers* and social echelons, between the champagne and the cheap red wine, the Metropolis and the colonies."[38] Appearing first in October 1928, with an editorial team directed by Georges Kessel (brother of Joseph), *Détective* recast the minor news item as a point of entry into the city by providing coverage of politics, crime, and entertainment in the register of scandal and spectacle. Within three years, the weekly's initial run of 300,000 copies tripled to almost a million.

Over the following decade, *Détective*'s "lurid reports of crime, investigation into the underworld, and reports on the seamier side of society" fueled its notoriety and sales to a point where, in 1932, the Paris police prefect, Jean

Chiappe, banned the posters that advertised it within the city limits.[39] The tabloid weekly was yet another venture undertaken by Gaston Gallimard to expand his commercial operations. As with *Marianne*, contributors to *Détective* included prominent literary figures such as Francis Carco, Pierre Mac Orlan, Albert Londres, and Georges Simenon. After André Gide ran a column of *faits divers* in the *Nouvelle Revue Française* and published two books covering criminal cases, it was evident that the literary mores he and the *NRF* had upheld for two decades had evolved. *Détective* was typical of interwar publications that straddled literature, the illustrated press, and the tabloid. Much like *Vu*, *Détective* exploited new production technologies to feature a high degree of visual content. But whereas *Vu's* layouts were aesthetically innovative, the lurid and graphic photographs in *Détective* strive instead for shock value.

Eugen Weber confirms the place of the illustrated press as a nexus of cultural practices when he evokes the mood of France in early January 1934, less than a week before Stavisky was found dead in a ski chalet outside Chamonix. Weber notes, as we mentioned in our Introduction, that some spectators attending a production of Shakespeare's *Coriolanus* at the Comédie Française took the play's critique of corrupt government in ancient Rome as a thinly veiled reference to the French parliament under Radical Party leadership. He juxtaposes this reference to conventional literary culture and the front page of the January 4, 1934, issue of *Détective*. The page consists of a medium close-up of a young woman looking out wide-eyed from behind what appears to be a curtain made of long bamboo beads.[40] The woman's facial expression and posture convey concern, if not fear. Weber describes her face as terrified. A caption in the lower left corner of the page reads: "1934 opens anxious, panicked eyes on a future heavy with hatred, tragedies, and catastrophes."[41]

The change of register and medium, from theatrical performance to tabloid weekly, displays Weber's grasp of the cultural moment in its complexity. But the topicality that Weber ascribes to the *Coriolanus* production obtains with equal complexity for the cover of *Détective*, which he describes only in passing. The woman's left hand raised to her cheek parts the curtain, while a shadow from one of its strands marks her face like a slash over the inner corner of her left eye. The effect is akin to an illumination by camera flash or strobe light, the sort of light one uses to pierce the dark and expose the unseen—light that is a metaphor for (in Rifkin's words) "the transience of the flash."[42]

93–94. *Détective:* glamor and scandal (January 4 and 11, 1934).

Another way to read the same *Détective* cover is to consider the figure of the young woman as an avatar of the allegorical Marianne, the female incarnation of Republican France. This particular Marianne, however, owes more to the conventions of glamour in film and fashion than to the classical pose she adopts in paintings, sculptures, and monuments. The bamboo curtain evokes an aura of overseas territories like those occupied as colonies by the French. By extension, it connotes the orientalism prevalent in interior set designs for colonial films of the period to the moral decadence played out in those films, in which the lure of glamour invariably leads to melodrama and violence. Examples of such interiors and the doom they foretell include the seedy hotel and bar in Morocco run by Blanche (Françoise Rosay) in *Le Grand Jeu* and the apartment in the Casbah of Algiers that Pépé shares with Inès in *Pépé le Moko.*

The tacky underside of the moment is exactly what *Détective* and peer publications such as *Voilà* (which billed itself as "the weekly of reportage") sought to exploit for commercial ends. But violence and criminality succeeded only in conjunction with scandal, especially when the scandal was political. On January 11, 1934, a week after the front page featuring the young blonde, the cover of *Détective* showed a tight close-up of Stavisky. The cropped image cuts off his left ear and chin, in a gesture of editorial violence that is enhanced by a slight tilting of the image to the left. The facial expression is flat, with eyes directly facing the camera and thin lips pressed together. A two-part caption along the bottom and right hand margins of the page—"Stavisky: The Man with the Golden Fingers"—lends an elements of mystery to the seemingly neutral affect of the portrait. Since one can assume that most readers already knew of Stavisky's death two days earlier and of the circumstances surrounding it, the image and title can be read, respectively, as a death image and an epitaph. With allegations of a government cover-up already circulating in right-wing publications such as *L'Action Française*, the prospect of major political scandal transforms the flat affect of the photo portrait into an image of inscrutability: What might be behind this face?

The interplay of word and image continues on the back page of the issue, which shows the photo of a woman, Lucette Alméras, beneath a headline, "Le Suicide de Stavisky." A caption below the photo reads: "Feeling cornered in the villa where he had taken refuge with some associates, Stavisky decided to cheat the hangman. And Lucette Alméras was the only witness of his despairing act." The portrait is of a round-faced woman whose heavy makeup, fashionably curled hair, and pearl necklace exude the sort of glamour seen on the cover of the January 4 issue. The woman is Lucette Alméras, not Stavisky's widow, Arlette, whose work as a fashion model gave her striking good looks frequent visibility in the press. Stavisky's death in Chamonix was linked to many sites in Paris, ranging from his Empire Theater on the Place Saint Georges to his apartment at the Hôtel Claridge on the Champs-Elysées. Later disclosure of Stavisky's involvement with Radical Party members of the Chautemps government added sites such as the Senate building and the Chamber of Deputies, on the Left Bank.

The attention elicited by the use of photo images, headlines, and captions goes well beyond that generated by the use of the same materials in daily newspapers. The design of the covers engages prospective readers in ways that recall Vogel's innovations with *Vu*. In addition, these images record the very underside of urban life in Paris that conventional dailies and specialized weeklies addressed at most only in passing. *Détective* inaugurated a distinctive perspective on the period by using illustrations and layout to give a form to everyday life as the narrative basis of the extraordinary and the spectacular.

This distinctiveness stemmed from the broadened range of culture and politics that the magazine included on a regular basis. Even when, as in the case of Stavisky's death, its coverage led to the rural provinces, *Détective*'s perspective was consistently Parisian and tied to the topography of the city. Altogether, the urban realism found in *Détective*, as in Dabit and Carné, popularized the upsurge of the marvelous that made the streets of Paris a prime setting for the kind of encounters that Aragon and Breton had cultivated.

Sociology, current events, and fiction converge to trigger multiple ways of imagining this other side of Paris. This convergence appears first in a predilection for locales like those where Dabit's novel and Carné's film are set, and others near the neighborhoods of Pigalle, Montmartre, and the Place Blanche, whose nightlife Breton and his cohorts frequented. Second, the stark juxtaposition of the real and the surreal that is so evident in various types of discourse, including the academic, hints at a latent violence in mass culture that is most clearly concentrated in fantastic popular fiction and sensationalist journalism.[43] Whether, as Robin Walz contends in his study of the Surrealists, these popular sites and expressions harbored genuine revolutionary potential, they undoubtedly convey the tense atmosphere of a Parisian underclass that fascinated Dabit, Carné, Aragon, and Breton, not to mention Céline, Mac Orlan, Carco, and a whole generation including Gide.

The pressure felt by those "others" in the *quartiers populaires* as depicted by Dabit and Carné was relieved only by fantasies of "another other" beyond civilization. For many Parisians like Raymonde and Edmond, with whom we began, the colonies offered a hope of renewal tinged with erotic appeal. Raymonde dreams of visiting faraway places, but scarcely gets outside the capital. Edmond works his way to Marseilles and a brief chance to leave for Port Said, but his fatalism—in the form of a death drive—draws him back to Paris. Through characters like these, literature and film produced cognitive maps in which a concrete Paris coexists with its marvelous underside, as well as with its exotic outer limits.

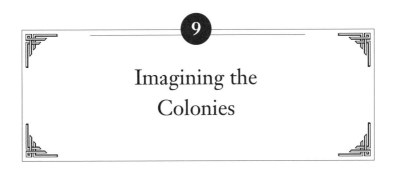

Imagining the Colonies

Greater France in Paris

The idea of the French nation from 1871 to 1962 was inseparable from a belief that overseas territories occupied by soldiers, settlers, and administrators were part of Greater France *(la plus grande France)*. This coincidence of nation and empire spawned policies of control and a form of government under which colonial expansion served as a measure of national consciousness. Through the mid-1930s, what the historian Raoul Girardet calls the "colonial idea" was debated on the political left and right.[1] This idea was nearly unavoidable. Vivid images of an imperial France circulated in advertisements, commercial films, newspapers, state-sponsored exhibitions, and other public displays. Not simply offshoots of policy, these images cast Greater France as a colonial empire of 100 million people in Europe, Africa, Asia, and the Americas.

Over the first three decades of the Third Republic, advocates of the colonial idea often found their cause dismissed as a fantasy more suited to the American Far West than to the everyday concerns of the French. But in 1885 the noted statesman Jules Ferry adopted a different approach in a speech before the Chamber of Deputies: he set colonial expansion in line with a "humanitarian" mission of transmitting Enlightenment values to the rest of the world.[2] It was a mission to which others, such as Paul Reynaud, Albert Sarraut, and Louis-Hubert Lyautey, would aspire over the next fifty years. Ferry was a legendary reformer of domestic education who had instituted compulsory schooling and uniform curricula that centralized the primary-school system throughout France. He also advocated gradual integration of the occupied territories into the nation, following a model previously applied to

France's provinces and regions. Just as Ferry's educational policies assimilated provincial populations within a national system, so he believed that administrative uniformity could extend to France's overseas territories.

By 1900, an infrastructure of state and private institutions was promoting the occupied overseas territories as essential to France's economic, political, and military concerns. This infrastructure included the Union Coloniale Française consortium, which monitored financial ventures related to the overseas territories, and the Ecole Coloniale, a state-run institution where future administrators were taught the finer points of "colonial sciences." In 1920, Sarraut, minister of the colonies, spoke of a sustained campaign to showcase France's colonial domain in the press and the educational system: "It is absolutely indispensable . . . that a systematic, serious, and constant propaganda of word and image have an impact on each adult and child in our country. . . . We must improve and broaden the narrow teaching that our primary schools, *lycées*, and *collèges* currently provide of our history and the constitution of our colonial domain."[3]

Girardet acknowledges that the interplay of idea and image went far beyond the classroom: "A page from a serialized novel, an adventure story for children, or a polemical tract can thus be considered more indicative of certain attitudes or behavior than the assertions of a statesman or the speculations of a political philosopher."[4] These remarks only begin to contend with the way such informal images tended to circulate within a colonial culture that sustained paternalism and privilege. Billboards, posters, and print advertising continually related the colonies to the material products of everyday life, such as food, drink, and clothing. The smiling face of the Senegalese rifleman on boxes of Banania breakfast food and the turbaned male sporting a goatee on the label of Arabica coffee were so much a part of the domestic sphere that they were seldom challenged. Not all of those who purchased Banania knew that the image on the box drew on the reality of the hundreds of thousands of soldiers from overseas territories who had served on behalf of France in World War I, before being sent "home" following the November 1918 armistice.[5]

The trajectory of the colonial idea during the Third Republic can also be traced through state-sponsored efforts to display the material benefits the colonies provided to consumer-citizens. Starting in 1851 at London's Crystal Palace, large-scale fairs and expositions made mass consumption "unthinkable apart from the maintenance and extension of empire."[6] In the logic of capitalism, display was a means to promote eventual sales. It is always also an end in itself, selling the comforting idea of order in idealized platforms. In this case, entire cultures were encapsulated visually through artifacts, fine arts, and—especially—architecture.[7] The growth of these fairs and expositions coincided with the emergence of science museums and enclosed shopping arcades, which provided object lessons in power through which individuals, transformed en masse into a citizenry of spectators, came to know and regulate themselves.[8] Throughout the Third Republic, the colonial sections at universal expositions transposed displays of difference into encounters with otherness. These encounters took concrete form as spaces of controlled interaction, which Mary Louise Pratt calls "contact zones": spaces in which "peoples geographically and historically separated come into contact with each other and establish relations, usually involving conditions of coercion, radical inequality, and intractable conflict."[9]

From May through November 1931, Paris staged a memorable contact zone on the land surrounding the Lac Daumesnil in the Bois de Vincennes. This was the site of the International Colonial and Overseas Exposition, where some eight million fairgoers, invited to go "around the world in a single day," visited pavilions and exhibits built for the occasion.[10] When the French government approved final plans for the exposition in 1929, advocates of colonial expansion were defending their cause with renewed vigor. From abroad, the 1925 Rif War in Morocco inaugurated a first wave of antiimperialism that was to evolve three decades later into full-scale decolonization, notably in Indochina and Algeria. In 1926, the French Communist Party helped to launch the Etoile Nord-Africaine (North African Star), a movement that promoted solidarity and independence in the occupied territories of Morocco, Algeria, and Tunisia. Further East, the same year was marked by a revolt of Annamite (Vietnamese) sharpshooters against the French officers who commanded them, and by the creation in Hong Kong of an Indo-Chinese Communist Party led by Nguyen Ai Quôc, later known as Hô Chi Minh. An insurrection at Yen Bay led to the creation in France of a Comité de Défense des Indochinois, whose members included André Malraux, Paul Rivet, and Andrée Viollis.[11]

Other problems closer to home were evident among advocates of expansion, whose words rang increasingly hollow. The "Address to the Visitor" that opened the 1931 exposition's official guidebook asserted that the heroic period of colonization had ended and that French colonists were now able to interact with affluent, free, and happy natives of the occupied territories. Yet in a striking reversal, this address echoed the patronizing tone of Jules Ferry almost a half-century earlier:

A bit of advice: in the presence of what is foreign or local, do not laugh at things or people you initially fail to understand. The mocking laughter of some Frenchmen has made more enemies for us abroad than cruel defeats or demeaning treaties. The ideas of other men are often your own, but expressed in a different way. Think about it. May you be filled, dear Visitor, with the most worthy delight—a delight that is quite French—and may it stay with you long after your visit has ended. Before you enter, I can give you no better watchword than that of Maréchal Lyautey, the great Frenchman of lofty human conceptions: "In this exposition one must seek, along with the lessons of the past, the teachings of the present as well as those of tomorrow. One should leave this exposition resolved to make oneself better, broader, greater, stronger, and more adaptable."[12]

Demaison may have been sincere, but the condescension of his remarks masked the inequalities of wealth and power on which colonization was founded and which it exploited. This mixture of good intentions and arrogance was typical of attempts to justify France's imperial presence by displaying the contributions of "its" overseas territories to the French population "at home." A speech by Louis-Hubert Lyautey, resident governor of Morocco from 1912 to 1925 and honorary director of the 1931 exhibition, described the goal of colonization: to win over the fierce hearts (*coeurs farouches*) of the savannah and the desert to a belief in human kindness.[13] His vision of enlightened colonialism cast the Bois de Vincennes exposition as a model space of Greater France, neither fully in Paris nor fully outside it. This was evident in early plans for the exposition, as described in Marcel Ollivier's official report:

The initial idea [for the exposition] goes back to 1910. In 1910, we naturally turned to exoticism, which by then had become an immensely popular novelty. We dreamed of renewing, with more brilliance and more sincerity, the picturesque ambience—although quite false and sometimes excessive—of the successful colonial sections at the 1878, 1889, and 1900 expositions. Why not transport once again, in a larger setting in the middle of Paris, this vision of the Orient and the Far

95. The Avenue des Colonies at the 1931 Colonial Exposition.

East? . . . The original idea for an Exposition of Exoticism was later enriched, amplified, and led toward more elevated goals. It was no longer a matter of artificially reconstituting an exotic ambience, with architectural pastiches and parades of actors; it was now a question of placing before the eyes of the exposition's visitors an impressive summary of the results of colonization, its present realities, and its future.[14]

Ollivier's disclaimer reveals the lure of exoticism as a supplement to government policy, especially when it enhanced the promotion of colonial expansion with elements of spectacle and entertainment.

The exhibition site, at the eastern end of the 12th *arrondissement* on the Right Bank, was on a section of former fortifications built in the mid-nineteenth century that encompassed a *zone non aedificandi*—a cleared space, not to be built on. Other possible sites had included space adjacent to the Ecole Militaire and the Eiffel Tower, in what proponents saw as a potential linear park creating a Left Bank equivalent of the Champs-Elysées. The final choice—the Bois de Vincennes—had the advantage of drawing attention to a neglected area of Paris that could benefit economically from the exposi-

96. Exoticism as marketing ploy.

tion, in contrast to the more elegant Bois de Boulogne in the posh 16th *arrondissement.*

The exposition site was divided into four sections, devoted, respectively, to metropolitan France, overseas territories, national pavilions, and a permanent museum of the colonies.[15] Additional space was assigned to an information center, two amusement areas, restaurants, and a number of commercial pavilions whose sponsors ranged from the automobile manufacturers Renault and Citroën to the state-controlled tobacco and cigarette industries. Their presence also marked a link between empire and commerce that the lofty rhetoric of Lyautey and Ollivier carefully elided.

A memorable image from a poster for the tobacco-industry pavilion features the portrait of a striking Mangbetou woman, reproducing a photograph from the book *La Croisière noire* (The Black Expedition—an account of a Citroën-sponsored motorized trek down the African continent in 1924–1925), except for the added detail of a cigarette, which transforms the woman into a smoker. This poster might pass as a playful recycling of an image recognizable to fairgoers who already knew about *La Croisière noire* or who could see it at the exposition, where its director, Léon Poirier, was in charge of the cinema section. This first transmutation was followed by a second, in which the portrait was used on the package of a new cigarette called Congo. A final transmutation, with overtones of hunting trophies, occurred in three dimensions in the form of a radiator cap on the hood of a luxury car.[16]

Following an itinerary recommended in the official guidebook, visitors entered the exposition at the Porte de Picpus, near the new Porte Dorée station, terminus of the number 8 line of the Paris Métro. Visitors reached the main gate by crossing an area bordered by stone columns that funneled them from the street toward the entrance. A painting by the gate's designer, Henri Bazin, shows visitors dressed in the kind of robes and tunics worn by natives of occupied territories in North and sub-Saharan Africa. A cloudless blue sky more typical of the Mediterranean than of northern France clashes with contemporary reports of that rainy Parisian spring. Even more out of place in this painting is a tall palm tree, one of many transplanted especially for the exhibition. Viewed after the fact, this depiction of native dress, blue sky, and palm tree is unsettling because it gives the impression that Arabs and Africans came to Paris to visit exhibitions of their homelands. Whereas documentation shows that the overwhelming majority of fairgoers were French—and white. Bazin included only two female figures, at the far right of the image. One appears to be carrying a child on her back, wrapped in the folds of a scarf or dress.

Who is depicted in Bazin's painting? One reading of the painting holds that it portrays employees rather than visitors, presumably natives of North and sub-Saharan Africa, on their way to the exposition. But this reading would suggest, rather crudely, that the employees often or always wore their traditional clothing in Paris. Unless, of course, they were simply coming to their jobs already dressed for their roles. Openly demeaning, both readings set French identity against the identities of the figures represented. Herman Lebovics notes that "everything [in the painting] is conflated and turned upside down. The line between here and there, between metropolitan France and the colonies, is erased; it is a pictorial representation of an ethnically diverse but politically unified and centralized French empire."[17]

Bazin's painting of the main gate—the Porte d'Honneur—fashions a space of collective experience within which fairgoers would be simultaneously educated and entertained. To this end, they entered through a monumental space that seemingly set the exhibition apart from the city surrounding it. Efforts to design the exposition as an autonomous space failed to detach it either from the city around it or from images in popular culture whose flagrant orientalism belied the ideals of empire associated with Greater France that organizers of the Vincennes exposition had meant to preach.

Physically separating the exhibit space from the capital repeats a principle of segregation in line with the colonial urbanism developed under Lyautey's 1912–1925 tenure as governor-general of Morocco. It also raises questions concerning the symbolic significance of the space within the exposition area. Patricia Morton argues that organizers planned the Vincennes exposition as a phantasmagoric microcosm of the French colonial empire, "a collection of objects taken from their contexts and reassembled into a whole: an ideal colonial world based on classifications of visible difference."[18] Even more to the point, what Morton terms "phantasmagoria" occurs as the incongruity of a reordering of objects for display within the new order (Morton uses the term "domain") of Greater France.

Beyond state policies, control and exploitation also derive from claims to objective knowledge. Johannes Fabian argues that practices of anthropology invariably distance those whom it claims to observe from "the Time of the observer."[19] This dual temporality is exactly what fairgoers experienced at the Bois de Vincennes as a double separation. First of all, they crossed a monumental entrance that served as a zone of transition between the city and the exposition. Once inside, they were guided by a suggested itinerary to the colonial pavilions clustered together in a corner of the exposition area, as though in a different time zone. Egregiously, the colonial section was placed next to the zoo, a juxtaposition that recent commentators have scrutinized.[20]

Visitors following the itinerary moved toward the Lac Daumesnil, then passed an information center just south of the main gate before coming to pavilions devoted to Madagascar, the Indochinese Union (Laos, Annam, Cambodia, Tonkin, Cochinchina), and the islands of Saint Pierre and Miquelon, off the Atlantic coast of Canada. The highlight of the colonial section—and the expo's great visual draw—was a full-scale replica of the Cambodian temple complex at Angkor Wat, which occupied some fifteen acres of the Indochina exhibit.[21] An internal framework of wood and reinforced concrete supported a central tower that rose fifty-five meters, amid four shorter towers. In keeping with the exposition's ethos of authenticity, the sandstone statues of minor divinities (*apsaras*) and fabulous snakes had been reproduced from molds cast during archaeological expeditions organized between the years 1873 and 1912. As a result, the ornamentation at the Bois de Vincennes was true to the temple as it had been some twenty to sixty years earlier, rather than to the temple in 1931.[22]

Fairgoers who entered the temple found eighty dioramas, in rooms illuminated from above by a vaulted ceiling of translucent glass blocks that formed a giant lotus blossom. Also on display were maps, small-scale models of indigenous buildings, mannequins dressed in authentic costumes, and a permanently illuminated "wall of images" consisting of nearly a thousand slides. A large upper gallery contained thirty original Khmer sculptures brought back from Cambodia by members of the Compagnie Française d'Extrême-Orient.[23] Robert de Beauplan, technical director of the colonial section, confessed that in order to draw fairgoers and hold their attention, he had followed Marcel Ollivier's strategy of exploiting "all the seductiveness of the picturesque and the irresistible magic of art."[24] This doctrinaire use of exoticism is clear in the architectural simulation of a Cambodia that no longer existed, especially when fairgoers were asked to note how France had "rescued" traditional Cambodian culture. An article in *L'Illustration* (May 23, 1931) assigns the French credit for this rescue in terms that add a note of anti-Communism to the compulsory invocation of France's civilizing mission:

> By unfurling the flag of the [French] Republic over the ruins that are today's Cambodia, and in forcing the Siamese to return Angkor to the oppressed and pillaged Cambodians, we have committed an act not of imperialism, but of liberation. And the temples of Angkor symbolize much less Indochina—one and indivisible according to the childish notion of Soviet politicos and the know-nothings who are their dupes—than a dead civilization which was murdered by the most terrible violence and which owes its rebirth today to France.[25]

Other exhibits along the Grande Avenue des Colonies likewise exploited the picturesque in the form of stylized architecture. The main French West African pavilion was a fortified king's palace *(tata)* built of red mud with a central tower forty-five meters high. Within the palace walls, fairgoers found a scale-model reconstruction of a settlement in the Malian town of Djenné, whose back streets contained the boutiques and workshops of jewelers, blacksmiths, weavers, and potters. Alongside the replica of a *quartier* in Djenné was a second village temporarily housing more than two hundred natives from parts of Ivory Coast, Sudan, Dahomey, and the Mandingo area of the Upper Niger River, as yet untouched by Islam. The official guidebook concluded: "Let the young hold on to these names and men and countries, whose resonance may seem bizarre at present. In ten, twenty, or thirty years, when fourteen million men on the move and their unworked land are linked by rail to our provinces of North Africa, when aviation will have developed to its fullest potential, these names will be more familiar to our ears than Provençal or Gascon names were to the ears of seventeenth-century Parisians."[26]

In contrast to the emphasis on authentic reproduction in the pavilions devoted to Cambodia and French West Africa, those devoted to Morocco and Algeria were designed to correct misperceptions of disorder, poverty, and backwardness associated with local cultures in these two occupied territories. The Moroccan pavilion featured a white-walled palace modeled on the Makhzen palace of Dar el-Beïda in Marrakesh. Its design was stunning, but hardly typical of the local architecture in urban Morocco. Displays within the pavilion supported ex-governor Lyautey's mandate to turn Morocco into a vast workplace for industry, commerce, and agriculture—so much so, that photographs of fields planted for harvest were seen as reminiscent of the plain of La Beauce between Paris and Chartres.

The Algerian pavilion, modeled on the sanctuary of the patron saint (*marabout*) of Algiers, Sidi-Abderrahmane, strove for formal authenticity by displaying a cupola and a minaret. But as with the Moroccan pavilion, realist details on the outside clashed with exhibits inside that portrayed a nation transformed through industry, commerce, and the promise of prosperity. The words used by organizers of the exposition to describe this transformation cast economic realities within a rhetoric of self-fulfillment: "Modern Algeria, such as France has created it, is in fact an immense vineyard, a giant wine press from which flows, like a natural spring, a river of wine. Wine is the future of Algeria, it is the great benefit France has given to this land of sunshine, which is also a land of thirst."[27]

The verisimilitude of all these reproductions became an object of curiosity in its own right. It is safe to say that no one mistook the reproduction of Angkor Wat for the real thing. Yet the reproduction exercised its own attraction by virtue of the skill that went into its creation. Because few fairgoers had been to North Africa and fewer still to Cambodia, the illusion of faithful reproduction had much to do with attitudes and expectations brought to the exposition. And while many people may not have realized it at the time, these responses inverted the conventional priority assigned to the original over its copy.

Timothy Mitchell writes that the space of the exhibition appeared "not just to mimic the real world outside but to superimpose a framework of meaning over its innumerable races, territories, and commodities."[28] This superimposition drew on a notion of the world-as-exhibition that coincided with the colonial age and the dream of a single world economy to which it laid claim. Nowhere was the force of this notion more evident than in accounts of non-European visitors to universal exhibitions: "Non-Europeans encountered in Europe what one might call, echoing a phrase from Heidegger, the age of the world exhibition, or rather, the age of the world-as-exhibition. 'World exhibition' here refers not to an exhibition of the world but to the world conceived and grasped as if it were an exhibition."[29] The immediacy of architecture and human display on the grand scale of world exhibitions makes for compelling expressions of what Sylviane Leprun has characterized as a plastic ethnology "at the edge of the imaginary."[30] Colonial powers always map and categorize their territorial acquisitions, thus opening them to political and economic calculation. Colonized lands and their inhabitants thus become legible, "readable like a book."[31]

Such questionable attitudes, together with the overt propaganda visible everywhere at the Bois de Vincennes, triggered two memorable tracts. The first, "Ne Visitez pas l'Exposition Coloniale" ("Do Not Visit the Colonial Exhibition") appeared in May 1931 under the signatures of André Breton, Paul Eluard, André Thirion, René Crevel, Louis Aragon, René Char, and others. Citing the recent arrest of an Indochinese student by the Paris police as the latest in a series of repressive actions, the tract called for a boycott of the Colonial Exposition, which was seeking to justify the violence of colonial rule by invoking the integrity of Greater France. These leftist intellectuals were not fooled: "The fact that the president of the Republic, the emperor of Annam, the cardinal archbishop of Paris, and several governors and thugs were present on the Colonial Exposition's inaugural platform, opposite the pavilion of the missionaries and those of Citroën and Renault, clearly reveals the complicity of the whole bourgeoisie with the birth of a new and especially repugnant idea of 'Greater France.'"[32] A second tract, "Premier Bilan de l'Exposition Coloniale" ("First Appraisal of the Colonial Exhibition"), appeared on July 3, several days after a major fire at the Dutch Indies pavilion had destroyed artworks from Malaysia and Melanesia brought to Paris by Dutch colonizers, much as the French had brought back art objects from Cambodia. As the tract's writers saw it, the fire was consistent with a pillaging of local cultures whose products came to France as trophies of colonialism.

According to André Thirion, at least 5,000 copies of the two tracts were distributed in factories, in working-class neighborhoods, and at the Porte Dorée Métro station. Whereas the first tract took a strong anticolonialist position against the luminaries who embodied the values of Greater France, the second supported the Surrealists' advocacy of art in the service of revolution: "Just as the opponents of nationalism must defend the nationalism of oppressed peoples, so the opponents of that art which is the fruit of the capitalist economy also have a duty to place the art of the oppressed peoples dialectically in opposition to it."[33]

In what we term "the other of the other," the stances set forth in the tracts also inspired a counter-exposition, La Vérité sur les Colonies (The Truth about the Colonies), held in a building that had served as the Soviet Constructivist pavilion at the 1925 Exposition of Decorative Arts. Often attributed to the Surrealists alone, the venture was a collaboration among various groups, including the Ligue Internationale contre l'Oppression Coloniale et l'Impérialisme, the French Communist Party, and the Confédération Générale du Travail Unitaire. Originally scheduled for August 1931, the counter-expo opened to the public on September 20.

La Vérité sur les Colonies was a collective venture, with Louis Aragon in charge of cultural issues and Georges Sadoul in charge of information. Yves Tanguy, Eluard, and Aragon filled the main room on the second floor with primitive objects and a few devotional ornaments.[34] André Thirion contrasted the motivation and effort he brought to the counter-expo with the more frivolous attitude of Aragon and Elsa Triolet:[35]

> The exhibit drew a lot of visitors, although it did not benefit from any strong publicity. The members of the Communist Party's Political Bureau stayed away, except for one syndicalist who came by for other reasons. I had installed loudspeakers to broadcast political commentaries from time to time and to urge passers-by climbing to Buttes-Chaumont to stop in at La Vérité sur les Colonies. Aragon and Elsa bought records of any Polynesian or Asian music they could find at specialty shops. Elsa had added a few hit songs, including a nice rhumba (or some other Caribbean rhythm that had just become the rage).[36]

In fact, the driving force behind La Vérité sur les Colonies was Alfred Kurella, a German national, delegate to the Communist International and head of the Anti-Imperialist League, whose intention to disclose the political agenda of the exposition drew on exactly what its organizers knew they had to avoid if they were to "sell" the colonies to the French citizenry.[37] For their part, the radicals who staged the counter-exposition often reverted to binary oppositions, including some that replicated stereotypes of the occupied territories and their inhabitants. In trying to preserve the corrosiveness of difference, the colonies became—even for the Surrealists—"an inexhaustible reservoir of strange objects and exotic images to be exploited."[38]

Today, the geographic setting and internal space of the Vincennes exposition seem highly problematic. Press coverage during and following the exposition was—with the notable exceptions cited above—largely favorable, a fact due in part to the advertising and government subventions that the daily newspapers received.[39] As might be expected, a writer for the neo-royalist *L'Action Française* described his hope that "the French, in leafing through this marvelous album, may come to know and to appreciate the wealth and potential of a colonial domain that is vaster than Europe and that belongs to them."[40] Most visitors to the Bois de Vincennes came away less with a respect for France's civilizing mission than with wonder at the spectacle based on the illusion of bringing the colonies to the outskirts of Paris. "Seeing" the colonies by seeing colonized peoples up close was a terminal instance linking the local peoples of France's overseas territories to an aesthetic category of the primitive whose political implications anticolonialists would soon reveal. If, as Charles-Robert Ageron and others argue, the physical presence of colonial places and peoples at Vincennes marked the apogee and apotheosis of a colonial expansion soon to be challenged, documentary and feature films provided spectators at home with other ways of seeing the colonies.[41]

Screening North Africa

Those in France who saw North Africa in the 1930s likely saw it on film, in the guise of a visual excursion. Of the 1,305 feature films produced in France between 1930 and 1939, eighty-five portrayed their central story as occurring outside France, with a majority set in Africa. Among films set in North Africa, seventeen took place in Morocco, seven in Algeria, and three in Tunisia.[42] Regardless of their themes and plots, when combined with the numerous documentary and ethnographic films that accompanied them at theaters or played in other venues, these features made the colonial imaginary palpable and unavoidable in 1930s Paris.[43]

Colonial cinema is largely an interwar genre whose growth coincided with the inflated nationalism of that period. Most often depicted were melodramatic tales of men caught up by alluring women in ungovernable terrain. Historians and critics have shown that many such films, and the genre as a whole, were indirectly tied to France's colonial mission (sometimes directly benefiting from government subsidies of one sort or another). Yet cinema used the colonies as it used all topics, to further its own expansion as modernity's dominant purveyor of information, attitudes, entertainment, and consensus.

Prospecting in rich terrain already mined by the adventure novel, Jacques Feyder hit the richest vein possible in 1920 when he brought Pierre Benoît's bestselling novel *L'Atlantide* to the screen. Daring to shoot on location—thereby consuming a year's effort and a fortune in production costs—Feyder attracted the largest film audiences of the entire decade in France. *L'Atlantide* was an international hit of astounding proportions.[44] Every film thereafter shot in North Africa would contend with the mythical values evoked in this film, whose fanciful adventure brought some of France's most popular stars into the desert to the "lost city of Atlantis." Insisting on removing his cast and his crew from France throughout the lengthy production, Feyder even shot the many interior sequences in Algerian studios, certain in his belief that the actors would catch the feel of a locale that amplified a conventional love story. *L'Atlantide* would go through numerous remakes, one by G. W. Pabst just after the Colonial Exposition. And its formula would govern a host of films, the most important of which in the 1930s was Julien Duvivier's *La Bandera*.

A forerunner of the poetic realism that would take French cinema to the apex of film art later in the decade, *La Bandera* distilled the murky psychological flow of exotic romance into what most critics regard as the essence of the colonial genre. It was adapted from a 1931 novel that Pierre Mac Orlan wrote in the flush of the aesthetic he had baptized *le fantastique social*. Mac Orlan was on hand to help Duvivier discover this aesthetic in the mysterious Rif Mountains of Morocco. And Duvivier was there to capture the encounter of two of France's greatest romantic stars, Jean Gabin and Anabella, amid odd geological formations, strange props, a genuine army (Francisco Franco's legionnaires), and a merciless sun.[45] Unlike pure ethnographic films and unlike hybrid docudramas, which grant their geography independent status, French colonial features—*Le Bandera* at their head—aim to join landscape and sentiments to produce a "unity of expression" that is all the more powerful for the disparity between the human and the geological. André Lang, a key critic of the time, could feel blood flowing through the six hundred cells of Duvivier's découpage, while Graham Greene was affected by the fluid camera that joined atmosphere to moral drama.[46] Produced through the artistry of writing, camera, editing, and music, this total integration of elements is in fact the film's overarching theme: the quest for personal wholeness achieved through the device of the Conradian double, and the quest for social fusion achieved at the end of the film as the brigade of foreign legionnaires is decimated. *La Bandera* lashes the mesmerized spectator to its hero, who is tracked by an implacable fatality from Paris to Barcelona to Morocco, then deeper still into the Rif Mountains. The common myth of Africa as a locus of spiritual regeneration here joins the film's disturbing ideology of brotherhood in the Foreign Legion, where pasts are forgotten and the future belongs to those who give the orders.[47]

La Bandera portrays Africa as indefinite, lawless, and unforgiving, but also as a female body whose veiled contours are ready to trap men who race across its sands or hide in its unmappable redoubts. In the absence of markers or of distinguishing features, the Foreign Legion cut roads into the landscape, tattooing it just as the film's two lovers tattoo themselves to etch visible boundaries of behavior. This eroticized space is utterly mythical; nevertheless, it seemed authentic to French spectators. An article in *Pour Vous* showed the film's female lead in her carefully researched Berber costume.[48] Yet the picture was not of a foreign woman at all, but of Annabella, France's most popular female star, playing a Berber courtesan who had acquired her perfect French from the many legionnaires passing through her room. When Annabella and Gabin sucked each other's blood in a bonding ritual taken from the Foreign Legion, audiences were meant to be aroused by the sexual connotation rather than shocked by the racial one. Indeed, the religious and racial difference coded in Annabella's costume and gestures depended on and doubled the power of sexual difference that was the cornerstone of French and international filmmaking. The strangeness of North Africa was tamed when it was romanced and possessed, and *La Bandera* extended but did not rewrite the usual promise of hypnotic experience that fiction films have always advertised.[49] And so the North African terrain was nothing other than a double of the flesh of the female star. To die in the Sahara was to die in a lover's arms—deliciously, picturesquely, and in cinematographic comfort.

The Spirit of Africa, the Spirit of Patriotism

The spiritual life is a quest and a risk, Charles Péguy had preached, and so, too, should be the life of art. Clearly, Léon Poirier agreed. Thus, it was to counter the comforts of the studio and of genre that in 1924 he joined La Croisière Noire, an expedition financed by the advertising wing of Citroën to promote its engineering prowess by featuring a powerful new half-track vehicle, combining conventional tires in front with tank treads in the rear. Poirier cared little about the automotive side of the adventure; he wanted to overcome the postwar lethargy that still afflicted him and the cinema. In contrast to feature films, even those shot on location, the ethnographic enterprise was meant to be uncomfortable from start to finish, including the production and the audience experience. In addition to long journeys undertaken without amenities, foreign treks proved socially unnerving. Unknown foods and customs, strange rites supplicating obscure deities—all this awaited the traveler who deployed the latest machinery to drive into the heart of disturbingly different worlds, where such machinery (indeed, where such drive) was out of place. This tension haunted the sort of ethnographic cinema which Poirier helped to invent but which he took as pure difference rather than as contradiction: "The world is a wheel. Those of us in the West are on its outside, thrown by centrifugal force in a continuous movement, condemned by an agitation that often vainly leads us to death without ever giving us time to comprehend why in truth we are agitated. At the center, on the other hand, is the Orient, whose people, attracted by centripetal force, tend with all their being toward the immobility of the interior life."[50]

Poirier was agitated enough to plow across an entire continent, seeking to capture what he knew only stillness could provide. Symptomatically, his film *La Croisière noire* breaks readily into images of the arduous journey on the one hand, and images of the strange lands traversed on the other. Like other ethnographic diary films of the period, it lurches from location to location, interspersing extended picture postcards of people and terrain with the tale of the trek—anecdotes of dangers, logistical obstacles ingeniously overcome, and so on. True, at one point Poirier expresses the majesty of a native dance by slipping momentarily into slow motion. He also moves in for close-up profiles of Mangbetou women whose elongated heads turned them into sculpture, into living bronzes. In this case, he presented an Africa to be possessed.

97. Alexandre Iacovleff, Portrait of
Marabout Aïm Gabo, Sultan of Birao
(1927).

Seven years later, a similar split between technology and spirit, between agitation and stillness, would vex the organizers of the Colonial Exposition (one of whom was Poirier). They arranged for the pavilions of colonized cultures (lit up by the abundant electrical power pouring into the Bois de Vincennes) to encircle a central metropolitan pavilion featuring technologies of progress. Poirier believed that a kind of parity could be reached between centrifugal and centripetal cultures, as if the huge French generators might illuminate an Orient that could become a natural reservoir of spiritual energy. When Poirier made his most ambitious film, *L'Appel du silence* (1936), it was with the intention of tapping that reserve, for he referred to the film's hero, Father Charles de Foucauld, as "a veritable accumulator of spiritual energy."[51] And that energy, as Foucauld embodied it, exploded from a fusion of military and religious discipline, which Poirier sought to pass on to his fellow French citizens. He believed that the West should pursue a heroic quest to penetrate the unknown parts of the world, where it would surely encounter revelations unavailable at home.

A stalwart of the film industry for thirty years, Poirier spent a lot of time in Paris, but he did so reluctantly. Compared to the rest of the country, Paris may have seemed secular, modern, and politically progressive, but it was still a very Catholic city, hosting many militant right-wing groups and a huge number of unaffiliated citizens who were conservative at root. Poirier spoke to and for those who were witnessing the erosion of traditional spiritual values on the streets and screens of modernity.

Poirier knew turn-of-the-century Paris, having worked his way up in the theater world there. The tragedy and glory of the Great War made the Parisian theater appear paltry, self-satisfied, and false. He pressured Gaumont, where he served as artistic director, into releasing him from its studios, which had been built to mime the stage. He would make grand films on sites of grandeur, initiating his directorial career in 1922 with an adaptation of Alphonse de Lamartine's *Jocelyn*. No matter that the silent screen muted the sinuous verse.

> Poetry and the screen had the same goal: expressing ideas and feelings by means of images, silent film should have found it much easier than stage drama to transpose a poem. In addition, a specific character appealed to me in Lamartine's work—neither the tender Laurence nor the shy bishop nor the heroic Jocelyn. It was the Mountain. What a magnificent means of rendering Lamartine's lyricism into screen images—by showing mountain peaks and eternal snows! The visual score completely wrote itself.[52]

Poirier would sing to the Alps with the longing and respect of a troubadour. His modest, Franciscan style relied on extreme long shots, as though he wanted the pinhole of the camera's iris to gather light from every corner of the widest possible field of view. Poirier's spiritual ambitions were boundless, as was his faith in the power of cinema to convey the oceanic fantasy representing the sublime that moved him. How small the camera lens, how vast the light it gathers into focus! And something analogous could be said of the human soul—so humble, yet so capable of being majestically filled.[53]

Jocelyn proved a commercial and critical success. The Société des Auteurs des Films designated it the best film of the year, and Gaumont financed a second adaptation from Lamartine. The result was *Geneviève*, an atmospheric meditation whose isolated rural settings strongly recall nineteenth-century realist painting. A reviewer for *Cinémagazine* compared the effect to "a Corot-like study of Nature's magnificence: wooded landscapes, fields, and mountains" that tempered the tragic experience of "the poor peasant girl."[54] Next came the ineffable *La Brière* (The Salt Marsh; 1924), taken from a novel by Alphonse de Châteaubriand set in lower Brittany. As with the adaptations from Lamartine, its pictorial realism and vivid footage shot on location transposed literary romanticism into a commercial version of cinematic impressionism. Poirier's treatment of the novel is as much "a visual essay on water, light, and fog as it is . . . the story of a peasant family dominated by a brutal, embittered patriarch"[55]—but dominated as well by the implacable dictates of industrial progress set to drain the marsh, and with it the mystery of the land. The dénouement turns on the discovery (on a misty isle inhabited by a madwoman) of a lost letter dated 1493 from the queen of France giving perpetual rights over the land to those living there. Poirier vaunts his undisguised distrust of modernization and his belief in France both as land and as inherited tradition—inherited in this case directly from a benevolent monarch.

All three of these early efforts reveal hints of the sacred deep within the French countryside, distant from Parisian street life and politics. Poirier wanted more than hints; he wanted to find the source of the sacred, just as Paris was to him the source of the secular. So, while *La Brière* was enjoying a fine run in the theaters, and before he agreed to participate in the motorized Citroën trek through Africa, Poirier began developing a project whose scale equaled that of his own religious and patriotic ambitions. *Le Puits de Jacob* (Jacob's Well) was to have been a tale of Christ set in the rugged hills of Palestine.[56] Poirier thought of it as a personal pilgrimage, believing that this film would resolve his crippling religious doubts. But logistical difficulties proved insurmountable. Citroën, on the other hand, offered unprecedented logistical support for their proposed adventure, and Poirier convinced himself that his pilgrimage could be diverted to Africa. First he had to dismiss his reservations about the outright commercial goals of the venture. He reminded himself that Robert Flaherty had been working for the Révillon fur company when he shot *Nanook of the North* (1921), and this was a film whose sublime images clearly outweighed any commercial or scientific value it may have delivered as a bonus. Poirier had a premonition that Africa would seize him as the Arctic had taken Flaherty, lifting him onto a plateau above the fog he had been dwelling in. His devout wife assured him that the African journey would provide the pure water needed to fill *Jacob's Well*. His mother, he recalls, blessed him on the forehead and ritualistically lit candles as he departed.

Poirier would ultimately film mysterious religious rites, but it was the continent more than its people that cured his angst. As Poirier would later detail, a sacred light in the darkness poured like water over his parched soul early in the journey, when he became separated from his comrades in the mountains of Algeria. Terrified in the pitch-dark Saharan midnight, he was startled by an eerie light emanating from a nearby peak. Poirier, it turned out, was seeing the phosphorescence that the rocks of these mountains sometimes release. The scientific explanation, however, would never account for the power that this light exerted on his soul. It was his burning bush, and North Africa would ever after be sacred ground to him. He would associate it—this initial call of silence *(appel du silence)*—with cinema, with the purifying effect of sound and light.[57]

Touched by this encounter, Poirier went on to chronicle the Citroën expedition with fervor. He found native dances and shamanistic esoterica to be powerful expressions answering the same needs he was certain all but jaded Europeans also felt. In addition, he believed that Christianity had gradually become a more blessed form of precisely the same human urges that African peoples still dealt with through their rites, including cannibalism. When André Gide consulted Poirier before embarking on the trip that inspired the book and the film *Voyage au Congo*, Poirier frowned on the writer's bemusement in the face of native rituals of circumcision and excision. Poirier considered Gide's attitude obscene and arrogant, since Gide refused to put aside his European self-assurance even when floating down the Congo.[58] One had to become dispossessed and humble in order to sink into a different (and purer) sensibility.[59]

Poirier wanted to reacquaint a decadent France with the purity it had given up for sophistication, and for this reason he set great store by his epic, *L'Appel du silence*. In effect, he would make Charles de Foucauld into a nonconformist whose conversion to Christian faith and whose hermitage in North Africa were immediately linked to colonial expansion. Foucauld had been born in Strasbourg in 1858 and orphaned as a child. In early scenes of the film, he displays a sense of independence that clashes with the conformity required of future officers destined for the elite national military academy at Saint Cyr. Having completed his studies at the rival academy for cavalry officers at Saumur, Foucauld is sent to North Africa in 1878. Another clash of wills with superiors results in his resignation and a return to France, after which he volunteers for desert assignment in 1881. Two years later, he resigns from the army again and undertakes an undercover mission in Morocco. It is during this 1883 mission that Foucauld first relates the silence and open space of the desert to the promise of a society of new men *(hommes nouveaux)*, which an acquaintance from his student days at Saumur had described to him with fervor several years earlier.[60]

Foucauld returns to Paris in 1886, but quickly rejects the hypocrisy and mechanization of a modern life at odds with the spiritual values he has come to hold. In 1889 he leaves France for good and follows his vision of Christ to the Middle East, where he volunteers to work at the monastery of the Sisters of Clarisse in Nazareth. By 1903 Foucauld has established his retreat in the Algerian Sahara, where he aims to convert the local inhabitants. Some of these inhabitants are the ones who in 1916 take his life.

Numerous scenes and images in Poirier's film uphold the values of a conservative nationalism and spiritual history of colonial France. Foucauld is shown utterly alienated from science and technology, for instance. In Paris he scorns the material progress contaminating urban life, including the telephone, the steam engine, and even the zoetrope. When a glib journalist asks him to comment on what his experience in North Africa has taught him about the differences between Muslims and "us," Foucauld states that the Muslims truly believe in God, while "we" (Christians) merely pretend to. The only words that impress Foucauld during his stay in Paris come from Jean Jaurès—the future leader of the French Socialists—who praises the advent of a new world in which technology would allow men to devote their efforts to the peaceful establishment of a future community *(cité future)*.

The idealism Foucauld lauds in Jaurès recalls an earlier conversation he has with a military school acquaintance, the marquis Antoine de Morès, during which the latter announces his intention to travel to the United States in search of the society of ardent and sincere men he cannot find in France. Foucauld responds that he has no interest in cowboys, preferring the desert and rural villages. As he puts it, "Je me charge du bled" ("I'll take care of the backlands"). Later in the film, Foucauld learns that de Morès has died in the Sahara, prefiguring his own fate.[61] In fact, de Morès' youthful idealism turned sour; he became an outspoken anti-Semite, an ally of Edouard Drumont, author of the notorious *La France juive* (1886). A syndicalist of sorts, de Morès organized the butchers of Paris. In *Le Secret des changes* (1894) he advocated a fusion of the labor union movement and anti-Semitism under what he termed "the doctrine of the *faisceau*" (meaning "sheaf," from the Latin *fasces*, symbol of authority in ancient Rome)—an early formulation of a native French fascism.[62]

Foucauld's response to the disenchantment he shared with Jaurès and de Morès was to leave Europe and secular modernity, answering a call to silence and spirituality. Poirier's bio-pic lines up perfectly with Lyautey's efforts in Morocco to develop a site of true cultural reconciliation, where Islamic and

French cultures would come together under the values of Christianity. *L'Appel du silence* emphasizes Foucauld's conversion from tactics of militant pacification to those associated with a spiritual, civilizing presence. Yet the film also discloses the ineradicable prejudice of the social privilege he never truly sheds. This is evident in Foucauld's haughty interactions with military officers and with the insensitive way he treats his female companion. In relation to the society he encounters in Africa, the film records a telling instance of religious prejudice, when Foucauld prepares his year-long reconnaissance mission in Morocco to help the military. Laying out his projected itinerary, he is advised to take extreme care with his disguise, without which any stranger in Morocco would immediately be assassinated, or kidnapped for ransom. His options are to become Arab or Jew; Foucauld answers without hesitation, "Je préfère Arabe."[63] Warned that any hint of Western accent or minor infraction of Islamic practices might prove fatal, Foucauld is counseled to consider the option he initially rejected: "As a Jew you can speak a mishmash [*un sabir*] of many languages. Besides, Jews are so despised in Morocco that no one will pay attention to you. This way, you could also find shelter in synagogues."[64]

And so Poirier portrays the future Christian mystic and martyr of Tamanrasset making his way into Morocco dressed as Joseph Aleman, an itinerant Muscovite rabbi who has come to North Africa to raise funds for "the wretched Jews of Russia."[65] This scene illustrates how a minor yet necessary anti-Semitism (consistent with the religious and military elements crucial to colonial expansion) enhances Poirier's portrait of Foucauld.[66] Anti-Semitism unquestionably heightened the appeal of *L'Appel du silence* among political conservatives, for whom the ideal of an imperial France was increasingly at odds with the 1936 Popular Front government under Léon Blum, a Socialist who was also Jewish.

The stunning commercial success of *L'Appel du silence*—second in box-office receipts, behind Marcel Pagnol's *César*—beclouds what is too often taken to be a pervasive Parisian leftism at the moment of the Popular Front victory. Controversy over the film's value tarnished the first Louis Delluc Prize for best French director. Film industry sponsors, who had blithely planned a ritual of self-congratulation asserting the preeminence and cultural value of France's cinema, saw their event degenerate into a fracas with political pressures, name calling, and resignations from the prize committee. For a time, six directors were in competition. Days of debate ended with a compromise

98. Charles de Foucauld (Jean Yonnel) disguised as a Muscovite rabbi in Léon Poirier's *L'Appel du silence* (1936).

and the startling announcement that there would be two winners. Sharing the Delluc Prize—but little else—were Jean Renoir and Léon Poirier.

L'Appel du silence's ticket sales went far beyond the combined total of Renoir's three films that year.[67] Yet Poirier is nearly forgotten, while Renoir has come down to us as the greatest filmmaker of that generation. This ultimate judgment may have been inevitable, given Renoir's complexity and genius, but Poirier in fact was to lose his reputation because of the very politics that brought him to prominence at the height of the Popular Front. In 1943, he unflinchingly produced a pure Pétainist work, *Jeannou*, casting himself on the side of pro-German collaborators. How can it be that his overt religious and political sentiments, tied to his sympathy for a figure like Charles de Foucauld, should have resonated with a large segment of the French populace in 1936, including the Parisian critics and cultural pundits who lavished such praise on him?

Poirier recognized the irony of sharing the Delluc Prize with someone so different from himself:

Renoir is my opposite: he is sensual, I am cerebral; he is Parisian and sociable, I am rural and solitary; he vacations on the Riviera, while I go to a lonely farm in the Périgord. He is internationalist and Russified; I am Catholic. . . . I believe that the French tradition, which I want to uphold, must go through the church. That is why I am so exhilarated by the recognition given to *L'Appel du silence* and feel that the Grand Prize of French Cinema has justly honored a film that seeks quite rightly to enlarge France. . . . I'm pondering these two prizes given out at the same time. I find this simultaneity excellent; it clarifies things. The ferment needed in every society is felt through opposition.[68]

Let us accept Poirier's invitation to see the dual prizes as a convenient way of dividing the opinions of the day. Renoir would next make *La Grande Illusion* and *La Marseillaise*, both of which asserted an egalitarian brotherhood of common interests over and against aristocratic hierarchies. When grouped with his Frontist trilogy of 1936 (*Le Crime de Monsieur Lange*, *Les Bas Fonds*, and the undistributed *La Vie est à nous*), this set of five films certifies a leftist humanism even down to our own day. On the other hand, Poirier's *L'Appel du silence* retains a cult appeal for a fringe of the French right by extending France's civilizing mission outward "through the church" toward colonial expansion. During an interview upon winning the prize, the lean Poirier refused the offer of a drink, refused both coffee and a cigarette; he spoke of the purity of his hero and of the rigorous film he had made to honor him. Seen beside the stout Renoir, always the accommodating artist who loved bouillabaisse and mixed his sauces, Poirier's asceticism conveyed a self-discipline in line with the conservative politics and morals of the Pétainist Etat Français that he was to support five years later.

Poirier's cultural politics were already on the table in 1936, when he was the toast of Paris. In a speech written to raise funds for *L'Appel du silence*, he made sure to mention his admiration not just for Charles de Foucauld, but for Count de la Rocque, leader of the Croix-de-Feu.[69] While the Vichy regime would ban Renoir's films, the 1943 re-release of *L'Appel du silence* prompted one reviewer to praise it as "a work of art of the highest moral and spiritual standards, which deals with a pioneer of French colonization in North Africa and which takes on special and deep significance given today's circumstances."[70] The same reviewer described the re-release's first screening as a gala attended by Vichy cabinet members, generals, rectors, and the heads of many religious orders. By 1943, Renoir had left France and was in the United States.

At the start of the 1930s, as they both prepared their first sound films, Renoir and Poirier had recognized the deep ideological divide between them. At that time, they lived next door to each other. Moreover, both were related to Impressionist painters: Renoir through his illustrious father, Pierre-Auguste, and Poirier through his aunt, Berthe Morisot, who also happened to be Edouard Manet's sister-in-law. Working at the edge of the film industry on projects motivated by personal and social ambitions, both directors routinely raised money through ingenious schemes. *L'Appel du silence* would be financed by national subscriptions and by collections in parishes, with Poirier canvassing France and Belgium to deliver homilies on Le Père Foucauld. As we have seen, Renoir would use a similar tactic to finance *La Marseillaise*, by asking labor unions and the CGT to contribute to a film representing their interests.

Although their respective film styles had little in common, both men felt more at home on location than in the hothouses of the studios, where 98 percent of French feature films were shot in the 1930s. Both considered studios to be an index of everything artificial in modern life. Midway through *L'Appel du silence*, Foucauld renounces his inherited position in the effete Parisian society of his day for the authenticity of a hermitage in the Hoggar Mountains of Algeria. In this he resembles the protagonist of Poirier's film *Caïn* (1931), who leaps from a steamship taking him to France. Turning his back on a fortune in Europe, he is shown swimming to the wild Madagascan isle that has become his home. In their instinct for the uncertainty and freedom of the outdoors, Poirier's heroes are kin to Boudu, the drifter in Renoir's *Boudu sauvé des eaux* (1932), who capsizes his wedding boat and swims to shore, where he is shown at home with the dogs and goats he so resembles. Then there are the heroes of the 1936 films that earned Renoir his Delluc Prize— Amédée Lange (of *Le Crime du Monsieur Lange*) and Pepel (of *Les Bas Fonds*)— both of whom ultimately leave their social groups and head off into an open frontier.

The most striking similarity between the two directors was their participation in events marking the 1930–1931 centennial of France's presence in Algeria. In an episode Renoir soon regretted, he took a commission from the Algerian cultural ministry to direct *Le Bled*. The finished film, which depicts the colonizers as brave, amiable men, contributed to the near hysteria of patriotism culminating in the 1931 Colonial Exposition, whose film section

Poirier headed. In light of Renoir's political positions over the next fifteen years, his association with the celebration of the centennial of French Algeria illustrates how pervasive Africa's presence was between the wars, even among sophisticated Parisians. Africa was in the air of the capital. Poirier helped waft it in like a Harmattan wind.

Split Screens

The remarkable team of Jean Benoît-Lévy and Marie Epstein, a Polish émigrée and France's major female director of the 1930s, left their mark on the decade with a series of films that were deemed humanist, progressive, and leftist. Their reputation soared in 1933 with *La Maternelle*, starring Madeleine Renaud and a band of urchins—a film that drew attention to the plight of abandoned children in Paris. The next year Benoît-Lévy and Epstein set out for Morocco to make *Itto*, a unique film whose split perspectives confound our standard conception of colonial cinema tied to right-wing ideology.

Itto is set in the French protectorate of Morocco during the years 1914–1920, when Maréchal Lyautey was pacifying the native inhabitants by acculturation more than by military force. The film recounts an armed uprising against French authority by the Chleuh Berber people. In the process, it dramatizes a number of conflicts over authority, including challenges to patriarchy asserted in both the French camp and native villages by women, who are portrayed as at least equal to their male counterparts. The film follows conventions that displace the power struggle of politics and of opposed cultures onto domestic melodramas of romantic love and family; yet it takes an unusual risk when it introduces pressing issues of health and hygiene to advance and seal the plot. For the dramatic conflicts cannot be solved by decisions at the level of politics or of domestic life until another drama is worked out. This pits the French military doctor *(toubib)*, assigned to a rural area of the Middle Atlas region, against the native sorcerer-healer in village markets.

Itto is framed from the start as a historical account of the Moroccan pacification, narrated after the fact. The film openly endorses the presence of the French military and the protectorate administrators by emphasizing policies intended to promote the physical well-being of all local peoples. A founding principle of this policy appears at the very start of the film in an epigraph attributed to Lyautey: "Other men are perhaps different from us, but observation shows that they are not inferior to us."

The emphasis on health care also advocates paternalistic colonization by setting the French in their self-assigned civilizing mission against the local Berber tribes, who, in a prefatory text following the epigraph, are described in terms recalling traditional myths of the noble savage. Their backwardness is said to have a distinctive beauty and dignity that needs preservation and protection:

> The story you are about to see is one of a struggle for independence and civilization. The Chleuh Berbers, shepherd-warriors fiercely attached to their land and to their freedom, were living under a truly feudal regime, forever at war among themselves, when the French arrived. Fighting for their individual ideals, the Arabs [*sic*] and the French—first known as *Roumis*, or "infidels"—quickly came to know and to respect each other, despite differences of race and of mind. Soon their hearts beat as one.

Contrary to what today's viewer might infer, this "struggle for independence and civilization" refers not to native self-determination, but to colonial policies that the French considered liberating for the presumably backward local peoples.

Itto thus reflected and promoted colonial expansion, despite the progressive credentials of its directorial team. The very genesis of the film reveals numerous ties to Lyautey and to the Moroccan protectorate. The plot was adapted by the politician and colonial administrator Georges Duvernois from the fiction of Maurice Le Glay, who had served as an emissary representing French military forces approved by the powerful sultan of Marrakesh, Si Abdallah al-Glaoui. Over the next decade, Le Glay was Lyautey's chief advisor on native affairs. It was he who devised the notion that the country should be divided into a land of order *(bled Makhzen)* and a land of dissonance *(bled s siba)*.[71] Etienne Rey, who wrote the film's dialogue, likewise served under Lyautey during World War I as an ordinance officer. Even the female lead, Simone Berriau, the one-time Opéra Comique actress cast in the role of Princess Itto, had personal ties to the protectorate, for she was the widow of Colonel Henri Berriau (1870–1918), director of Morocco's political affairs and intelligence services. Lyautey reputedly treated him as a surrogate son, and assigned him to head a native-officers' training school whose curriculum included language instruction in Arabic and Berber, as well as readings in Arabic literature and law. Unquestionably, Simone Berriau, who was fluent in

99–100. Princess Itto (Simone Berriau) and her chieftain father, Hammou (Moulay Ibrahim).

Berber and trained as a nurse, embodied the complex relations between the film's dramatic elements and the historical events on which they drew.

The film's portrait of the earnest military *toubib* was inspired by Lyautey's medical units *(groupes sanitaires)*, created almost as soon as he arrived in Morocco. Lyautey wrote to his mentor, General Joseph Gallieni, that if he had four more doctors assigned to him he could relieve four battalions from their task of suppressing local resistance: "Doctors assigned to rural clans . . . made French political authority palatable. They traveled the length of the country, and Lyautey consulted them because they were astute, independent observers."[72]

Itto recounts the final submission of the Zaiane Chleuh Berber clans of the Middle Atlas region, who resisted the protectorate administration *(dawla)* until 1920, fighting under their leader, Moha ou Hammou el Zaiani. The film develops chiefly as the Romeo-and-Juliet story of Princess Itto and her fiancé, Miloud, whose father, Hassan, heads a clan that Itto's father, Hammou, seeks to enlist to fight against the French. On the French side, similar issues of gender and family are played out in the figures of a French military doctor, Pierre Darrieu, and his wife, Françoise, who arrives from France early in the film.

Cultures collide when a French surveillance plane passing over Hassan's camp is shot down during the betrothal announcement of Itto and Miloud. The crash strands the plane's pilot and his passenger behind enemy lines. Miloud accompanies the passenger to the French camp under a flag of truce, after agreeing to return with a doctor to treat the wounded pilot. Upon a request from Hassan, the doctor—whom the natives refer to as the white sorcerer *(le sorcier blanc)*—agrees to inoculate Hassan's sheep, which are dying of an unknown disease. Thus begins the action in a contact zone.

But first, the drama must develop in segregated spaces. In one scene, Françoise whispers to Pierre that she is pregnant; and Itto too becomes pregnant, after she and Miloud, increasingly at odds with their respective families, spend a night together at Miloud's camp. In a time-jump of nine months, Itto gives birth to a daughter in a mountain tent away from her father's Casbah. Under simulated moonlight, Itto's tender maternity is laid out in tableau. Nearby, a dog nurses her newborn pups. When Itto's nurse, Aïcha, carries the infant down to the stream where she means to drown one of the puppies, Itto fears the worst. (In a later scene, Hammou is ready to kill a baby, until he shown that it is not a girl.) After Itto's daughter falls ill with diphtheria, a local sorcerer ties a paper charm around the baby's neck. When the charm proves ineffective, Itto breaks with tradition and takes the child to the *toubib* in the local market outside Hammou's Casbah. As the French doctor applies his "amulet" (injected serum), Miloud is re-united with Itto and the baby daughter whose existence she had not revealed to him.

Françoise likewise gives birth, to a son. But when he too falls ill, Pierre finds to his dismay that he no longer has enough vaccine to save the boy's life. Itto and other women at Hammou's Casbah salvage medication that Hammou's men have stolen from the market after mistaking it for ammunition. They return it to the doctor just as a snowstorm breaks out in the mountains. Afterward, Françoise welcomes Itto into her house; in a crucial display of empathy between the women, Françoise extends her hand to thank Itto. This gesture echoes an earlier gesture in which an officer in the French military camp had held out a cigarette to the conflicted Miloud. Whereas the two women come together because they share maternity, the cigarette that links the men symbolizes compromise and betrayal.[73]

Itto returns to her native town, Tidikelt, where she learns that her father has ordered his sons away so that he can take a final stand and die a warrior's death. Determined to keep faith with her father, she abandons her baby on the windowsill of Pierre and Françoise's home. An initially hesitant Françoise cannot resist the baby's cry; as she nurses her, a voice-over repeats Lyautey's statement (shown onscreen at the start of the film) about tolerance. Meanwhile, Itto has joined her father on the ramparts of Tidikelt, where, despite their heroic resistance, local riflemen under French command kill them both.

In a final scene, Françoise agrees to remain with her husband in Morocco and serve alongside him to raise Itto's child among the Chleuh.

This end is troubling, for arguably it illustrates that Princess Itto regresses from the independence she had attained through rebellion and motherhood to the traditional role of dutiful daughter. Her decision to entrust her child to the French doctor and his wife entails a future for her daughter (and, by extension, for her people) removed from the values of paternal authority in whose name she sacrifices her own life. Her action also acknowledges the prospect of better health for her child through the Western medicine that Pierre and Françoise embody. In addition, the final scenes focus on the newfound capacities of Itto and Françoise to act with a compassion that the males surrounding them—Hammou, Miloud, and Pierre—fail to match. Her baby's illness marks a turning point for Itto, since the inability of the Berber *sorcier* to cure the baby's fever sends her to the *sorcier blanc*. Françoise's decision to serve as surrogate mother to Itto's child marks a commitment in direct response to Itto's. Instead of continuing to bemoan her discomfort as a doctor's wife living in the hinterlands, she ends by supporting the cause to which her husband is committed. The presence of Lyautey's words at the very moment of Francoise's conversion would seem to recruit (in the full sense of the term) France's maternal response to the colonial mission through the benevolence of Western medicine.

While upholding the colonial mission, *Itto* stands out against the exotic "white-hat" legionnaire melodramas that dominated the genre of *le cinéma colonial*. Shooting on location in the Atlas Mountains and using untrained natives in all roles (except for Simone Berriau as Princess Itto), Benoît-Lévy and Epstein moved their film toward documentary and filmed ethnography. They enhanced its authenticity by including portions of dialogue in Berber, with French subtitles. Yet just as the Berber language ultimately yields to the pervasive presence of French (whether spoken or scripted in subtitles), so the protofeminist elements of the film are contained within a broader narrative of pacification justifying the French presence because of the hygiene it brings to less developed societies. Princess Itto's particular story, no matter how progressive it may be at its edges, echoes the general monumental account of colonial expansion.

Who Is French in *La Plus Grande France*?

When Pierre Chenal referred to his 1938 feature film *La Maison du Maltais* as his "little Sternberg," he was thinking of Josef von Sternberg's *Morocco*

101. Cover of Jean Vignaud and Henri Fescourt's *ciné-roman* (1926).

(1931), in which French Legionnaire Gary Cooper encounters a world-weary Marlene Dietrich. Chenal saw the film with his friend Pierre Mac Orlan, who likewise admired it and who characterized it as utterly European in tone despite the fact that it was a Paramount production.[74] At the time, Mac Orlan was just finishing his own novel about Morocco, *La Bandera*, and writing the voice-over for a short that Chenal was busy shooting in the back alleys of Paris.[75] Besides *La Bandera*, other colonial films of the decade such as *Le*

Grand Jeu and *Pépé le Moko* featured white males who die after fleeing from France to North Africa.[76]

Rather than extending the scenario of a loss of male identity in Africa, Chenal's film reverses direction by recounting the failed assimilation and then the death of an "African" in France. Matteo, a fey Maltese storyteller (played by Marcel Dalio), pursues Safia (played by Viviane Romance), a white prostitute from Marseilles, after they meet by chance in the native market of the Tunisian port of Sfax. Transfixed by this stunning woman, who walks into his life like a princess out of one of his tales, Matteo follows and watches over her. Safia is touched by this would-be guardian angel who spoils her with tenderness. She finds Matteo's devotion a pleasant break from the harsh treatment to which she is accustomed. And when she is stricken with sadness by the death of her fellow prostitute Greta, he takes her to the house that he shares with his father (hence the film's title, *The House of the Maltese*) at the edge of the desert, where they live happily for several weeks.

Safia tells an elated Matteo that she is pregnant, just as he is leaving to fish for sponges off the island of Djerba. In fact, he has agreed to partake in a smuggling scheme to earn money that will secure his new life with Safia. But the operation goes awry, and when Matteo is arrested and fails to return as expected, his father curses Safia and throws her out of his house. Desperate to ensure the future of her child, Safia accepts an invitation to go to Paris with a French anthropologist, Chervin (Pierre Renoir), who finds her distraught, wandering in the desert. With melodramatic mistiming, she leaves for France with Chervin just before Matteo returns. When her daughter, Jacqueline, is born in Paris, she raises her as if Chervin were the father.

Three years later, Matteo arrives in Paris, knowing vaguely that Safia is somewhere in the city. One day in the Parc Monceau, Matteo, by now nearly a tramp, finds himself surrounded by children drawn to his bizarre appearance. Impulsively he launches into a favorite story, unaware that one of the children is Jacqueline, his daughter. When the girl retells the story to her parents that night, Safia is frightened. Using a false name to keep the matter from Chervin, she hires a private detective, Rossignol (Louis Jouvet), to locate Matteo. Because Safia fears losing the privileges she has earned for her daughter by raising her as Chervin's child, she deceives Matteo first by meeting him in a hotel where she pretends to work as a prostitute, and then by telling him that her pregnancy did not come to term.

But Rossignol has secretly followed her to the hotel, overheard her conversation with Matteo, and discovered that she is Chervin's wife. He tries to blackmail her, claiming to represent Matteo. Safia is forced to sell a ring to buy Rossignol's silence. Of course Chervin notices the missing ring, confronts Safia, and insists that they separate. Safia returns to the hotel—called the Eden—where Matteo is staying. When he shows up that night accompanied by rowdy friends—some of the Montmartre band of petty criminals he has moved in with—Safia confesses that she has been raising their child as Chervin's daughter. Matteo now understands her behavior and sacrifice. He meets with Chervin to reconcile him with Safia. Validated in his love, yet ashamed at the sufferings his actions have caused, Matteo dons his "native" shirt and turban before praying to Allah and shooting himself, in a symbolic return to Sfax and to his father's house.

The pathos of this suicide resounds well beyond the mere melodrama of the plot, for Chenal rendered Matteo (played to full effect by a Jewish actor) as both chimerical and complex. Matteo may be introduced as an innocent storyteller, but a quick series of encounters makes him the linchpin of a conflicted rebus, involving questions of race, class and gender. First he meets a French friend (Gaston Modot), who tries to interest him in colonial labor. Having rejected this form of assimilation, he next runs into his father, Ibrahim, who, invoking Islamic tradition, berates him for his idleness. Matteo scorns work, and presumably religion, as distractions from the poetry of the present. He prefers to listen to the birds sing while he awaits his princess. He doesn't have long to wait. In their unforgettable first meeting, he cannot keep from staring at Safia up and down. Hardened to such looks, she mocks Matteo—"Ma parole, c'est un muet. Merci quand même" ("My word, he's a mute. Thanks all the same")—before pointing to her breasts and saying, "Ah! ça, mon bébé, c'est les grenades du jardin d'Allah!" ("Ah! These, baby, these are pomegranates from the Garden of Allah!").

Matteo is oblivious to Safia's "work" as a prostitute. He also seems blind to the fact that she is white, and thus exotic among prostitutes in the native sections of a colonial port such as Sfax.[77] Ironically, the fairy tale that he begins to live with her drives him to join the port's laboring force, while she retires from being a "working girl." In the pointed words of her landlady, Rosina (played by *chanteuse réaliste* Fréhel): "Madame est devenue honnête" ("Milady has become respectable").

Matteo's decision to join the colonial workforce initiates a shift in identity whose implications he understands only later, in Paris, after he has adopted additional marks of assimilation. Chenal signals this shift through clothing. In the port, Matteo trades in the turban and billowing shirt he wore as a "native" and "exotic" storyteller for the standard work shirt, slacks, and leather jacket. On the surface of his body, then, the difference of the nonwhite has been reduced, if not completely elided. A second shift occurs in Paris, when Matteo exchanges his "native" garb for a "French" suit. Later he borrows a more elegant outfit for his meeting with Safia, and even wears a tuxedo for a night out on the town with his gangster friends.

Yet the appearance Matteo gives through his costume of complete French assimilation is never anything more than a disguise to help him locate Safia. And she comes back from Tunis to readopt French culture only by putting on airs with her fancy gowns. In her daughter's interests, she is upwardly mobile. (At one point, she reveals to a delighted Chervin that she is auditing courses at the Sorbonne on the positivist philosophy of Auguste Comte.) But in what sense other than by birthplace is Safia French? In Sfax, she had been down and out within a marginal community in a colonial port. Is she really, as she claims, a white woman from Marseilles? Her name, unusual and exotic, throws her identity in doubt.

Assumptions concerning identity are the source of a cruel moment in Paris, when Matteo's gangster accomplices tell him they have found Safia and that she is waiting for him in the basement of their hangout. Matteo rushes downstairs, where he sees a shapely leg sticking out from around a corner. What he finds instead of Safia is a female mannequin dressed in veil and "native" garb. Knowing that Matteo was pining over a woman (the French word used is *poule*, a derogatory term for prostitute) whom he had come to Paris to find, the gang assumed that she was neither French nor white. More than an instance of good-natured hazing, the incident is one of a series of humiliations that Matteo undergoes in Paris that destabilizes him.

Chenal skillfully transcended the formulas of picturesque exoticism in his film's dual sources: Jean Vignaud's 1926 novel, *La Maison du Maltais*, and Henri Fescourt's silent feature of the same title. Unlike Benoît-Lévy and Epstein in *Itto*, Chenal displaced historical issues onto an isolated protagonist unsure of his ethnic and religious identity. Never taken with Jean Vignaud's nationalist novel, he nonetheless recognized that it could support an audacious exploration of psychology in which "style . . . could become more important than the story."[78] Whereas Fescourt had filmed mainly on location in North Africa, Chenal achieved theatrical effects in the studio by rubbing "canned" (sound-stage) exoticism up against an "authentic" tale of dual assimilations. In the end, he chose atmosphere and melodrama over the larger questions that Vignaud's novel had raised, questions pursued by Fescourt and even by an eighty-page *ciné-roman*, composed of passages from Vignaud's novel and twenty-one photos from Fescourt's film.[79] We can thus see—five years before the 1931 exposition—how a constellation of media was mass-marketing the colonial imaginary, with few scruples. By the time Chenal made his film in 1938, it was only with some irony that he tapped into the colonial genre. The film's stylistic self-consciousness points to the nearly schizophrenic behavior of the main characters as they struggle with assimilation. This can be seen notably during the latter two-thirds of the film, set in Paris, where class differences stifle both Safia and Matteo.[80]

The differences between the films in plot, characterization, and tone are striking. From the start, Fescourt's silent version casts Matteo as a hybrid ("carrefour de deux races") offspring of a Maltese father and a young Bedouin woman. Matteo must live under the pall of the fate of his father, whose renown as a sponge fisher ended with the scandal caused by an interracial marriage that made him a prisoner in his house: "Old Matteo had said goodbye to the sea, to the world, to everything . . . . He was still expiating a mistake, one that went back twenty-six years; this mistake, brought back from the South, had at the time a sixteen-year-old body and saffron skin. Unforgettable scandal in the Maltese clan! Despite the indignation of the parish, despite the mockery of his friends, the fisherman had brought the young Bedouin, Massouda ben Lakdhar, to his house . . . and Matteo had been born."[81]

Matteo's devotion to Islam in the silent film is a form of rebellion against a father who had turned in shame against him. Matteo's subsequent devotion to Safia overcomes neither the Islamic tradition that subjugates women to the will of a forceful master nor the advantages of the *Roumis*, whose wealth Matteo knows he can never match.

Matteo's desire to please Safia leads him to steal pearls that his father has hidden in his house. The pearls represent the capital the elder Matteo accumulated during his career as a sponge fisher, as well as the identity he had sacrificed to marriage. When Matteo's father catches him with the pearls, Matteo runs to Safia, only to discover that she has left Sfax without him. Forsaken by his father and abandoned by his lover, Matteo realizes that his theft has brought him only despair. He vows vengeance on Safia by swearing to seek her out and bring her back, even if it means crossing the universe on his knees.

As in Chenal's film, Fescourt has Matteo follow Safia to Paris. But unlike the remake, in which Matteo kills himself, the silent version portrays a Matteo driven by the righteous vengeance he feels as a Muslim son and husband. Once in Paris, Matteo uses the "inheritance" of the stolen pearls to establish himself among dealers in jewels and precious metals. He sells the pearls to fill his bags with the money he hopes will win back Safia. The pearls also attract the attention of Chervin, a major Parisian dealer who asks Matteo to become his partner and assume control of the company while he works out a personal matter. Ever on the lookout for Safia, Matteo intuits that, like someone fishing in the waters off the coast of Tunisia, he has netted his tuna and needs only to find the right place to throw his harpoon. When Chervin asks Matteo to buy a necklace for his mistress, Matteo is unable to hide his curiosity about its recipient, whom Chervin seems to keep in a golden cage: "Being the eunuch of the harem," Matteo thinks, "I should have the right to know the pasha's favorite."[82]

Matteo learns that Safia is indeed Chervin's mistress, and hardens his resolve to destroy her by ruining her lover. To this end, he invests heavily in risky ventures that threaten the consortium created by his partnership with Chervin. Safia confronts Matteo to learn the true motives of his actions, but he rejects her. After the investments fail and Chervin kills himself, Matteo carries a small trunk from his room in Paris to the house in Neuilly that Safia shared with Chervin. Inside the trunk are the clothes she was wearing the first time Matteo saw her in Sfax. Matteo enters the house, orders Safia to put on the clothes in the trunk, and carries her off for the return trip by boat to Tunisia. Once they are back in the native section of Sfax, Safia puts on a veil before throwing herself at Matteo's feet to beg him to let her be his slave in the Casbah. He turns away without answering:

> Safia felt that all was useless and that she had to yield to her destiny. She got to her feet. Like a soldier, Matteo raised the almond-green trunk on his shoulder and they walked toward the house of the Maltese. The lock was rusted; the heavy key turned with difficulty. Then Matteo leaned against the heavy door to make it yield. When it was open, he spoke to Safia for the first time since their arrival in Sfax. "Enter," he commanded. Safia went in without turning around, her shoulders hunched as if the doorway threatened to crush her. And Matteo closed the door behind her—forever.[83]

The two versions of *La Maison du Maltais* differ especially in their treatment of gender and religion. Fescourt casts Matteo as totally devoted to

Safia. Yet even after she laments her life, Matteo fails to see that his oath to take her away from Sfax obligates her to him and results in the opposite of the independence she wants. Matteo's blindness to this truth is borne out when he learns of her departure for Paris with the British *Roumi* whom she had met in the Casbah, misconstruing this as an infidelity he must avenge. Fescourt's Matteo reverts to the role of the master who aims to bring "his" woman to submission, very different from the self-destructive Matteo portrayed a decade later in Chenal's remake.

Three examples from the 1926 film reinforce significant elisions of cultural difference in Chenal's remake. Fescourt portrays Sfax as multifaceted and multiracial. In doorways illuminated by a single candle, prostitutes of all shapes and races attract potential customers into rooms adorned with portraits of His Highness the Imperial Bey and President Gaston Doumergue, cut out from illustrated magazines. The walls are also hung with African and Bedouin fetishes, such as lamb bones. At the stand run by Matteo's friend, the Sudanese Blanchette, where visiting foreigners are as likely to be offered a bargain on "hot" pearls as a shoeshine, the novelization includes colorful pidgin French: "Ti parles franci, ti parles angli un petit peu. Ti parles macaroni. Ti montres mouquères de la Kasbah aux étrangers. La livre sterling, c'est bon, ti sais, mon ami" ("Ya talk Frenchie, ya talk a little Engli. Ya talk Macaroni. Ya show Casbah women to foreigners. The sterling pound is good, ya know, my friend").[84]

Fescourt's Paris is likewise filled with displaced foreigners. In the Marais, on the Right Bank, Matteo finds himself passing storefronts whose shingles bear Jewish names such as Shirman, Aaron, Sonnemberg, and Bonner. Inside the Café Carrefour, where pearls are sold and traded, Matteo is struck by another list of names—Eschmann, Cadir, Brekof, Hamara—on a mounted panel, whose gold inscription says that they died for France. He is unable to restrain a smile as he wonders what France might have meant to them: "They had died in order to conserve their scales and magnifying glasses, these people come from every distant horizon. Matteo, crossroads of many races, could not understand anything else! Their fatherland was this café with its marble tables, this counter, and this pyramid of stacked oranges. Each one fashioned his fatherland to the measure of his interests."[85]

Matteo's obsession with Safia turns romance into an expression of cultural specificity. In the silent film, Matteo's fatherland has less the dimensions of a country than those of a woman's body: "Safia, the lost provinces! In order to locate and reconquer her, Matteo was ready to spill his blood on every battlefield."[86] Such military vocabulary suggests that Matteo's isolation is a necessary condition of his mission. Whereas Chenal will portray Matteo donning Sunday-best attire, looking very much the part of a proper Parisian bourgeois, the Western clothing worn by Fescourt's Matteo does little to destabilize his identity as a Muslim male working mainly among Europeans.

Fescourt portrays Matteo as self-possessed, decked out in his Westernized clothing. But one striking scene reveals his vulnerability: "He had bought a phonograph and records with the kinds of processed Arab melodies [*aux airs simili arabes*] that are piped into movie houses every time a camel or a veiled woman comes onscreen. The twang of the machine transported him to Sfax . . . next to a bucket of crabs and a glass of *boukha* on the narrow channel, on the shore of the glittering sea where he had sworn to bring back Safia. And he raised his arms to repeat his oath."[87] Ironically, Matteo's homesickness is triggered by a sound technology that silent film can reproduce in visual terms only. And while Fescourt elsewhere portrays Matteo as stable in his sense of self, this time his desire to simulate the sounds of Sfax in Paris suggests that, even if only for a moment, his resolve has weakened.

The two versions of *La Maison du Maltais* make explicit the extent to which all colonial films reasserted the subjugation of inferior others while continuing all the time to provide spectators in France with a safe exoticism. Slippage between these two desires points to the complex gaze of spectators in metropolitan France whose attitudes and assumptions mimed those of real-life colonizers. For Marc Augé, this ambivalence persists in residual forms of an ill-defined bad conscience among ethnographers, who "would prefer not to concern themselves with the conditions under which those they study are directly or indirectly colonized, dominated, or exploited."[88] Accordingly, Chenal's film contributes to an exercise of subjection articulated linguistically in terms of racial and sexual difference. During his stay in Paris, Matteo's interactions with members of the gang into which he is drawn are marked by the hostility of the gang's leader, who continually refers to Matteo as *crouillat*, a word derived from the Arabic *khouya* ("brother"). The term and its alternate, *crouille*, were brought to France by North Africans in the French military. As with *sidi* ("sir"), the term in French had a pejorative meaning (via ironic inversion) that was not there in the Arabic.

The remake by Chenal featured established stars Viviane Romance and Marcel Dalio, alongside Louis Jouvet and Pierre Renoir, in a romantic adventure Chenal termed "Tristan and Isolde in Sfax."[89] Like the 1927 silent version, Chenal exploited popular perceptions of the exotic overseas territories in North Africa, in contrast to scenes in Paris played out largely in the mode of domestic melodrama. But whereas Fescourt's Matteo goes to Paris to retrieve Safia and to avenge what he takes to be her infidelity, Chenal's Matteo embodies the dilemma of unstable identity that assimilation imposes on foreigners, even those who adopt nothing more than the superficial trappings of French language and dress. Notably, this dilemma occurs not merely in the case of Matteo and the Parisian criminals he gets mixed up with, but also in Safia's apparent transformation into a middle-class Parisian housewife and mother who audits courses at the Sorbonne.

Assimilation is usually thought to be a matter of ethnicity and religion. Chenal's remake adds the pressures of class and gender. Because Viviane Romance's Safia is presumably a French (that is, "white") woman, Chervin shows no hesitation in asking her to accompany him when he leaves Tunisia for Paris. In Chenal's film, a white female of indeterminate class can assimilate into the Parisian upper middle class by marriage or cohabitation with far greater ease and success than can a foreign male who attempts to make—or buy—his way by other means. In his effort to transcend mere melodrama, Chenal has condensed attitudes toward colonial culture and assimilation gnawing at French audiences of 1938.

By feminizing Dalio's character and placing it between cultures and classes, Chenal preceded Jean Renoir's extraordinary use of this actor the following year in *La Règle du jeu*. Both films destabilized character and type. For Renoir, this destabilization conveyed a debilitated France caught inside its borders. The France that Chenal portrayed was confused about those borders too—about what "France" and "French" should mean. A Brussels-born Jew who moved his career to Argentina during the war, Chenal would make his most emblematic film a dozen years later. In 1950, he daringly adapted Richard Wright's *Native Son* and cast the famous African-American novelist himself in the lead role. The crisis of identity so poignant in that novel, as well as its naked expression of racial fears and attractions, had already touched the director of *La Maison du Maltais*. Chenal's ambivalent fascination with "the other" stands out in *Native Son*, permitting us to position *La Maison du Maltais*, in retrospect, at the antipodes of Léon Poirier's confident attitude toward France and toward those beyond France's borders.

Expressions of the colonial imaginary in *L'Appel du silence*, *Itto*, and *La Maison du Maltais* overlap in multiple ways. Poirier and Epstein/Benoît-Lévy provide ample images of the desert, feeding an appetite for what might be termed the "authentic exotic," yet this imagery enlivens narratives that uphold the values of France's civilizing mission.[90] Chenal forgoes authenticity of location in favor of studio sets that exude a formulaic exoticism more in line with melodrama in the vein of Sternberg. But even here, Matteo's failed assimilation points to seemingly unbridgeable differences in ethnicity, gender, and class that colonial expansion had reinforced.

The commercial appeal of colonial films is grounded on the exploitation of a picturesque (and thus nonthreatening) exoticism added to conventions of popular genres like the melodrama, the romance, and the military film. While few spectators saw them as direct expressions of governmental policies, these films were doubtless central to a visual culture that made display of the colonies and their native peoples integral to the cause of colonial expansion. This is especially the case for didactic elements of *L'Appel du silence* and *Itto*. It extends as well to Chenal's *La Maison du Maltais*, where contrasts between colonial Sfax and bourgeois Paris magnify the obstacles that Matteo and Safia must overcome if they are to assimilate. But more than mere obstacles are involved, for the division between home and colony is only one of the many divisions this genre of film tries in vain to ignore.

One can track evolving attitudes toward identity and difference by looking at the types of divisions that haunt colonial films in successive years. Look again at the two versions of *La Maison du Maltais*. Fescourt's Matteo remains a stable character in the confusing cities of Sfax and Paris, both of which harbor diverse cultures. Indeed, Fescourt went to great lengths to depict rival cultures in Sfax, using local inhabitants as extras and masking the presence of his camera so that the contrasts of this city would surround his limpid hero. Chenal's Matteo and Safia, on the other hand, are characters acutely aware of their marginal status in both cities. But it is especially within the hierarchical environment of bourgeois Paris that their personalities unravel, as they don a succession of costumes, masks, and assumed roles to anchor their lives. Such a shift from the divided space of the earlier version to the divided characters of the later version can be felt in the difference between Dabit's 1929 novel, *L'Hôtel du Nord*, and Carné's 1938 adaptation. Dabit's characters invariably focus on the short term, on getting by from day to day and week to week. Together they comprise a variety of social types in this *quartier* of Paris, but individually they are not conflicted; each plays his or her role. Nine years later, however, Carné found it crucial to add characters not found in Dabit's novel, especially Louis Jouvet's fatalist Edmond, who enters the dark mood of poetic realism. An extreme self-consciousness gnaws at the inner wholeness of all these poetic realist figures and afflicts them with a debilitating passivity. Edmond's stalking of his own death is on a par with the suicide of François (Jean Gabin) in *Le Jour se lève*, cornered in his upper-story room, and of Matteo, dislocated in his Montmartre basement.

Could these representations of paralyzing consciousness point to a corresponding shift in collective identity visible in the "two Frances" (one rural, the other urban) that were on display at the 1937 International Exposition? France in the era of the Popular Front was, regardless of political positions, an internally riven nation.

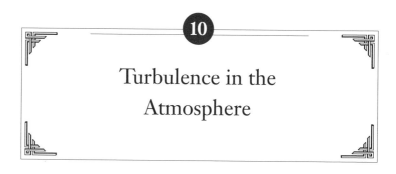

Turbulence in the
Atmosphere

The split identity that tortures Matteo in Chenal's *La Maison du Maltais*, and that characterizes the notion of the colonial imaginary in its various expressions, makes a mockery of convenient binary divisions. This holds as well for our book, which we organized perhaps all too readily in two parts. For the ambience of Paris in the 1930s affected all who lived there, including the writers and intellectuals discussed in Part I who went down into the streets hoping to make history. Everyone breathed the same atmosphere; everyone was subject to the changes brought on by the fronts, storms, and high-pressure zones that passed through. And so we return to the privileged caste with which we began—authors, artists, and thinkers—but this time viewing them more as historical subjects than as putative makers of the decade. They were subjected to the popular press and to the songs and voices broadcast over Parisian airwaves; they could not avoid the city's visual surround, including magazines, billboards, and movies. Nor could they escape the smoke of ideology that pervades every era and every place, though with varying chemical pollutants.

As for ideology, we have seen that in France the colonies constituted an interwar dreamscape—sometimes vague, sometimes vivid—floating at the horizon of the political. Colonial politics can be seen as state-sponsored involvement, as when the Popular Front government promised to overhaul colonial administration (a promise it did not keep). It can also be seen as a factor in the agendas of individuals and collectives, as when the Surrealists dated the coalescence of their movement to rallies protesting military action in Morocco in 1925. But the case of Léon Poirier clearly demonstrates that politics represents only one way of dealing with a far-flung geography that was frighteningly unfamiliar. Poirier openly pursued colonial politics—he headed the film section of the 1931 exposition—but only in order to broadcast the potent nonpolitical experience that contact with Africa offered. In his vocabulary, that experience was spiritual, even religious. He set out to demonstrate this priority of the spiritual in his major effort of the decade, *L'Appel du silence*. Yet while he deliberately transported the film's action and its audience beyond Parisian politics into the solitude of the desert, in order to finance and distribute the film Poirier had to preach from pulpits as though for a crusade. His efforts paid off. Surely Poirier must have felt deeply involved in, yet also beyond Parisian politics. Likewise, our concluding chapter sails in waters whose tides run alternately toward and beyond the public life of the Third Republic's final decade.

One did not have to be fanatical to place religion on a level with or above politics. The leftist Catholic journal *Esprit* maintained relative neutrality on many political issues during its first five years, including the issue of the Popular Front itself. This followed from Emmanuel Mounier's desire to foreground spiritual and cultural renewal, whose effects he believed would show up secondarily in politics. Once the Spanish Civil War drew toward its disastrous conclusion and Hitler's every move seemed unopposed, Mounier advocated more direct political action. Nevertheless, whether to retain the support of fervent Catholics like Jacques Maritain and Georges Rouault (both associated with the journal in its early days) or because he recognized it as a semi-autonomous realm of experience, Mounier gave religion a long tether so that it could roam largely free of day-to-day events in the temporal realm.

Our study has scarcely touched on the religious dimension of individuals or of French culture. But we have encountered another realm of experience whose value, some would argue, stands to the side of politics: the aesthetic. Here André Gide continues to serve as the central figure, since he was indisputably the bellwether of the literary establishment before, during, and beyond the interwar period. Originally a devotee of literature as sacred trust, he turned toward social concerns in the 1930s and became a crucial convert to those who forged the Popular Front. Although he defected after his disillusioning 1936 visit to the Soviet Union, his efforts to relate literature to the politics of culture continued until his death in 1951. Still, this relation was never direct, and Gide asserted the autonomy of the writer from partisan and ideological orthodoxies, even in the face of political crisis. In this he served as a model for so volatile a figure as André Breton, who, while affiliating briefly with the Parti Communiste Français, never submitted his imagination to political authority. Hence his famous break with Aragon and many others.

It seems heretical today to assert the transpolitical value of religion, of art, or of any social practice in a period known as the decade of the Popular Front. To assess the reach and the limits of the public sphere, however, we conclude our study with a look at aesthetic utopias. Was there room left for artists and writers to entertain private obsessions without shame, to hover within a milieu of ideas and aesthetic concerns distant from the unavoidably intense local conversations of those years? To return to the analogy of the newspaper, let us imagine a column or section oblivious to politics, fashion, and quotidian life, yet still able to hold the attention of the public. Even today, religiously affiliated dailies and journals routinely include theological ruminations and edifying anecdotes. And deluxe journals published by literary and art presses often feature poems, stories, photographs, and prints as "original contributions" whose rapport with current events is rarely obligatory. But what exactly are "original contributions," and to what do they contribute if not to public life and thus to politics? This is the question driving our concluding reflections.

Our plan is to glance summarily at the status of the aesthetic in the three moments that have conveniently parsed the decade in our study all along: the years immediately preceding the Stavisky riots; the ascendancy of the Popular Front from 1934 into 1937; and the decline of the Front in 1938, leading toward the fall of the Third Republic. In each moment, we sample figures who often had politics on their mind, yet who just as clearly inhabited a realm beyond the public—a realm of experience, of writing, and of art, personal enough to be linked to dream. Public issues may have absorbed every important personality of the time, but they did so incompletely. *Engagé* those figures may have been, but engaged with more than Paris and more than politics.

Before the Front: The Politics of Dream

"Documentary—Paris—1929." A series of six newspaper articles bearing this title appeared in *La Publicitat* (Barcelona), signed by an unusual reporter, Salvador Dalí. Banking on an increased popular appetite for the exotic, yet certain that the strangest things, images, and experiences lay close at hand, he wrote in his preface: "My document, I guarantee, will be in the most antiliterary style possible. My readers should not expect poetic images. . . . Today, industry offers us the most perfect and exact metaphors, ready-made and already objective."[1] Dalí's unexpected offering on the eve of the thirties signals a new role and a new direction for the Parisian avant-garde: from the book of poems to the newspaper column, from the colonial exotic to the metropolitan exotic, from art to industry, from the human to the object, from the spectacle to the document, and above all from the eye to the hand. This is the place to begin our conclusion.

Léon Poirier used the camera as a prosthetic super-eye, an organ taking in light and possessing the world spread out before it. In contrast, Luis Buñuel and his co-conspirator Dalí thought of cinema as a hand, favored organ of the Surrealists, which "feels" by touching and being touched. Buñuel's scandalous entry onto the Parisian scene came in 1928, in the very first sequence of *Un Chien andalou*, with his own hand wielding the straight-edge razor that slices into a bulbous eyeball: the colonial eye, let's call it. He deliberately turned the stomachs of the bourgeoisie, cutting threads in the delicate web of their precious subjectivity. Whereas Poirier's camera looks on with awe at a spectacle he desires, Buñuel's enters into the guts of what is desired—even into the guts of cinematic signification, which he manipulates through cutting, enlarging, splicing.

When Jacques Brunius—actor and Surrealist fellow traveler—chronicled 1925–1931 as the glory years of experimental cinema, he pummeled Poirier's pious approach in favor of the aggressive avant-garde represented by Buñuel. Brunius mocked the current art cinema for its reliance on the extreme long shot as the cornerstone of a style that respected natural vision and spatial contiguity.[2] The physical distance Poirier's camera maintains from the amazing and exotic material he went in search of, not to mention his uplifting plots, protects the viewer from the direct sensual power that might leap like static electricity from the foreign onto the screen and from the screen into the audience. To use categories that Walter Benjamin would develop in 1936 with explicit reference to Poirier's compatriot, Abel Gance, Poirier stands back from the body of reality; he spreads his hands over its awesome spectacle like a magician. Buñuel, the surgeon, penetrates the bodies of foreign organisms:

How does the camera operator compare with the painter? In answer to this, it will be helpful to consider the concept of the operator as it is familiar to us from surgery. The surgeon represents the polar opposite of the magician. The attitude of the magician, who heals a patient by a laying-on of hands, differs from that of the surgeon, who makes an intervention in the patient. The magician maintains the natural distance between himself and the person treated; more precisely, he reduces it slightly by laying on his hands, but increases it greatly by his authority. The surgeon does exactly the reverse; he greatly diminishes the distance from the patient by penetrating the patient's body, and increases it only slightly by the caution with which his hand moves among the organs.[3]

Having worked antagonistically with Gance and especially with Jean Epstein, theorist of a soft, impressionistic style, Buñuel determined to wield a razor rather than a paintbrush. He cuts into the body of his subject, moving "his hand . . . among the organs" in order to affect the nerves (our nerves) directly. Amid the fawning and flaccid films of the day, including those of the artistic avant-garde, his prototype "cinema of cruelty" constituted a ferocious anti-aesthetic.[4] So concerned was Buñuel not to play into the art market, that, on Breton's command, he tried to stop the scenario of *Un Chien andalou* from being published in *La Revue du Cinéma* (a trendy Gallimard publication), going so far as to break into the printing plant to smash the plates with a hammer.[5]

But the art market was unstoppable, and a taste had developed even for this kind of tastelessness. *La Revue du Cinéma*, to take the case at hand, boldly published essays on films that aimed to disturb as well as to intrigue. The most shocking essay appeared in 1929, just as Buñuel and Dalí's short was scandalizing Paris. Entitled "Le Film chirurgical" (The Surgical Film), it literalizes Benjamin's metaphor, describing a film that graphically depicts

> the most terrible operation a woman can undergo, a hysterectomy. . . . White coats. The stomach smeared with iodine. The suffocating odor of ether. . . . A slit marking the place where the scalpel will penetrate. And suddenly . . . the stomach is opened, there's a moment of apprehension, the skin is pulled back, the interior organs appear with their mysterious precision. . . . A large steel plate is inserted into the opening to keep the lower organs in place. . . . No need to "frame" all this. . . . The most passionate attention is saved for the interior of the black square in the white sheet, whose border little by little reddens with blood.[6]

Surgical films promise to shock adventuresome viewers by taking them beyond the threshold of culture into natural processes that are at once violent and mysterious. A spate of entomological films, including the quasi-Surrealist efforts of Jean Painlevé,[7] amazed viewers with macro-images of organic processes, some repellent. Sadism and a certain misogyny unquestionably operate in all such films, sometimes explicitly, as when Buñuel cuts into the woman's eye or when the author of "Le Film chirurgical" mentions as an aside: "Only at the end of the operation did it occur to me to look at the face of the young woman lying on her stomach, being given chloroform constantly by a nurse. A young working girl, not very pretty, her nose dilated, her mouth deformed by the hiccups continually bringing up white phlegm."[8] A comparably sadistic voyeurism often accompanies ethnographic cinema, as filmmakers and spectators strain their eyes to glimpse the naked bodies of women or to soak up the naked violence of beasts and unspeakable rituals.

All forms of early exotic cinema—whether scientific, Surrealist, or colonialist—deployed an erotics of vision, often exploiting, even manhandling the female body. But whereas the genre of colonial cinema (just like much of the Colonial Exposition) turned the "other" into a spectacle that the audience could gaze at and merge with, the Surrealists presented the "other" in what they referred to as "documents" to be handled. This difference hinges precisely on the status of *difference*, with Poirier aiming to dissolve it, the Surrealists to sharpen it.

In the tradition of Impressionism and Symbolism, filmmakers such as Jean Epstein, Gance, and Poirier wanted to transport themselves and their audiences into the world they filmed, where subject and object lose definition in moments of *photogénie*.[9] The latent rapport between things and psychological states can be brought out through the specific operations of light and camera lens. Objects flow into one another in the quasi-subjective atmosphere of the cinematic gaze. Poirier's extreme long shots and panoramas testify to the continuity of space and to the interrelation of all objects, just as the lure of spiritual identification invites the spectator inside the wholeness of spectacle. The goal is identity through identification—that is, Oneness.

Documents, in contrast, assert difference and multiplicity. As material evidence of human thought, they need not address the interpreter, but remain obtuse, separate even from the contexts in which they were produced. Whatever its form (thing, image, text), the document is at once complete in itself, like a found object, and a metonymy that signals some larger world from which it has been abruptly excised. The Cubists, in their synthetic phase, were the first to include documents (fragments of newspapers, especially) in their paintings. Cubism exchanges the satisfactions of optical unity for a more complex experience of the *thingness* of the world, expressing not so much the eternal as the transitory (hence the "news"). Confronting a document in the glass case of an ethnographic museum, or inspecting a photograph, or seated before a Surrealist film, the viewer is drawn not to its satisfying meaning but to its insistent material presence.

To maintain and strengthen the force field of difference, to produce a Cubist effect beyond the realm of aesthetics, the Surrealists took on something of the ethos of ethnography. They stripped away artistic conventions and niceties from the odd or obscure objects they displayed as documents in harsh light. Eugène Atget had insisted that his prints be termed "documents," greatly increasing their value to the Surrealists, who came upon them in the late 1920s. By then the term was in fashion, especially in conjunction with the scientific display of exotica. Even before *La Croisière noire* was released in 1926, Léon Moussinac had identified a specific category of *films documentaires*, although the designation would not show up in English until years later.[10] About half of the twenty titles he listed are records of journeys into little-explored lands, including *Nanook of the North* as well as *Chez les anthropophages* (1921), *Au coeur de l'Afrique sauvage* (1923), and *En Afrique équatoriale* (1923). A second subcategory that one can pull from his list comprises documentaries on natural processes, such as *La Germination des plantes* and *La Formation des cristaux*.[11] These two types of documentaries seem specifically concocted to satisfy Surrealist taste broadly conceived, including the predilection of those who in 1929 and 1930 would be reading or contributing to Georges Bataille's aptly named *Documents*, an avant-garde journal full of bizarre photos and articles.[12]

Surrealist taste is, in a strict sense, an oxymoron. And the document, as opposed to the art object, fascinates by its obtuse power in resisting assimilation to the viewer's norms and expectations. The document can be any human record whatever. Once it is cut off from its context, its significance outpaces its original meaning. The viewer, like the ethnographer, can suspend judgment concerning its function, and thereby short circuit the mind's attempt to place or rationalize it. In isolation or in unusual contexts, when it no longer serves some system to which it is putatively connected, the document releases its latent material power. This is the power of the scorpion's tail seen in huge close-up in the "found film" that serves as prologue to Buñuel and Dalí's *L'Age d'or* (1930); it is a tail broken into five prismatic articulations capped by a final articulation, a vessel holding deadly venom. To the Surrealists, the stark power of the found film is no different in kind from the scenes directed and photographed by Buñuel and Dalí. In a 1941 exchange with Claude Lévi-Strauss, Breton would exalt authenticity and spontaneity as the prime qualities sought in Surrealist art-making, qualities that documents share with geological evidence or animal leavings. Because human leavings (our term) can be beautiful, banal, or disgusting, Lévi-Strauss hoped to reserve a more transcendent place for artworks, but Breton found "the distinction arbitrary."[13]

Photography's stock rose dramatically at the end of the 1920s, in the ambience of Surrealism and under the general fascination with documents. Atget, previously ignored as a hobbyist, became overnight a saint of the mysterious "other Paris" that Breton and Aragon were evoking in their innovative novels. Atget chiefly inspired (in the full sense of the term) the vogue for bohemian photography, including the work of Kertész, of the young British genius Bill Brandt, and of Brassaï, whose "secret" and "nocturnal" Paris of the 1930s marks its apotheosis.[14] Atget's photos were chosen by Man Ray to startle readers of *La Revolution Surréaliste* (1929), just as were the photos taken specifically for the journal *Documents* the same year by Eli Lotar and Jacques-André Boiffard. The latter rendered, among other odd images, the illustration for Bataille's key essay "Le Gros Orteil" (The Big Toe).

Dalí, often denigrated as an opportunist riding the fame of Surrealism to fortune, actually grasped the importance of photography before Buñuel, before Breton, and even before Atget had been lionized. "Nothing has come to prove Surrealism more correct than photography," declared Dalí. "O Zeiss, lens so full of uncommon faculties of surprise!"[15] This most modern medium appealed to his "precisionism," and it flew in the face of the overblown subjectivity that painters and novelists of the day increasingly advertised. Photography could be exact while being both accidental and automatic. This formula accorded perfectly with one strain of Surrealism. The fact that one cuts photos directly from the surface of the visible world, and then can manipulate them on walls or in books to utterly change or obliterate their contexts, made them even more valuable in the aggressive game of provoking the unconscious. Dalí imitated their effect in his six-part newspaper series,[16] concluding the first section of "Documentary—Paris—1929" like this: "Let us consider documentary, without taking it to be antagonistic to Surrealism, as one more proof of the delicate and constant osmosis which develops between Surreality and reality: that reality of the objective world which is increasingly more submissive, more docile, and more blurred, all the more able to obey the violent reality of our mind."[17] While Dalí's stock as a serious, rather than merely theatrical, provocateur would soon tumble, from 1928 to 1931 he herded the wayward spirit of Surrealism. These were transition years, during which the "Second Manifesto" came into its own, when Surrealism was in danger of melting into a growing pool of rowdy artistic groups like Le Grand Jeu. Dalí upheld a mission (the supra-subjective state of reverie), a way of thinking (the paranoid-critical method), and most important a special way of conceiving art (the Surrealist object), which for a while distinguished the Surrealist endeavor.

It was the Surrealist object that most caught the attention of Walter Benjamin, who took full notice of the group in a 1929 essay that also references photography: "Surrealism: The Last Snapshot of the European Intelligentsia." Benjamin cared little for Surrealism's cult value, its idealist fancy, and its adolescent pranks. But the Surrealist object startled him; its material density, holding an undisclosed history, made it capable of giving off that "profane illumination" which meant so much to him.[18] In a telling phrase, he said: "[Breton] is closer to the things that Nadja is close to than to her."[19] Photography documents the world by isolating "things" and scenes that harbor haunting qualities (see Benjamin's "Little History of Photography," written at about this time). Benjamin implies that the character Nadja—and the desire she stirs up—is but a contrivance for encountering objects and photographed images in Paris whose mystery and possibility illumine existence by stimulating errant thought.

Surrealism, photography, and cinema: to Benjamin, their joint ascendancy after the First World War constituted the most hopeful sign of a changing of the guard. The Surrealists were intent on producing a revolution that would finish off, once and for all, bourgeois art and thought. It was the poetic life that concerned them, not poetry itself. (Hence Breton's later condemnation of Dalí's careerism.) Benjamin praised this readiness to revolutionize life even at the expense of art. In the anarchist tradition of the journal ironically baptized *Littérature* (dating from 1919), the Surrealists embraced the lottery of modern life by making use of "objective chance," "automatic writing," and other practices that denigrated artistic control and *objets d'art*. They were artists who despised artfulness, striving to tap into another level of consciousness; and so photography suited them, as did the dubious pleasures of cinema. The messages they read off the silver screen and which they took most seriously were those authored not by a creative intelligence but by the medium—

that is, by reality imprinting itself on celluloid through the lens of a camera pointed by even the most brutish producer, or pointed accidentally by no one in particular.

Benjamin and the Surrealists agreed that if cinema was an art at all, it belonged not to the producers of movies but to the spectators, who used it as they knew how, without lessons from critics or teachers, without heeding the directions of directors. The Surrealists ensured their consumer rights when they hopped mid-film from theater to theater, breaking the chain of images so that no single film or filmmaker could control their experience or could discipline the way their hyperactive perception arrived at chance meaning. Curiously, the ostentatious freedom of Surrealist *flânerie* meets up in the movie theater with the rote automatism of the assembly line, which Benjamin mentions as characterizing working-class life and entertainment. Both were apt preparations for a kind of spectatorship alert to mechanical, as opposed to human, signification.

The movies were prime material for the exercise of Dalí's paranoid-critical method, by which he intentionally introduced short-circuits in perception. This method, which helped to shape the ideas of the young Jacques Lacan,[20] can be seen at play in *Nadja*. There Breton activates the very clues that haunt him, and this haunting then produces the heightened perception of a Paris replete with still other clues. This form of objective chance, developed fully in *L'Amour fou*, distinguishes it from avant-garde styles like Cocteau's which claim to be oneiric by imitating the memory we have of dreams. But imitations can never produce the direct power of dreams, first because they exist to remind us of experiences rather than to produce them outright, and second because they occur entirely within the human realm, whereas dreams, according to the Surrealists, bypass human logic, including myth. They bring the inhuman into play, the dreamer serving as relay for objective processes and messages that can scarcely be controlled.

Surrealism meant to correct for the subjective sway of Impressionism by handing over control to things in the world. Hence the promotion of chance over myth. The latter subsumes the individual to a vast drama of the human spirit, whereas the former makes consciousness submit to material processes that pass through the subject without being resolved by consciousness. Breton would write: "Chance is the form of manifestation of exterior necessity, which traces its path in the human unconscious."[21] Photography, and above all cinema, can produce uncanny effects by tracing the path of desire within the dense material world (the cityscape), where it wanders seeking its object. In this heightened state of expectation and emptiness, desire is subject to "chance, the encounter of an external causality and an internal finality."[22] In contrast, Cocteau's concerns remain with myth and culture—that is, with what humans have already produced. His cinema stands as another link in the cultural chain, whereas Breton, Buñuel, and Dalí aimed explicitly to de-link subjectivity from culture, so it could be open to the inhuman processes of "modern materialism" at work mysteriously in the city.[23]

This difference between these avant-gardes is apparent in something as technical as range of focus. In *L'Age d'or* Buñuel and Dalí aim to release the potential within the world via the sharpest possible attention to things ("precisionism" is Dalí's term), while Cocteau's gauzy pictures encourage the viewer's vision to drift from the hard world of objects and fade into a softer one ruled by ancient mythology. Cocteau's dreamer is lured into a predestined world—like that of Orpheus or Oedipus—which, even when tragic, is transcendent. Cocteau's life as well as his work showed how moderns can rise above modernity when buoyed by culture. Yet his was precisely the notion of culture from which the Surrealists sought release. They made use (and fun) of classical mythology to clear the ground for the astoundingly new, for the marvelous. Theirs would be a mythology of the future. Paris was its capital.

One need only compare *L'Age d'or* to the film Cocteau made less than a year later (both financed by the count de Noailles). Cocteau's very title, *Le Sang d'un poète* (The Blood of a Poet), immediately calls up the topos of the martyred artist, presented in slow-motion shots languidly linked by long, meaningful dissolves. Its first episode opens with the title "The Wounded Hand" and culminates in an artist gazing at his palm, which speaks to him.[24] Hardly the violent, impulsive hand of instinct or a putrefying hand with ants crawling from it (a dream-image of Dalí's), Cocteau's hand is a benevolent artistic muse whispering to him familiarly. His film relays the muse's heroic message to an applauding audience. That audience honored this ciné-poet for taking them to the thrilling brink of modernism while anchoring them safely in the immutable lessons of Greek mythology.

Cocteau's next film, *L'Eternel Retour* (1943), a reworking of the Tristan myth, would be the most popular French film of the entire Occupation period. Cocteau, the presumed avant-gardist, here played into the most common and insistent theme the movies have offered, that of adultery so passionate it immolates the lovers acquiescing to it. Denis de Rougemont, as we have

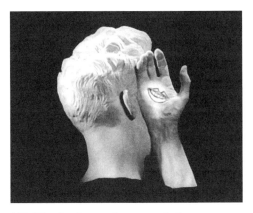

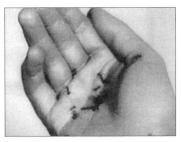

103. Hand as malignant menace in *Un Chien andalou*, by Luis Buñuel and Salvador Dalí (1929).

102. Hand as benevolent muse in Jean Cocteau's *Le Sang d'un poète* (1930).

104. Pickled hands: the sublime surrealism of Jean Vigo in *L'Atalante* (1934).

seen, traced this complex from the troubadours to its degraded form in political rallies and in popular films (*Mayerling* and *La Maison du Maltais*, to take two of our strongest examples). Cocteau, the avant-garde poet, was here in phase with the masses and the market.

This fact must have both amused and annoyed the Surrealists (though in 1943 Dalí had already sold himself to the highest bidder and was ready to sign on with both Walt Disney and Alfred Hitchcock). For one thing, Cocteau exploited a vein that they had gotten to first. Benjamin had claimed in his prescient article on Surrealism that "Provençal love poetry comes surprisingly close to the Surrealist conception of love." Dalí and Buñuel had likewise put Wagner's *Tristan und Isolde* "Liebestod" dead center in *L'Age d'or*, after using the music during projections of *Un Chien andalou*. De Rougemont seems vindicated, for whether deployed with Surrealist irony or in a mythic belief in its innate potency, the attraction of the love suicide pervades modern Western culture, be it popular, avant-garde, or corrosively Surrealist.

With his deep spiritual and social commitments, de Rougemont must have found both Cocteau's aestheticism and Dalí's gratuitous gestures impotent and repellent. These were associated in his mind with (respectively) homosexuality and masturbation, which, in his 1938 lecture to the Collège de Sociologie, he claimed were vices incubating in modernity, especially within the military. De Rougemont, ever vigilant about the pleasure principle that Dalí worshipped, had titled his foundational 1936 text *Penser avec les mains* (Thinking with Your Hands).[25] From his Protestant perspective, hands are to the mind what good works are to faith: proof and consequence. Hands should reach out from the self first toward a beloved and then toward the social body; they should join other hands, then build community and institutions. To de Rougemont, Surrealism could appear only self-centered and inconsequential.

Dalí made an easy target, for he famously built an entire aesthetic around onanism, turning the self into a site of exploration and discovery. The masturbator elects to give his hand independence, so that it can surprise him beyond his control. Yet he does control it, to the point that he can feel guilty about his pleasure, can consider it sinful, can fantasize his (red) hand severed by his father when caught in the act.[26] His 1929 essay "L'Alliberament dels dits" (The Liberation of the Fingers) directly joins the automatism of the digits to the Surrealist project of an errant rationality.[27] Literary production must be anti-artistic, the essay says in its opening paragraph; it must be "photographic" in its objective annotation of the world of facts, so as to register occult meanings that human rationality has previously missed or repressed. And so Dalí lets his mind follow the index of the pointing finger, even as his mind produces the image of that finger's liberation. "Probably due to a hypnagogic image of pre-sleep in which I confessed to having seen a detached and floating finger, the image of an isolated finger was frequently in the texts to which I devoted my reading. . . . Often my own thumb would suddenly surprise me as a rare, disturbing thing."[28]

To be surprised by one's own body as an independent entity: this is the shock and the goal of Surrealist art—of *Gadget and Hand* (1927) and *The Great Masturbator* (1929), for instance. This latter painting derives from a strange autobiographical poem, easily related to Dalí's passion for cinema.[29] The obtuseness of the painting, which, like his thumb or big toe or nose, both does and does not belong to him, disturbs Dalí (he never sold this particular painting) and gives him an odd sensation. At the limit, Dalí loses definition of himself, is engorged by his own fantasy. (An important study on his work from this period bears a telling title: "Swallowing Dalí").[30] He called his fantasies "reveries," describing one graphically. First comes a calculated setup: retiring to his sofa to rest after eating, Dalí distractedly hollows out a crust of bread and lies down in a state of excitation. Deliberately he conjures up Arnold Böcklin's painting *The Isle of the Dead*, but finds that this image slips into Vermeer's *The Letter*, whose meaning he is sure emanates from the scarlet curtain on the left-hand side of the canvas. He writes: "Then, I make my (very) little penis automatically jerk up, leaving on the sofa the small crust of bread that I had been picking at. With one hand I play with the hair underneath my testicles, with the other, I accumulate a bit of the soft part of the bread that has been removed from the crust. Despite several completely sterile efforts to return to my thought, an absolutely involuntary reverie begins."[31] The cycle of reverie continues for pages, as images and thoughts produce "automatic" reflexes of hand, then penis; new images and thoughts in turn are stimulated. Mind and body, inside and outside, stimulation and response commingle in those ineffable experiences that he and other Surrealists cultivated.[32] *Nadja* develops the same structure as Dalí's shameless reverie; in both texts, mystery (signaled by an isolated hand)[33] is not just sought out, but is deliberately concocted and then experienced as real.

Surrealism might be called the autoeroticism of the spirit. This has been both its boast and its vulnerability. Louis Aragon, for instance, whose break with Surrealism can be dated to 1930, found it easiest to attack Dalí's manner of self-inflation.[34] He denigrated the obsession with isolated objects and body parts and hence with psychoanalysis. Aragon proposed Marxism as a healthy, consequential substitute for psychoanalysis, whose chief concern had always been with the spiritual and sexual liberation of the bourgeois male. Dalí's reveries, based exclusively on the pleasure principle, were impotent when it came to what Aragon thought of as a genuine Surrealist revolution, one that would transcend the anxieties of the alienated individual in an arc culminating in street politics. The impulses of the severed hand or the detached finger, grasping this or that charged object, would never overturn history. Most often, the charged object grasped or manipulated by the hand was nothing other than a simulacrum of the charged self, as in the famous print by M. C. Escher in which a hand doubles back to create itself or, more pertinent here, Valentine Hugo's 1931 painting of two gloved hands (one white, one black) on a green roulette cloth; the supple fingers of one hand are inserted into the wrist of the other, lifting it slightly. Both hands are covered with a fine white netting.[35]

Aragon wanted Surrealism to change historical reality, while Dalí wanted it to engender simulacra that would underscore the triviality of historical reality. And so Aragon could imply that Dalí's flaccid reveries, no matter how grotesque and uncensored, pandered to the middle class. Through his very success in selling dreams, Dalí would become linked, in some minds, to the contemptible Cocteau, that well-paid performer hired to astonish with clever tricks an audience of decadent aristocrats and fey intellectuals.[36]

Ostensibly Dalí's fall from Surrealist favor occurred because of his outrageous defense of Hitler and of racism. Breton called him on the carpet for official sanction on February 5, 1934, the day before the Stavisky riots.[37] Dalí would continue to denounce all politics, including Communism ("sentimental humanism"), as bureaucratic repression of desire. His flagrant intransigence and corrosive wit appealed to Breton, even in his role as head of this Trotskyite tribunal. Nor did it surprise Breton that the painter ridiculed leftist alliances like the AEAR. But what Breton could not condone was Dalí's pandering and self-promotion. When, despite Breton's proscription, he submitted *The Enigma of William Tell* to be hung in the Grand Palais as part of the fiftieth anniversary of the Salon des Indépendants, Breton denounced him viciously.[38]

And so it surprised no one that Dalí, always courting a larger public, should begin to court Hollywood. On a visit there in late 1936, he claimed he had met "the three American Surrealists" (the Marx Brothers, Cecil B. De Mille, and Walt Disney).[39] Hollywood was, after all, a dream factory, and the studios had engaged Buñuel in 1930. Domesticated versions of psychoanalysis were becoming common in screenplays (Alfred Hitchcock's *Spellbound*, with a set by Dalí, would mark the apotheosis of this trend in 1945). Moreover, Dalí's disturbing images—the severed hand a case in point—were drawn from a European repertoire that Hollywood was siphoning straight into its horror genre. There had already been Robert Wiene's *Orlacs Hände* (The Hands of Orlac; 1924), with Conrad Veidt.[40] This tale was remade in 1935 when Karl Freund directed Peter Lorre in what was the first Hollywood vehicle for both. Titled *Mad Love* (Breton was just then writing his book of that name), it allowed Lorre to reprise his role in *M* as a compulsive psychopath. In *Mad Love* his mania is displaced into the pair of hands he maliciously amputates from the corpse of a strangler and attaches to a pianist, whose career had been wrecked by an injury. The impulses of the hands win out over the delicate sensibility of the musician; the artist is convulsed by the violence he unintentionally yet automatically causes.

Whether or not Breton and his gang saw *Mad Love* in 1935, they did see another Hollywood production of that year, *Peter Ibbetson*, for Breton cites it in a footnote in *L'Amour fou*. There he declares it an "enterprise of exaltation of total love," the only film worthy of *L'Age d'or*, that "triumph of Surrealist thought."[41] *Peter Ibbetson*, directed by Henry Hathaway from George du Maurier's popular romance, likewise features potent hands, but in this case they are a synecdoche for the soul. When the title character, played by Gary Cooper, lies beaten (presumably to death) in prison, where he has been put away for the accidental murder of the husband of his one true love, Mary, she steals into his cell each night. Mary's glowing hands, gloved and seemingly detached, draw him through the bars so they can wander till daylight in the rapturous haunts of the childhood estate where they had become soulmates.[42]

Peter Ibbetson may be naive melodrama, but Breton found it easy to promote a film that so directly exhibited the resurrection of a victim who had nothing to lose but his chains, and who breaks those chains via dream and erotic encounter, each substantiating the other. The Surrealists relished such popular images of liberation. Dalí especially lauded their commercial, industrial character, as precision products. Aside from selected Hollywood vehicles, the entire group also stood up passionately for the few genuinely aggressive Surrealist efforts (effectively those of Dalí and Buñuel). Why, given these preferences, did Breton & Co. not immediately latch onto Jean Vigo, whose films shared their values of rebellion and oblivious love? Vigo's only full-length feature, *L'Atalante*, improvises wildly on the commercially confected script that he was handed by his producer. Especially given the censorship to which his earlier *Zéro de conduite* had been subjected, Vigo, known to many in the Surrealist orbit, should have become a *cause célèbre* long before his post-war apotheosis as a *ciné-poète maudit*.

L'Atalante is "one of the most penetrating dreams of love in all cinema," wrote Ado Kyrou in his 1963 compendium of Surrealist tendencies in cinema. "Aboard a barge *l'amour fou* is born—a love whose grandeur is sung by the poetry of the curious and terrifying objects belonging to Michel Simon, the old sailor."[43] Vigo injected mystery into those objects, filming in a feverish state that worked its way onto the set and killed him at age twenty-nine. He recruited members of the Prévert band and other Surrealist fellow travelers to locate bizarre props and to serve as extras in a production fabled for its freshness and spontaneity. As the most thorough study of Surrealism and cinema puts it: Breton should have seen in *L'Atalante* the far more potent expression of the elements he adored in *Peter Ibbetson*.[44] He should have preferred its politics too. Rather than upper-crust youngsters mystically bound together by childhood experiences, Vigo's couple represent the peasant class and the working class. Their prison is the barge that carries them through France, seeming to confine them within the conventions and drudgery of ordinary life—that is, until the Surrealist object and gesture intervene.

How to conjure the marvelous out of such a repressive domestic situation is both a structural problem to be solved in the script and a spiritual problem facing most human beings. Stanley Cavell could type *L'Atalante* a "comedy of remarriage," for it involves a temporary separation, then a change of vision, before the couple can reunite in an embrace that is at once mature and marvelous. Their salvation comes at the hands (literally and figuratively) of Père Jules, the craggy ship's mate—crude, superstitious, and instinctive—whom Michel Simon turns into a Surrealist being of the first order.

Vigo's career began under the umbrella of Buñuel, whom he praised without qualification in his only public statement on cinema.[45] Yet *L'Atalante* marks an aesthetic and moral advance over *Un Chien andalou* and *L'Age d'or*. Vigo shared with Buñuel (and, as it happens, with Michel Simon) an impulse to pornography, to the direct sensory manipulation and gratification of his spectators. In a remarkably frank sequence, he turns the simultaneous masturbation of the separated couple, Jean and Juliette, into a most glorious expression of oblivious conjugal lovemaking. The pornography comes not just from the acting and editing, but also from his use of a grid over the lights to produce polka-dot blotches on the bodies. This visual arousal, supported by Maurice Jaubert's surging music, makes the spectator feel not just the feline writhing of each character but the greater excitement of the director, who both watches and creates (through lighting and montage) what is projected before us on the screen. In a later scene, superimposition rather than montage unites the couple in the amniotic fluid of the river into which Jean has dived so as to have a vision of Juliette. This is his baptism, after which he is prepared for the miracle of remarriage, something that only the preternatural powers of Père Jules can bring about.

Id-figure and Surrealist godfather, Père Jules blesses the couple's *amour fou* by sharpening Juliette's appetite for the mysterious world we all inhabit.[46] When Juliette stumbles into his cluttered cabin, her eyes widen at his collection of marvels. The litany of Surrealist objects includes an old phonograph, lavish oriental fans, photographs taken around the world, music boxes, huge seashells, "and even some old wrought-iron wreaths Vigo and his friends had stolen from the Montparnasse cemetery."[47] There are also enormous fish teeth and a dilapidated—but very phallic—puppet. "Handmade," Père Jules insists of one of his treasures, a "Navaja" dagger, as he tests its blade on his palm. When the blood oozes from the slit, Juliette recoils, her tongue jutting out spontaneously. At once attracted and repelled, she turns to open a cupboard looking for first aid. Instead, she discovers with horror the fetish object Vigo has held in reserve all along: in close-up, we see a pair of hands pickled in a jar of brine (a gift to Vigo from Jean Painlevé, as it happens).

A Surrealist seemingly from birth, Vigo, like Père Jules, let fly his imagination in an all-out assault on the restrictions of conventional life, and in this case on a conventional script. He discovered, as surely as did Breton, that the exotic dwells not only in far-off lands but wherever we are, on the barge we call home. And the exotic, when embraced, can forge rather than undo social cohesion. Vigo died early, in 1934, envisioning just such cohesion.

A few months before he passed away, he had been one of ninety people who signed the tract composed by Breton in the aftermath of the Stavisky riots, a document that foresaw a Popular Front in the making. With even the government up for grabs, Paris was now openly a field of action, wilder in some respects than the colonies. Quick to sign Breton's tract alongside Vigo were Michel Leiris and André Malraux, who, having made their names in Africa and the Far East, respectively, now realized that Paris was as risky and adventurous as any place on earth. The politics of dream had dissolved into a dream of politics.

The Front: The Dream of Politics

Michel Leiris (1901–1989) was as explicit about his shameful fantasies as was Salvador Dalí, if less grandiose. Surprisingly, their lives coincide on many counts. Born just before Dalí, Leiris outlived him by a few months. Both men came from privileged Catholic and politically conservative families. Both made their living in the art world; both felt the magnetic pull of André Breton; and both flagrantly exposed the demeaning anxieties and desires to which they were prey. Why is it, then, that Dalí is often reviled as a charlatan and exhibitionist, while Leiris is credited as a dauntless excavator of the soul's secrets?

One answer, recognized at the time by Breton among others, is politics. Dalí's politics were egomaniacal; other people seemed only to stand stupidly in his way, or else they existed to contribute to his desires and anxieties. Leiris, more in line with Breton, deemed self-analysis an instrument through which to engage an immeasurable outer world vibrating with human desire. Only by tracking the vicissitudes of his own desires could he take the larger social world into account and be "of service to the revolution." Dalí certainly looked intently into geology, botany, mythology, and entomology, but he did so as a solipsist, to stimulate his private reveries. In contrast, Leiris mobilized his personal obsessions as a tactic to wring from the world its human or inhuman possibilities, finding them most often in the unconscious and the exotic. If this be narcissism, it is a most instrumental version.

Margaret Cohen ties Leiris' *L'Age d'homme* (translated as *Manhood*; begun in 1934 and first published in 1939) to Breton's *Nadja*, as the two books which best constitute Surrealist historiography, "a revision of the autobiographical project following Freud," according to Walter Benjamin.[48] Whereas standard history rides on the momentum of sequence and commonplace, autobiography can drift at any moment into dream, desire, memory, or sheer happenstance. Such drifting disconnects the present from what is commonly believed to constitute it; this in turn permits hidden causes, parallels, and rapports to relate disparate moments. If private life in the insipid Third

Republic can be so readily interrupted through this feat of autobiographical unlinking, why can't the entire social system also be publicly overthrown? Breton's politics ride exactly along this trajectory when he "stresses the need for individual tactical disruptions of reigning social orders in what he calls 'unchaining.' [. . .] Socially transformative activity becomes . . . the province of subjects who no longer define themselves according to their work."[49] This parallel between psychoanalysis and social analysis involves the preservation and the liberation that are part of every act of "unchaining." As one of Benjamin's celebrated historical theses has it: "Nothing that has ever happened should be regarded as lost to history."[50]

Benjamin was drawn to *Nadja* as a kind of socially instructive autobiography—that is, as both *flânerie* and as an experiment in what Breton would later call "lyric behavior."[51] Instead of the flashback, Breton stages moments that permit the "flash-now," where the past enters the present through an encounter with a place or an object, or—best of all—through photographs of places and objects harboring ghosts of earlier encounters and of their origin. In danger of floating toward subjective self-portraiture like any autobiography, *Nadja* is anchored by forty-four photographs that exhibit a public Paris of identifiable sites and streets. At the same time, these photographic documents release emotions and meanings into the "now" of the present. The city grows progressively dense with possibilities—some lustrous, others ominous—when experienced in the aura of encounters with Nadja and, some years later, with the mysterious woman of *L'Amour fou*. Both women serve as oracle and muse through whom Breton experiences a world where past, present, and future frequently fuse.[52]

This climate of urban expectation allows other photographs to emerge. Many of Eugène Atget's innumerable prints, for instance, after lying inert and unseen, returned to haunt the Surrealists as documents not only of the moment they were taken, but also of the deeper past that they disclose. Photography's relation to psychoanalysis and thus to autobiography could hardly be clearer. The extended afterlife of an Atget print, as representation and document of a certain past, may be said to apply as well to various images (*clichés*) that Leiris evokes in *L'Age d'homme*. Some of what Leiris brings to consciousness through writing have origins dating as far back as his youth in the Belle Epoque (Atget's period). Through psychoanalysis in the 1930s—and in what Benjamin might term a "state of emergency"[53]—Leiris scours the past, animating the present with incidents deliciously or shamefully recalled.

He spotlights personal moments in the decade ("The evening of December 17, 1934, when I saw *Salome* at the Opera") when the living presence of the past floods his "now" through precise images that release their ghosts. Leiris identifies his ghosts as Judith, Lucretia, and Holophernes, each figure powerful enough to redirect or derail his future.

L'Age d'homme, whose form Leiris once described as a negation of the novel, employs precise dates and events without aspiring to the linear format of the diary. One of the events he invokes occurs "toward the beginning of July 1925, . . . at the end of a literary banquet which ended in a fight. I was roughed up by the police." The banquet, history books tell us, was held in honor of a visit to Paris by the poet Saint-Pol-Roux (Paul Roux). It coincided with a collective statement in *L'Humanité* (July 2, 1925) condemning the war waged by the French army in the Rif Mountains of Morocco. From this defining moment of Parisian Surrealism, Leiris derived only personal consequences: he notes how the bruises he received during the fight helped him in his pursuit of a girl.

A similar ratio of past to present and of private to public is found in *L'Amour fou*, when Breton records meeting his woman of destiny on May 29, 1934, and wandering with her all night through a Paris that less than five months before had been a battleground of rioters. Indeed, this meeting occurred about a month before Trotsky was expelled from France. Thus, the dates of *L'Amour fou* are tied to erotic assignation rather than to political drama; yet four years later Breton headed for Mexico, where he and Trotsky hammered out their shared belief in the autonomy of the imagination and of art.[54]

What Breton calls "lyric behavior" kept Benjamin near the Surrealists into the early years of the 1930s. They all believed in the flash-now of encounters and episodes, and they were prepared to career through life in zigzags, touching the present with the past and bringing private obsession into political expression. But the revolutionary potential that Benjamin attributes to the "dialectical image" was increasingly at odds with the figure of the zigzag, which Breton invokes in the "Second Manifesto" (1930) in order to subordinate political activity to language:

> It is normal for Surrealism to appear in the midst of, and perhaps *at the cost of*, an uninterrupted series of zigzags and defections. . . . The problem of social action, I would like to repeat and to stress the point, is

only one of the forms of a more general problem which Surrealism set out to deal with, and that is *the problem of human expression in all its forms*. It should therefore come as no surprise to anyone to see Surrealism almost exclusively concerned with the question of language at first, nor should it surprise anyone to see it return to language, after some foray into another area, as though for the pleasure of traveling to conquered territory.[55]

Thus, language remains the material core of the revolutionary ambitions to which Breton aspires, even and especially when he wants Surrealism to be taken seriously as a political movement. A year earlier, Benjamin had noted with admiration Breton's conviction that language takes precedence over all.[56]

Following Hitler's 1933 accession to power, Benjamin's antennae turned away from Breton toward the cohort of one-time Surrealists who were beginning to lay the foundation of the Collège de Sociologie by exploring the power of collective irrationality—even of fascism, a phenomenon that they both feared and admired. Leiris was just such a dissident Surrealist. This timid soul had a horror of street demonstrations. He had also experienced the concentration of the irrational in bullfights and in trance dances in Mali, and so was ready to leave the analyst's couch and join this pointed effort to change history by exploring "extreme value" in social formations and group activity, "whose etiology he traced to the unifying movements of attraction and repulsion characterized as sacred."[57] Benjamin watched closely as the *zig* of Surrealism evolved into the *zag* of the Collège.

Call it a round-trip. Leiris' efforts in the thirties to put his psychological compulsions to work in the world can be plotted as a line from Paris to Africa and back. The monumental result of these efforts was *L'Afrique fantôme*, Leiris' 1934 account of the 1931–1933 Dakar-Djibouti Mission for which Marcel Griaule recruited him as secretary-archivist. Leiris produced another document covering the same period—a diary he refers to as *le cahier bleu* (the blue notebook)—in which he recorded dream fragments, notations on his professional activities as ethnographer, a log of books read, and entries of a more personal nature about his marriage, his sexual fantasies, and concerns about his virility. This diary, which he kept virtually all his adult life, was not intimate in the sense of disclosing emotional states.[58] His detached tone never ventures into the charged politico-historical moment that utterly consumed the writings by others in Leiris' literary generation, such as Nizan, Mounier, and Lefebvre. A diary entry for October 29, 1933, lists the origins of a deep depression, including anguish caused by fear of war and of his mother's death, as well as ideas of escape (running away to somewhere peaceful, no longer calling himself a revolutionary, abdicating all pretense to virility).[59] The three entries for January 1934 (with none afterward until March 18) record Leiris' obsession with a woman whom he decides to call Léna in a novel he plans to write. The diary makes no mention whatsoever of Stavisky, the February 6 demonstrations, or their aftermath. And this despite the fact that Leiris signed the February 11, 1934, "Call to Struggle" manifesto printed in the Socialist daily *Le Populaire*.

Leiris' self-analysis extends to his professional writing. For example, the short text "L'Oeil de l'ethnographe" ("The Ethnographer's Eye"; 1930) signals his expectations about the upcoming expedition across Africa: the rigors of the journey may dissipate errors and prejudices resulting from his European (white) "mentality."[60] Much like the desire to lose oneself—specifically, the self as a rational construct—that Roland Barthes was to record forty years later on the basis of three trips to Japan, Leiris wanted those who leave Paris for Dakar to strip themselves of their "white ways" and thus of their identities as European intellectuals.[61] Yet even here Leiris frames the hoped-for encounter with otherness in more personal terms, when he characterizes the trip as the realization of childhood dreams and a momentary escape from writers and artists all too similar to himself.

Leiris' personal trajectory measures temperature shifts in the intellectual atmosphere of the day. For the Paris Leiris had left in May 1931 was regrouping in the wake of splits and defections listed by Breton in the "Second Surrealist Manifesto" (Leiris himself broke with Breton in 1929). Over the decade to follow, he would be one among a nucleus of former Surrealists involved in collective ventures that produced *Documents*, *Minotaure*, *Cahiers de Contre-Attaque*, *Inquisitions*, and *Acéphale*. Even if Leiris was not always directly involved, he moved among such groups and ventures. All of these journals were short-lived, since they emerged from the force of dangerous circumstances and under conditions that unavoidably brought clashes of strong personalities. A new fluidity of intellectual and political positions among former Surrealists upended the more disciplined model of revolutionary politics that had dominated extremists from 1925 (the protest against the French intervention in Morocco) through 1935 (the Congress for the Defense of Culture). Breton was personally targeted for his role as nominal leader of the Surrealists, a group that seldom disguised its culturally imperial designs. At the same time, the new groups widened the front of dissidence against a general (and generally intolerable) political condition, extending far beyond squabbles with Surrealism. The fact that Breton himself brazenly opposed the bourgeois conventions of family and nation only multiplied the stakes of anti-authoritarian stances everywhere, even among those who left or who were rejected by the group.

Parallel to the Surrealists and bands of their dissident offshoots, there were also groups formed by young Catholic intellectuals to promote political, economic, and spiritual renewal. These brazen nonconformists (whom we encountered in Chapter 3) looked desperately for alternative means to militate against what they considered the established disorder institutionalized in the church and the government.[62] Thus, dissidence directed toward institutions of state and religious authority was rife, crossing the spectrum from right to left, but mainly involving young intellectuals who had given up on the Sorbonne as just another institution deserving opprobrium.

A high-profile attempt to mobilize dissent occurred in the fall of 1935, when Bataille and Breton set aside their differences long enough to participate in Contre-Attaque, an antifascist group that cast itself as Union de Lutte des Intellectuels Révolutionnaires (Union of Struggle of Revolutionary Intellectuals). After the June 1935 Congress for the Defense of Culture, where Breton and his views were dismissed by hard-line Communists and their sympathizers, he had yet to find an adequate means of responding to the bankruptcy and impotence of the partisan left.[63] The new venture styled itself as anti-authoritarian; it publicly opposed both fascism and, more broadly, the political institutions of capitalist authority.[64] At the more personal level, it marked a final collaboration and definitive parting of ways. Contre-Attaque offered Breton a last-ditch chance to contend with a critical impasse, first for himself following the rebuff at the 1935 Congress and, second, for the fading vision of direct political activity formulated in the name of the Surrealist group. It offered Bataille a focus for his preoccupation with the energy of mass movements unleashed by fascist regimes in Italy and Germany. In particular, Bataille was struck less by the phenomenon of nationalist ideology sweeping Europe than by the nature of mass force and frenzy as an end in itself.

Contre-Attaque's ambitions went beyond organized politics at the very moment the Popular Front was building momentum, and it remains unclear to what extent it added to or complemented the leftist coalition. This ambiguity was not lost on Dalí, who voiced his doubts in a letter to Breton in which he described the venture as too utopian ("a political party of NUANCES").[65] By March 1936, just two months before the elections, this self-styled minority of men was blasting away at right and left: "WE BELONG TO THE HUMAN COMMUNITY, BETRAYED TODAY BY SARRAUT JUST AS IT WAS BY HITLER, AND BY THOREZ JUST AS IT WAS BY DE LA ROQUE."[66] A month earlier, the group had issued a more pointed call to action in a tract exhorting workers to organize against the watchdogs of capitalism. But that tract, penned by Bataille, fell flat when the Communist and Socialist dailies failed to reprint it. A movement grounded in anti-fascism yet somehow also above politics, Contre-Attaque was doomed when it failed to enlist support from the organized parties it sought to transcend. Politically rebuffed, members of the group recognized, even from the beginning, that its significance lay elsewhere, at a critical remove from direct intervention. Contre-Attaque would operate at a level of inquiry and analysis that would lead Bataille to the form the secret society Acéphale and the Collège de Sociologie.

What moves people to collective activity? Where does unity come from? The primordial lure of solidarity that led to Contre-Attaque can best be felt in a text in which Bataille presents contrasting responses to the violent demonstrations on the Cours de Vincennes on February 12, 1934. It reflects a complete lack of confidence among militant revolutionaries on the one side, and the contagious emotion of the masses on the other: "This is how revolutionary activity can be expressed *in the street* with force and at the same time with an incomparable certainty, when from the poisoned atmosphere of committees and editorial offices nothing comes but political directives testifying to a scandalous blindness."[67] This text appeared little more than a month after Surrealist adherents broke with Contre-Attaque over Bataille's willingness to adopt fascist techniques in a battle against fascism. They concluded that his critical strategy derived from a dangerous fascination. The split, seen from the start as inevitable, is a definitive zigzag taken by Breton, whose vision of revolutionary politics became increasingly isolated from partisan and militant practices. In Bataille's evolution, the dialectic of sublation and cancellation (*Aufhebung*) was yielding to a more abrupt and sovereign overcoming (*Überwinden*) of Nietzschean inspiration. The dissolution of Contre-

Attaque isolated Breton once and for all from political intervention, beyond tracts, position papers, and topical statements to the press. With Trotsky across the Atlantic, Surrealist dissidence toward nation and patriotism no longer marched alongside the revolutionary politics (and art) upheld by the Communists. Nor was it in line with the nascent group around Bataille that moved progressively from Contre-Attaque toward and beyond Acéphale.

The Collège de Sociologie emerged from its gestation period (1934 to 1937) much in the way that Surrealism had emerged from postwar disillusionment between 1918 and 1924. And just as the 1924 "Surrealist Manifesto" was a call to action against the symbolic authority of family, country, and religion oppressively reasserted after the war, so the founding statements of the Collège react to the symbolic authority of a bogus parliamentary democracy called into question in February 1934, when thousands mobilized in the streets. But whereas Breton anchors the 1924 manifesto in a concept of *the marvelous* that he models on the individual's experience of dreams, childhood, and madness, the Collège explores the active cohesive presence of *the sacred*, understood—in the 1937 formulation by Roger Caillois—as "the points of coincidence between the fundamental obsessive tendencies of individual psychology and the principal structures that govern social organization and are in command of its revolution."[68]

Tensions between individual and group agency are already evident in Bataille's 1935 talk "Popular Front in the Street," where the potential for revolutionary activity is said to build on the force of energy unleashed by crowds of demonstrators, the power of the group being patently greater than the sum of its parts. Caillois explicitly linked historical and social circumstance to the critical work of the Collège when he wrote in 1937 of the germ of a contradiction that had come to paralyze intellectuals in his generation: he saw them "awkwardly or arrogantly trying their hand at taking part in political struggles, and seeing their intimate preoccupations so out of tune with the demands of their cause that they quickly had to give in or give up."[69] Was he referring to writers in general? More pointedly to the Surrealists? Or perhaps also to himself and other former Surrealists? Less accusatory than self-critical, the statement candidly expresses the very shortcomings that he—and presumably others in the Collège—were looking to overcome in a group dynamic that would be more open and less hierarchical than what existed among the Surrealists under Breton.

It would be an exaggeration to describe Leiris in 1937–1938 as having abandoned Surrealism (and Breton) and having completely adopted the Collège (and Bataille). Of particular interest is his January 1938 talk "Le Sacré dans la vie quotidienne" (The Sacred in Everyday Life), delivered at a session of the Collège—a talk that Denis Hollier sees as constituting the pivot linking *L'Age d'homme* to the future volumes of the autobiographical series, *La Règle du jeu*.[70] An opening paragraph asks pointed questions that unfold in scope and generality from the first-person singular ("what, for me, is the *sacred?*") toward objects, places, and occasions. These questions awaken in Leiris "that mixture of fear and of attachment, that ambiguous attitude caused by the approach of something simultaneously attractive and dangerous, prestigious and outcast—that combination of respect, desire, and terror that we take as the psychological sign of the sacred."[71] The outward movement in the first paragraph extends throughout the talk, as Leiris evokes memories of his childhood, starting with the spatial configuration of his family house, which he transposes into a topography of the sacred.

Outside the house, Leiris recalls a sort of bush-country or *no-man's land* between the fortifications and the Auteuil hippodrome. Consciously or not, the description of this *no-man's land*—Leiris uses the English expression—reads like an afterword to the Dakar-Djibouti Mission. It supplements "L'Oeil de l'ethnographe" and *L'Afrique fantôme* by recasting the Parisian *zone* as "a place apart, extremely taboo, an area heavily marked by the supernatural and the sacred."[72] To the extent that it tempers self-analysis with categories adopted from anthropology and the study of myth, this text locates Leiris somewhere between Surrealism and the Collège—somewhere, that is, between the marvelous and the sacred.

Leiris' ambivalent intellectual position, it turns out, is hardly eccentric. For "The Sacred in Everyday Life" appeared in the July 1938 issue of the *Nouvelle Revue Française*, alongside "Vent d'hiver" (Winter Wind) by Caillois, "L'Apprenti Sorcier" (The Sorcerer's Apprentice) by Bataille, and a manifesto written by Caillois in the name of the group: "Pour un Collège de Sociologie" (For a College of Sociology). This defining dossier of the Collège came at the invitation of Jean Paulhan, the *NRF*'s editor, who, between 1936 and 1940 opened the pages of the Gallimard monthly to Leiris, Caillois, Bataille, and Kojève. For us, it constitutes a follow-up—a bookend—to the *Cahier de revendications* dossier that Paulhan had commissioned Denis de Rougemont to organize five and a half years earlier for the *NRF*'s December 1932 issue. These two dossiers mark the changing seasons of the Popular

Front that they surround: its rambunctious springtime (the authors de Rougemont recruited were nearly all under twenty-five and dreaming of a new France) mutated into its fall (the Collège ruminating over the fate of France from the perspective of an institute concerned with larger ethnographic questions). Leiris lived this transition, as his obsession with self increasingly gave way to a quest to understand the workings of social organization.

If literature is a bullfight, full of violence and ritual, as Leiris unforgettably wrote in 1938, then his perspective wavered over the decade between that of toreador and that of (engaged) anthropologist. Two years later, he would see the arena invaded by something more menacing than a bull: Nazi tanks, occupation forces, and collaborators. But even as early as September 1938, when the Munich Accords signaled the inevitability of renewed war between France and Germany, Bataille's and Leiris' respective interests in ritual and violence converged at a critical remove from the redemption that Breton had projected for the Surrealist movement as early as the 1924 manifesto. True, Breton had suffered political setbacks during the 1930s. But worse was the loss of faith in the redemptive potential of political activity signaled by the dissolution of the Contre-Attaque group. Then came the nonredemptive collective activity that the Collège de Sociologie explored and represented. This marked a definitive break with the optimism that inspired and sustained the Popular Front from 1934 to 1938. Much as Leiris wanted *L'Age d'homme* to be the negation of the novel, so the transition from revolutionary Surrealism to Acéphale and the Collège was the negation of a redemptive militancy.

After the Front: From Revolution to Art

Next to the grotesquely over-inflated dandy Salvador Dalí and the rather pathetically deflated Michel Leiris, André Malraux stands out as a robust, well-proportioned figure, his magnificent shadow falling across the entire decade. Malraux was thoroughly Parisian, but as Paris stood proudly at the forefront of the world, he felt international by birthright. Shuttling from Paris to Indochina, Egypt, Iran, Afghanistan, Arabia, Berlin, Moscow, Madrid, London, and New York, he returned each time to France's capital, his beloved home city that in the 1960s, as Minister of Culture under Charles de Gaulle, he would cleanse, building by building. A truly prominent figure, he nonetheless operated in the same cultural world as Breton, Leiris, and even the marginal immigrant Walter Benjamin. In a lengthy 1933 overview called

"The Present Social Situation of the French Writer," probably occasioned by the huge successes of the novels by Malraux and Céline discussed in the piece, Benjamin unsparingly dismisses two generations of authors since Dreyfus for their bogus social and political pretensions. Malraux he saves for last, the pure example of a troubled individual from the privileged class allaying his solitude by involving himself in adventures with the proletariat, whose interests he doesn't really understand.[73] Benjamin clearly admires Malraux's heroic gestures, yet finds them blind to the genuine needs of workers and thus of the revolution. He concludes his essay by lauding a single group of writers, the Surrealists, each of whom, in contrast to Malraux, understands and works beyond his own class position. He writes:

> A petty bourgeois who means business with his libertarian and erotic aspirations. . . . The more uninhibitedly and resolutely he asserts his claims, the greater the certainty that he will find himself on the road to politics. . . . At the same time, he will cease to be the petty bourgeois he once was. "Revolutionary writers," Aragon maintains, "if they are of bourgeois stock, are essentially and crucially traitors to the class of their origins." They become militant politicians. . . . They know from experience why literature—the only literature they still think worthy of the name—is dangerous.[74]

Benjamin insinuates that Malraux and virtually all French authors merely toy with revolution, in comparison to the genuinely dangerous situation the Surrealists put themselves in. Fifteen months later, when many of the most "engaged" authors of the day (Malraux, Gide, Benda, Barbusse) testified at the 1935 Writers' Congress for the Defense of Culture, Breton found himself uncivilly disinvited. He lashed out at the pretensions of this event, mocking Malraux's "moving declaration" as "a veritable bath of useless repetitions, infantile considerations, and toadying" to a conformist ruling class of bureaucrats.[75]

Benjamin and Breton were being unfair. Malraux, first of all, did not by any means come from a privileged family—certainly not from the "ruling class." As for political activism, in the years since Benjamin's article, hadn't he met with Trotsky in the Atlantic coast city of Royan, flown to Berlin with Gide to negotiate with Goebbels, traveled to Moscow to participate in the First Congress of Soviet Writers, and been present at the founding of the World League against Anti-Semitism? As for his writing, between October

1933 and December 1936, Malraux published four pieces in the AEAR monthly, *Commune*, and another two in the Gallimard weekly, *Marianne*, where Communists and non-Communists found common ground on domestic and international matters. Then, in July 1936, just two days after the full-scale eruption of civil war in Spain, he turned from writing and advocacy toward direct involvement and personal risk. Forming the España squadron, he flew immediately to Spain and took off on missions over battle sites around Madrid, Toledo, and Teruel.

Breton, it seems, could have had Malraux in mind when, in the speech that he had prepared for the Writers' Congress (but that was delivered for him by Eluard), he underwrote the following "lapidary formula: We must dream, said Lenin; we must act, Goethe said."[76] Malraux, artist and adventurer, visibly did both. Breton might boast in his second manifesto that Surrealism offered the average citizen "books, paintings, and cinema . . . to begin to shake up his settled way of thinking."[77] But Malraux had gotten there first; he had published novels that were both serious and popular, and he was changing the art world by promoting Asian artifacts from his travels (albeit dubiously acquired); as he left for Spain, he was outlining his groundbreaking *musée imaginaire*, which would have the greatest consequences for democratizing art. As for cinema, Malraux would not just make a film but would do so in the heat of civil war, firing his camera like a machine-gun to turn back Franco's forces. What did Benjamin think of this gesture? What did Breton think—Breton for whom the ultimate Surrealist gesture would be firing a revolver indiscriminately into a crowd? Was Malraux merely indulging the needs of his own useless class by joining up with the Republican cause? Was this nothing but a displaced dream of politics?

Breton, for his part, excused himself from participating in the Spanish conflict altogether: he had just become a father and felt that his duty to his daughter took priority.[78] What really took priority, however, were Paris and the struggle over imaginative expression in the arts, which we have seen Breton explicitly put ahead of direct political or military campaigns. But even here, it was Malraux who was in the trenches. The man who was perhaps the most successful novelist of his generation found himself making a zigzag not just to Spain but to cinema, so as to unite thought and action, imagination and deed. *Espoir*, conceived in 1937 before being financed and shot the next year, was completed just as Franco declared complete victory. The film's single theatrical showing took place in July 1939, the same untimely month that saw the notorious première of *La Règle du jeu*.[79] (These two films, so different from the entire prewar French canon, would reappear powerfully after the Liberation, provoking, among other things, André Bazin's awakening of modernist film theory.)[80] Even as war against Hitler was being declared, postponing *Espoir*'s commercial release for six years, Malraux found time in September to write up a series of profound reflections on cinema. Appearing as "Esquisse d'une psychologie du cinéma" (Sketch for a Psychology of the Moving Pictures) in the art journal *Verve* in late 1940, these speculations, together with his exceptional film, amount to an aggressive intervention in the theory of representation.[81]

With this essay, Malraux is positioned between the two great essayists of classical film theory, Walter Benjamin and André Bazin. Bazin was at just the right age to be smitten by the dashing intellectual Malraux. He mentions him in his letters; he joined an "André Malraux study group" at the Maison des Lettres near the Sorbonne during the Occupation; most important, he cites him in the first paragraph of his stupendous debut essay, "Ontologie de l'image photographique" (Ontology of the Photographic Image; 1945).[82] There he speculates about cycles in the psychology of art, ideas triggered by a series of short essays that Malraux had published in *Verve*'s splendid first issues.[83] Bazin ends—or rather upends—his "Ontology" argument by mimicking Malraux's conclusion to his film essay: "Par ailleurs le cinéma est une industrie" ("Also we must never forget—the cinema is an industry") becomes in Bazin "D'autre part, le cinéma est un langage" ("On the other hand, of course, cinema is also a language").

Walter Benjamin would have appreciated both of these concluding sentences, but he seems not to have directly inspired them. Bazin never mentions him, and Malraux would have been too illustrious and too busy to have encountered him socially.[84] Still, Rosalind Krauss argues that Benjamin supplied the final ingredient for Malraux's vast project on art, a project that she dates from the watershed year 1936. Pierre Klossowski translated "Das Kunstwerk im Zeitalter seiner technischen Reproduzierbarkeit" (The Work of Art in the Age of Its Technological Reproducibility) into French in the spring 1936 issue of Max Horkheimer's *Zeitschrift für Zozialforschung* (Journal of Social Research), published in Paris.[85] Malraux, she implies, read it there and took notes, as he was outlining what he called at the time his vast *Psychology of Art*. This would have been just before flying off on his dangerous missions in Spain.

In 1937 and 1938, *Verve*'s first issues include tantalizing "fragments of the *Psychology of Art* on which André Malraux has been engaged for several years."[86] One wonders how, between sorties, he found the time and the concentration to put it all together. Perhaps it was only "all together"—that is, as man of action and as intellectual—that Malraux could operate in this age of anxiety. He entered the Spanish cause to help protect the fledgling republic from barbarous fascism but also to keep the values of El Greco and Goya alive, and to accomplish this through a medium, the cinema, that was revitalizing narrative and visual expression, and doing so for a mass audience.

Malraux seemed successfully to have lived out Breton's declaration that politics should drive the search for radical techniques of representation, which in turn are the precondition for any new social order. To some extent, he subscribed to Breton's strategy of "de-linking" in politics and aesthetics, for it breaks the chain of command that rules language, the self, and society. Of course, Benjamin took this Surrealist method more seriously and practiced it in his "fragmentary" approach to history, to art, and to rhetorical composition. It also lay behind his enthusiasm for photography and for its effect on art and culture.

But "fragment" is precisely the word appearing beneath many of the reproductions in Malraux's *Psychologie de l'art*. Morseling artworks into their significant "details," morseling the world of art into photographs (whether of entire works or details), is a necessary violence the art historian inflicts on what he loves in order to give it meaning. Claude-Edmonde Magny wrote of an "odor of death emanating from this accumulation of fragments, of debris juxtaposed in an album of art."[87] Like Benjamin, Malraux points to an earlier violence, by which many artworks were uprooted and brought together on the "neutral" walls of the secular museum.[88] Photography next leveled the scale of every work to the size of the print, permitting an indefinite number of works (or pertinent fragments of them) to be moved about. Malraux's introduction to *Le Musée imaginaire* boasts of this necessary photographic operation, which physically prepares the terrain for the design of the art historian. Paintings from the Prado and the Louvre, as well as sculptures and frescoes impossible to move to museums, now enter into a dialogue. Certain elements of style communicate more clearly in their black-and-white reproductions than when looked at in their original media. Details on portals can be isolated so as to answer massive tapestries, since photographs bring everything literally into the hands of the historian on 8 x 11 sheets or (more commonly today) on 35mm slides, projected side by side at the same scale in lecture halls, or in the multiple windows of a computer screen among which we toggle.

Malraux understood that such "neutralization" (the neutron bomb of photographic reproduction) distorts texture, color, scale, dimension, and context. Yet look at the gains for art history and for the democratization of culture. The object of the art historian shifts from adulating superior works of art to rendering the spirit of art—the epic response of humans to their ultimately tragic plight—and this is registered in the evolution of style visible when artifacts of all sorts are properly surveyed, including those that were never conceived entirely for contemplation: African masks, ornamental pottery, and so forth. The art historian puts in play all sorts of artifacts, now that the single format made possible by photographic reproduction has rendered them equally available (and in a certain sense equivalent). With his myriad fragments before him, Malraux laid down the drama of civilization as on the storyboard of a great film, one image beside the next.

Benjamin and Malraux (one of them dreading the future, the other intoxicated by it) understood the metamorphoses not just of art, but more profoundly of art's role for mankind. They knew the future of the museum was now in question (witness the corrosive effects of Duchamp and Surrealism), especially in the wake—or bright light—of photography and cinema. Benjamin promoted a democratic aesthetic, a vulgate of ubiquitous reproductions. Its aura having evaporated, art could now be handled by ordinary people for their enjoyment, but also as a means for them to understand and criticize the world.

Malraux's scenario, in contrast, started top-down. Rather than a popular revaluation of art, he anticipated that once it was widely diffused in reproductions, art would elevate the people, bringing them to consciousness and action under the redemptive blessing of the great spirits who had preceded them. He fought the debilitating vulgarity of popular uses of art (even predicting that television would mesmerize the next generation). Yet he wanted art to be revered in every home, not on the altar of a museum pedestal but in books of art history or in series of prints. Although he didn't employ the term, "aura" was not to be dispersed but was to drift from authentic *works* to the authentic *story (histoire)* of art, illustrated in books of reproductions. Even poor copies, if properly ordered, remain capable of transmitting the silent voice of art's indomitable quest.

Despite Malraux's sublation of pastiche into unified expression, Benjamin would no doubt have applauded this pedagogical use of photography as a gain for the notion of artistic signification over that of artistic beauty and uniqueness. Photographs encourage the semiotic use of paintings, each one of which takes its place as a unit in a differential, comparative system.[89] Such a system was precisely what Benjamin believed the working class could begin to deploy on its own, without the lead of an expert, in its search for a relevant aesthetic. On the eve of the barbaric Hitlerian onslaught, Malraux, guided by civilization, became a resistance leader and later a cultural minister. Sadly, it was otherwise for Benjamin.

Malraux's vast *Psychology of Art* culminated in the Pléiade edition of *Les Voix du silence* (The Voices of Silence), bearing the composition dates 1935–1951. The year 1935 was also when Benjamin drew up the outline of the *Arcades Project*.[90] Thus, in the midst of the democratic swell of the Popular Front, two aggressive techniques of creative fragmentation made possible these stupendous but distinct undertakings, both of which wanted to hand art over to the people.

Benjamin's program was the more radical. His "modern materialism" initiates an atomic fission that decomposes every text, institution, and idea it goes in search of, destroying the gods of culture. Yet an undeniable strain of idealism complicates this "negative theology," as Terry Eagleton astutely recognized.[91] Benjamin's crude technological determinism shows photography and cinema upending the culture that produced such machinery. Yet Benjamin also holds to a "culturalism" whereby bits of material evidence taken from a huge variety of cultural sources (the Arcades) indicate a devolution of life experience *(Erfahrung)* for individuals within modern society. Fragmentation names the twentieth-century result of this devolution; it also names the process by which it can be recognized and reversed in those messianic moments when pieces culled from different eras and zones of experience come together in congruence and prophecy. Benjamin wanted to fashion significant, revolutionary history out of his fragments, rather than anecdotes or mere intertextual play. He had neither the time—nor perhaps the ability— to bring it off. Eagleton wonders if his modernist historiography is even feasible, warranted though it may be. Surely Benjamin wanted more than the recent "primitivist and unpalatable" alternatives to standard history (Marxist or otherwise) that have canonized him. Surely he would have been allergic to much postmodern cultural history that, often calling on his method and assumptions, "has ended up by abandoning all hopes of [revolutionary] change."[92]

Eagleton is not the first to link the tragic, uncompromising Marxist intellectuals Benjamin and Trotsky, who both suffered violent political deaths in 1940, caught between fascism and Stalinism.[93] Breton stands as their go-between, friendly as he had been with Benjamin from as far back as 1928 and then joining Trotsky in Mexico a decade later to produce position papers that combined Surrealism's radical aesthetics with Trotsky's political aspirations. In fact, as Eagleton notes, Benjamin's turn of mind was closer to Breton's Surrealism than to Trotsky's more traditional view of art and ideas. Trotsky was happy to recruit the energy of younger rogue intellectuals, but his own frame of reference remained the Enlightenment project of classical Marxism, not their "modernist Marxism."

Trotsky was more comfortable with Malraux, whom he treated as someone to be contended with, though certainly not as an equal. They had kept one another in view since that famous night meeting in 1933 captured in *Stavisky* . . . . In 1937, however, Malraux riled his former idol in a New York City speech to raise money for the Spanish Republican cause.[94] Feeling the need to defend Stalin as the only head of state sending military aid to Spain, he denigrated Trotsky's importance, and this in the midst of the Moscow show trials. A clumsy sparring match took place in *The Nation* when Trotsky hit back. This high-profile political debate suited Malraux nonetheless, who always lived on the main stage of history. Impatient with frivolous avant-gardes, he implied that Trotsky had been shunted off to a sideshow. He no doubt felt sadly vindicated when the next year Trotsky forged an alliance with the tiresome and constitutionally adolescent Breton.[95]

Effectively dismissing Trotsky and Breton, as if after 1936 their roles were over, Malraux concerned himself with major characters in the drama of contemporary history. Whereas Benjamin collected forgotten bits of culture, superimposing them rather than drawing a line between them, Malraux compulsively connected those fragments that he felt participated in the big picture. Evidently Trotsky and Breton, the former exiled, the latter reduced to stunts and manifestos, had become inconsequential "fragments," chips that had fallen off the big fresco.

A Nietzschean ethos can be felt in the three massive endeavors Malraux embarked on during the Popular Front (as though its goals and rhetoric were too modest for someone of his ambitions). Nietzschean—or Promethean—he took on responsibilities that God had forsaken: first, to help peasants and workers coalesce into a Communist Spain; second, to gather from all places and all ages the evidence of man's struggle for redemption from absurdity and present that evidence in *The Psychology of Art*; third, to construct a monumental film out of the innumerable characters, perceptions, incidents, and images that came to him in the intense days of the Spanish struggle. In each of these endeavors, scattered bits of material fact are brought together as fragments whose undeniable reality sustains the larger picture they form when properly connected. As squadron leader, art historian, and film director, Malraux helped to lift individual elements into ecstatic totality. As early as his first editorials in Indochina, back in 1925, Malraux understood this principle: "that one doesn't govern men at all; that one may—with great tact—direct an evolution; that to guide it is a worthy role."[96]

On his 1934 trip to Moscow and the First Writer's Congress, where he delivered his speech "Art is a Conquest," Malraux visited Sergei Eisenstein, who had recently returned from Mexico and was preparing his ill-fated film *Bezhin Meadows*. Over the next few days, allegedly in a fever of perfect collaboration, they composed a full adaptation of *La Condition humaine* (Man's Fate), Malraux's masterpiece. This novel owes much to the films of the Soviet silent period, with its multiple, alternating sketches of a revolutionary moment, its collective hero, and its vivid and violent images, all orchestrated into a powerful symphony of noble suffering. Both *Espoir* and "Esquisse d'une psychologie du cinéma" would stand confidently in the light of Eisenstein's theory and praxis. Even critics of the time recognized this. Evidently Malraux did too, for in a note to Volume 2 of *The Psychology of Art*, he links the culmination of his film, the great descent of the wounded aviators from the mountain, to an equivalent sequence in *Potemkin*, when the body of a martyred sailor is brought to shore. The glory of these sequences is the glory both of gallant subject matter and of modernist expression. "The function of Malraux's images is precisely that of projecting a series of multiple perspectives upon reality, so that every aspect is mirrored against every other, to be refracted finally against the membrane of a single consciousness, that of the author himself."[97] As in Eisenstein, the fragments are said to come together at a higher level than that of plot or character which they produce on their way toward an unmistakable representation—what Eisenstein referred to as the "single image hovering before the artist," which isn't merely delivered to the audience, but which in fact they experience by completing it themselves, leaping from fragment to fragment in bursts of understanding.[98]

Eisenstein thus confirmed Malraux's belief in the function of modern art and in the place of cinema within the art world. Against the vulgarity of most films, Eisenstein's glowed with the aura of traditional painting (including the spirit of rebellion, by which every real artist struggles to go beyond the tradition). It must have gratified Malraux that Eisenstein so often called on El Greco, a painter about whom Malraux had written so passionately that Bazin deemed his writing on the painter to be not so much art history as an artistic co-creation with El Greco.[99] In Malraux's view, every artist begins by making a personal pastiche of past masterworks, gradually rearranging them into an order whose value extends beyond the past, culminating in an artistic gesture that constitutes the next step in the evolution of style, the next accretion on the coral reef of art.

Malraux's "gesture" can be seen at work in the two most memorable sequences of *Espoir*. For although *Espoir* takes as its subject history in the making, it is history intensified in the frame of art, history experienced as Goya and El Greco might have imaged it. Malraux would later call El Greco's *Storm over Toledo* the first Christian landscape, because its tormented Spanish vista directly figures the suffering of Christ. In the terms that Eisenstein was developing at the time, *Espoir* reaches a "pathetic" (pathos-filled) level of expression, especially in its representation of villages and mountains. The figure of the Crucifixion enlarges the human agony included in the frame, the agony of innocent peasants dying for their freedom. In the film's glorious final sequence, one of the planes that courageously took out a key bridge and neutralized a Franquist airfield has crashed in the mountains. Several members of the crew have died; others are hurt and would die without aid from the peasants who inhabit the lowlands around the mountain. Accompanied by Darius Milhaud's emotional score, with its sacred overtones, the eleven-minute descent from the mountain—with the wounded borne on makeshift stretchers—becomes a descent from the Cross, a deposition. James Agee wrote that "a whole people and a whole terrain become one sorrowing and triumphal *Pietà* for twentieth-century man."[100] In the final moments of the descent, shifting visual planes and compositions produce a modern agony that echoes the style and subject of Tintoretto's *Ascent to Calvary*,[101] but even more of El Greco's work, whose crucifixions and views of Toledo vividly hovered before Malraux's imagination as he shot his film.

With Goya, as critics have noted, the subject matter is that much closer.[102] In the most famous of the "Disasters of the War" cycle, *The Third of May*, a defiant Spanish rebel throws open his arms before the French guns that execute him. This single image condenses what Malraux presents in the dramatic sequence in which a Republican suicide squad drives a car into a firing cannon (where the camera has been placed). Malraux here draws power from Goya, who referenced El Greco before him, implying a crucifixion whose violent agony radiates hope through its lighting. Malraux's light bursts forth only as the scene ends: a flock of pigeons suddenly fly up in the sacred aftermath of death.

On the heels of making *Espoir*, Malraux declared in his "Esquisse d'une psychologie du cinéma" that the art of cinema was born with the practice of editing, where mechanically recorded pictures, of no importance in themselves except as "identity cards," submit to design: "The means of reproduction in the cinema is the moving photograph, but its means of expression is a sequence of planes."[103] He would restate this conventional view in a response to André Bazin's stunning essay on *Espoir*, which promoted its mise-en-scène and documentary value over its cutting. Editing rendered cinematographic Malraux's favorite literary figure, the ellipsis.[104] Here Bazin pursued a prophetic article that his predecessor at *Esprit*, Roger Leenhardt, published there in 1936. Leenhardt had opposed Eisensteinian and Surrealist fragmentation, which he surmised was premised on metaphor, in favor of a kind of cinema that aimed to keep the world intact, if necessarily providing only pieces of it. "Precisely because of its primordial realism, it is not in the cinematographic material, if I may say so, that the art of the cinema lies, but only in connections, comparisons, and ellipses."[105] Leenhardt then immediately identifies Malraux as the novelist who best realizes the potential of cinematic ellipsis in prose fiction.

We know what figure Walter Benjamin prized: allegory. He was indifferent to the natural world cinema claims to represent, if only elliptically. And he was suspicious of anything like "voices of silence" emanating from the past—voices that Malraux would release in a famous 1951 study. Against pious contemplation, Benjamin held to noisy dialectics. One of his recent exponents, Russell Berman, writes approvingly that "for the young Benjamin, nature represents a fallen world of graceless silence." He goes on to suggest that Benjamin disdains any visual display whose logic leaves no room for "fragmentation or commentary, [so that] the passive recipient is condemned to a silence that excludes the redemptive moment of language."[106] Malraux, for his part, found in cinema a means "other than language" for linking mankind and the cosmos. He congratulated Bazin as being the first to have understood this, and for having subtly understood the aesthetic effect of the ellipses that allows *Espoir* to be a complete expression of a historical situation while only sampling the far more numerous incidents and perspectives represented in the novel.[107] This great film expresses the novel (and the historical moment) by doing something impossible in language: it shows human beings existing and acting within a landscape of current danger and of enduring art.

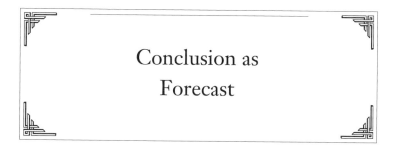

Conclusion as
Forecast

Let's leave Paris and our chosen decade for the South of France in the fall of 1940. For Paris is occupied by the Nazis, while Parisians by the thousands have relocated in the so-called free zone or are looking for ways to leave the country. Out of our cast of characters, most are desperate. In late August, Trotsky is assassinated. A month later, Benjamin takes his life while trying to enter Spain. In late October, Malraux escapes from a military detention camp near Sens and makes his way to the Côte d'Azur. Gaston Gallimard, realizing that his famous author must be near the top of the Germans' blacklist, destroys the records of Malraux's old plan to liberate Trotsky from Siberia.[1] Then he puts Pierre Drieu La Rochelle in charge of the *NRF*, replacing Jean Paulhan, who has resigned as editor rather than work under German censorship. The flagship monthly reappears in December, but under a new dispensation. There would no longer be royalties or editorial fees for Malraux and most other Gallimard authors. Nor did Malraux receive anything for his essay on cinema that appeared in *Verve* just as he was escaping into the Free Zone. Malraux thus needed American contacts to access the substantial funds that Random House owed to him for the sales of *Man's Fate*, the English-language translation of *La Condition humaine*. Special pleading was needed, since the U.S. government, fearing Nazi confiscation, was restricting the amount of cash that could be sent to France. Plus, there was the potential revenue bottled up in the still very timely film *Espoir*. Malraux's half-brother, Roland, smuggled a complete print to him in the South around Christmas.

It was inevitable under these conditions that Malraux should meet Varian Fry, the "American Schindler," who ran an antifascist mission in Marseilles. Fry arrived in late autumn 1940 and set up an underground railway that ultimately smuggled nearly 2,000 Jews and many prominent fugitives through the Pyrenees and Spain to freedom across the Atlantic. He came too late to save Walter Benjamin. But he was able to help Malraux, whom he invited to lunch in Marseilles. At the table was Victor Serge, the Belgian-born Trotsky-ite whose imprisonment by Stalin had been a cause of debate when Malraux was presiding over the June 1935 Congress for the Defense of Culture. Serge, now living in Fry's villa along with André Breton, had joined the Marxist workers' party (the POUM) in Spain during the Civil War and had objected to Malraux's courting of Stalin. This pair of activist-novelists might have argued about Spain and about Trotsky, but with Hitler bearing down on them they suddenly shared a great many values and concerns. Malraux had no intention of emigrating. He just wanted to access his U.S. funds and to deliver his film intact to a distributor and a paying public. He also wanted to be sure that his estranged (and Jewish) wife, Clara, and their daughter could leave. As for Victor Serge, Fry found him passage on a cargo ship that left Marseilles on March 25, 1941, for Martinique. Serge's destination was Mexico, where, among other things, he planned to write the biography of the just-martyred Trotsky. Among the other passengers on this grotesquely over-crowded refu-gee barge was his housemate Breton, who had much to tell him about Trotsky and Mexico from his own pilgrimage two years earlier. This time Breton's destination was New York, as it was for the young anthropologist Claude Lévi-Strauss, aboard the same ship.

Lévi-Strauss's diary of this voyage, colorfully reworked in the introduc-tion to *Tristes Tropiques*, recounts the friendship that he forged on board with Breton, a friendship that continued when in New York they both worked as broadcasters for the Voice of America.[2] Breton joined a covey of exiled Surre-alists including Yves Tanguy, Roberto Matta, André Masson, and Max Ernst (who scandalously arrived with his new lover, Peggy Guggenheim). They would all soon welcome Marcel Duchamp, but not Salvador Dalí, who, on his visits from Hollywood, was rebuffed by Breton and Ernst (very rudely by the latter).[3] Breton had been offered a position at the New School for Social Re-search, where he would have taught alongside Walter Benjamin's colleagues Theodor Adorno and Max Horkheimer; but he had no intention of mastering (or even studying) English. He survived on his broadcasting job and on the fame of Surrealism, holding forth memorably at Yale in December 1942. Meanwhile Lévi-Strauss was teaching at the New School, which immigrants from Europe made singularly vibrant.[4]

Though Lévi-Strauss's method, later dubbed Structuralism, took shape at the New School, it had been conceived in the 1930s. Indeed, in the chapter of *Tristes Tropiques* called "How I Became an Anthropologist," he gives a more precise date, one very familiar to us: February 1934. That tumultuous month following Stavisky's death found Lévi-Strauss leaving Europe for the first time, escaping the instabilities and cacophony of Paris as he embarked at Marseilles (destination Santos, Brazil) for what he deliberately designated a tracking mission *(une poursuite)*. As a budding intellectual caught in a familiar dilemma between "normal science" and its avant-garde alternative, Lévi-Strauss considered his options. He had been schooled in law, the social sciences, and philosophy as taught in the academy, all of which seemed doomed to widen knowledge in a most predictable fashion. He mercilessly ridiculed the pretense toward the forward march of knowledge conducted by the bureaucrats operating within the hothouse of the Sorbonne between the wars (reminding us how seldom the academy has seemed relevant to either the politics or the poetics of culture in that era).[5] And so he flirted with the Surrealists but found them too flighty and unpredictable, too concerned with experience over knowledge. Their methods were those of meandering, self-styled knights-errant who bank on the uses of error in a chivalric search for a more fundamental truth.[6] Proceeding by puns, connotations, and other zigzags of language, "errancy" is an acquired method that wanders or strays toward its goal. Lévi-Strauss found Surrealism inconsequential, its discoveries ultimately just self-discovery; haphazard flashes of illumination were neither "sequential" nor progressive. Lévi-Strauss didn't want to manufacture discoveries; he preferred to give them a chance to appear to him, after which he would pursue them wherever they might lead. Geology was his model discipline, for the terrain it encountered, while objectively outside the investigator, required historical imagination in order for one to clarify its surface confusion. As with the earth and the past in geology, so Lévi-Strauss would engage other worlds and worldviews in anthropology. Individual encounters mattered to him insofar as they could contribute to the larger discoveries of regularities and interconnections. His wide-ranging pursuit was "a *very* different thing from just walking or from the straightforward exploration of a given area. What seems mere incoherent groping to an uninformed observer is to me the very image of knowledge-in-action, with the difficulties it may encounter and the satisfactions it may hope to enjoy."[7]

Lévi-Strauss, who claimed to have been "collecting exotica since childhood," was quick to relate unknown continents to their counterparts in the

382 | Conclusion as Forecast

human psyche that Freud had learned to track with superior agility. In the
realm of sociology and economics, Marx had likewise navigated different layers of knowledge in excursions that dispensed with available scientific maps,
proceeding instead in a more abductive manner of discovery-by-tracking.
These nascent *human sciences* share a commitment to "Look, Listen, Read"
(Lévi-Strauss's adage)—that is, to scrutinize nature and culture equally in a
search for correspondences. As interpretive sciences, they mean to avoid
merely finding the singular or inflating the self (the danger of "just wandering" by whim, exemplified by Breton in *Nadja* and *L'Amour fou*). Yet they are
poised to apprehend relationships invisible to standard disciplines (the danger of the planned "straightforward exploration" of an academic area). Explicitly following Marx and Freud, and bearing his dubious visa allowing him
to track his intuitions, Lévi-Strauss aimed at a "super-rationalism" that sorts
through and interprets myriad elements collected during vaguely organized
and wide-eyed hunting expeditions.[8] These elements retain their singular
properties even as they are integrated into the wider perspective available to
someone who has explored but passed beyond the layers where they are
found. Modeling himself on the geologist, Lévi-Strauss goes back and forth
between fragments of rocks and a history of the strata in which they are embedded. Listening to the elements from the proper distance allows the "harmonies" of a larger system to be felt.[9]

Our book has substituted a meteorological analogy for Lévi-Strauss's geological one, as each chapter explored a semi-autonomous stratospheric level,
while keeping in view the fuller fluctuating pattern that produces fronts,
storms, and doldrums. Our conclusion has tracked several extravagant flights
through these levels. Each flight discloses an interaction of aesthetic and political concerns that are profoundly consequential for the writing of history:
from Dalí's paranoid-critical method and the allegorical impulse explicit in
Leiris and Benjamin to Malraux's Promethean expression (via lines drawn between stark fragments) of revolutionary history-in-the-making.

The tragic and messianic Benjamin appeals today to students of historiography, while no one apologizes for rejecting Salvador Dalí. Yet Benjamin
makes use of Dalí—and most certainly of Breton—when he announces the
value of detritus and when he ignores, indeed refuses, all logic of linkage.
Terry Eagleton may speak for us when he implies that, admirably radical
though Benjamin's historiography may be, no one has succeeded in producing a consequential account of historical experience in Benjamin's Messianic

mode.[10] We certainly haven't tried. But Benjamin, together with Breton, has forced on us a respect for the overlooked, the peculiar, the obtuse fact or idea that might burn brilliantly enough to reflect unpredictably but prophetically off other elements or moments.

Malraux, too, hunted down obscure telling details in art and history, arranging these selectively to indicate an expansive sweep. We have adopted something of his perspective by keeping in view the arc of the decade while trying to characterize aspects of life that are detached (or partly so) from the grand narrative of the Popular Front. As was the case for Malraux regarding the Spanish Civil War, so for us an expansive historical moment must be represented through precise treatment of certain of the elements that make it what it is. Each of the elliptical sequences in *L'Espoir* (both novel and film) is like a newspaper column, relating a discrete anecdote that constitutes only a section of "the daily." And how does one read history-as-newspaper? In zigzags, bouncing from one column to another. "Zigzag" is how Malraux describes the suicidal rush of the Republican car hurtling toward the firing cannon in his novel's justly famous scene. It was also, as we have seen, a significant term for Breton. Surrealist historiography zigzags erratically from attraction to attraction, from level to level, and from the personal, the idiosyncratic, even the aesthetic, to the political. Our account of the decade of the Popular Front has likewise zigzagged, though with far more sobriety.

Zigzags make connections, dot-to-dot; and despite Breton's injunction, they link the elements they touch. Malraux believed in the great chain of man, artworks forging the links that allow the revolutionary spirit of our day to communicate with the revolutions of the past. His materialism—call it Nietzschean—comes from an age earlier than that of Benjamin. It was not Brecht whom Malraux approached about adapting *La Condition humaine*, but Sergei Eisenstein, that master unifier of montage fragments. Eisenstein, he knew, would have made all characters, shots, and registers of expression vibrate harmonically in an orchestrated tragic expression of history. After all, it was Eisenstein who wrote about "overtones" and "harmonics" in his dialectical theory of cinema, well before Alain Resnais mentioned them. (Florence Malraux, we should note, André's only child, married Alain Resnais and was the assistant director of *Stavisky . . . .*)

We opened our study by adopting the viewpoint of a character in *Stavisky . . .* whose binoculars revealed History arriving with Trotsky on the shores of France in 1933. It takes two hours and hundreds of shots for His-

105. Nora Grégor (the Marquise) and Jean Renoir (Octave) as participant observers in *La Règle du jeu* (1939).

tory to settle into its place, in the period that concerned Resnais. We conclude with a rhyming image from Jean Renoir's 1939 masterpiece, *La Règle du jeu*, shot on the eve of war with Germany. Through a small spyglass, Christine, the Marquise, catches her husband kissing another woman as the hosts and guests make their way to the château after a vicious rabbit hunt. This image gives her both false and true information: false, since the kiss is a perfunctory, insipid, final parting, yet true, since the woman has indeed been her husband's mistress. The rest of the film spreads out from both sides of the spyglass in equal measures of truth and falsity, creating a harmonics of ambiguity that suits the age.

La Règle du jeu, as André Bazin was to note, signals a metamorphosis in the history of cinema, whereby representation and critique—hence conflicting points of view—are not dissociable. Tellingly, it opens not with an action or a character in the drama but with a reporter. More tellingly, this reporter has abandoned the newspaper for the radio. She speaks excitedly into a microphone, describing the transatlantic touchdown of a heroic aviator (one thinks of Jean Mermoz or Edouard Corniglion-Molinier, or even of Malraux). The purity of the aviator's romantic motives cannot penetrate the intricate fabrications that make French society from top to bottom impervious to authenticity. In the end, a blood sacrifice is unavoidable. The foolish hero is shot down like a rabbit, and no one is responsible.

And so, only a year after his partisan Popular Front production *La Marseillaise*, Renoir stands here as an anthropologist, spyglass in hand, to view the intricate and nearly incomprehensible social rules of *La Règle du jeu*. Just how closely does his method parallel that of the Collège de Sociologie? When he finally left a fallen France and made his way to New York in 1941, did he run into Denis de Rougemont, a leader in the community of Francophone exiles? If so, did he remark on the title of de Rougemont's lecture series at New York's vibrant Ecole Libre des Hautes Etudes? Yes, de Rougemont, former fellow of the Collège de Sociologie could be found holding forth on the topic of *La Règle du jeu*, zigzagging between "regulation" and "play" in a manner that Jeffrey Mehlman suggests was both proto-Structuralist *(règle)* and Surrealist *(jeu)*. Mehlman neatly characterizes de Rougemont's ambiguous (or balanced) position by noting that it was he who wrote the Voice of America programs that were spoken over the air in tag-team fashion by Lévi-Strauss and Breton, the respective fathers of Structuralism and Surrealism. Just as he had in the 1930s, de Rougemont served as a voice of passionate moderation, suspicious of the moral convenience that extremism affords. This is the attitude Renoir adopts as the character Octave in *La Règle du jeu;* and it is a virtue found in the autobiography that Michel Leiris would project into a multivolume opus and for which he chose the very same title, *La Règle du jeu*. Whether Leiris was intentionally citing either Renoir or de Rougemont (or maybe both), this title insists on the interplay between system and player and, more specifically, between participant and observer, which is Christine's double role as she looks anxiously through that spyglass. Such intense participatory observation imparts to anthropology its risk and glory, and it is the condition of all interpretation, including the kind of history to which we subscribe. The bold reflexivity of these ambitious projects (masterpieces, in the cases of Renoir and Leiris) are models of the moral, intellectual, and aesthetic perspectives adopted in this book, where we have done our best to put the Popular Front back into its time—its *temps*—its atmosphere.

Notes

PROLOGUE

1. Julian Jackson, *The Popular Front in France: Defending Democracy, 1934–38* (New York: Cambridge University Press, 1988), p. 8.

2. See the essays in Martin S. Alexander and Helen Graham, eds., *The French and Spanish Popular Fronts: Comparative Perspectives* (New York: Cambridge University Press, 1989). Joel Colton's essay in this collection lists relevant works in French and English. Jackson provides an account of three historiographic traditions—*gauchiste*, Socialist, and French Communist Party (Jackson, *The Popular Front in France*, pp. x–xii). See also the bibliography in his earlier study, *The Politics of Depression in France, 1932–1936* (New York: Cambridge University Press, 1985).

3. Stephen Bann, *The Clothing of Clio: A Study of the Representation of History in Nineteenth-Century Britain and France* (New York: Cambridge University Press, 1984), p. 3.

4. We were taken with the collective nature of projects across traditional specializations and disciplines, particularly *Yale French Studies*, 59 (1980), an issue that bore the collective title *Time, Myth, and Writing* and featured work by noted historians, literary scholars, and sociologists. In French, we looked to Jacques Le Goff and Pierre Nora., eds., *Faire de l'Histoire* (Paris: Gallimard, 1974); Jacques Le Goff, ed., *La Nouvelle Histoire* (Paris: Retz CEPL, 1978); and Thierry Paquot, ed., *L'Histoire en France* (Paris: La Découverte, 1990).

5. See Lynn Hunt, *The Family Romance of the French* Revolution (Berkeley: University of California Press, 1992); Robert Darnton, *The Great Cat Massacre and Other Episodes in French Cultural History* (New York: Basic Books, 1984); and Natalie Zemon Davis, *The Return of Martin Guerre* (Cambridge, Mass.: Harvard University Press, 1983).

6. Roger Chartier sharply questions reliance on such lists of objects, positing the greater importance of the manner by which they were appropriated—in this case, the varied ways such books were read. See Chartier, *Culture écrite et société: L'Ordre des livres, XVI–XVIIIe siècles* (Paris: Albin Michel, 1996), pp. 143, 218.

7. Four years earlier, Allio had made *Les Camisards*, a filmed history of a Protestant sect of the seventeenth century, drawing on the work of Emmanuel Le Roy Ladurie. See *Avant-Scène Cinéma*, 122 (January 1972). A decade later, film had become attractive to historians, as when Natalie Davis helped to script Daniel Vigne's successful 1982 movie of *The Return of Martin Guerre*.

8. Stephen Greenblatt, "Towards a Poetics of Culture," in H. Aram Veeser, ed., *The New Historicism* (New York: Routledge, 1989).

9. See especially Pascal Ory, *La Belle Illusion: Culture et politique sous le signe du Front Populaire, 1935–1938* (Paris: Plon, 1994); and Olivier Barrot and Pascal Ory, eds., *Entre deux guerres: La Création française, 1919–1939* (Paris: François Bourin, 1990). Significant studies in English include George Melly, *Paris and the Surrealists* (New York: Thames and Hudson, 1991); Herman Lebovics, *True France: The Wars over Cultural Identity, 1900–1945* (Ithaca: Cornell University Press, 1992); Adrian Rifkin, *Street Noises: Parisian Pleasure, 1900–1940* (New York: Manchester University Press, 1993); Eugen Weber, *The Hollow Years: France in the 1930s* (New York: Norton, 1994); Michael B. Miller, *Shanghai on the Metro: Spies, Intrigue, and the French between the Wars* (Berkeley: University of California Press, 1994); Romy Golan, *Modernity and Nostalgia: Art and Politics in France between the Wars* (New Haven: Yale University Press, 1995); Siân Reynolds, *France between the Wars, Gender and Politics* (New York: Routledge, 1996); and James D. Herbert, *Paris 1937: Worlds on Exhibition* (Ithaca: Cornell University Press, 1998).

INTRODUCTION

1. James Monaco has written that the pyramid became the metaphorical emblem of the film, because the scandal following Stavisky's death showed him to have been "the peak of a structure of fraud that reached deep into the bowels of French society." According to Resnais, the small stone pyramid that appears in certain scenes was filmed in the Parc Monceau, near Stavisky's home: "One can dream of the young Sacha walking in the park, passing that mysterious pyramid." James Monaco, *Alain Resnais* (New York: Oxford University Press, 1979), p. 170.

2. Janet Flanner, *Paris Was Yesterday, 1925–1939* (New York: Harcourt Brace Jovanovich, 1988), p. 111. Flanner devotes three entries to Stavisky: pp. 109–111 and 114–116 comment on his death and the ensuing scandal, while pp. 154–155 comment on the 1935 trial held twenty-two months after his death.

3. Statement attributed to the attorney Jean-Charles Legrand, cited by Raymond Thévenin in Joseph Kessel, *Stavisky: L'Homme que j'ai connu* (Paris: Gallimard, 1974), p. 137.

4. Monaco, *Alain Resnais*, p. 68.

5. Jorge Semprun and Alain Resnais, *Stavisky . . .* , trans. Sabine Destrée (New York: Viking, 1975), p. 150.

6. Monaco, *Alain Resnais*, p. 175. Monaco's listing continues: "We also have Serge

the romantic hero whose mad love for his wife, Arlette, colors everything he does. Alexandre the failed theatrical producer. Sacha the pre-eminent model of elegance, extravagance, and noble repose who had no trouble disposing of 22 million francs in two years. Then we have the Serge Dr. Mézy describes as schizophrenic, and finally the legend Stavisky Resnais and Semprun remember from the media" (Monaco, *Alain Resnais*, pp. 175–176).

7. Richard Seaver, "Interview with Alain Resnais," in Semprun and Resnais, *Stavisky . . .* , p. 162.

8. Ibid.

9. Curtis Cate, *André Malraux: A Biography* (London: Random House, 1995), p. 176.

10. Semprun and Resnais, *Stavisky . . .* , p. 20.

11. For Dr. Mézy, Alexandre/Stavisky is totally sincere, a typical case of schizophrenia: "The person he once was has become someone else: a ghost he despises. But a ghost who worries him."

12. See J. Salles, *"L'Empire": Un Temple du spectacle* (Paris: S.F.P., 1975), which recounts the extraordinary months when Stavisky owned the theater.

13. One should add to this Guitry's possibly Jewish origins. On June 19, 1925, two weeks after the death of his father, Lucien Guitry, a journal insisted that Sacha was indeed Jewish. During the Occupation, Sacha spent some time refuting the implication so that he could keep appearing on the stage, a fact that did not work to his advantage after the Nazis left Paris in 1944.

14. Semprun and Resnais, *Stavisky . . .* , p. 156.

15. Dominique Desanti, *Sacha Guitry: 50 ans de spectacle* (Paris: Grasset, 1982), p. 246.

16. *Comoedia* (9 December 1933).

17. Kessel, *Stavisky*, p. 36. The first edition of the book appeared in March 1934. A second edition, with an updated appendix and a photo of Stavisky on the jacket, was released about the same time as Resnais' film. Kessel (1898–1979) was born in Argentina to Russian Jewish parents. After studying in Russia and France, he worked in the theater and then served in the French air force during World War I. He wrote in many different genres, often mixing investigative journalism with romance and adventure fiction set in Asia and Africa. Elected to the Académie Française in 1962, Kessel was author of the 1928 novel *Belle de jour*, adapted for the screen in 1967 by Luis Buñuel.

18. *Comoedia* (9 January 1934).

19. Bettina Knapp, *Louis Jouvet, Man of the Theater* (New York: Columbia University Press, 1958), pp. 148–149.

20. Semprun and Resnais, *Stavisky . . .* , p. 43.

21. *Comoedia* (4 February 1934).

22. Barthes, *Camera Lucida: Reflections on Photography*, trans. Richard Howard (New York: Hill and Wang, 1981).

23. Kessel, *Stavisky*, p. 7.

24. Ibid., pp. 93–94.

25. Cited in Henri-Charles Tauxe, *Georges Simenon: De l'humanisme au vide* (Paris: Buchet/Chastel, 1983), p. 108. At a later point, Simenon claimed he'd been advised to carry a gun to defend himself from reprisals by the criminal underground.

26. Ibid., p. 112. For a slightly different version of the same anecdote, see Lucille Becker, *Georges Simenon* (New York: Twayne, 1977), p. 111.

27. See Zeev Sternhell, *Neither Right nor Left: Fascist Ideology in France*, trans. David Maisel (Berkeley: University of California Press, 1986).

28. Cited in Eugen Weber, *Action Française: Royalism and Reaction in Twentieth-Century France* (Stanford: Stanford University Press, 1962) p. 321.

29. Fred Kupferman, "L'Affaire Stavisky," *L'Histoire*, 7 (December 1978): 44. Kupferman is quite hard on Resnais' film, seeing it as an entertainment ("un film de divertissement") transforming of a real swindler into a romanticized Arsène Lupin figure. Kupferman's conclusion: the film represents Stavisky's second and presumably final death.

30. Cited in Weber, *Action Française*, p. 349.

31. Carlo Rim, in *Marianne* (8 May 1934): 8.

32. See André Kaspi, *Les Juifs pendant l'occupation* (Paris: Seuil, 1991), pp. 104–110; and Raymond Bach, "Identifying Jews: The Legacy of the 1941 Exhibition, 'Le Juif et la France,'" *Studies in Twentieth Century Literature*, 23 (1999): 65–92.

33. The account is taken from Raymond Thévenin's afterword to the 1974 edition of Kessel's *Stavisky*, pp. 120–121. See also the epilogue in Paul F. Jankowski, *Stavisky: A Confidence Man in the Republic of Virtue* (Ithaca: Cornell University Press, 2002), pp. 263–266.

34. Jean-Louis Comolli, "Historical Fiction: A Body Too Much," *Screen*, 19, no. 2 (1978).

1. FEBRUARY 6, 1934, AND THE PRESS OF DIRECT ACTION

1. Marc Augé, *Paris, Années 30: Roger-Viollet* (Paris: Hazan, 1996), p. 10.

2. Charles Rearick, *The French in Love and War: Popular Culture in the Era of the Two World Wars* (New Haven: Yale University Press, 1997), p. 183.

3. Augé, *Paris, Années 30*, p. 21.

4. Ibid., p. 18.

5. Serge Berstein, *Le 6 février 1934* (Paris: Gallimard/Julliard, 1975), p. 11.

6. Cited in Eugen Weber, *Action Française: Royalism and Reaction in Twentieth-Century France* (Stanford: Stanford University Press, 1962), pp. 321–322.

7. Cited in Olivier Bernier, *Fireworks at Dusk: Paris in the Thirties* (Boston: Little Brown, 1993), p. 175.

8. Berstein, *Le 6 février 1934*, p. 57.

9. Ibid., p. 64.

10. Jean-François Sirinelli, *Intellectuels et passions françaises: Manifestes et pétitions au XXe siècle* (Paris: Fayard, 1990), p. 5. Sirinelli adds a third category: incarnation-texts *(textes-incarnations)*. These symbolize, in preliminary form, the coalition of groups on the left that spawned the Popular Front as movement and as government.

11. *Le Populaire* (11 February 1934). José Pierre reproduces a version in *Tracts surréalistes et déclarations collectives, I: 1922–1939* (Paris: Terrain Vague, 1980), pp. 262–264.

12. Sirinelli, *Intellectuels et passions françaises*, pp. 87–88.

13. Yves Santamaria, "Amsterdam-Pleyel," in Jacques Julliard and Michel Winock, eds., *Dictionnaire des intellectuels français* (Paris: Seuil, 1996), pp. 63–64.

14. Reproduced in Nicole Racine-Furlaud, "Antifascistes et pacifistes: Le Comité de Vigilance des Intellectuels Antifascistes," in Anne Roche et Christian Tarting, eds., *Des Années trente: Groupes et ruptures* (Paris: Centre National de la Recherche Scientifique, 1985), pp. 58–59.

15. Ibid., p. 57.

16. Nicole Racine-Furlaud, "Comité de Vigilance des Intellectuels Antifascistes (CVIA)," in Jacques Julliard and Michel Winock, eds., *Dictionnaire des intellectuels français* (Paris: Seuil, 1996), p. 298.

17. Sirinelli, *Intellectuels*, p. 91.

18. Martyn Cornick, *The "Nouvelle Revue Française" under Jean Paulhan, 1925–1940* (Amsterdam: Rodopi, 1995), p. 5.

19. Benjamin Crémieux, "Hypothèses autour du 6 février," *Nouvelle Revue Française*, 246 (March 1934): 541.

20. Pierre Drieu La Rochelle, "Air de février 34," *Nouvelle Revue Française*, 246 (March 1934): 568.

21. Pierre Drieu La Rochelle, "Guerre et révolution," *Nouvelle Revue Française*, 248 (May 1934): 888.

22. Pierre Drieu La Rochelle, *Socialisme fasciste* (Paris: Gallimard, 1934), p. 93.

23. Georges Bataille, "Popular Front in the Street," in idem, *Visions of Excess: Selected Writings, 1927–1939*, ed. Allan Stoekl (Minneapolis: University of Minnesota Press, 1985), p. 166. The article is based on a November 24, 1935, lecture first published in *Cahiers de la Contre-Attaque* (May 1936) and reprinted in Georges Bataille, *Oeuvres complètes* (Paris: Gallimard, 1970–1988), vol. 1, pp. 402–412. See also Bataille, "En attendant la grève générale," in idem, *Oeuvres complètes*, vol. 2, pp. 253–263.

24. Maurice Blanchot, "La Fin du six février," *Combat*, 2 (February 1936): 2.

25. Henri Lefebvre, "France Decides Europe's Fate," *New Republic* (22 April 1936), pp. 306–308.

26. Alice Yaeger Kaplan, "1945, February 6: Condemned to Death for His Activities as a Collaborator, Robert Brasillach Is Executed by Firing Squad," in Denis

392 | Notes to Pages 72–84

Hollier, ed., *A New History of French Literature* (Cambridge, Mass.: Harvard University Press, 1989), p. 968. See also Kaplan, *The Collaborator: The Trial and Execution of Robert Brasillach* (Chicago: University of Chicago Press, 2000).

27. Claude Estier, *La Gauche hebdomadaire, 1914–1962* (Paris: Armand Colin, 1962), p. 96. See also Lars A. Peterson, "The Age of the Weekly: Contesting Culture in the *Hebdomadaires Politico-Littéraires*, 1933–1940" (Ph.D. diss., University of Iowa, 2003).

28. Michel Winock, *Le Siècle des intellectuels* (Paris: Seuil, 1997), p. 271.

29. Herbert R. Lottman, *The Left Bank: Writers, Artists, and Politics from the Popular Front to the Cold War* (Chicago: University of Chicago Press, 1998), p. 73.

30. The articles in *Marianne* are "SOS" (11 October 1933) and "Trotsky" (25 April 1934). They are reprinted in André Malraux, *La Politique, la culture: Discours, articles, entretiens, 1925–1975*, ed. Janine Mossuz-Lavau (Paris: Gallimard, 1996). Over the next two years, Malraux published three articles on the defense of culture in the AEAR's monthly, *Commune*.

31. Emmanuel Berl, *Mort de la pensée bourgeoise: La Littérature* (Paris: Grasset, 1929), p. 25.

32. Patrick Modiano, *Dialogue avec Emmanuel Berl* (Paris: Gallimard, 1976), p. 117.

33. Ibid., p. 49.

34. Modiano, *Dialogue*, p. 117. Charles Péguy edited the *Cahiers de la Quinzaine* from 1900 to 1914.

35. *Marianne* (16 November 1932), p. 4.

36. Modiano, *Dialogue*, p. 75.

37. Lucie Mazauric, *Vive le Front Populaire* (Paris: Plon, 1976), p. 37.

38. Quoted in Géraldi Leroy and Anne Roche, eds. *Les Ecrivains et le Front Populaire* (Paris: Presses de la Fondation Nationale des Sciences Politiques, 1986), p. 98.

39. *Vendredi* (8 May 1936), cited in Winock, *Siècle*, p. 273.

40. Winock, *Siècle*, p. 277.

41. Bernard Laguerre, "*Vendredi*," in Julliard and Winock, *Dictionnaire*, p. 1149.

42. *Vendredi* (2 April 1937), p. 1.

43. *Vendredi* (6 August 1937), p. 3.

44. *Vendredi* (4 February 1938), p. 1.

45. *Vendredi* (13 May 1938), p. 1.

46. Lottman, *The Left Bank*, p. 85.

47. Cited in Roger Shattuck, "Having Congress: The Shame of the Thirties," in idem, *The Innocent Eye: On Modern Literature and the Arts* (New York: Farrar, Straus, Giroux, 1984), p. 4.

48. Ibid., p. 7.

49. See David L. Schalk, *The Spectrum of Political Engagement: Mounier, Benda,*

Nizan, Brasillach, Sartre (Princeton: Princeton University Press, 1979). This work remains a key source.

50. Margaret Cohen argues convincingly for the seriousness of the Marxist content in Breton's prose trilogy, *Nadja, Communicating Vessels*, and *Mad Love*. See Cohen, *Profane Illuminations: Walter Benjamin and the Paris of Surrealist Revolution* (Berkeley: University of California Press, 1993).

51. André Breton, "Second Manifesto of Surrealism," in *Manifestoes of Surrealism*, trans. Richard Seaver and Helen R. Lane (Ann Arbor: University of Michigan Press, 1972), p. 151.

52. The postwar Sartre excoriates Breton and the Surrealists as negative examples of the program of *littérature engagée* whose model of prose journalism he opposes to a poetic attitude to which he is once more sympathetic. See Steven Ungar, "Sartre, Breton, and Black Orpheus: Vicissitudes of Poetry and Politics," *Esprit Créateur*, 17, no. 1 (Spring 1977): 3–18.

53. Régis Debray, *Teachers, Writers, Celebrities: The Intellectuals of Modern France*, trans. David Macey (London: Verso, 1981).

54. See Bernard-Henri Lévy, *Le Siècle de Sartre* (Paris: Grasset, 2000), pp. 142–143.

55. Daudet had been Benda's lycée classmate but had turned on "that Jew" in 1912 to keep *L'Ordination* from taking the Prix Goncourt, which by all accounts it deserved. See Michel Winock, *Siècle*, pp. 239, 245.

56. Schalk, *Spectrum of Political Engagement*, p. 41.

57. Gide read the book immediately, discussing it in a letter written July 18, 1932. See *Correspondence André Gide–Roger Martin du Gard*, vol. 1 (Paris: Jean Delay, 1968), p. 553. Gide returned to Nizan's book two years later, "entirely approving" of its attack on the Cartesian influence in French thought. See Gide, "Feuillets retrouvés," in idem, *Littérature engagée*, ed. Yvonne Davet (Paris: Gallimard, 1950), p. 51.

58. Shattuck, "Having Congress," p. 5.

59. Citation and commentary in Schalk, *Spectrum of Political Engagement*, pp. 43–44.

60. In 1948, Queneau published a compendium of notes taken by attendees of Kojève's lectures. See Alexandre Kojève, *Introduction à la lecture de Hegel* (Paris: Gallimard, 1947; English translation, 1969). See also Michael S. Roth, *Knowing and History: Appropriations of Hegel in Twentieth-Century France* (Ithaca: Cornell University Press, 1988).

61. Richard Terdiman, *Discourse / Counter-Discourse: The Theory and Practice of Symbolic Resistance in Nineteenth-Century France* (Ithaca: Cornell University Press, 1985), p. 120.

62. Ibid., p. 117.

63. Robin Walz, *Pulp Surrealism: Insolent Popular Culture in Early Twentieth-Century Paris* (Berkeley: University of California Press, 2000), p. 3.

64. The figure is potentially misleading. Five million readers does not mean five million copies sold, since it is likely that each copy had several readers. See Raymond Manevy, *Histoire de la presse, 1914–1939* (Paris: Corréas, 1943), p. 149n.

2. CÉLINE AND MALRAUX

1. Régis Debray, *Teachers, Writers, Celebrities: The Intellectuals of Modern France*, trans. David Macey (London: Verso, 1981).

2. Denis Hollier, Paper delivered at conference entitled "Legacies of *J'Accuse:* The Public Intellectual in France, 1898–1998 and Beyond," Harvard University, November 1998.

3. To be fair, as we mentioned in Chapter 1, Ramon Fernandez—one of the eleven authors vying for the Goncourt that year—composed a brief notice about the novel in *Marianne* (November 16, 1932). His remarks were curt and objective, linking Céline to the tradition of the picaresque novel, and praising the first half of the book over the second. After the Goncourt fiasco, Paulhan evidently offered Céline space to write in the *NRF,* an offer that was refused. See Nicholas Hewitt, *Life of Céline* (London: Blackwell, 1999), p. 123.

4. Curtis Cate, *André Malraux: A Biography* (London: Hutchinson, 1995), p. 107.

5. In a review of *Les Conquérants*, Paul Morand emphasized Malraux's authentic adventures, the risks he took in China and with his health, and the risks evident in his prose. See Cate, *André Malraux*, p. 128.

6. Ibid., p. 134.

7. Leon Trotsky, "La Révolution étranglée," *NRF,* 211 (April 1, 1931), in *Malraux: A Collection of Critical Essays*, ed. R. W. B. Lewis (Englewood Cliffs, N.J.: Prentice-Hall, 1964).

8. André Malraux, "Réponse à Trotsky," *NRF,* 211 (April 1, 1931), translated ibid.

9. Mary Rowan, "Asia out of Focus," in Brian Thompson and C. Viggiani, eds., *Witnessing André Malraux* (Middletown, Conn.: Wesleyan University Press, 1984), pp. 33–35.

10. André Malraux, *The Conquerors*, trans. Stephen Becker (Chicago: University of Chicago Press, 1992), pp. 154 and 179 (Afterword). We have altered the translation to retain the English for Malraux's term *lucidité*, in place of Becker's word "logic."

11. André Bazin later understood this technique as deriving from Malraux's innate feeling for cinema. See "On *L'Espoir,* or Style in the Cinema," in Bazin, *French Cinema of the Occupation and Resistance* (New York: Ungar, 1981).

12. Leon Trotsky, "Céline et Poincaré, Novelist and Politician," *Atlantic Monthly* (October 1935), translated in *Leon Trotsky on Literature and Art*, ed. Paul N. Siegel (New York: Pathfinder Books, 1970).

13. "Manifesto of the Surrealists Concerning *L'Age d'or,*" collected in Paul Hammond, ed., *The Shadow and Its Shadow: Surrealist Writings on the Cinema*, 3rd ed. (San Francisco: City Lights, 2000), p. 182.

14. See Christopher L. Miller, *Blank Darkness: Africanist Discourse in French* (Chicago: University of Chicago Press, 1985), ch. 6.

15. Louis-Ferdinand Céline, *Journey to the End of the Night*, trans. John Marks (New York: New Directions, 1960), p. 121. Hereafter referred to in the text as *Journey*.

16. See Michèle Richman, "Rejection and Renewal: Durkheim in the Twentieth Century," in *Modern and Contemporary France*, 5, no. 4 (1997): 409–419; and idem, *Sacred Revolutions: Durkheim and the Collège de Sociologie* (Minneapolis: University of Minnesota, 2002).

17. Hewitt, *Life of Céline*, pp. 124–133.

18. Pierre Drieu La Rochelle, *Gilles* (Paris: Gallimard, 1939), pp. 590–609.

19. Hewitt, *Life of Céline*, p. 123.

20. Céline responded to an invitation from Mauriac: "We have nothing and can never have anything in common. You belong to another species, you see other people, you hear other voices. For me, a simpleton, God is a trick to help us think more highly of ourselves." Cited ibid., pp. 123–124.

3. *ESPRIT* IN THE ARENA OF EXTREMIST POLITICS

1. Denis de Rougemont, *Journal d'une époque* (Paris: Gallimard, 1965), pp. 318–320 and 332–334.

2. According to Pierre Verdaguer, de Rougemont would later bristle when the term *engagé* was credited to Sartre, especially because the latter, who had no affection for de Rougemont, never set the record straight (Pierre Verdaguer, Interview with Dudley Andrew, College Park, Maryland, 2002). A main source cited by Verdaguer is Jean Starobinski, "Remédier à la défaillance," *Ecriture* (Lausanne), 29 (Autumn 1987): 19–28. Starobinski begins his essay:

"It bears repeating: commitment [*engagement*], starting with the beginning of the 1930s, was the central theme of de Rougemont's thought, a theme that was obviously impossible for him to reserve for his personal use. The notion had meaning only on the condition that it proved to be contagious. It spread so rapidly that it became the password of the postwar existentialism inspired by Sartre. De Rougemont might have been somewhat bitter about it, not because he did not receive credit for inventing it (he never claimed to have coined the word *engagement*, available in every dictionary) but because commitment became an official badge sported by people who had nothing more urgent to do than abdicate their freedom."

3. Marc claimed to have taken the term "personalism" from the German thinker William Stern (the word is *personnalisme* in French, *Personalismus* in German). See Alexandre Marc, preface to Denis de Rougemont, *Inédits* (Neuchâtel: La Baconnière, 1988), p. 13.

4. De Rougemont prefaces Philippe Lamour's contribution to the *Cahier* by mentioning that his group, organized around the journal *Plans*, while undoubtedly close

to the personalism of the groups affiliated with *Esprit* and *L'Ordre Nouveau*, "differs from these radically by its determinist, Marxist postulates." Lamour was certainly not nearly as doctrinaire as Nizan or Lefebvre.

5. Denis de Rougemont, Preface to *Cahier de revendications*, in *Nouvelle Revue Française* (December 1, 1932): 801.

6. Paul Nizan, ibid., p. 806.

7. Jean-Louis Loubet del Bayle, *Les Non-conformistes des années 30* (Paris: Seuil, 1969), p. 173.

8. Thierry Maulnier, writing in *Combat* (June 1936), at the time the Popular Front took control of the French government. See Zeev Sternhell, *Neither Right nor Left: Fascist Ideology in France*, trans. David Maisel (Berkeley: University of California Press, 1986), p. 12.

9. Sternhell, *Neither Right nor Left*, pp. 18–19. See also Robert Soucy, *French Fascism: The Second Wave, 1933–1939* (New Haven: Yale University Press, 1995), pp. 57–58.

10. Denis de Rougemont, in *Cahier de revendications*

11. This was the name of the ideology put in place during the German Occupation. Many of its positions seemed worthy, attracting idealists after the defeat. See John Hellman, *Emmanuel Mounier and the New Catholic Left, 1930–1950* (Toronto: University of Toronto Press, 1981), p. 201.

12. Maurice Blanchot's relation to such groups, particularly to Thierry Maulnier's publications like *Combat*, presents a more complex and troubling problem. See Steven Ungar, *Scandal and Aftereffect: Blanchot and France since 1930* (Minneapolis: University of Minnesota Press), pp. 104–125.

13. Marc, Preface to de Rougemont, *Inédits*, p. 11.

14. Emmanuel Mounier, in *Cahier de revendications*, p. 826.

15. Georges Izard, ibid., pp. 828–829

16. Ibid., p. 829.

17. Robert Aron, in *Cahier de revendications*, p. 836.

18. Loubet del Bayle notes that de Rougemont claims Hitler's Parisian contacts, Joachim von Ribbentrop and Otto Abetz, stole the name *L'Ordre Nouveau* for Nazi propaganda at just this time. See Loubet del Bayle, *Les Non-conformistes*, p. 403.

19. Mounier, quoted ibid., p. 402.

20. Denis de Rougemont, "L'Esprit n'a pas son palais," *Esprit*, 37 (October 1935): 25–44.

21. Denis de Rougemont, in *Esprit* (October 1935).

22. Denis de Rougemont, *Love in the Western World*, trans. Montgomery Belgion (New York: Pantheon, 1956), p. 8.

23. De Rougemont reviewed books by André Breton and Tristan Tzara for *Esprit* in 1934 and 1935. He agreed with their tone of alarm in the face of a decadent materialist culture, but he scoffed at the naïveté of their "Hegelo-Marxist" solutions, which

he found ludicrously "in error" in their extremist views of language, psychology, and politics. Still, his acquaintance with their works helped to bring him into the orbit of the Collège de Sociologie. See especially *Esprit*, 33 (1935): 430–432.

24. De Rougement, *Love in the Western World*, p. 16.

25. Ibid., pp. 34–37.

26. Ibid., pp. 44–46.

27. Ibid., p. 53. The same virile Hegelian philosophy of life-in-death drove Georges Bataille to claim: "What there is of tragedy, that 'blinding miracle,' can be encountered now only in bed." See Bataille, "The Sorcerer's Apprentice," in Denis Hollier, ed., *The College of Sociology, 1937–1939*, trans. Betsy Wing (Minneapolis: University of Minnesota Press, 1988), pp. 18–19.

28. De Rougemont, *Love in the Western World*, p. 52.

29. Ibid., pp. 68–69.

30. Ibid., p. 107.

31. Ibid., p. 122.

32. Jean-Paul Sartre would take him to task for subscribing to the "myth of myth" of the 1930s (Sartre, Review of de Rougemont, *L'Amour et l'Occident*, in *Europe* [June 1939]). Denis Hollier catalogs several other attacks on myth written at the same time. See Hollier, ed., *The College of Sociology*, pp. 160–164.

33. Hollier, ed., *The College of Sociology*, pp. 260–261.

34. James Clifford, "Ethnographic Surrealism," in idem, *The Predicament of Culture: Twentieth-Century Ethnography, Literature, and Art* (Cambridge, Mass.: Harvard University Press, 1988). Michèle Richman, "From Emile Durkheim to the Collège de Sociologie," in Marc Manganaro, ed., *Modernist Anthropology* (Princeton: Princeton University Press, 1992).

35. The essays by Bataille and Caillois are translated in Hollier, ed., *The College of Sociology*.

36. De Rougemont commented favorably on this issue of *Acéphale* in *Esprit* (May 1937), further linking the two journals and two dispositions with which he felt comfortable.

37. De Rougemont, *Love in the Western World*, p. 266.

38. Frank S. Nugent, in *New York Times* (14 September 1937).

39. Emmanuel Mounier, "Letter from France," *Commonweal* (25 October 1940): 8–10.

40. Loubet del Bayle, *Les Non-conformistes*, p. 415.

41. De Rougemont, in *Cahier de revendications*, p. 843.

4. JEAN RENOIR'S *LA MARSEILLAISE*

1. Jean-Baptiste Duroselle, *La Décadence, 1932–39* (Paris: Imprimerie Nationale, 1979).

2. Cited in Julian Jackson, *The Popular Front in France: Defending Democracy, 1934–38* (Cambridge: Cambridge University Press, 1988), pp. 114–115.

3. Ibid., p. 119.

4. See Pascal Ory, *La Belle Illusion: Culture et politique sous le signe du Front populaire, 1935–1938* (Paris: Plon, 1994), p. 448.

5. Jean Renoir, in *Paris Soir* (11 February 1937).

6. The alleged rapport between Popular Front politics and "poetic realism" (the films of lower- and middle-class life by Clair, Vigo, Duvivier, Carné, Renoir, Jean Grémillon, Pierre Chenal) has no material basis. Although many poetic realist films did represent (in a picturesque, literary way) current social conditions and impasses, and although a critic like Graham Greene could judge French cinema the most "adult" in the world (*Graham Greene on Film* [New York: Simon and Schuster, 1972], p 111), these films were commercial ventures from start to finish. See Dudley Andrew, *Mists of Regret: Culture and Sensibility in Classic French Film* (Princeton: Princeton University Press, 1995).

7. Léo Lagrange, "Le Cinéma et les loisirs," *La Critique Cinématographique* (5 December 1936).

8. Hardest to accept was the forty-hour work week, which effectively banned a producer's right to schedule shooting in the most economical way (pushing for the completion of a scene by working late into the night, let's say).

9. Marcel Ruby, *Jean Zay: Député à 27 ans, ministre à 31 ans, prisonnier politique à 36 ans, assassiné à 39 ans* (Orléans: Corsaire, 1995), pp. 280–283; and Ory, *La Belle Illusion*, pp. 434–438.

10. See Claude Aveline, "Nous voulons voir *Zéro de conduite*," *Ciné-Liberté*, 3 (August 1936).

11. Henri Jeanson, "Lettre non-censurée à Jean Zay," *Ciné-Liberté*, 3 (August 1936). See also Ory, *La Belle Illusion*, pp. 429–431.

12. *Almanach Populaire, 1937* (Limoges: Imprimerie Nouvelle, 1937), p. 154.

13. See Jonathan Buchsbaum, *Cinema Engagé* (Urbana: University of Illinois Press, 1988), p. 164.

14. Martin Quigley, ed., *Motion Picture Almanac* (New York: Quigley, 1936), p. 1079. Directors who were named include Maurice Tourneur, Jacques Feyder, René Clair, Julien Duvivier, Léonce Perret, André Berthomieu, Marcel L'Herbier, Jean Benoît-Lévy, and Marc Allegret. The following year, Renoir was still not on the short list but *Le Crime de Monsieur Lange* was among the twenty-five films mentioned.

15. André Bazin, "The Evolution of the Language of Cinema," in *What Is Cinema?* trans. Hugh Gray (Berkeley: University of California, 1967), p. 30.

16. Renoir's leftist reputation also attracted Kurt Weill, who left Germany for Paris in spring 1933 under the pretext of working with Renoir, presumably on *Toni*. Nothing ever came of the meetings they held in Paris that spring. Kim Kowalke, "A Tale of Seven Cities: A Chronicle of the Sins," in booklet accompanying CD of Kurt Weill, *The Seven Deadly Sins; The Berlin Requiem*, recorded by the London Sinfonietta, conducted by David Atherton (PolyGram Records, 1989), p. 4.

17. The October Group, which took its name from the starting month of the 1917 Russian Revolution, was part of an agit-prop network that militated after World War I to promote working-class culture in Europe and the Soviet Union. The group known as Octobre emerged in 1932 after members of a French group, Prémices (Premises), contacted the writer and ex-Surrealist Jacques Prévert to stage a spectacle, "Vive la Presse" (Long Live the Press), for the annual May 1 (Labor Day) celebration organized by the PCF daily, *L'Humanité*. In June 1933, the group traveled to Moscow, where it won first prize at the International Olympiad of Working-Class Theater. By the time it disbanded, in the fall of 1936, the political climate had changed: the group was now far too strident for the relative moderation that the Popular Front sought to promote through coalitions on the left. Prévert and others in the group such as Jean-Louis Barrault, Jean-Paul Le Chanois, Yves Allegret, and Mouloudji focused their energies instead on film. See Michel Fauré, *Le Groupe Octobre* (Paris: Christian Bourgois, 1977). In English, see Claire Blakeway, *Jacques Prévert: Popular Front Theater and Cinema* (Rutherford, N.J.: Farleigh Dickinson University Press, 1990); and Andrew, *Mists of Regret*, pp. 78–82.

18. By 1936 both Gaumont and Pathé had ceased production, as had the Paris wing of Paramount. No individual producer or company could be said to dominate France. Yet neither the liberal government nor the radical *Ciné-Liberté* could inflect the course of cinema to any visible degree.

19. Jonathan Buchsbaum, *Cinema Engagé*, pp. 258–269; and Dudley Andrew, "Revolution and the Ordinary: Renoir's *La Marseillaise*," *Yale Journal of Criticism* (Autumn 1990).

20. Jean Cassou, "De l'avant-garde à l'art populaire," *Ciné-Liberté*, 4 (November 1936).

21. We should take into account the context of this remark, however, for it was made to an American audience just before D-Day. Jean Renoir, "A propos du film *La Marseillaise*," Transcript, 18 May 1944, Jean Renoir Archive, Special Collections, University of California, Los Angeles.

22. Henri Noguères, *La Vie quotidienne au temps du Front Populaire* (Paris: Hachette, 1977), p. 207.

23. Jacques Prévert, in *Images et Son*, 189 (December 1965): 59, cited in Blakeway, *Jacques Prévert*, p. 78. Blakeway relies on Fauré, *Le Groupe Octobre*, p. 340.

24. Ory, *La Belle Illusion*, pp. 448 and 930, note 170, cites Jean Bruhat, *Il n'est jamais trop tard* (Paris: Albin, 1983). See also *Le Travailleur du Film* (9 April 1937).

25. Jean Renoir, *La Marseillaise: Inédits*, ed. Claude Gauteur, (Paris: CNC, 1989). This pamphlet contains the two early script outlines dealt with here, plus an early and revealing draft of the prologue sequence in which the king learns of the fall of the Bastille while eating. The Renoir Archives at the University of California, Los Angeles, contain a typescript that seems to combine both versions. More ample than either, it makes frequent use of the wealth of information gathered for the project.

26. Jean Renoir, "La Forme et l'esprit: *La Marseillaise*," *Cahiers de la Jeunesse*, 7 (15 February 1937), reprinted in Jean Renoir, *Le Passé vivant* (Paris: Cahiers du Cinéma, 1989), p. 30.

27. Sally Shafto first drew our attention to Przybyszewska in a seminar presentation at the University of Iowa in 1996.

28. Daniel Gerould, "Stanislawa Przybyszewska and the Mechanism of Revolution," Introduction to Stanislawa Przybyszewska, *The Danton Case; Thermidor*, trans. Boleslaw Taborski (Evanston: Northwestern University Press, 1989).

29. See Eric Rohmer, *The Taste for Beauty*, trans. Carol Volk (New York: Cambridge University Press, 1987). This anthology of Rohmer's film criticism concludes with an entire section devoted to the brilliance of Renoir's films.

30. Frédéric Bonnaud, "First Look: Eric Rohmer's First Digital Feature," *Film Comment* (September–October 2001): 11.

31. Eric Rohmer, interview in *Libération* (7 September 2001): 29.

32. Philippe Azoury, *Libération* (7 September 2001).

33. Ibid.

34. Bonnaud, "First Look," p. 11.

35. Ory, *La Belle Illusion*, pp. 455–457.

36. Particularly caustic in its dismissal of Renoir is François Poulle, *Renoir 1938, ou Renoir pour rien* (Paris: Cerf, 1969).

37. See Louis Marin, "The Royal Host: The Historic Medal," in idem, *Portrait of the King*, trans. Martha Houle (Minneapolis: University of Minnesota Press, 1988).

38. Jean Renoir, quoted in *Positif* (April 1968): 4.

39. François Truffaut, quoted in André Bazin, *Jean Renoir*, trans. W. W. Halsey II and William H. Simon (New York: Simon and Schuster, 1973), p. 252.

40. Celia Bertin, *Jean Renoir: A Life in Pictures* (Baltimore: Johns Hopkins University Press, 1991), p. 144.

41. Geneviève Guillaume-Grimaut, *Le Cinéma du Front populaire* (Paris: Lherminier, 1986), p. 112.

42. Jules Michelet, *Histoire de la Révolution francaise*, ed. Gérard Walter (Paris: Gallimard, 1939).

43. Gerould, Introduction to Przybyszewska, *The Danton Case*, p. 11.

44. Ben Kennedy, "France's Celebration of the Cent-cinquantenaire of the Revolution in 1939 and Georges Lefebvre's *Quatre-vingt-neuf*," paper presented at NEH Summer Seminar for College Teachers, "France between the Wars," University of Iowa (1991).

45. These materials are preserved at the Jean Renoir Archives, University of California, Los Angeles.

46. Guillaume-Grimault, *Le Cinéma du Front populaire*, p. 107.

47. Johann Wolfgang von Goethe, *Campaign in France, 1792*, trans. Robert Farie (London: Chapman and Hall, 1849), p. 77.

48. Renoir reports this incredible statistic a year after the fact in *Ce Soir* (15 May 1939).

49. See Pierre Bost, in *Vendredi* (15 February 1938): "Renoir composes each episode, each tableau, with awareness and with love. Every moment of his work is for him a perfect universe, with neither past nor future. And that, precisely, is the view of a painter."

50. See Roger Leenhardt, in *Esprit* (March 1938): "The film fails on its own aesthetic principles. It's a matter of grasping History via anonymous and obscure characters—of giving a full portrait of the Revolution by following a group of men from Marseilles as they travel up to Paris."

51. Maurice Merleau-Ponty, "Eye and Mind," trans. Carleton Dallery, in Merleau-Ponty, *The Primacy of Perception and Other Essays*, ed. James M. Edie (Evanston: Northwestern University Press, 1964), p. 179.

52. Henri Jeanson, in *La Flèche de Paris* (18 February 1938). In his autobiography, *70 ans d'adolescence* (Paris: Stock, 1971), Jeanson virtually accuses Renoir of embezzlement.

53. Marcel Achard, in *Marianne* (16 February 1938).

5. DAILY LIFE IN THE CITY

1. This shift also responds to ongoing efforts by historians, anthropologists, and architects surrounding the topography of social space, the ethnography of everyday life, and urban ecology grounded in relations between the physical environment and the people who inhabit it. See Daniel Roche, *A History of Everyday Things: The Birth of Consumption in France, 1600–1800*, trans. B. Pearce (New York: Cambridge University Press, 2000), p. 82; and Stanford Anderson, "People in the Physical Environment: The Urban Ecology of Streets," in Anderson, ed., *On Streets* (Cambridge, Mass.: MIT Press, 1978), p. 1.

2. The 250 percent increase in the combined circulation of Parisian dailies over the years 1880–1914 solidified the dual role of the newspaper: as a primary means of access to information, and also a powerful form of mass entertainment. See Vanessa R. Schwartz, *Spectacular Realities: Early Mass Entertainment in Fin-de-Siècle France* (Berkeley: University of California Press, 1999), pp. 27–28. Schwartz cites the circulation increase given in Anne-Marie Thiesse, *Le Roman du quotidien* (Paris: Chemin Vert, 1984), p. 17.

3. Henri Lefebvre, *The Production of Space*, trans. Donald Nicholson-Smith (Cambridge: Blackwell, 1991; orig. pub. 1974), p. 386.

4. David P. Jordan, "Haussmann and *Haussmannisation:* The Legacy for Paris," *French Historical Studies*, 27, no. 1 (Winter 2004): 88. The characterization of Paris as an "urban machine" appears in Patrice Higonnet, *Paris: Capital of the World* (Cambridge, Mass.: Harvard University Press, 2002), pp. 177–204. See also David Harvey, *Paris: Capital of Modernity* (New York: Routledge, 2003).

5. Rosemary Wakeman, "Nostalgic Modernism and the Invention of Paris in the Twentieth Century," *French Historical Studies*, 27, no. 1 (Winter 2004): 117. Wakeman sees the nostalgic modernism that culminated under the Vichy regime and the early postwar years as a variant of and counterpoint to high modernist doctrines, such as those upheld by the Bauhaus movement. The relevant distinction here is less between change and timelessness than among multiple rates of change at various sites within the geographic space of the city.

6. Alistair Horne, *The Seven Ages of Paris* (New York: Knopf, 2002), p. 329.

7. Eugen Weber, *From Peasants into Frenchmen: The Modernization of Rural France* (Stanford: Stanford University Press, 1976).

8. Ralph Schor, "Le Paris des libertés," in André Kaspi and Antoine Marès, eds., *Le Paris des étrangers, depuis un siècle* (Paris: Imprimerie Nationale, 1989), p. 16.

9. David H. Weinberg, *A Community on Trial: The Jews of Paris in the 1930s* (Chicago: University of Chicago Press, 1977), p. viii. See also Jonathan Boyarin, *Polish Jews in Paris: The Ethnography of Memory* (Bloomington: Indiana University Press, 1991). In 1939, the number of Jews in France was estimated at over 300,000, more than twice the figure reported twenty years earlier. Opposition to this influx occurred among French-born Jews as well as non-Jews. See Paula Hyman, *The Jews of Modern France* (Berkeley: University of California Press, 1999), p. 138.

10. Eugen Weber, *The Hollow Years: France in the 1930s* (New York: Norton, 1994), p. 109. Four pages earlier, Weber cites an incendiary claim in the reactionary weekly *Candide* which asserted that Paris was turning into Canaan-on-the-Seine. See also Hyman, *The Jews of Modern France*, pp. 145–148.

11. See Philippe Dewitte, "Le Paris noir de l'entre-deux-guerres," in Kaspi and Marès, pp. 157–169; and Pascal Blanchard, Eric Deroo, and Gilles Manceron, *Le Paris noir* (Paris: Hazan, 2001). Relevant studies in English include Tyler Stovall, *Paris Noir: African Americans in the City of Light* (Boston: Houghton Mifflin, 1996); and Petrine Archer-Straw, *Negrophilia: Avant-Garde Paris and Black Culture in the 1920s* (New York: Thames and Hudson, 2000).

12. Alastair Phillips, *City of Darkness, City of Light: Emigré Filmmakers in Paris, 1929–1939* (Amsterdam, Holland: Amsterdam University Press, 2004), p. 53.

13. Benjamin Stora, "Les Algériens dans le Paris de l'entre-deux-guerres," in Kaspi and Marès, p. 144.

14. See David Henry Slavin, *Colonial Cinema and Imperial France: White Blind Spots, Male Fantasies, Settler Myths* (Baltimore: Johns Hopkins University Press, 2001), p. 201.

15. On such mapping, see Marc Augé, *In the Metro*, trans. Tom Conley (Minneapolis: University of Minnesota Press, 2002). Augé's account straddles ethnography and personal memoir. On circulation in areas surrounding the city, see François Maspero, *Roissy Express: A Journey through the Paris Suburbs*, trans. P. Jones (New York: Verso,

1994). Annie Ernaux's *Journal du dehors* (Paris: Gallimard 1994) and *La Vie extérieure* (Paris: Gallimard, 2001) are diary accounts of her experiences commuting on regional express trains of the RER—Réseau Express Régional—system between Paris and the new town (*ville nouvelle)* of Cergy.

16. Norma Evenson, *Paris: A Century of Change, 1878–1978* (New Haven: Yale University Press, 1979), p. 272.

17. Ibid., p. 208.

18. Henri Noguères, *La Vie quotidienne en France au temps du Front populaire, 1935–1938* (Paris: Hachette, 1977), p. 100; and Ian Walker, "Terrain vague," in Walker, *City Gorged with Dreams: Surrealism and Documentary Photography in Interwar Paris* (New York: Manchester University Press, 2002).

19. Higonnet, *Paris: Capital of the World*, p. 186.

20. Walter Benjamin cites the term *artiste démolisseur* in *The Arcades Project*, trans. Howard Eiland and Kevin McLaughlin (Cambridge, Mass.: Harvard University Press, 1999), p. 12. Critical accounts of Haussmann's projects include Howard Saalman, *Haussmann: Paris Transformed* (New York: Braziller, 1971); and David P. Jordan, *Transforming Paris: The Life and Labors of Baron Haussmann* (New York: Free Press, 1995).

21. The current avenue de l'Opéra, which extends to the north-northwest from the Place Colette near the Palais Royal and the Louvre to the Place de l'Opéra, was constructed in the years 1864–1873. Before its completion, it was known as the boulevard Napoléon (Jacques Hillairet, *Dictionnaire historique des rues de Paris*, 10th ed. [Paris: Minuit, 1997], vol. 2, p. 197). On the emergence of the Parisian department store, see Rosalind H. Williams, *Dream Worlds: Mass Consumption in Late Nineteenth-Century France* (Berkeley: University of California Press, 1982); Michael B. Miller, *The Bon Marché: Bourgeois Culture and the Department Store, 1869–1920* (Princeton: Princeton University Press, 1981); and Beatrix Le Wita, *French Bourgeois Culture*, trans. J. A. Underwood (Cambridge: Cambridge University Press, 1994).

22. See Marc Augé, *Non-Places: Introduction to an Anthropology of Supermodernity*, trans. John Howe (London: Verso, 1995).

23. Horne, *The Seven Ages of Paris*, p. 330.

24. Wolfgang Schivelbusch, *The Railway Journey: The Industrialization of Time and Space in the Nineteenth Century* (Berkeley: University of California Press, 1986), p. 188.

25. Louis-Ferdinand Céline, *Journey to the End of the Night*, trans. John Marks (New York: New Directions, 1960), pp. 70–71. Ralph Manheim's 1983 translation of the *Voyage* renders the end of the passage more concisely: "All the rest is shit."

26. René Duval, "Ondes," in Olivier Barrot and Pascal Ory, eds., *Entre deux guerres: La Création française, 1919–1939* (Paris: François Bourin, 1990), p. 129.

27. Cecile Méadel, *Histoire de la radio des années trente* (Paris: Anthropos / Institut National de l'Audiovisuel, 1994), p. 32.

28. Duval, "Ondes," p. 141.

29. Jonathan Buchsbaum, *Cinema Engagé: Film in the Popular Front* (Urbana: University of Illinois Press, 1988), pp. 68–72.

30. Pascal Ory, *La Belle Illusion: Culture et politique sous le signe du Front populaire, 1935–1938* (Paris: Plon, 1992), pp. 571–573; and Méadel, *Histoire de la radio des années trente*, p. 103. On the politics of programming, see also Joëlle Neulander, "Broadcasting Morality: Family Values and the Culture of the Radio in 1930s France" (Ph.D. diss., University of Iowa, 2001). For a discussion of the aspirations for radio entertained by the Surrealists and others of the avant-garde who worked in this new industry, see Anke Birkenmaier, "Radio y surrealismo: La diseminación de un movimiento," in Birkenmaier, "Alejo Carpentier y la cultura del surrealismo en América Latina" (Ph.D. diss., Yale University, 2004).

31. Méadel, *Histoire de la radio des années trente*, p. 9.

32. Jacques Kergoat, *La France du Front populaire* (Paris: La Découverte, 1986), 355.

33. Ibid., p. 359.

34. Josephine Baker, who was born in St. Louis, Missouri, warrants special mention because the Parisian persona she fashioned exploited an exoticism that homegrown ("white") stars such as Fréhel, Damia (née Marie-Louise Damien), and Arletty (née Léonie Bathiat) were simply unable to convey. On Baker in the context of interwar Paris and the transition from live entertainment to sound film, see Elizabeth Ezra, "A Colonial Princess: Josephine Baker's French Films," in idem, *The Colonial Unconscious: Race and Culture in Interwar France* (Ithaca: Cornell University Press, 2000), pp. 97–128.

35. Kelley Conway, "'Les Goualeuses' de l'écran," in Emmanuelle Toulet, ed., *Le Cinéma au rendez-vous des arts: Années 20 et 30* (Paris: Bibliothèque Nationale de France, 1995), p. 171.

36. Elizabeth Wilson, *The Sphinx in the City: Urban Life, the Control of Disorder, and Women* (London: Virago, 1991), p. 9.

37. Denis Hollier, "Birthrate and Death Wish," in Hollier, ed., *A New History of French Literature* (Cambridge, Mass.: Harvard University Press, 1989), pp. 919–924.

38. Mary Louise Roberts, *Civilization without Sexes: Reconstructing Gender in Postwar France, 1917–1927* (Chicago: University of Chicago Press, 1994), p. 154.

39. Ibid., p. 85.

40. Weber, *The Hollow Years*, p. 62. Weber adds that in those days the cost of a washer-dryer in France was the equivalent of about 1,200 hours of a cleaning woman's wages, which was three to four times the labor cost of an equivalent appliance in the United States.

41. Anne-Marie Sohn, "Between the Wars in France and England," in Françoise Thébaud, ed., *A History of Women, Volume 5: Toward a Cultural Identity in the Twentieth Century* (Cambridge, Mass.: Harvard University Press, 1994), p. 102.

42. Siân Reynolds, *France between the Wars: Gender and Politics* (New York: Routledge, 1996), p. 86.

43. Ibid., pp. 85–86.

44. Richard Cobb, *People and Places* (New York: Oxford University Press, 1985), p. 159.

6. POPULAR ENTERTAINMENT AND THE DECAY OF INTIMACY

1. Louis Chevalier, *Montmartre du plaisir et du crime* (Paris: Robert Laffont, 1980), p. 443.

2. For a thorough analysis of this effect, see the discussion of *Le Million* in Marcia Butzel, "Choreography and the Camera" (Ph.D. diss., University of Iowa, 1984).

3. Pierre Dufay, "De l'Alcazar au cinéma," *Mercure de France* (1 September 1933): 302.

4. Ibid., p. 302.

5. Charles Rearick, *The Pleasures of the Belle Epoque* (New Haven: Yale University Press, 1985), p. 75.

6. T. J. Clark, *The Painting of Modern Life: Paris in the Art of Manet and His Followers* (New York: Knopf, 1984), pp. 205–258.

7. Clark cites the disgust with which this morally altered Paris was received by the Goncourt brothers in their journals. They specifically lamented the lost private values of the 1832–1848 period, which had given way to a completely public life, most visible in the public houses of these cafés. See ibid., pp. 212–214.

8. Dufay, "De l'Alcazar au cinéma," pp. 317–320.

9. Ibid., p. 330.

10. Pierre Loiselet, "Défense du music-hall," *Paris Soir* (1933; precise date uncertain), collection of the Bibliothèque de l'Arsenal (Paris), Fonds Rondel, Ro 15.643.

11. François Caradec and Alain Weill, *Le Café-Concert* (Paris: Hachette, 1980), p. 7.

12. See Rearick, *Pleasures of the Belle Epoque*, pp. 57–60.

13. See X. Hochlein, "The Berlin Café" (Ph.D. diss., New York University, 1978).

14. Caradec, *Le Café-Concert*, pp. 86–88.

15. Pascal Sevran, *Le Music-Hall français, de Mayol à Julien Clerc* (Paris: Olivier Orban, 1978), p. 49.

16. Eugène Dabit, *Journal intime* (Paris: Gallimard, 1989), pp. 253–254.

17. Ibid., p. 253.

18. The modernity of Georgius helped him to outlive the *caf'conc'* itself. While so many other big names of the prewar era maintained their visibility after World War II only by appearing in nostalgic re-creations of vaudeville, he turned instead to another medium altogether, one that was right up to date: the detective novel. According to Caradec and Weill, Georgius published *Tête-blonde* (translated as *My Fair Lady*) in 1947, and then, after 1955, under the pseudonym Jo Barnais, he turned out a complete

collection of novels for the Série Noire edited by Marcel Duhamel. Duhamel had been a fan of Georgius' cabaret routines. See Caradec and Weill, *Le Café-Concert*, pp. 86–88. In the 1950s Marcel Duhamel, then editor of the Série Noire at Gallimard, would publish three detective novels that Georgius wrote after ending his career as a performer. See Marcel Duhamel, *Raconte pas ta vie* (Paris: Mercure de France, 1972), p. 205.

19. Ibid., p. 140.

20. Dufay, "De l'Alcazar au cinéma," p. 302.

21. Rearick, *Pleasures of the Belle Epoque*, p. 83.

22. Jacques-Charles, *Le Caf'Conc'* (Paris: Flammarion, 1966), p. 16.

23. See Rearick, *Pleasures of the Belle Epoque*, p. 74.

24. Legrand-Chabrier, "Le Music-Hall," in *Les Spectacles à travers les âges* (Paris: Cygne, 1931), p. 256.

25. See Tom Gunning, "The Cinema of Attractions: Early Film, Its Spectator, and the Avant-Garde," in Thomas Elsaesser and Adam Barker, eds., *Early Film* (London: British Film Institute, 1989).

26. Pierre Bost, *Le Cirque et le music-hall* (Paris: Sans-Pareil, 1931), p. 28. Bost, who would later write novels, was clearly aware of the import of this idea.

27. Bost, *Le Cirque et le music-hall*. We take the phrase "single overall effect" from his book.

28. Dufay, "De l'Alcazar au cinéma," p. 334.

29. *Paris Music-Hall* (15 February 1925).

30. Loiselet, "Défense du music-hall."

31. Bost, *Le Cirque et le music-hall*, p. 136. Bost, a young novelist, would become an architect of the notorious *cinéma de qualité*, which was excoriated by François Truffaut and defended by Bertrand Tavernier.

32. Bost, *Le Cirque et le music-hall*, p. 25.

33. *Paris Music-Hall* (1 September 1930).

34. Legrand-Chabrier, "Le Music-Hall," p. 256.

35. The Folies Bergère showed movies early on, but resisted a final annexation by cinema. La Cigale and the Trianon became movie palaces in 1927 and 1939, respectively. The Eldorado, which had shown films in 1896, became a cinema in 1932 and the Ba-ta-clan was converted in 1932. The Olympia (where in 1896 the Lumière brothers had displayed their apparatus) was absorbed by a film exhibitor in 1930.

36. *La Cinématographie Française*, 986 (24 September 1937): 89.

37. In 1936 movie theaters paid more than 17 percent of their income in the form of taxes, while music halls paid less than 13 percent and theaters only around 10 percent. (Ibid.)

38. See Alexander Sesonske, *Jean Renoir: The French Films, 1924–1939* (Cambridge, Mass.: Harvard University Press, 1980), pp. 185–186.

39. The sensational murder of the music-hall czar Oscar Dufrenne, director of the Casino de Paris and a municipal councillor, rocked the entertainment world a few months before the Stavisky revelations. See Chevalier, *Montmartre du plaisir et du crime*, p. 420.

40. Théodore de Banville, *Souvenirs*, quoted in Dufay, "De l'Alcazar au cinéma," p. 307.

41. Ibid.

42. Georges Tabet, *Vivre deux fois* (Paris: Robert Laffont, 1979), p. 155.

43. Ginette Vincendeau, *Pépé le Moko* (London: British Film Institute, 1998), p. 119.

44. This kind of media rivalry is the subject of Jim Collins, *Uncommon Cultures: Popular Culture and Post-Modernism* (New York: Routledge, 1989).

45. Important analyses of Josephine Baker's impact on cinema include Elizabeth Ezra, "A Colonial Princess: Josephine Baker's French Films," in *The Colonial Unconscious: Race and Culture in Interwar France* (Ithaca: Cornell University Press, 2000); Felicia McCarren, *Dancing Machines: Choreographies in the Age of Mechanical Reproduction* (Stanford: Stanford University Press, 2003); and Terri Francis, "Josephine Baker's Museum: Black Dance, French Cinema, Harlem Renaissance" (Ph.D. diss., University of Chicago, 2004).

46. Maurice Chevalier, in *Le Music-Hall*, 3 (11 October 1935).

47. See *Le Music-Hall*, 2 (27 September 1935).

48. See Ginette Vincendeau, "French Cinema in the 1930s: Social Text and Context of a Popular Entertainment Medium" (Ph.D. diss., University of East Anglia, 1985), p. 81. Of course, a ticket to a first-run film could cost as much as an inferior seat at a music hall.

49. Bost, *Le Cirque et le music-hall*, pp. 28–33.

50. Ibid., p. 21.

51. Both the music hall and the theater made this appeal to authority, as a response to the talking cinema and to the radio. Drama journals, engaged in what Jean Fayard called the "querelle du cinéma," continually reminded theater to be faithful to its mission of uplifting individuals through the communication of ideas, as opposed to the mindless spectacle that infatuates the masses who flock to the movies (see Fayard, *La Querelle du cinéma* [1933]). But the theater had already succumbed in other ways to modern, mass-entertainment practices. Charles Dullin (*Ce sont les dieux qu'il nous faut* [Paris: Gallimard, 1967]) summed up the standard view when he blamed the weakness of twentieth-century theater on the loss of the family atmosphere within companies. Before World War I, every significant acting troupe was led by a key actor who also served as its administrator. This dual role gave definition to the troupe's style and its choice of repertory, and maintained consistency and morale among the actors. But the 1920s brought a new breed of theatrical entrepreneur, modeled on the Hollywood

producer or music-hall magnate. Plays were chosen, actors engaged, and sets designed with nothing but immediate proceeds in mind. Of course, small theaters based on traditional or avant-garde values continued to attract a small elite audience, but popular theater had indeed been corrupted by the business practices and appeals with which the cinema overwhelmed all competitors in this era.

52. In fact, the melodramatic style that fanned the growth of the *caf'conc'* fifty years earlier had been derailed by the joyous, often irreverent, and scintillating songs of Mistinguett, among many others. The music hall's fabulous growth just after the First World War coincided with the arrival of American jazz. Josephine Baker, Mireille (née Mireille Hartuch), Charles Trenet, and many others recruited the energy of jazz for their own purposes.

53. Pascal Sevran has made this link between the *chanson réaliste* and poetic realist cinema in his entry on Fréhel in *Le Music-Hall français, de Mayol à Julien Clerc*. See also Ginette Vincendeau, "The Mise-en-Scène of Suffering: French *Chanteuses Réalistes*," *New Formations*, 3 (Winter 1987): 107–128; Kelley Conway, "Flower of the Asphalt: Popular Song, Gender, and Urban Space in 1930s French Cinema," in Pamela Robertson and Arthur Knight, eds., *Soundtrack Available: Essays on Film and Popular Music* (Durham: Duke University Press, forthcoming); and Kelley Conway, *Chanteuse in the City: The Realist Singer in French Film* (Berkeley: University of California Press, 2004).

54. Florelle's song references the part of Paris evoked by Jean Gabin and Mireille Balin during their litany of Métro stops in *Pépé le Moko*. But theirs is already a nostalgic dialogue, for the Right Bank *quartier* just south of Montmartre had changed. Writing in 1932, Maurice Sachs rued the post–World War I shift in music-hall clientele that he noticed in 1923. "The concert and music halls built their success on visiting foreigners. . . . Oh, my American friends, how greedily you trotted toward that Montmartre brilliant with promise, and were properly deceived!" Maurice Sachs, *A Decade of Illusion, 1918–1928*, trans. Gladys Matthews Sachs (New York: Knopf, 1933), p. 36. For a thorough history of the entire Montmartre scene, see Louis Chevalier, *Montmartre du plaisir et du crime*, pp. 321–451.

55. See Chevalier, *Montmartre du plaisir et du crime*, pp. 343–346. Chevalier gives ample evidence for Montmartre and its *bals* as the nexus of various families of anarchists, criminals, and bohemians right up to World War II. Part V, chapter 4, discusses the various *bandes* (gangs) from Corsica, Poland, and elsewhere. Part VI, chapter 2, treats "La Signification du bal," "La Misère et le crime," "Le Plaisir plus que la misère," "Tournées des bals," and so on. Chapter 3 continues with a discussion of "Les 'Vrais' du milieu."

56. For a discussion of these writers in relation to the cinema, see Dudley Andrew, "The Impact of the Novel on French Cinema of the 1930s," *L'Esprit Créateur* 30, no. 2 (Summer 1990): 3–13.

57. This *bal* in fact is a seedy bar in Dakar. The choice of a colonial setting for Mistinguett's dark past plays into an ideology that we will discuss in Chapter 9.

7. THE LOOK OF PARIS IN THE AGE OF ART DECO

1. See Chapter 6 for a discussion of the rivalry between these forms of entertainment—a rivalry whose balance was swiftly falling on the side of cinema at precisely this time, in the early 1930s.

2. Francis Lacloche, *Achitectures de cinémas* (Paris: Moniteur, 1981), p. 97.

3. Its reputation endures. In 1998, for instance, the Rex was the ideal site for the long run of *Titanic*, until then the most expensive film ever made.

4. *L'Illustration* (1 December 1934): xxxix.

5. James Herbert, *Paris 1937: Worlds on Exhibit* (Ithaca: Cornell University Press, 1998), pp. 46–48, 64–67.

6. Twenty studios paid taxes during the 1930s, but most were not large enough for full-scale sound productions.

7. The Rex opened its doors in December 1932 with Diamant-Berger's blockbuster *Les Trois Mousquetaires*. Its 1933 season featured lighter French films, like those starring the singer and comedian Bach (né Charles-Joseph Pasquier).

8. Composed during the Commune in 1870, "Le Temps des cerises" can be heard in a series of working-class films, right up to Alain Tanner's 1975 feature, *Jonah Who Will Be 25 in the Year 2000*. Jean-Paul Le Chanois' film uses the song as its title to complement Renoir's *La Marseillaise*. The nostalgia the song evokes in its title and theme became mingled with regret for the passing of the Popular Front. Jacques Becker used the song to reference Le Chanois' film in his 1951 *Casque d'or*; and Tanner, in reprising the song in 1975, was thus citing Becker's 1951 reference to the 1937 glory years. And so this sentimental song carries the echo of decades of social movement in France, resonating most powerfully with the 1930s. See Andrew, *Mists of Regret*, pp. 344, 389.

9. More ironic still is the fact that until 1997, when it was moved, the Palais de Chaillot was where the Cinémathèque had offered bargain tickets to the elderly men and women of Paris, who perhaps had been poor young lovers themselves back in 1937. In their later years, they came there to relish the films of their youth—Hollywood products, of course, but French films above all, many of which showed them a Paris that had been inaccessible to them during the Depression. Ironically, *Le Temps des cerises* would eventually be screened in this "palace." By then, Le Chanois would be known not as the PCF's designated director but as a bankable studio stalwart, responsible for the popular Don Camillo series and for the 1956 version of *Les Misérables*.

10. *Paris 1937: L'Art indépendant*, Exhibition catalogue, Musée d'Art Moderne, Paris (June–August 1987), p. 44.

11. Ibid., p. 45.

12. Herbert, *Paris 1937*, p. 100; and *Paris 1937: L'Art indépendant*. Escholier's rather direct challenge can be found on page 5 of his preamble to the 1937 original catalogue of his exhibition.

13. Jeanne Laurent, *Arts et pouvoirs en France de 1793 à 1981: Histoire d'une démission artistique* (Saint-Etienne: Université de Saint-Etienne, Centre Interdisciplinaire d'Etudes et de Recherches sur l'Expression Contemporaine, 1983), p. 112.

14. A rundown of all the painters, along with the number of pieces displayed, can be found in *Paris 1937: L'Art indépendant*, p. 48.

15. Louis Gillet, writing in *Revue des Deux Mondes* (15 July 1937). Herbert (*Paris 1937*, pp. 105–108) discusses Gillet's notion of the continuity of French art under the equilibrium of "intelligence and sensuality," which can be thought of as constituting a human totality at the base of the global totality of the International Exposition.

16. *Paris 1937: L'Art indépendant*, p. 44.

17. For a discussion of realist tendencies in 1930s painting, see *L'Art dans les années 30*, Catalogue of exhibition, March–May 1979 (Sainte-Etienne: Musée d'Art et Industrie, 1979); *Les Réalismes, 1919–1939*, Catalogue of exhibition, December 1980–April 1981 (Paris: Editions Centre Georges Pompidou, 1980); and *Force Nouvelle, 1935–1939*, Catalogue of exhibition, February–March 1980 (Paris: Musée d'Art Moderne de la Ville de Paris, 1980). Also see Raoul-Jean Moulin, "La Longue Marche de Tal-Coat," in *Tal-Coat: Oeuvres de 1926–1946* (Paris: Galerie Fanny-Laffaille), pp. 6–7. For a discussion of Taslitzsky in relation to social realist painting of the period, see *Années 30 en Europe: Le Temps menaçant, 1929–39* (Paris: Paris-Musées, 1997), pp. 369–414. A color reproduction of *Les Grèves de juin 1936* appears on p. 381.

18. Harold Osborne, ed., *The Oxford Companion to Art* (New York: Oxford University Press, 1970), p. 814.

19. Romy Golan, *Modernity and Nostalgia: Art and Politics in France between the Wars* (New Haven: Yale University Press, 1995).

20. Ibid., p. 143. For evidence, Golan points to the many paintings and sculptures bearing the motif of the accordionist playing at *bals populaires* in Montparnasse.

21. This museum in Boulogne-Billancourt opened in 1998 to great fanfare. See Emmanuel Bréon and Michèle Lefrançois, eds., *Le Musée des années trente* (Paris: Somogy, 1998), especially p. 18.

22. Ginette Vincendeau, "French Cinema of the 1930s: Social Text and Context of a Popular Entertainment Medium" (Ph.D. diss., University of East Anglia, 1985).

23. François Garçon, *De Blum à Pétain: Cinéma et société en France, 1936–45* (Paris: Cerf, 1984).

24. As an additional irony, Clair contrived to include the Epinay Studios (where the film was made) in the ugly landscape shot displaying the visual impoverishment of modernity.

25. Dudley Andrew, *Mists of Regret: Culture and Sensibility in Classic French Film* (Princeton: Princeton University Press, 1995).

26. Claude Vermorel, in *Pour Vous*, 481 (2 February 1938): 4.

27. Jonathan Buchsbaum, *Cinema Engagé: Film in the Popular Front* (Urbana: University of Illinois Press, 1988), p. 268.

28. Marcel Carné, "When Will the Cinema Go Down into the Street?" in Richard Abel, ed., *French Film Theory and Criticism*, vol. 2 (Princeton: Princeton University Press, 1988), pp. 102–103. Originally published in *Cinémagazine*, 12 (November 1932).

29. Pierre Chenal failed to start a trend when, in 1933, he shot *La Rue sans nom* entirely on location.

30. See the discussion in Edward Turk, *Child of Paradise: Marcel Carné and the Golden Age of French Cinema* (Cambridge, Mass.: Harvard University Press, 1990), p. 65.

31. Andrew, *Mists of Regret*, chs. 7 and 8.

32. Siân Reynolds has documented two exhibitions featured the work of "exiles and outsiders." One of these, "Les Dix" (1936), treated Kertész, François Kollar, and other bohemian photographers as modern-day equivalents of Emile Zola. Reynolds, "Exiles and Outsiders Photographing Paris," Address at conference entitled "Picturing Paris: Visual Cultures and Urban Identities in the Paris of the 1930s," University of Warwick, March 7, 1998.

33. Jerrold Seigel, *Bohemian Paris: Culture, Politics, and the Boundaries of Bourgeois Life, 1830–1930* (New York: Viking, 1986), p. 392. Seigel links artists, social outcasts, and dropouts as allied groups who inhabited a zone geographically on the margins of the city, where they lived isolated from the bourgeoisie (whom they despised) yet where they were also cut off from the proletariat (whose conditions of life they did not really share). World War I effectively ended the innocent age of *la bohème*—the bohemian world—of Montmartre, after which it became self-conscious and even commercialized. But *la bohème* persisted into the 1930s as a lifestyle (Henry Miller) and a style of art (Brassaï) set against the official face the city turned to the world.

34. See Marie de Thézy, *Marville Paris* (Paris: Hazan, 1994).

35. Teri Wehn-Damisch interviews Trauner in her 1991 film, *Voyage surprise d'Alexandre Trauner.*

36. Dominique Baqué, *Les Documents de la modernité: Anthologie de textes sur la photographie de 1919 à 1939* (Paris: J. Chambon, 1993), p. 161.

37. Jean Vétheuil, in *Photo-cinématographie*, 21 (November 1934), reprinted in Baqué, *Les Documents de la modernité*, p. 165.

38. Pierre Mac Orlan, Preface, in *Paris vu par André Kertész* (Paris: Plon, 1934). See also Dabit, "Paris par André Kertész," *NRF* (March 1935).

39. *L'Illustration* (2 December 1933). Dunoyer de Segonzac is one of the chief *terrien* artists discussed by Romy Golan.

40. Paul Fierens, in *Variétés* (15 November 1929): 508, reprinted in Baqué, *Les Documents de la modernité*, p. 168.

41. Mallet-Walton, "La Rue et le photographe," *La Revue Française de Photographie*, 144 (15 June 1938): 134, reprinted in Baqué, *Les Documents de la modernité*, p. 167.

42. Robert Short, Lecture on committed photography in Popular Front France, University of Iowa (Spring 1993).

43. See Chapter 6, above. See also Andrew, *Mists of Regret*, pp. 216–225.

44. Golan, *Modernity and Nostalgia*, p. 148. Golan takes her cue from Kim Sichel, "Les Photographes étrangers à Paris," in André Kaspi and Antoine Marès, eds., *Le Paris des étrangers depuis un siècle* (Paris: Imprimerie Nationale, 1989), pp. 257–267.

45. Mallet-Walton, "La Rue et le photographe."

46. Benjamin had recourse to the Baudelairean term *flânerie* to characterize his friend Franz Hessel, whose book *Spazieren in Berlin* had just appeared. Hessel was one of those modern types who wanders aimlessly through the city noting whatever strikes his fancy, thus both a parasite and a consumer of the visual environment. See Anke Gleber, *The Art of Taking a Walk: Flânerie, Literature, and Film in Weimar Culture* (Princeton: Princeton University Press, 1999).

47. Paul Fierens, in *Variétés*, 7 (15 November 1929): 507–508, reprinted in Baqué, *Les Documents de la modernité*, pp. 167–168.

48. Brassaï (born Gyula Halász in 1899) was a journalist and writer who turned to photography soon after he moved from his native Hungary to Paris, where his friends in the 1930s included Henry Miller and Pablo Picasso. His 1976 book *Le Paris secret des années 30* (The Secret Paris of the '30s) promoted his reputation as the "eye of Paris" (Miller's phrase) whose moody black-and-white images of streets and nightlife captured how many non-Parisians all over the world saw Paris. The book drew largely on his first major success, *Paris de nuit* (Paris by Night), a 1933 collection of sixty-four photos, with an introduction by Paul Morand. Other books include *Conversations with Picasso*, trans. Jane Marie Todd (Chicago: University of Chicago Press, 1999); *Proust in the Power of Photography*, trans. Richard Howard (Chicago: University of Chicago Press, 2001); and *Letters to My Parents*, trans. Peter Laki and Barna Kantor (Chicago: University of Chicago Press, 1997). In English, see Marja Warehime, *Brassaï: Images of Culture and the Surrealist Observer* (Baton Rouge: Louisiana State University Press, 1996).

49. Gilbert Salachas, *Le Paris d'Hollywood: Sur un air de réalité*, photographs by Séeberger Frères (Paris: Caisse Nationale des Monuments Historiques et des Sites, 1994), introduction.

50. This collection is housed at the Mission du Patrimoine Photographique, in Paris.

51. Roy Elston, ed., *Cook's Traveller's Handbook to Paris* (London: Simpkin Marshall, 1931).

52. Mac Orlan in Baqué, *Les Documents de la modernité*, pp. 163 and 169, originally in Mac Orlan, "Les Sentiments de la rue et ses accessoires," *L'Art Vivant*, 145 (February 1931): 21.

53. Cited in J. G. Kennedy, *Imagining Paris* (New Haven: Yale University Press, 1993), p. 151. On its way to gentrification today, along with the entire Bastille neighborhood, the rue de Lappe still excites the smart set, who stroll by its innumerable bars soaking up the "real thing" after an evening at the nearby Opéra.

54. Salachas, *Le Paris d'Hollywood*, p. 83.

55. Jean-Claude Gautrand, *Les Séeberger: L'Aventure de trois frères photographes au début du siècle* (Paris: La Manufacture, 1995).

56. Donald Albrecht says outright that "France in particular took advantage of modern architecture's potential for the cinema. . . . They treated the screen as modern painters did their canvases. [Experimental cinema found] representation in many of the most important Expositions during the 1920s, including the 1921 Salon d'Automne, the 1924 Exposition de l'Art dans le Cinéma Français, and . . . the 1925 Paris Exposition, at Mallet-Stevens' cinema studio on the Champ de Mars." Donald Albrecht, *Designing Dreams: Modern Architecture in the Movies* (New York: Harper and Row, 1986), p. 44. See also Howard Mandelbaum and Eric Myers, *Screen Deco* (New York: St. Martin's, 1985), p. 85.

57. See Lucy Fischer, *Designing Women: Cinema, Art Deco, and the Female Form* (New York: Columbia University Press, 2003).

58. Mandelbaum and Myers, *Screen Deco*, p. 4. See also Charles Affron and Mirella Affron, *Sets in Motion: Art Direction and Film Narrative* (New Brunswick, N.J.: Rutgers University Press, 1995); and Albrecht, *Designing Dreams*.

59. Andrew, *Mists of Regret*, pp. 93–99.

60. Salachas, *Le Paris d'Hollywood*, introduction.

61. Mandelbaum and Myers, *Screen Deco*, p. 37.

62. Ibid., pp. 26–27.

63. Ibid., p. 13.

64. Ibid., p. 34.

65. Suzanne Tise, "Art Deco," in Jane Turner, ed., *The Dictionary of Art*, vol. 2 (New York: Grove, 1996), p. 522.

66. Mandelbaum and Myers, *Screen Deco*, p. 121.

67. Tise, "Art Deco," p. 522.

68. Bréon and Lefrançois, *Le Musée des années 30*, p. 174.

69. Tise, "Art Deco."

70. See Donald Kirihara, *Patterns: Mizoguchi in the 1930s* (Madison: University of Wisconsin Press, 1992).

71. Tise, "Art Deco," pp. 519–520.

72. Nataša Ďurovičovà, "Empire of Taste: The 1925 International Exhibition of Modern Decorative and Industrial Arts" (Unpublished paper, NEH Summer Seminar for College Teachers, University of Iowa, 1986).

73. The composers in the group were Georges Auric, Louis Durey, Arthur Honneger, Darius Milhaud, Francis Poulenc, and Germaine Taillefer.

74. Robert Pincus-Witten, "Art Deco," *Artforum*, 9, no. 4 (December 1970), p. 69.

75. Donald Albrecht, "Thirty Little-Known Facts about Modernism," *New York Times Magazine* (10 April 1994).

76. Dominique Gagneux, "Art décoratif en France: Rationalisme ou nationalisme?" in *Années 30 en Europe: Le Temps menaçant, 1929–1939*, Exhibition catalogue, Musée d'Art Moderne (Paris: Paris Musées / Flammarion, 1997), pp. 504–507.

77. Editorial, *Interior Architecture and Decoration* (January 1932).

78. Extract from André Bloc's manifesto, on display at the Musée des Années 30, Boulogne-Billancourt.

79. Howell Cresswell, "Decoration at the Paris Autumn Salon," *Interior Architecture and Design* (January 1932): 4.

80. Howell Cresswell, "Made in France," *Interior Architecture and Design* (March 1932): 63–66.

81. Ibid.

82. Gagneux ("Art décoratif en France," p. 506) suggests that Mallet-Stevens, who submitted a manifesto on *le style-paquebot* ("ocean-liner style") in *Acier* (July 1935), soon had to accept a reconciliation of the purity he demanded with ordinary terrestrial palaces, which required sumptuous ornamentation.

83. Mandelbaum and Myers, *Screen Deco*, p. 122.

84. Pincus-Witten, "Art Deco," p. 71.

85. Siân Reynolds, Lecture at the University of Warwick, March 7, 1998. See also Baqué, *Les Documents de la modernité*, p. 438.

86. Jean-Noël Marchandiau, *L'Illustration, 1843–1944: Vie et mort d'un journal* (Toulouse: Privat, 1987).

87. Jacques Guenne, "Sougez, ou L'Ennemi du hasard," in Baqué, *Les Documents de la modernité*, pp. 396–397.

88. "Paris qui s'en va," *L'Illustration* (3 April 1930).

89. Marie-Loup Sougez and Sophie Rochard, *Emmanuel Sougez: L'Eminence grise* (Paris: Créaphis, 1993), p. 18.

90. "Les Puits perdus," *L'Illustration* (Autumn 1937).

91. One can sense this mission in the organizing categories of the special issue on the city that *L'Illustration* published in 1937: (1) The Development of Paris; (2) Atmosphere; (3) How Paris Supplies Itself; (4) The Paris of the Intelligentsia; (5) The New Face of Paris; (6) Dangerous Streets; (7) Le Plus Grand Paris. (The suburbs—*la banlieue*—are equated with the colonies!)

92. *L'Illustration* (11 May 1935).

93. Part of international modernist fashion, Leroy spectacles were variants of those round black glasses made famous by Harold Lloyd. As David Bordwell points out in *Ozu and the Poetics of Cinema* (Princeton: Princeton University Press, 1988), this style of eyeglasses even crossed to Japan, where they were known as Rroydos.

94. *L'Illustration*, 200 (30 July 1938): 445. Or see its annual coverage in, for instance, the issue of 7 February 1931, where that year's contestants are displayed.

95. *L'Illustration*, 4779 (1934): 238. In *Le Grand Jeu*, Marie Bell insists that Pierre-Richard Willm take her yachting.

96. See Andrew, *Mists of Regret*, pp. 189–191.

97. Idole Vaillant, "Robert Mallet-Stevens: Architecture, Cinema and Poetics," in François Penz and M. Thomas, eds., *Cinema and Architecture: Méliès, Mallet-Stevens, Multimedia* (London: BFI, 1997).

98. For a full treatment of this style in the cinema, see Fischer, *Designing Women*.

99. An exception would be Feyder's 1928 film *Les Nouveaux Monsieurs*, which dealt with the highlife of the monied class.

100. Andrew, *Mists of Regret*, pp. 96, 126–127.

101. *Stavisky . . .* makes reference to *L'Illustration:* a close-up shows a vintage two-color cover of *Le Petit Journal Illustré* displaying Serge Alexandre's melodramatic first arrest in 1926.

102. *L'Illustration* (4 and 11 October 1933). In fact, every year during the 1930s this magazine would run a large spread picturing the new models of automobiles, each with a stylish woman in the frame.

103. *Pour Vous*, 427 (21 January 1937).

104. For a fuller analysis of the film, see Ginette Vincendeau, *Pépé le Moko* (London: BFI, 1998); and Andrew, *Mists of Regret*, pp. 255–257.

105. In French usage, the term *spahi*, which referred originally to a member of the Turkish cavalry, designates a cavalryman—usually but not always a native of North Africa—serving in the French army.

106. Mandelbaum and Myers, *Screen Deco*, pp. 38–40.

107. Ibid., p. 32.

108. Even before the Nazis took it over, the Rex had become "politicized." On August 11, 1939, the producer Edouard Corniglion-Molinier booked it for the only full showing that Malraux's film *Sierra de Teruel* received until after the war (when it would be reissued under the title *Espoir*).

109. Note again the title of Romy Golan's book, *Modernity and Nostalgia: Art and Politics in Interwar France*. In our view—though perhaps not in hers—the terms "modernity" and "nostalgia" must be taken as an ensemble.

8. THE LOWER DEPTHS

1. *Hôtel du Nord*, screenplay in *L'Avant-scène cinéma*, 374 (October 1988): 97. A more literal translation of the final sentence would be, "Do I have an atmosphere kind of face?" The French term *gueule* refers primarily to the mouth or maw of certain mammals. Colloquial usage with reference to the human face builds on verbs such as *gueuler* ("to speak or sing loudly") and *dégueuler* ("to vomit"), as well as the adjective

dégueulasse ("disgusting"). The noun is also a synonym for *tête* ("head"), as a reference to facial expression. When Arletty asks her question, the term *gueule* conveys an animal crudeness reminiscent of Balzac's typology of characters in *Goriot* and other novels of *La Comédie humaine*.

    2. Here is the entire footbridge sequence in English:

> Raymonde: Why don't we leave for Toulon? You're in a rut, in a rut. It'll never stop making trouble.
> Edmond: And then what?
> R: Oh, you weren't always so fatalitary.
> E: Fatalistic.
> R: If you say so—the result's the same. What's bugging you? Aren't we happy, the two of us?
> E: No.
> R: Are you sure?
> E: Yeah.
> R: You don't like our life?
> E: Do *you* like our life?
> R: I'd better like it; I've become used to it. Except for the black eye, you're a swell guy. Downstairs we argue, but in bed we make up and get along. So?
> E: So nothing. I've had enough, get it? I'm suffocating. Do you hear? I'm suffocating, suffocating!
> R: In Toulon, there's fresh air because of the sea. You'll breathe better!
> E: Everywhere we went, it would smell of rot.
> R: Let's go abroad, to the colonies.
> E: With you?
> R: Whad'ya think?
> E: Well, it would be the same everywhere. I need a change of atmosphere, and my atmosphere is you.
> R: This is the first time anyone ever called me an atmosphere. If I'm an atmosphere, you're a funny hick-town. Oh, give me a break! Guys who only look tough and who make a big deal out of what they used to be—they should all be rubbed out! Atmosphere, atmosphere. Do I look like an atmosphere kind of girl? If that's the way it is, go off to La Varenne on your own! Good fishing and good atmosphere.

    3. *Hôtel du Nord*, p. 96.

    4. Ibid., p. 97. An earlier scene provides a hint of Edmond's displeasure, when he states with eloquence that he needs a change of air because he's just existing and he needs a life.

    5. Ibid., p. 96.

6. The word *bled*, meaning "land" or "countryside," derives from Arabic. In French it was first used among nineteenth-century colonial troops in North Africa. Standard English translations of the term include "boondocks" and "hick-town." The Oxford-Hachette dictionary (first edition, 1994) gives the British equivalent as "god-forsaken hole." Suggested to Carné by the scriptwriter Henri Jeanson, *bled* signifies not only a difference of affect, but also differences of class and culture. Raymonde seems unlikely to use the term *atmosphère* on an everyday basis, but she clearly intuits Edmond's meaning, and responds with the term *bled*, from the opposite end of the cultural spectrum. Urban youths in the United States today might use "turf" or "'hood."

7. *Hôtel du Nord*, p. 45.

8. Ibid. In a 1989 interview with Pierre-Edmond Robert, Arletty (1898–1992; born Léonie Bathiat) recalled her pleasure in working on *Hôtel du Nord* with Jouvet, whose Edmond Henri Jeanson had sought to portray as an intellectual pimp. Concerning her dialogue with Jouvet on the footbridge, she reiterated that the whole thing had been Jeanson's idea: "And it was Jeanson who came up with that word [*atmosphère*]—because it isn't in Dabit, not once! Jeanson, who wanted to find a use for the word, which he must have had in his head for a long time, has Jouvet and several others say it in *Entrée des artistes*. But it didn't catch on at all—nobody paid attention to it. He used it again in *Hôtel du Nord*, and there . . . It's curious, the fate of a word." Arletty, "Le Tournage d'*Hôtel du Nord* en 1938," *Jungle*, 12 (1989): 69.

9. Francis Ramirez and Christian Rolot, "Hôtel(s) du Nord: Du Populisme en littérature et au cinéma," *Roman 20/50*, 18 (1994): 72. Melodrama abounds in both the novel and the film. Dabit includes a character named Lucie who attributes a nagging cough to what she calls "a change of air" (Eugène Dabit, *L'Hôtel du Nord* [Paris: Gallimard, 1993], p. 169). Like Raymonde in Carné's film, she dreams of a healthier life in the countryside. But Lucie's cough persists, and she dies without leaving the city.

10. Dabit retained the subtitle at least through July 1927, but seems to have dropped it from published versions of the novel. Pierre-Edmond Robert, *D'un Hôtel du Nord l'autre: Eugène Dabit, 1898–1936* (Paris: Bibliothèque de Littérature Française Contemporaine de l'Université de Paris–VII, 1986), p. 65.

11. Dabit initiated contact with Gide in a February 1927 letter—the first of some seventy between them—in which he asked to show Gide his poetry. Four months later, he wrote to Gide of a new project, a novel based on his experiences as a night clerk at his parents' hotel on the Quai des Jemmapes. See Robert, *D'un Hôtel du Nord l'autre: Eugène Dabit, 1898–1936*, pp. 62–70.

12. Cited ibid., p. 91.

13. Eugène Dabit, "Tous les secrets de la culture," *Commune*, 25 (September 1935): 58–62. Reprinted in *Jungle*, 12 (1989): 60–64.

14. See Eugène Dabit, review of Céline's *Voyage au bout de la nuit*, in *Nouvelle Revue Française* (December 1932). A translation appears in William K. Buckley, ed., *Critical Essays on Louis-Ferdinand Céline* (Boston: G. K. Hall, 1989), pp. 23–24.

15. Dabit, *L'Hôtel du Nord*, pp. 16–17.

16. Magic-City was a dance hall at 180 rue de l'Université, built in the mid-1920s on the former site of an amusement park, near the Esplanade des Invalides. It was shut down in 1939, until the Germans requisitioned it in 1943 for use as a television studio. See Emmanuel Lemieux, *Cognac-Jay 1940: La Télévision française sous l'Occupation* (Paris: Calmann-Lévy, 1990).

17. Dabit, *L'Hôtel du Nord*, p. 173.

18. Ibid., p. 214.

19. Edward Baron Turk, *Child of Paradise: Marcel Carné and the Golden Age of French Cinema* (Cambridge, Mass.: Harvard University Press, 1989), p. 140.

20. Marcel Carné, *La Vie à belles dents*, rev. ed. (Paris: Jean Vuarnet, 1979), p. 122.

21. Dudley Andrew, *Mists of Regret: Culture and Sensibility in Classic French Film* (Princeton: Princeton University Press, 1995), p. 5.

22. Taken as a pair or complementary set, the figures of the anarchist and the homosexual in Dabit's novel incarnate fears and fantasies about national decline in light of ethnicity, politics, and sexuality a decade after the Treaty of Versailles ending World War I. See Carolyn J. Dean, *The Frail Social Body: Pornography, Homosexuality, and Other Fantasies in Interwar France* (Berkeley: University of California Press, 2000). Government attempts to reverse the low birthrate followed the deaths of hundreds of thousands of French soldiers in World War I.

23. It lacked the authenticity that Poulaille promoted in the years 1931–1936 through a series of journals—*Nouvel Age Littéraire, Prolétariat, À Contre-Courant*, and *Cahiers de Littérature Prolétarienne*—advocating a maverick socialist realism at odds with French Communist Party doctrines. See J. E. Flower, *Literature and the Left in France: Society, Politics and the Novel since the Late Nineteenth Century* (London: Methuen, 1985), p. 79.

24. Pierre Mac Orlan, *Masques sur mesure* (Paris: Gallimard, 1965), p. 27.

25. Dabit, *L'Hôtel du Nord*, p. 217.

26. Other texts by Dabit, such as *Petit-Louis* (1930), *Villa Oasis, ou Les Faux Bourgeois* (1932), *Faubourgs de Paris* (1933), *Un Mort tout neuf* (1934), *L'Ile* (1935), *La Zone verte* (1935), and *Trains de vies* (1936), continue to explore urban spaces within and surrounding Paris. His posthumous publications include *Les Maîtres de la peinture espagnole* (1937) and *Journal intime* (1939). *Hommage à Eugène Dabit* (Paris: Gallimard, 1939) includes contributions by Gide, Jean Giono, Max Jacob, and Maurice Vlaminck. See Robert, *D'un Hôtel du Nord l'autre*; David O'Connell, "Eugène Dabit: A French Working-Class Novelist," *Research Studies*, 41 (1973): 217–233; and Mary Jean Green, "Writers of the Working Class: Guilloux and Dabit, in idem, *Fiction in the*

Historical Present: French Writers and the Thirties (Hanover, N.H.: University Press of New England, 1986).

27. André Bazin, *"Le Jour se lève:* Poetic Realism," in *Le Jour se lève: A Film by Jacques Prévert and Marcel Carné*, trans. Dinah Brooke and Nicola Hayden (New York: Simon and Schuster, 1970), p. 10.

28. Edward Turk writes that the street is purportedly in the city of Amiens, about sixty miles north of Paris (Turk, *Child of Paradise*, p. 154). But it would be easy to mistake the neighborhood in question for an outlying area of Paris, such as those depicted in Céline's *Voyage au bout de la nuit.*

29. See Andrew, *Mists of Regret*, pp. 3–6 and ch. 8. Trauner's stylization of urban space reached its most forceful expression a decade later in his sets for the boulevard du Crime in *Les Enfants du paradis* (1945) and the elevated Métro station in *Les Portes de la nuit* (1946). Over the next forty years, his sets re-creating Paris for Billy Wilder's *Irma La Douce* (1962), Joseph Losey's *Monsieur Klein* (1975), Claude Berri's *Ciao Pantin* (1983), Luc Besson's *Subway* (1985), and Bertrand Tavernier's *Autour de minuit* (1986) evolved from the poetic realism of the 1930s to the glossy *cinéma du look* championed by Besson and others. See Alexandre Trauner, *Décors de cinéma* (Paris: Jade-Flammarion, 1986).

30. Marcel Carné, "When Will the Cinema Go Down into the Street?" in Richard Abel, ed., *French Film Theory and Criticism, 1907–1939, Vol. 2: 1929–1939* (Princeton: Princeton University Press, 1988), pp. 127–129. The article was first published in *Cinémagazine*, 13 (November 1933).

31. Ibid., p. 129.

32. Marc Augé, *In the Métro*, trans. Tom Conley (Minneapolis: University of Minnesota Press, 2002), pp. 4 and 8.

33. Michel de Certeau, *The Practice of Everyday Life*, trans. Steven Rendall (Berkeley: University of California Press, 1984), p. 104.

34. See Steven Ungar, "Narration et pratique spatiale dans deux récits surréalistes," in C. W. Thompson, ed., *L'Autre et le sacré: Surréalisme, cinéma, ethnologie* (Paris: Harmattan, 1995), pp. 93–111.

35. See Margaret Cohen, *Profane Illumination: Walter Benjamin and the Paris of Surrealist Revolution* (Berkeley: University of California Press, 1993); Hal Foster, *Compulsive Beauty* (Cambridge, Mass.: MIT Press, 1995); Victor Burgin, "Chance Encounters," in idem, *In/Different Spaces: Place and Memory in Visual Culture* (Berkeley: University of California Press, 1996); and Robin Walz, *Pulp Surrealism: Insolent Popular Culture in Early Twentieth-Century Paris* (Berkeley: University of California Press, 2000).

36. Walz, *Pulp Surrealism*, p. 26.

37. Henry Luce acknowledged that *Vu* was the model for the American illustrated weekly *Life*, which he launched in 1936. Ironically, Vogel was hired in 1937 as a tech-

nical advisor to *Marianne*, after Berl resigned as editor and Gaston Gallimard sold the weekly to Raymond Patenôtre. See Pascal Ory, *La Belle Illusion: Culture et politique sous le signe du Front populaire, 1935–1938* (Paris: Plon, 1992), pp. 542–543; and Claude Bellanger et al., eds., *Histoire générale de la presse française, vol. 3: 1871–1940* (Paris: Presses Universitaires de France, 1972).

38. Adrian Rifkin, *Street Noises: Parisian Pleasure, 1900–1940* (New York: St. Martin's, 1993), p. 124.

39. David H. Walker, "Cultivating the 'Fait Divers': *Détective*," in idem, *Outrage and Insight: Modern French Writers and the "Fait Divers"* (New York: Berg, 1995), p. 34. See also Pierre Assouline, *Gaston Gallimard: A Half-Century in Publishing*, trans. Harold J. Salemson (New York: Harcourt Brace Jovanovich, 1988).

40. Rifkin (*Street Noises*, p. 89) shows the cover in a full-page reproduction whose lighting from the side and front enhances the woman's facial expression, hairdo, and makeup against the dark background.

41. Eugen Weber, *The Hollow Years: France in the 1930s* (New York: Norton, 1994), p. 134.

42. Rifkin, *Street Noises*, p. 120.

43. Walz, *Pulp Surrealism*, p. 3. See also Philippe Azoury and Jean-Marc Lalanne, *Fantômas: Style moderne* (Paris: Centre Pompidou / Yellow Now, 2002); and Ian Walker, "Surrealism in the Street," in Walker, *City Gorged with Dreams: Surrealism and Documentary Photography in Interwar Paris* (New York: Manchester University Press, 2002).

9. IMAGINING THE COLONIES

1. Raoul Girardet, *L'Idée coloniale en France, 1871–1962*, rev. ed. (Paris: Hachette, 1991).

2. Jules Ferry, Speech to the Chamber of Deputies, 28 July 1885, cited in Guy Pervillé, *De l'Empire français à la décolonisation* (Paris: Hachette, 1991), pp. 47–48.

3. Cited in Jacques Marseille, *L'Age d'or de la France coloniale* (Paris: Albin Michel, 1986), p. 5.

4. Girardet, *L'Idée coloniale en France*, p. 12.

5. If many (white) French people found these images innocuous at the time, anticolonialists subsequently were quick to denounce them as oppressive. In *Black Skins, White Masks* (1952), Frantz Fanon wrote that he had discovered his blackness in France when battered down by "fetishism, race defects, slave ships, and above all *Y'a bon Banania*."

6. Robert W. Rydell, *Worlds of Fairs: The Century-of-Progress Expositions* (Chicago: University of Chicago Press), p. 62.

7. Zeynep Çelnik, *Displaying the Orient: The Architecture of Islam at Nineteenth-Century World's Fairs* (Berkeley: University of California Press, 1992), p. 11. See also

Lynn E. Palermo, "Identity under Construction: Representing the Colonies at the Paris *Exposition Universelle* of 1889," in Sue Peabody and Tyler Stovall, eds., *The Color of Desire: Histories of Race in France* (Durham: Duke University Press, 2003), pp. 285–301.

8. Tony Bennett, "The Exhibitionary Complex," in idem, *The Birth of the Museum: History, Theory, Politics* (New York: Routledge, 1995), pp. 60–61.

9. Mary Louise Pratt, "Introduction: Criticism in the Contact Zone," in idem, *Imperial Eyes: Travel Writing and Transculturation* (New York: Routledge, 1992), pp. 1–11.

10. Catherine Hodeir and Michel Pierre, *L'Exposition Coloniale* (Brussels: Complexe, 1991), p. 101. Because some scholars have calculated attendance on the basis of entrance tickets (which varied in number, depending on the day of the week) rather than on the actual number of admissions, the oft-cited figure of thirty-three million suggests the total number of tickets rather than the number of actual fairgoers. An estimate of eight million visitors seems accurate.

11. Viollis (born Françoise d'Ardenne de Tizac; 1879–1950) was a journalist and writer best known as the author of *Indochine S.O.S.* (Paris: Gallimard, 1935), for which André Malraux wrote a preface. In 1931, she was assigned by the large-circulation daily *Le Petit Parisien* to accompany the Minister of the Colonies, Paul Reynaud, on an official trip to Indochina, the first such trip by a French government official. While her articles on the visit were straight reportage, a December 1933 article in *Esprit* was more critical of French rule in the region. (Emmanuel Mounier himself contributed a piece, "Pour la vérité en Indochine" [Toward Truth in Indochina], to the same issue, and *Esprit* followed through in 1934 with petitions and short articles calling for an end to repressive French practices and greater freedoms leading to eventual autonomy for local peoples of Cochinchina, Annam, Tonkin, Cambodia, and Laos.) After the openly critical *Indochine S.O.S.* appeared in 1935, Viollis stated that it was an accurate account of the 1931 trip that her duties as a reporter for *Le Petit Parisien* had not allowed her to write. Controversy surrounding the book labeled Viollis alternately as "Communist" and "anti-French." As noted above in Chapter 1, Viollis was a member of the CVIA, as well as an early organizer for and contributor to *Vendredi*. In English, see Kimberley J. Healey, "Andrée Viollis in Indochina: The Objective and Picturesque Truth about French Colonialism," *Asian Journal of Social Sciences*, 31, no. 1 (2003): 19–35.

12. André Demaison, "Adresse au visiteur," in *Guide officiel de l'Exposition Coloniale Internationale* (Paris: Mayeux, 1931), p. 20.

13. Louis-Hubert Lyautey, "Le Sens d'un grand effort," *L'Illustration*, 4603 (23 May 1931).

14. Marcel Ollivier, ed., *Exposition Coloniale Internationale de Paris: Rapport général* (Paris: Imprimerie nationale, 1931), vol. 1, pp. xi–xiii, cited in Patricia A. Morton, *Hybrid Modernities: Architecture and Representation at the 1931 Colonial Exposition, Paris* (Cambridge, Mass.: MIT Press, 2000), p. 70.

15. The latter, which still stands, houses the Musée National des Arts d'Afrique et d'Océanie. The matter of its permanence depends at present on how much of its collections will become part of a new museum due to open in 2005 or 2006 on the Quai Branly, next to the Eiffel Tower. See Catherine Hodeir, "Le Musée des Arts Africains à l'Exposition Coloniale: Un Musée permanent pour une exposition éphémère?" in Dominique François, ed., *Le Palais des colonies: Histoire du Musée des Arts d'Afrique et d'Océanie* (Paris: Réunion des Musées Nationaux, 2002).

16. We thank Panivong Norindr for providing us with documentation of this last transmutation.

17. Herman Lebovics, *True France: The Wars over Cultural Identity, 1990–1945* (Ithaca: Cornell University Press, 1992), p. 69.

18. Morton, *Hybrid Modernities*, p. 79.

19. Johannes Fabian, *Time and the Other: How Anthropology Makes Its Object* (New York: Columbia University Press, 1983), pp. xi and 25–29.

20. See Nicolas Bancel, Pascal Blanchard, Gilles Boetsch, Eric Deroo, and Sandrine Lemaire, eds., *Les Zoos humains* (Paris: La Découverte, 2002). The novelist Didier Daeninckx has taken on this topic, writing of human display at the Colonial Exposition in *Cannibale* (1998). For an analysis of the ideology of human display in Luis Buñuel's 1933 avant-garde film *Las Hurdes: Land without Bread*, see James Lastra, "Why Is This Absurd Picture Here? Ethnology/Heterology/Buñuel," in Ivone Margulies, ed., *Rites of Realism: Essays on Corporeal Cinema* (Durham: Duke University Press, 2003).

21. In fact, the Angkor Wat pavilion at Vincennes was a full-scale re-creation of the central Angkor pavilion, and thus only a partial re-creation of the actual complex of structures that made up the temple in Annam (the country known today as Cambodia). According to Pierre Guesde, the commissioner of the Indochinese section of the Colonial Exposition: "The architect, Charles Blanche, has striven to re-create the exact physiognomy of this masterpiece of Cambodian art, as remarkable for the grandeur of its conception and the harmony of its forms as for the magnificence of its decoration. The palace will keep its two floors, its 150-meter-long façade, and its 60-meter height—the height of the towers of Notre Dame in Paris. The interior of the monument, by contrast, will be resolutely modern and perfectly adapted to its purpose, with vast halls where air and light will penetrate abundantly, spacious passageways, and wide staircases permitting the crowds to move about easily." See Pierre Guesde, "L'Indochine à l'Exposition de Vincennes," *La Dépêche Coloniale et Maritime* (7 November 1928): 1, cited in Morton, *Hybrid Modernities*, p. 246. Our thanks to Pat Morton for pointing us to this passage in her book.

22. Albert Le Bonheur, *Angkhor: Temples en péril* (Paris: Herscher, 1989), cited in Hodeir and Pierre, *L'Exposition Coloniale*, p. 40.

23. Hodeir and Pierre, *L'Exposition Coloniale*, p. 43

24. Robert de Beauplan, "Les Palais de l'Indochine," *L'Illustration* (24 May 1931): 109, cited in Lebovics, *True France*, p. 76.

25. Claude Farrère, "Angkor et l'Indochine," *L'Illustration* (23 May 1931). The stated goal of saving a native culture on the point of extinction was essential to ongoing attempts to justify France's interventions overseas, defining the civilizing mission as a secular variant of early modern Christian missions. This was certainly the ideology of *L'Illustration*, as is argued by Lynn E. Palermo in "Mixed Marriages: *L'Illustration* on the Exposition Coloniale of 1931," *Proceedings of the Annual Meeting of the Western Society for French History*, 25 (1998): 196–206.

26. *Guide officiel*, p. 68. These remarks tranfer to the airplane the progressive annihilation of space by time that the railroad had initiated a century earlier. See the fascinating account of this phenomenon in Wolfgang Schivelbusch, *The Railroad Journey: The Industrialization of Time and Space in the Nineteenth Century* (Berkeley: University of California Press, 1986).

27. Quoted in Hodeir and Pierre, *L'Exposition Coloniale*, p. 51.

28. Timothy Mitchell, *Colonising Egypt* (New York: Cambridge University Press, 1988).

29. Ibid., p. 13.

30. Sylviane Leprun, *Le Théâtre des colonies* (Paris: L'Harmattan, 1986), p. 17. Leprun's invocation of ethnology is a reminder that the opening of the Colonial Exhibition coincided with the departure of the Mission Dakar-Djibouti, which was led by Marcel Griaule on behalf of the Musée d'Ethnographie du Trocadéro and which Michel Leiris chronicled in *L'Afrique fantôme* (1934).

31. Mitchell, *Colonising Egypt*, p. 33.

32. André Breton et al., "Do Not Visit the Colonial Exhibition," in Michael Richardson and Krzysztof Fijalkowski, eds., *Surrealism against the Current: Tracts and Declarations* (London: Pluto Press, 2001), p. 184. See also Adam Jolles, "'Visitez l'exposition anti-coloniale!': Nouveaux Eléments sur l'exposition protestataire," *Pleine Marge*, 35 (2002): 107–116.

33. Richardson and Fijalkowski, *Surrealism against the Current*, p. 186.

34. André Thirion, *Revolutionaries without Revolution*, trans. Joachim Neugroschel (New York: Macmillan, 1975), p. 289.

35. Elsa Triolet (born Ella Kagan; 1896–1970) was trained as an architect in her native Moscow, where early friendships with Roman Jakobson and Vladimir Mayakovsky introduced her to literary Futurism and Formalism. In 1930, two years after she met Aragon in Paris, Triolet accompanied him to Russia for the first of many visits to promote cultural exchanges between France and the Soviet Union. They militated together in high public profile throughout the decade. Often considered a fellow traveler of Communism, Triolet was never a party member. Following World War II, she experimented with fictional forms, collaborated with Aragon on joint nov-

els *(romans croisés)*, and often intervened both as a feminist and as a critic of Soviet Cold War policies.

36. Ibid., p. 289.

37. Lebovics, *True France*, p. 106; and Morton, *Hybrid Modernities*, p. 102.

38. Panivong Norindr, *Phantasmatic Indochina: French Colonial Ideology in Architecture, Film, and Literature* (Durham: Duke University Press, 1996), p. 71.

39. Pascal Blanchard, "L'Union nationale: La 'Rencontre' des droites et des gauches à travers la presse et autour de l'exposition de Vincennes," in Pascal Blanchard et Sandrine Lemaire, eds., *Culture coloniale: La France conquise par son empire, 1871–1931* (Paris: Autrement, 2003), p. 230.

40. Cited ibid., p. 213.

41. Charles-Robert Ageron, "L'Exposition Coloniale de 1931: Mythe républicain ou mythe impérial?" in Pierre Nora, ed., *Les Lieux de mémoire, I: "La République"* (Paris: Gallimard, 1948), pp. 561–591.

42. These figures are based on Raymond Chirat's findings, cited in Geneviève Nesternko, "L'Afrique de l'autre," in Michèle Lagny, Marie-Claire Ropars, and Pierre Sorlin, eds., *Générique des années 30* (Paris: Presses Universitaires de Vincennes, 1986), p. 127. Pierre Boulanger counts 210 films shot totally or partly in Africa from 1911 to 1962. See Boulanger, *Le Cinéma colonial: De "L'Atlantide" à "Lawrence d'Arabie"* (Paris: Seghers, 1975), p. 15.

43. The full corpus of colonial cinema should also include the significant body of educational films that provided information to the populations of occupied territories on topics ranging from agricultural methods to personal and public health. These, however, were not routinely seen in Paris. See Alison Murray, "Documentary Fiction: Images of Sub-Saharan Africa in Colonial Film between the Wars," in Barry Rothaus, ed., *Proceedings of the Western Society for French History* (Boulder: University of Colorado Press, 1999), pp. 186–195.

44. For details of *L'Atlantide*'s production and exhibition, see Henri Fescourt, *La Foi et la montagne, ou Le Septième Art au passé* (Paris: Paul Montel, 1959), pp. 271–273.

45. Mac Orlan (1882–1970) was a reporter and literary figure. Much as Duvivier had done with *La Bandera*, Marcel Carné adapted Mac Orlan's novel *Le Quai des brumes* into the film *Quai des brumes* (1938), a classic of poetic realism. Mac Orlan wrote the screenplay from his novel and then penned some laudatory interviews about the results. See *Mac Orlan et le cinéma* (Reims: Maison de la Culture, 1982); and Andrew, *Mists of Regret*, ch. 8.

46. André Lang, in *Pour Vous*, 57 (19 September 1935); and Graham Greene, review of *La Bandera*, in *The Spectator* (6 December 1935).

47. Duvivier dedicated the film to Franco, who supplied the production unit with costumes and extras when the French military refused to do so.

48. Anonymous, "Le Visage d'Islam, fidèlement refleté par le cinéma français, travesti par Hollywood," *Pour Vous*, 494 (4 May 1938): 8–9.

49. For a slightly different view concerning this assertion, see Charles O'Brien, "The 'Cinéma Colonial' of 1930s France: Film Narration as Spatial Practice," in Matthew Bernstein and Gaylyn Studlar, eds., *Visions of the East: Orientalism in Film* (New Brunswick: Rutgers University Press, 1996).

50. Léon Poirier, *Pourquoi et comment je vais réaliser "L'Appel du silence"* (Paris: Comité d'Action Charles de Foucauld, 1935), p. 16.

51. Ibid., p. 25.

52. Léon Poirier, *24 Images à la seconde: Du studio au désert* (Tours: Paris, 1953), p. 49.

53. For a consideration of Poirier's early career, see Fescourt, *La Foi et la montagne*, pp. 319–326.

54. Cited in Richard Abel, *French Cinema: The First Wave, 1915–1929* (Princeton: Princeton University Press, 1984), p. 104.

55. Ibid., p. 104.

56. Poirier reviews his career in the aptly titled *A la recherche d'autre chose* (Brussels: Desclée de Brouwer, 1968).

57. Ibid., p. 247.

58. See Jacques Wolgensinger, *L'Aventure de la Croisière Noire* (Paris: Robert Laffont, 2002), pp. 223–224.

59. Poirier, *24 Images à la seconde*, pp. 93–94.

60. The reference to *les hommes nouveaux* recalls the title of Marcel L'Herbier's feature film *Les Hommes nouveaux*, also made in 1936, in which a simple French worker makes his fortune in Morocco during Lyautey's term as governor.

61. See Donald Dresden, *The Marquis de Mòres: Emperor of the Bad Lands* (Norman: University of Oklahoma Press, 1970).

62. Zeev Sternhell, *La Droite révolutionnaire: Les Origines françaises du fascisme, 1885–1914* (Paris: Seuil, 1978). See also Jeffrey Mehlman, *Legacies of Anti-Semitism in France* (Minneapolis: University of Minnesota Press, 1983), p. 7.

63. Léon Poirier, *Charles de Foucauld et l'Appel du silence* (Tours: Mame, 1936), p. 127.

64. Ibid., p. 127.

65. Ibid., p. 132.

66. Abdelkader Benali, *Le Cinéma colonial au Maghreb: L'Imaginaire en trompe l'oeil* (Paris: Cerf, 1998), p. 247.

67. Ginette Vincendeau, "French Cinema of the 1930s: Social Text and Context of a Popular Entertainment Medium" (Ph.D. diss., University of East Anglia, 1985), p. 173. Third and fourth on the 1936 list were Pierre Colombier's *Le Roi* and Anatole Litvak's *Mayerling*.

68. Léon Poirier, Interview in *Pour Vous* (31 December 1936).

69. Poirier, *Pourquoi et comment je vais réaliser "L'Appel du silence."*

70. *Le Film*, 56 (9 January 1943).

71. David Henry Slavin, *Colonial Cinema and Imperial France: White Blind Spots, Settlers Myths* (Baltimore: Johns Hopkins University Press, 2001), pp. 116–117.

72. Ibid., p. 121.

73. Sandy Flitterman-Lewis makes a similar point in *To Desire Differently: Feminism and the French Cinema* (Urbana: University of Illinois Press, 1990), p. 162.

74. Pierre Mac Orlan, Review of *Morocco*, in *Pour Vous*, 146 (3 September 1931).

75. Chenal's *Les Petits Métiers de Paris*, a twenty-minute "picturesque" short, was made in September and October 1931. See Pierre Chenal, *Souvenirs du cinéaste*, ed. Pierrette Matalon et al. (Paris: Editions Dujarric, 1987), p. 38. Mac Orlan narrated as well as composed the text.

76. Chenal's film was explicitly likened to *Pépé le Moko* because of its elaborately constructed décors and because of the *cassoulet* of humanity populating the scenes in Sfax. See Lucie Cerain, in *La Cinématographie Française*, 1020 (20 May 1938).

77. Safia's whiteness is an exception to the rule in colonial films of the period, in which the white French male (e.g., Gabin as Pierre Gilieth in *La Bandera* and Pépé in *Pépé le Moko*) more often takes up with a native woman. In *La Bandera*, the native woman is played by a white French actress, Annabella. In *Pépé*, the role of Inès, who loses Pépé to the white Parisian, Gaby (Mireille Balin), is played by Line Noro, a white actress whose character identity as a Gypsy is marked by her bandana and her hooped earrings.

78. Chenal describes his initial lack of interest in the novel, then his realization that "the style . . . could become more important than the story." See Chenal, *Souvenirs du cinéaste*, p. 117. Also in 1938 André Hugon remade the silent film *Sarati le terrible*, likewise based on the work of novelist Jean Vignaud. In 1932 G. W. Pabst had remade the most successful French film of the 1920s, *L'Atlantide*, once again an exotic tale of North Africa. Pierre Mac Orlan was predictably effusive in his praise of Pabst's remake; see Mac Orlan, in *Pour Vous*, 187 (16 June 1932).

79. See Jean Vignaud, *La Maison du Maltais* (Paris: Plon, 1926), published in conjunction with the Société de Ciné-Romans de France.

80. Even Safia's apparent assimilation is tenuous. After marrying Chervin to ensure her daughter's future, Safia finds that his friends treat her like one of the exotic artifacts he brings back to Paris from his research travels. See Denise Brahimi, "Le Cinéma colonial revisité," *CinémAction*, 111 (2004): 12.

81. Vignaud, *Maison*, p. 6.

82. Ibid., p. 57.

83. Ibid., pp. 79–80.

84. Ibid., p. 19.

85. Ibid., p. 57.

86. Ibid., p. 38.

87. Ibid., p. 67.

88. Marc Augé, *The Anthropological Circle: Symbol, Function, History*, trans. Martin Thom (New York: Oxford University Press, 1982), p. 78.

89. Chenal, *Souvenirs du cinéaste*, p. 119.

90. The expression appears in Assenka Oksiloff, *Picturing the Primitive: Visual Culture, Ethnography, and Early German Cinema* (New York: Palgrave, 2001), p. 40.

10. TURBULENCE IN THE ATMOSPHERE

1. Salvador Dalí, "Documental—París—1929," *La Publicitat* [Barcelona] (1929). An English version appears in Dalí, *Oui: The Paranoid-Critical Revolution—Writings, 1927–1933*, ed. Robert Descharmes, trans. Yvonne Shafir (Boston: Exact Change, 1998), p. 95.

2. Jacques Brunius, Surrealist actor and filmmaker, should be remembered for his role in Renoir's 1936 film *Une Partie de campagne*, where he plays the lecher who cavorts with the young girl's mother. His book *En Marge du cinéma français* (Paris: Arcane, 1948) is among the best discussions of the culture of alternative cinema between the wars.

3. Walter Benjamin, "The Work of Art in the Age of Its Technological Reproducibility" (Third Version), trans. Harry Zohn and Edmund Jephcott, in Benjamin, *Selected Writings, Vol. 4: 1938–1940* (Cambridge, Mass.: Harvard University Press, 2003), p. 263.

4. Buñuel's name appears in the subtitle of André Bazin's posthumous collection, *The Cinema of Cruelty, from Buñuel to Hitchcock* (New York: Seaver, 1982). In a preface to his wonderful interview with Buñuel that appears in the volume, Bazin notes that the director's favorite adjective is "ferocious" (p. 101).

5. Luis Buñuel, *My Last Sigh*, trans Abigail Israel (New York: Vintage, 1983), p. 109.

6. Paul Sablon, "Les Films chirurgicaux, d'hier et d'aujourd'hui," *La Revue du Cinéma* (8 March 1930), pp. 12–13.

7. Adored by Chagall, Le Corbusier, Léger, and Prévert, Painlevé was the son of a prime minister of France. Beginning in the late 1920s he made many films about bizarre creatures, and in 1931 he established the society and archive known as Les Documents Cinématographiques, in Paris. See Andy Bellows and Marina McDougall, eds., *Science Is Fiction: The Films of Jean Painlevé* (Cambridge, Mass.: MIT Press, 2000).

8. Sablon, "Les Films chirurgicaux," p. 13.

9. Jean Epstein made the evocative term *photogénie* famous in the title of a 1924 film associated with his article of the same year, "On Certain Characteristics of Photogénie," translated in Richard Abel, ed., *French Film Theory and Criticism, 1907–1939*, vol. 1 (Princeton: Princeton University Press, 1988), pp. 314–320.

10. Léon Moussinac, *Naissance du cinéma* (Paris: J. Povolozky, 1925), p. 177.

11. These films, made in the early 1920s, have their roots in the series of scientific short subjects Eclair Studios had turned out from 1911 to 1917.

12. Denis Hollier points out that Bataille used the word *document* in a 1922 thesis. See Hollier, "The Use-Value of the Impossible," *October,* 60 (1992): 4.

13. Claude Lévi-Strauss reproduces his exchange with Breton in *Look, Listen, Read* (New York: Basic Books, 1997), pp. 143–151.

14. See Chapter 9 for a discussion of Brassaï's bohemian photography.

15. Salvador Dalí, "La Dada fotogràfica," *Gazeta de les artes,* 6 (February 1929): 152.

16. Dalí, *Oui: The Paranoid-Critical Revolution,* pp. 93–107.

17. Ibid., p. 95.

18. Benjamin uses the phrase in his essay "Surrealism: The Last Snapshot of the European Intelligentsia." See Margaret Cohen, *Profane Illumination: Walter Benjamin and the Paris of Surrealist Revolution* (Berkeley: University of California Press, 1993). Cohen stresses the importance of photography and of the "haunting" of Paris by Surrealism, as well as the haunting of the Surrealists by the dialectical objects scattered throughout the city.

19. Walter Benjamin, "Surrealism: The Last Snapshot of the European Intelligentsia," trans. Edmund Jephcott, in Benjamin, *Selected Writings, Vol. 2: 1927–1934* (Cambridge, Mass.: Harvard University Press, 1999), p. 210.

20. Elisabeth Roudinesco, *Jacques Lacan and Co.,* trans. Jeffrey Mehlman (Chicago: University of Chicago Press, 1990), p. 110.

21. André Breton, *Mad Love,* trans. Mary Ann Caws (Lincoln: University of Nebraska Press, 1987), p. 23.

22. Ibid., p. 21.

23. See Cohen, *Profane Illumination,* ch. 5.

24. Cocteau could boast a pair of the most beautiful and most identifiable hands of the twentieth century.

25. Denis de Rougemont, *Penser avec les mains* (Paris: Albin Michel, 1936). See especially pp. 149–151. The phrase originated with Thomas Aquinas.

26. The mutilated hand symbolizes "the renunciation of childhood onanism," according to Sarane Alexandrian. See Alexandrian, *Le Surréalisme et le rêve* (Paris: Gallimard, 1974), p. 179. The key painting by Dalí would surely be the 1927 *Gadget and Hand.*

27. Salvador Dalí, "L'Alliberamente dels dits," *L'Amic de les arts,* 31 (March 1929), reprinted in Dalí, *Obra Catalana completa* (Barcelona; Quaderns Crema, 1995), pp. 159–162.

28. Dalí, *Oui: The Paranoid-Critical Revolution,* p. 84. Originally published in *L'Amic de les arts* (Sitges, Spain), 31 (31 March 1929).

29. Haim Finkelstein, *Salvador Dalí: Art and Writing, 1927–1942* (New York:

Cambridge University Press, 1996). Part 3 of Finkelstein's study, "Under the Sign of 'The Great Masturbator,'" traces the impact of cinema on Dalí's developing aesthetic.

30. Carter Ratcliff, "Swallowing Dalí," in *Art Forum* 21, no. 1 (September 1982): 33–39, deals with such paintings as *Object Cannibalism* and *The Sacrament of the Last Supper*. Thanks to Tracy Biga for drawing our attention to this article.

31. Salvador Dalí, "Reverie: Port-Lligat, October 17, 1931, 3 o'clock in the afternoon," in Dalí, *Oui: The Paranoid-Critical Revolution*, pp. 139–141.

32. The isolated, mutilated, severed, and gloved hand signals Surrealism. Its discovery in prehistoric caves tempted some to see the hand as the primordial figure of the artistic impulse. It receives a full entry in the *Dictionnaire du Surréalisme*, where Man Ray's photos, Eluard's poems, and Breton's 1959 homage to the hand are referenced. The title character of Breton's *Nadja* draws a woman's face in the palm of a hand, just as Dalí, in *Unsatiated Desire*, suggested female genitals in the palm of a hand with one finger forming a "flying phallus." Yves Tanguy, Alberto Giacometti, Léon Malet, and other Surrealists come back to the delicacy of the hand.

33. Cohen analyzes the passage where Nadja hallucinates: "That hand, that hand on the Seine—why that hand which is flaming over the water? It's true that fire and water are the same thing. But what does that hand mean? How do you interpret it? Let me look at that hand." (Cohen, *Profane Illumination*, pp. 102–103.) She reminds us that Breton, through Nadja, here resurrects Gérard de Nerval's tale "La Main enchantée," in which citizens of the capital are subject to—haunted by—its bloody, insurrectional past.

34. Dawn Ades, *Dada and Surrealism Reviewed* (London: Arts Council of Great Britain, 1978), pp. 259–260.

35. Ibid., p. 262.

36. Dalí's flagrant self-indulgence won him no friends. Henry Miller, in ranking *L'Age d'or* the greatest film ever made, attributed it entirely to Buñuel, a clear-eyed man of the future. Dalí he took to be a paid performer. See Miller, "The Golden Age," in idem, *The Cosmological Eye* (New York: New Directions, 1939), pp. 54–55.

37. Ian Gibson, *The Shameful Life of Salvador Dalí* (New York: Norton, 1998), p. 379.

38. Despite his irregular status, Dalí was still a major draw at the 1938 International Surrealist Exposition at the Galerie Beaux-Arts. See Gibson, *The Shameful Life of Salvador Dalí*, p. 434; and James Herbert, *Paris 1937: Worlds on Exhibition* (Ithaca: Cornell University Press, 1998), p. 139.

39. Gibson, *The Shameful Life of Salvador Dalí*, p. 426.

40. The source of this film was a popular 1920 novel by Maurice Renard, *Les Mains d'Orlac*. See Ruth Goldberg, "Orlac's Dance," *Kinoeye*, 2, no. 4 (February 2002).

41. Breton, *Mad Love*, p. 128, note 2. Breton was sufficiently struck by the film to

mention it years later in his essay "Comme dans un bois," published in *L'Age du cinéma*, 4–5 (August–September 1951): 29.

42. The film *Peter Ibbetson*, today largely forgotten, gave its title to a magnificent Surrealist painting which the Czech artist known as Toyen (1902–1980; born Marie Čermínová) produced just after World War II. In it, two hands reach out through an opaque surface and grasp each other, the fingers of the hand on the left actually penetrating and emerging from the back of the hand on the right. Though cut off from any body, these hands, unlike those figured by Dalí, communicate; they interlock with each other, in a gesture of heterosexual union. Toyen had been a member of the Surrealist group since her first trips to Paris in the early 1930s, and it was because of her that Breton—elated by *Peter Ibbetson* and in the midst of composing *L'Amour fou*—made his notable journey to Prague to consecrate the Czech Surrealist circle. After his departure, Toyen was excoriated in her home city for her forthright erotica. Chief among her explicit works is a drawing that displays a series of free-standing hands, each recognizably female, each in dynamic relation with an erect penis.

43. Ado Kyrou, *Le Surréalisme au cinéma* (Paris: Ramsay, 1985; orig. pub. 1963), p. 158.

44. Alain and Odette Virmaux, *Les Surréalistes et le cinéma* (Paris: Seghers, 1976), pp. 89–90.

45. Jean Vigo, "Vers un cinéma social" ("Toward a Social Cinema"; 1930). This brief lecture, delivered at the première of his first film, *A Propos de Nice*, was devoted almost exclusively to the virtues of *Un Chien andalou*. In English, see Jean Vigo, "Toward a Social Cinema," trans. Stuart Liebman, in Richard Abel., ed., *French Film Theory and Criticism, 1907–1939, vol. 2: 1929–1939* (Princeton: Princeton University Press, 1988), pp. 60–63.

46. For a fuller interpretation of *L'Atalante*, see Dudley Andrew, *Film in the Aura of Art* (Princeton: Princeton University Press, 1984), pp. 59–77; Marina Warner, *L'Atalante* (London: BFI, 1992); and idem, *"L'Atalante": Un Film de Jean Vigo* (Paris: Cinémathèque France, 2000).

47. P. E. Salles-Gomes, *Jean Vigo* (Berkeley: University of California Press, 1955) p. 164.

48. Cohen, *Profane Illumination*, p. 81.

49. Ibid., p. 107.

50. Walter Benjamin, "On the Philosophy of History," in idem, *Selected Writings*, vol. 4, p. 390.

51. Breton makes the claim in *Mad Love*, first published as *L'Amour fou* in 1937.

52. The first sentence of *Nadja*—"Qui suis-je?"—conveys the ambiguity of this quest through its first-person singular present-tense verb. The sentence translates as both "Who am I?" (from the infinitive *être*) and "Whom do I follow?" (from the infinitive *suivre*).

53. Benjamin, "Thesis VIII," in "On the Philosophy of History," in idem, *Selected Writings*, vol. 4, p. 392.

54. Breton's presence in Mexico initially had less to do with revolutionary politics than with financial need, which led him in late 1936 to apply to the French Ministry of Foreign Affairs for a visiting professorship abroad. The application was turned down because Breton lacked the necessary university diplomas. More than a year later, the diplomat-poet Alexis Léger (better known under the pen name Saint-John Perse) intervened and Breton was assigned to give a series of historical lectures on French literature and art. Five years after Leiris left for Africa, and only months after the Popular Front's electoral victory Breton "dreamed of his own escape to distant shores." Mark Polizzotti, *Revolution of the Mind: The Life of André Breton* (New York: Da Capo, 1997), p. 439.

55. Breton, *Manifestoes of Surrealism*, trans. Richard Seaver and Helen R. Lane (Ann Arbor: University of Michigan Press, 1972), pp. 151–152.

56. Walter Benjamin, "Surrealism: The Last Snapshot of the European Intelligentsia," p. 208.

57. Michèle H. Richman, *Sacred Revolution: Durkheim and the Collège de Sociologie* (Minneapolis: University of Minnesota Press, 2002), p. 111.

58. Michel Leiris, *Journal, 1922–1989*, ed. Jean Jamin (Paris: Gallimard, 1992). Unlike Leiris' retrospective autobiographical writings, the *Journal* is prospective, addressing what Leiris holds in reserve for the future. It thus marks a preliminary phase of introspection preceding explicit interactions with others. See Guy Poitry, "La Part réservée," *Critique*, 547 (December 1992): 927. See also the discussion involving Jamin, Denis Hollier, and Aliette Armel, published as "Un Homme du secret discret," *Magazine Littéraire*, 302 (September 1992): 16–23.

59. Leiris, *Journal, 1922–1989*, p. 243.

60. Leiris, "L'Oeil de l'ethnographe," in idem, *Zébrage* (Paris: Gallimard, 1992), pp. 26–34. The piece, which appeared in *Documents*, 7 (1930), was commissioned by one of the journal's editors, Georges Henri Rivière, who was also assistant director of the Musée Ethnographique du Trocadéro. An undated entry listed after 1929 appears to have been a note Leiris wrote in conjunction with the essay. The next diary entry is dated April 21, 1933, after Leiris returned to Paris and while he was helping to prepare an exhibition based on the Dakar-Djibouti Mission. The catalogue that Leiris and Albert Skira produced for the exhibition was published in June 1933 as the second issue of *Minotaure*.

61. Leiris, "L'Oeil de l'ethnographe," p. 34. The references to "white ways" and "white mentality" are not merely passing barbs. Leiris once inscribed a copy of *L'Afrique fantôme* with the statement: "This book might have been called *Moi, un Blanc*" (see Michel Delahaye, "La Règle de Rouch," *Cahiers du Cinéma*, 120 [June 1961]). The Dakar-Djibouti Mission was not Leiris' first extended stay abroad. In

1927, he had spent more than five months traveling in Egypt and Greece. Barthes' comments on Japan are from his book *L'Empire des signes* (Paris: Skira, 1970).

62. See Chapter 3 above, where we rely heavily on Jean-Louis Loubet del Bayle, *Les Non-Conformistes des années 30* (Paris: Seuil, 1969); and on Robert Aron and Arnaud Dandieu, *La Révolution nécessaire* (Paris: Jean-Michel Place, 1993).

63. André Breton, "Position politique du surréalisme," cited in Helena Lewis, *The Politics of Surrealism* (New York: Paragon House, 1988), p. 136.

64. Georges Bataille et al., "Counter-Attack: Union of Struggle of Revolutionary Intellectuals," in Michael Richardson and Krzysztof Fijalkowski, eds., *Surrealism against the Current* (London: Pluto Press, 2001), pp. 115–116. Discrepant French versions appear in volume 1 of José Pierre, *Tracts surréalistes et déclarations collectives, 1922–1969*, and in volume 1 of Georges Bataille, *Oeuvres complètes* (Paris: Gallimard, 1970), implying that ambiguity extends even to attribution of authorship.

65. Pierre, *Tracts surréalistes et déclarations collectives*, p. 500. Pierre includes the undated letter, which he believes was written in October, November, or December 1935—in his notes for Contre-Attaque's October 7, 1935, tract. He retains the numerous misspellings that add irreverence to the letter, which Richardson and Fijalkowski have rectified in their translation of the tract.

66. Pierre, *Tracts surréalistes et déclarations collectives*, p. 298.

67. Bataille, "Popular Front in the Street," in Allan Stoekl, ed., *Visions of Excess: Selected Writings, 1927–1939* (Minneapolis: University of Minnesota Press, 1985), p. 163. The text of the talk was published in May 1936, in the first (and only) issue of *Cahiers de Contre-Attaque*.

68. Roger Caillois, "Note on the Foundation of a College of Sociology," trans. Betsy Wing, in Denis Hollier, ed., *The College of Sociology* (Minneapolis: University of Minnesota Press, 1988), p. 3.

69. Roger Caillois, Introduction, in Hollier, *The College of Sociology*, p. 9.

70. Hollier, *The College of Sociology*, p. 100.

71. Michel Leiris, "The Sacred in Everyday Life," in Hollier, *The College of Sociology*, p. 24.

72. Ibid., p. 27. The *zone* and the sacred carry an aura of dangerous sexuality; Leiris recalls being warned as a child to beware of strangers (whom he realizes were pederasts) who might, under false pretenses, try to take him off into the buses. In *Les Mots* (The Words), the young Sartre recalls receiving a similar warning, about older men who stalked children in the Luxembourg Gardens.

73. Walter Benjamin, "The Present Social Situation of the French Writer," trans. Rodney Livingstone, in *Selected Writings, Vol. 2: 1927–1934* (Cambridge, Mass.: Harvard University Press, 1999), pp. 761–762.

74. Ibid., p. 763.

75. Breton, *Manifestoes of Surrealism*, pp. 245–246. Breton's rapport with Malraux

is complex. Among Malraux's first publications is a spiteful attack on Lautréamont clearly aimed at the young group of Dada rebels, of which Breton was a charter member. But it was Breton who came to his aid when he was jailed in Saigon. See Curtis Cate, *André Malraux* (London: Hutchinson, 1995), pp. 21, 72–76.

76. Breton, *Manifestoes of Surrealism*, p. 235.

77. Ibid., p. 152.

78. Helena Lewis, *Dada Turns Red* (Edinburgh: Edinburgh University Press, 1990), p. 141. This excuse seems ironic, given Breton's attack on the family that concludes his diatribe against the 1935 Writer's Congress. (See Breton, *Manifestoes of Surrealism*, p. 253.) But was this the real reason? See Polizzotti, *Revolution of the Mind*, p. 435.

79. An invaluable timeline relating to this film has been compiled by John Michalczyk, *André Malraux's "Espoir": The Propaganda/Art Film and the Spanish Civil War* (University, Miss.: Romance Monographs, 1977), pp. 168–173.

80. Vigo's work should also be mentioned here, for *Espoir* was paired with *Zéro de conduite* in its commercial release, the latter not having been seen since it had been banned in 1932. See *André Bazin, French Cinema of the Occupation and Resistance*, trans. Stanley Hochman (New York: Ungar, 1981), p. 157, note 3.

81. The 1937 novel *L'Espoir* (Man's Hope) lent its name to the film, which was retitled *Sierra de Teruel* for its summer 1939 première in Paris. Since its march 1945 re-release, it has been known as *Espoir*. We have adopted the latter title in reference to the film.

82. See Dudley Andrew, *André Bazin* (New York: Oxford University Press, 1978), pp. 52 and 69–70. Bazin penned several short articles for student journals during the war, but "Ontologie de l'image photographique" was his first major piece.

83. The first issue of *Verve* brought together texts by Gide, Bataille, Caillois, and Elie Faure, along with an extended fragment from Malraux's *Psychologie de l'art*. The cover was done specially by Matisse; Léger and Miró contributed original work. Precious photos were also included: Matisse's studio, by Brassaï, and Picasso's *Guernica* in his studio, by Dora Maar. In the second issue, Malraux once again found himself in the company not only of Gide (this was expected), but of Bataille and Caillois. Other notable contributors included Valéry, Pierre Reverdy, James Joyce, Ernest Hemingway, and Henri Michaux.

84. Benjamin was not utterly cut off from the luminaries of Paris. He interviewed André Gide, for example, in his hotel in 1928. See Benjamin, *Selected Writings*, vol. 2, p. 91.

85. See Rosalind Krauss, "Reinventing the Medium," *Critical Inquiry*, 25 (1999): 291. Krauss calls the original publication a shortened version of Benjamin's German text. In fact, this 1936 version consisting of nineteen sections is longer than the "third version," which Benjamin wrote in spring 1936 and which appeared in the 1969 *Illu-*

minations anthology years after his death. The French agrees nearly exactly (minus the epigraph and a few words at the outset) with the "second version," which Benjamin prepared in German around December 1935 and which likewise was never published in his lifetime. Because no German version was published until the 1955 *Schriften*, Pierre Klossowski's French translation would have been the only one available to Malraux or to anyone else.

86. Publisher's note to André Malraux, "The Psychology of Art," *Verve*, 1, no. 1 (December 1937). This was the first installment of what would be four "fragments" from Malraux's project *La Psychologie de l'art*, eventually published in three volumes.

87. Claude-Edmonde Magny, "Malraux le fascinateur," *Esprit*, 16 (October 1948): 525.

88. Rosalind Krauss, "Postmodernism's Museum without Walls," in Reesa Greenberg et al., eds., *Thinking about Exhibitions* (New York: Routledge, 1996), p. 342. Krauss condenses this argument in "The Ministry of Fate," in Denis Hollier, ed., *A New History of French Literature* (Cambridge, Mass.: Harvard University Press, 1988), p. 1001.

89. Krauss, "The Ministry of Fate," p. 1001.

90. Translators' Foreword, in Walter Benjamin, *The Arcades Project*, trans. Howard Eiland and Kevin McLaughlin (Cambridge, Mass.: Harvard University Press, 1999), p. x.

91. Terry Eagleton, *Walter Benjamin, or Towards a Revolutionary Criticism* (London: New Left Books, 1981), pp. 151, 175.

92. Ibid., p. 175.

93. Eagleton is careful to temper his affection for Benjamin's mind and ideas with the historical reality of Trotsky's infinitely more important political and social role. See Eagleton, *Walter Benjamin*, p. 174.

94. Cate, *André Malraux*, p. 256.

95. It should be noted that Trotsky remained ambivalent, embarrassed, and sometimes hostile when it came to Breton's insistence that they shared a vision of the world. See Lewis, *Dada Turns Red*, p. 145.

96. Walter Langlois, *André Malraux: The Indochina Adventure* (New York: Praeger, 1965), p. 74.

97. Michalczyk, *André Malraux's "Espoir,"* p. 48, quoting from Ralph Tarica, "Imagery in the Novels of Malraux: An Index with Commentary" (Ph.D. diss., Harvard University, 1966), p. 179.

98. Sergei M. Eisenstein, "Word and Image," in idem, *The Film Sense*, trans. Jay Leyda (New York: Harcourt Brace, 1947), pp. 11, 30–31. See also Dudley Andrew, *The Major Film Theories* (New York: Oxford University Press, 1976), pp. 72–73.

99. André Bazin, "Painting and Cinema," in idem, *What Is Cinema?* p. 169.

100. James Agee, in *The Nation* (1 February 1947).

101. Michalczyk, *André Malraux's "Espoir,"* pp. 80–81, collects this and other pic-

torial references, noting their frequent recurrence in Malraux's *Les Voix du silence*, where the Tintoretto appears on p. 443. On p. 434 Malraux inserted a color plate of El Greco's *Storm over Toledo* next to his *Crucifixion (with View of Toledo)*.

102. Violet Horvath, *André Malraux: The Human Adventure* (New York: NYU Press, 1969), p. 97.

103. André Malraux, "Esquisse d'une psychologie du cinéma," *Verve*, 8 (1940), in English as "Sketch for a Psychology of the Moving Pictures," in Susanne K. Langer, ed., *Reflections on Art: A Source Book of Writings by Artists, Critics, and Philosophers* (Baltimore: Johns Hopkins University Press, 1958), p. 320.

104. Bazin, "On *L'Espoir*, or Style in the Cinema," in idem, *French Cinema of the Occupation and Resistance*, pp. 176–188. Bazin, in his view of Malraux and ellipsis, relies on Claude-Edmonde Magny's contemporaneous study, *The Age of the American Novel*, trans. Eleanor Hochman (New York: Ungar, 1972).

105. Roger Leenhardt, "Le Rythme cinématographique," *Esprit* (January 1936), reprinted in idem, *Chroniques de cinéma* (Paris: Cahiers du Cinéma, 1986), pp. 42–43.

106. Russell Berman, Foreword to Alice Kaplan, *Reproductions of Banality: Fascism, Literature, and French Intellectual Life* (Minneapolis: University of Minnesota Press, 1986), p. xviii.

107. See André Malraux, "Reply by André Malraux to André Bazin," in Bazin, *French Cinema of the Occupation and Resistance*, trans. Stanley Hochman (New York: Ungar, 1984), pp. 158–160.

CONCLUSION AS FORECAST

1. Pierre Assouline, *Gaston Gallimard: A Century in Publishing*, trans. Harold Salemson (New York: Harcourt Brace, 1988), p. 216.

2. During this voyage, Lévi-Strauss and Breton exchanged views on the question of "art versus document." This exchange has been preserved in Claude Lévi-Strauss, *Look, Listen, Read* (New York: Basic Books, 1997), pp. 143–151.

3. Mark Polizzotti, *Revolution of the Mind: The Life of André Breton* (New York: Farrar, Straus and Giroux, 1995), p. 503.

4. See Martica Sawin, *Surrealism in Exile and the Beginning of the New York School* (Cambridge, Mass.: MIT Press, 1995); and Jeffrey Mehlman, *Emigré New York: French Intellectuals in Wartime Manhattan, 1940–1944* (Baltimore: Johns Hopkins University Press, 2000).

5. Lévi-Strauss, *Tristes Tropiques*, trans. John Russell (London: Hutchinson, 1961; orig. pub. 1955), pp. 54–67.

6. Lévi-Strauss claims to have been taken with Surrealist thought as a young student in 1928 ("I viewed myself as a revolutionary in all fields at the time"), but later, especially after public discord with his theories, he distanced himself. See Roger Caillois, *The Edge of Surrealism: A Roger Caillois Reader*, ed. Claudine Frank (Durham: Duke University Press, 2003), p. 48.

7. Lévi-Strauss, *Tristes Tropiques*, p. 59.

8. Ibid., p. 61.

9. Lévi-Strauss wrote of the "search for unsuspected harmonies," echoing the "harmonics" that Alain Resnais sees governing *Stavisky*. . . . See ibid., p. 59.

10. Terry Eagleton, *Walter Benjamin, or Towards a Revolutionary Criticism* (London: New Left Books, 1981), p. 175.

Credits

1–5. *Stavisky . . .* (Alain Resnais, 1974).
6. Roger-Viollet.
7–8. *Stavisky . . .* (Alain Resnais, 1974).
9. ACRPP (Association pour la Conservation et la Reproduction de la Presse par la Photographie), Paris.
10–13. *Stavisky . . .* (Alain Resnais, 1974).
14. ACRPP.
15–16. *Stavisky . . .* (Alain Resnais, 1974).
17. ACRPP.
18. *Stavisky . . .* (Alain Resnais, 1974).
19. ACRPP.
20. *Stavisky . . .* (Alain Resnais, 1974).
21–24. Roger-Viollet.
25–26. ACRPP.
27. Roger-Viollet.
28. Alexandre Iacovleff, *Portrait of André Gide* (1927). Sanguine on paper, 48.5 x 39 cm. Private collection, Paris. Photo by Suzanne Nagy. Courtesy of the Photothèque du Musée des Années 30, Boulogne-Billancourt, France.
29. ACRPP.
30–31. Roger-Viollet.
32. Institut Mémoire de l'Édition Contemporaine, Paris.
33. ACRPP.
34. Roger-Viollet.
35–36. *Mayerling* (Anatol Litvak, 1936).
37. Roger-Viollet.
38. *La Vie est à nous* (Jean Renoir, 1936).
39. *Napoléon vu par Abel Gance* (Abel Gance, 1927).

40. *Danton* (Andrej Wajda, 1983).
41. *L'Anglaise et le duc* (Eric Rohmer, 2001).
42–43. *La Marseillaise* (Jean Renoir, 1938).
44. Poster by Maurice Toussaint, 1938. Copyright © Alain Gesgon. All rights reserved.
45–47. *La Marseillaise* (Jean Renoir, 1938).
48. Roger-Viollet.
49. *Sous les toits de Paris* (René Clair, 1930).
50–51. *A Nous la liberté* (René Clair, 1931).
52–53. Roger-Viollet.
54–55. *Le Crime de Monsieur Lange* (Jean Renoir, 1936).
56. Sterling Memorial Library, Yale University.
57–59. *Rigolboche* (Christian-Jacque, 1936).
60–61. *Le Crime de Monsieur Lange* (Jean Renoir, 1936).
62. Courtesy of Monsieur Bernard Chevojon.
63–65. Roger-Viollet.
66. Association Française pour la Diffusion du Patrimoine Photographique.
67. Photo by Séeberger Frères. Courtesy of the Photothèque du Centre des Monuments Nationaux, Paris.
68. *Love Me Tonight* (Rouben Mamoulian, 1932).
69. Photo of the Hôtel Prince de Galles, Paris, by Séeberger Frères. Courtesy of the Photothèque du Centre des Monuments Nationaux.

70. *Trouble in Paradise* (Ernst Lubitsch, 1932).
71. Le Corbusier and Georges-Henri Pingusson, Maquette of the Villa Ternisien, 5 Allée des Pins, Boulogne-Billancourt (1923–1927). Collection of the Musée des Années 30, Boulogne-Billancourt, France. Photo by Philippe Fuzeau.
72. Photo by Collas. All rights reserved.
73. *L'Illustration* (1937).
74. *Bonne Chance* (Sacha Guitry, 1936).
75. *L'Illustration* (May 11, 1935).
76. Trademark image for Leroy, 1930s.
77. *L'Illustration* (1933).
78. *Bonne Chance* (Sacha Guitry, 1936).
79. *L'Illustration* (July 30, 1938).
80. *Prix de Beauté* (Augusto Genina, 1930).
81–82. *L'Illustration* (1935 and October 4, 1933).
83. *Hôtel du Nord* (Marcel Carné, 1938).
84. Courtesy of Monsieur Yves Blacher.
85–87. *Hôtel du Nord* (Marcel Carné, 1938).
88. Association Française pour la Diffusion du Patrimoine Photographique.
89. *Hôtel du Nord* (Marcel Carné, 1938).
90. Association Française pour la Diffusion du Patrimoine Photographique.
91. *Le Jour se lève* (Marcel Carné, 1939).
92. Association Française pour la Diffusion du Patrimoine Photographique.
93–94. ACRPP.
95. Roger-Viollet.
96. Bibliothèque de Documentation Internationale Contemporaine, Paris.
97. Alexandre Iacovleff, *Portrait of Marabout Aïm Gabo, Sultan of Birao* (1925). Mixed media on paper, 75 x 56 cm. Collection of the Musée des Années 30, Boulogne-Billancourt, France. Photo by Dominique Genet.
98. *L'Appel du silence* (Léon Poirier, 1936).
99–100. *Itto* (Jean Benoît-Lévy and Marie Epstein, 1933).
101. Cover of Jean Vignaud and Henri Fescourt, *La Maison du Maltais* (Paris: Plon, 1926).
102. *Le Sang d'un poète* (Jean Cocteau, 1930).
103. *Un Chien andalou* (Luis Buñuel and Salvador Dalí, 1929).
104. *L'Atalante* (Jean Vigo, 1934).
105. *La Règle du jeu* (Jean Renoir, 1939).

Portions of the text were previously published, in very different form, as follows:
Introduction: Andrew and Ungar, in *Hors Cadre*, 10 (1992).
Chapter 4: Andrew, in *Yale Journal of Criticism*, 4 (Fall 1990); Andrew, in Robert Stam and Alessandra Raengo, eds., *A Companion to Literature and Film* (Oxford: Blackwell, 2004).
Chapter 6: Andrew, in Richard Dyer and Ginette Vincendeau, eds., *Popular European Cinema* (London: Routledge, 1992).
Chapter 8: Ungar, in *Studies in Twentieth-Century Literature*, 21 (1997).
Chapter 9: Ungar, in *Journal of Film Preservation*, 63 (2001); Ungar, in Pascal Blanchard and Sandrine Lemaire, eds., *Culture coloniale: La France conquise par son empire, 1871–1931* (Paris: Autrement, 2002); Ungar, in Dina Sherzer, ed., *Cinema, Colonialism, Postcolonialism: Perspectives from the French and Francophone World* (Austin: University of Texas Press, 1996); Andrew, in Matthew Bernstein and Gaylyn Studlar, eds., *Visions of the East: Orientalism in Film* (New Brunswick, N.J.: Rutgers University Press, 1997).

Index

Acéphale (group), 364, 365, 367. *See also* Bataille, Georges
Acéphale (journal), 133, 362, 397n36. *See also* Bataille, Georges
Achard, Marcel, 172, 270, 401n53
ACI (Alliance du Cinéma Indépendant), 146, 148–149
Action Française (group), 61, 84, 114, 117, 390nn28,6. *See also* Maurras, Charles
Action Française, L' (daily), 32, 43, 60, 63, 68, 72, 75, 78, 86, 280, 297, 311
Adorno, Theodor Wiesengrund, 380
AEAR (Association des Ecrivains et Artistes Révolutionnaires) 65–66, 68, 69, 78, 145, 153, 280, 354, 368, 392n30. *See also* Journals, scholarly and specialized: *Commune*
Affaire est dans le sac, L' (1932), 200. *See also* Prévert, Pierre
Africa (sub-Saharan), 14, 69, 91, 101, 103, 274, 299, 304–305, 311, 313, 317, 324, 335, 358, 361, 389n17, 424n42, 431n54. *See also* North Africa
Age d'or, L' (1930), 101, 152, 346, 352, 356, 429n36. *See also* Buñuel, Luis
Agee, James, 376, 434n100
Ageron, Charles-Robert, 311, 424n41
Alain (Emile-Alain Chartier), 65, 66, 67, 69, 88
Alexander Nevsky (1938), 146. *See also* Eisenstein, Sergei
Algeria, 181, 301, 308, 311, 318, 319, 323, 324. *See also* North Africa
Algiers, 296, 306. *See also* Pépé le Moko
Alibi, L' (1937), 275. *See also* Chenal, Pierre
Allégret, Marc, 270, 398. *See also* Hôtel du libre échange; Lac aux dames; Voyage au Congo; Zou Zou
Allegret, Yves, 399n17
Alméras, Lucette, 297
Amour l'après-midi, L' (1972), 160. *See* Rohmer, Eric
Amsterdam-Pleyel (group) 65–66, 68, 391n13
Angkor Wat, 94, 306–308, 422n21, 423n25. *See also* Exposition Coloniale Internationale

Anglaise et le duc, L' (2001), 159–160. *See also* Rohmer, Eric
Annabella (Suzanne Charpentier), 313, 426n77
Annales School (historians), 6, 157
A Nous la liberté (1931), 189, 192–194, 242. *See also* Clair, René
Anti-Semitism, 32, 37, 180, 319–320, 368. *See also* Drumont, Edouard; Judaism
Appel du silence, L' (1936), 315, 320–323, 337, 338, 341, 425nn50,63,69. *See also* Poirier, Léon
Aragon, Louis, 75, 78, 83, 87, 88, 145, 148–149, 153, 240, 293, 294, 308, 309–310, 341, 353, 354, 368, 423n35. *See also* Surrealism
Arletty (Léonie Bathiat), 185, 278, 404n34, 416n1, 417n8
Aron, Raymond, 86, 87
Aron, Robert, 110, 112, 116, 120, 123, 127, 396n17, 432n62
Artaud, Antonin, 152
Art Deco (style, aesthetic), 17, 228, 229, 231, 233–236, 239, 241, 243, 245, 247, 249, 251–253, 263, 265–266, 269–271, 273–276, 310, 413nn57,65,67,69,72, 414nn74,84. *See also* Exposition des Arts Décoratifs
Art Nouveau (style, aesthetic), 258, 260
Association Radio-Liberté (ARL), 183–184
Atalante, L' (1934), 351, 356, 430n46. *See also* Vigo, Jean
Atget, Eugène, 245, 247, 249, 346–347, 359
Atlantide, L' (1920), 312, 424n42, 426n78. *See also* Feyder, Jacques
Aurenche, Jean, 279, 286
Autant-Lara, Claude, 252
Aymé, Marcel, 72

Baker, Josephine, 185, 186, 404n34, 407n45, 408n52
Bal (*bal populaire*, local dance hall), 198, 226–227, 408n55, 409n57
Balin, Mireille, 230, 273, 408n54, 426n77
Ballets Russes, 200, 258